D1604539

APR 1 8 2008

AFRICAN AMERICAN PIONEERS OF BASEBALL

AFRICAN AMERICAN PIONEERS OF BASEBALL

A Biographical Encyclopedia

Lew Freedman

GREENWOOD PRESS
Westport, Connecticut • London

Library of Congress Cataloging-in-Publication Data

Freedman, Lew.
    African American pioneers of baseball : a biographical encyclopedia / Lew Freedman.
      p. cm.
    Includes bibliographical references and index.
    ISBN 978-0-313-33851-9 (alk. paper)
    1. African American baseball players—Biography—Dictionaries. I. Title.
    GV865.A1F68 2007
    796.3570922—dc22
    [B]   2007000420

British Library Cataloguing in Publication Data is available.

Copyright © 2007 by Lew Freedman

Library of Congress Catalog Card Number: 2007000420
ISBN-13: 978-0-313-33851-9
ISBN-10: 0-313-33851-5

First published in 2007

Greenwood Press, 88 Post Road West, Westport, CT 06881
An imprint of Greenwood Publishing Group, Inc.
www.greenwood.com

Printed in the United States of America

The paper used in this book complies with the
Permanent Paper Standard issued by the National
Information Standards Organization (Z39.48-1984).

10 9 8 7 6 5 4 3 2 1

Copyright Acknowledgment

We would like to thank the National Baseball Hall of Fame Library, in Cooperstown, New York,
for the use of the photographs that appear in this encyclopedia.

CONTENTS

PREFACE

For the baseball fan who has grown up since the 1950s, it is inconceivable that the sport was once a segregated game. But once Jackie Robinson signed with the Brooklyn Dodgers organization in 1946 and broke the Major League color barrier in 1947, African Americans showed instantly that they belonged.

The impact was dramatic and significant. Between 1949 and 1959, blacks won the National League Most Valuable Player award nine times. A black player won the first Cy Young award. Between 1947 and 1953 blacks won the rookie of the year award six times.

Nearly all the African American pioneers of baseball discussed in this volume have been selected to the Baseball Hall of Fame—something considered unfathomable in 1945. All have made unique contributions to the sport and several have done so in ways that transcend the dugout. Hank Aaron, who is on all experts' short list of the greatest players of all time, claimed the most cherished baseball record of all. After a life begun in racist Alabama, Aaron got his taste of the Negro Leagues, vituperativeness in the minor leagues, and persevered to become the greatest home-run hitter of all time.

Careers of players profiled here began in the 1920s and stretched into the 1970s. Even those whose careers extended well into the period of baseball integration featured roots in the Negro Leagues. These men were selected to represent a time period when blacks suffered discrimination in the sport and a time period when baseball was undergoing change. The talents of many of these players far exceeded those of many whites, yet no team would allow them onto a roster.

Careful thought was given to the arrangement of the order of those profiled in *African American Pioneers of Baseball: A Biographical Encyclopedia*. The order is neither chronological nor alphabetical, but laid out in a manner that best illustrates the African American baseball experience through the Negro Leagues and the barrier-breaking period in the major leagues. Even avid, youthful baseball fans may not be familiar with the achievements of some of the outstanding players profiled here. It is a goal to remedy that.

Buck O'Neil was chosen as the man to kick off this collection because he was the longest-living member of a dying fraternity—those who excelled in the Negro Baseball Leagues. Not only was O'Neil a top player and manager, he witnessed first-hand much history that has only been sketchily recorded and made himself a vocal and very available testifier to what he saw. The early black stars of baseball in America often plied their trade in the shadows. O'Neil worked to keep the flame of memory alive as long as possible.

Judy Johnson, Buck Leonard, Cool Papa Bell, and Josh Gibson were the elite of the elite in the Negro Leagues—all of them recognized for their accomplishments by organized baseball long after retirement. But they never had a sniff of Major League play because the majors' unwritten law of segregation banned them in their primes because of their skin color. The heart of all of their careers played out between 1920 and 1946, when Robinson signed his barrier-breaking contract. When the majors opened the doors to blacks, these stars were too old to play.

Jackie Robinson represents the breakthrough, the player who was built on the labor of the O'Neils, Leonards et al. His signing by Branch Rickey with the Brooklyn Dodgers' organization in 1946 and his rise to the majors in 1947 to become the first black player in the twentieth century symbolized society's first widespread acceptance of blacks in the National Pastime. Roy Campanella and Don Newcombe, Dodger teammates of Robinson's, were part of the first wave of African Americans in the minors and majors.

Although the American League was generally behind the National League in integration efforts, Larry Doby did become the first African American player in the American League with the Cleveland Indians months after Robinson broke the color line. Satchel Paige is a crossover. In most ways Paige's career parallels Johnson's, Bell's, and the like, but he retained his youthful vigor just long enough to make his mark in the American League and join Doby on the Indians.

The New York Giants were not far behind the Dodgers integrating their team, and their first black star was Monte Irvin, who went on to even greater accomplishments in the Baseball Commissioner's office. Whereas once the commissioner's office was complicit in banning blacks, Irvin became involved in the game's most important decisions. He also served as a de facto big brother to Willie Mays with the Giants. Mays was probably the first mainstream black superstar, but he also had his roots in the Negro Leagues. Willie McCovey was the linear descendent of Irvin and Mays with the Giants. He was the Giants' first homegrown San Francisco superstar, and the community's embracement of him was notable for its lack of racism.

Ernie Banks was the first black Chicago Cub—after being signed by scout Buck O'Neil. Elston Howard battled to become the first black New York Yankee—after playing for O'Neil with the Kansas City Monarchs.

Minnie Minoso symbolizes the struggle for acceptance of the black Latin player, whose first language is Spanish. He was the first black Chicago White Sox player. Frank Robinson became the first black manager with the Cleveland Indians. Bob Gibson used pride and a stirring fastball to defeat racism where he saw it. Curt Flood took a stand for all baseball players, challenging baseball's restrictive contract reserve clause in a case that went to the Supreme Court.

Many of the careers chronicled in this book date to a time when records for the Negro Leagues were incomplete. Many of the players had no biography written about them. It was imperative in many instances to quote first-hand witnesses to accurately form impressions about each man. Newspaper and magazine stories were reviewed, but for the most part they were not contemporary. In an era when box scores could be scarce, in-depth profiles were scarcer. The journey of today's major leaguer is recorded from first at-bat to last. Even the most significant events in older African American players' careers must be recounted from anecdote and memory. Selected players such as the late Buck O'Neil, Minnie Minoso, Monte Irvin, Carl Long, and the late Charles Johnson contributed recollections in one-on-one interviews with the author. The Baseball Hall of Fame Library Archives has massive amounts of material in individual player files. For further information on resources cited in this book, the reader is encouraged to visit www.baseballhalloffame.org.

Written for students and general readers alike, this biographical encyclopedia chronicles the history of African American baseball through the life stories of twenty of the game's greatest players, legends who played a significant role in the integration of the major leagues. Sometimes achievements alone account for their inclusion—the magnificence of performance recorded through numbers—and sometimes the flamboyance of their personalities help merit inclusion. It is most important that these men's contributions be recognized in the context of the National Pastime.

Each entry hopefully offers illumination about each man, but does not represent a complete biography. There is an attempt to bring out the personality and accomplishments of each player within the framework of several thousand words, but no man's life can be encapsulated in a limited space. Additional readings about each player can be found in "Further Reading" at the end of each entry, as well as in the Bibliography at the back of the book.

In gathering material for this volume, the National Baseball Hall of Fame Library in Cooperstown, New York, was of paramount support. In addition, the Negro Leagues Baseball Museum in Kansas City offers rare perspective on the African American baseball experience.

INTRODUCTION

On March 2, 2005, President George W. Bush greeted Rachel Robinson in the Capitol rotunda in Washington, D.C., and gently placed into her hand the Congressional Gold Medal in the name of her deceased husband, Jack Roosevelt Robinson.

The ceremony of awarding the gold medal—the highest civilian honor that can be presented by Congress—took place nearly fifty-eight years after Robinson played his first Major League baseball game for the Brooklyn Dodgers. On that day in April 1947, Robinson's presence in the lineup represented a giant step for integration. Merely by setting foot on the field of play, Robinson broke the sport's color barrier and ignited a torch of hope in African Americans.

When Robinson became the first black player in organized ball in the twentieth century, elbowing aside Major League policies of segregation that had been inviolate for sixty years, he became a symbol of opportunity and acceptance for his countrymen. Robinson withstood insult and hatred to persevere and establish himself as a Hall of Fame player, and to lead future generations of black players into the previously all-white world of organized ball.

Before Robinson, even the absolute best black baseball players were confined to the Negro Leagues. After Robinson, Major League teams signed the best ballplayers regardless of skin color. He faced down vituperative shouts, vicious mail, and physical threats at extreme cost to his well-being and long-term health, but left the sport more forward thinking than it was when he entered it.

Some 600 people attended the ceremony where President Bush quoted civil rights leader Martin Luther King Jr.'s viewpoint of Robinson's impact on society. " 'He was a freedom rider before freedom rides,' " Bush repeated. "To me, that says courage and decency and honor."[1] Baseball commissioner Bud Selig, U.S. senator John Kerry, and the Reverend Jesse Jackson were among those who attended. "He was a transforming figure who made life in America better," Jackson said.

From the vantage point of six decades in the future, and the way society has evolved, without the reminders of special awards to pioneers like Robinson, and to those who toiled in obscurity in the Negro Leagues, younger baseball fans might forget baseball's ugly past. They might be unaware of a time when blacks were not welcome to play with whites and when many of the greatest stars suffered prejudice because of skin color when they traveled the country's roads, when they tried to rent a hotel room to rest, or when they sought a hot meal to fill their stomachs.

Black baseball stars like Josh Gibson, Buck Leonard, Judy Johnson, Buck O'Neil, and Cool Papa Bell were shut out of the majors until they grew too old. Satchel Paige got to dip his toe in the water. A new generation of stars like Hank Aaron, Willie Mays, Ernie Banks, Monte Irvin, Roy Campanella, Larry Doby, Don Newcombe, Elston Howard, and Minnie Minoso followed them and made their marks in the majors, but did not forget their own experiences in the Negro Leagues. The stars who followed them—a third generation of black players—like Frank Robinson, Bob Gibson, Curt Flood, and Willie McCovey, never played a minute in the Negro Leagues, but did not evade the still-prevalent racism in the minor leagues' small-town homes.

All of them were African American pioneers of baseball for different reasons. Jackie Robinson was the first black to play in the majors in the twentieth century. Doby was the first black player in the American League. Howard was the first black New York Yankee; Minoso was the first black White Sox player, who also felt the sting of discrimation as a black Cuban trying to make it in the United States.

Campanella and Newcombe continued Robinson's Dodger legacy by integrating minor league teams. Aaron, Mays, Banks, and Irvin made their professional debuts in the Negro Leagues, then became nationally famous in the National League. Frank Robinson became the first African American manager. Bob Gibson refused to sublimate his personality to get along. McCovey showed that a black man could become a homegrown hero. Flood carried the weight of the entire sport on his shoulders when he challenged owners in court over player contract restrictions.

Josh Gibson, Cool Papa Bell, Buck Leonard, Buck O'Neil, Judy Johnson, and Satchel Paige were acknowledged great baseball players denied Major League opportunities because of their skin color, but who through their talents still laid the foundation for Robinson's acceptance and others' success in the majors.

All of these men, those who preceded Jackie Robinson, those who were contemporaries, and those who followed, were building blocks in the monument that now stands to the ability of African American baseball players. They suffered so others could prosper. They paid more than their share of dues so others could become millionaires.

This examination of African American pioneers of baseball is designed to highlight the careers of some of the best black baseball players in American history, including several who were prohibited from pursuing careers in the major leagues because of their skin color.

Some of the greatest baseball players of all—as supported by their later admittance to the Baseball Hall of Fame—were banned from the game they loved and consigned to competition in the Negro Leagues, the so-called shadow leagues of big-time baseball for lesser wages. They never received the acclaim and attention they deserved. If racism is the greatest American sin perpetuated officially and unofficially on the society's own people, players born too soon to be accepted into the simple world of professional baseball paid a terrible price. Buck O'Neil, Buck Leonard, Cool Papa Bell, Judy Johnson, and Josh Gibson never played a moment in the majors, although all were deserving. Satchel Paige's best years played out in obscurity, and only through his remarkable longevity did he outlast Major League baseball's unconscionable unwritten rules of prejudice to make it to the top in his forties.

It is important to shed as much light as possible on the lives of those men. Baseball is a far more pluralistic society in the 2000s than it was in the 1930s or 1940s, and players and fans of the game who were born much later should appreciate the sacrifices made by men like these. Theirs is not solely a sports story, but an American story, and it veers back and forth from the inspirational to the shameful.

Many of the other stars included in this book are players who straddled the world of the Negro Leagues player and the majors. It is probable that only a tiny percentage of baseball fans who recognize the fabulous gifts of these All Stars realize that they experienced professional baseball careers before making their marks in the majors. Hank Aaron is revered as the all-time home-run king, but he played in the Negro Leagues before the majors, likewise Willie Mays, Minnie Minoso, Don Newcombe, Roy Campanella, Larry Doby, Monte Irvin, Ernie Banks, and Elston Howard. If they ever knew it, the average baseball fans may not remember the formative years that made them into the men they became. But those players never forgot their beginnings and the racism that they faced. Experiences outside the limelight shaped the lives they led after their ascension to the majors. Even Jackie Robinson, the man who broke the color line and suffered his abuse in the public arena, began in the Negro Leagues.

These men were selected for inclusion not only because they demonstrated extraordinary talent, but also because their pasts could be shared, to offer insight into a world now gone, as displays of character in showing what it took to achieve what they had achieved in the big leagues. Minnie Minoso's was a unique story. He faced the complex challenge of being a dark-skinned Cuban. He faced prejudice not only because of his skin color, but also because his first language was Spanish. Latin American players are stars on every Major League team now, but Minoso's career, during which he became the first black player for the Chicago White Sox, is symbolic. He was black and Latin.

Frank Robinson was not only a great player, but also a different kind of pioneer. He became the first African American manager in history. Bob Gibson, Curt Flood, and Willie McCovey came along a little bit later. They were African American players who made the leap into the majors as the Negro Leagues were fading out. Yet, they did not escape discrimination in the low minors of the American South. If racism was, at least, being diluted on the Major League level, the experience of latecomers showed that it remained just as vicious in other locations. Flood was a special case, a pioneer for his activities off the field. When he refused a trade in 1969 and sued Major League baseball to overturn the reserve clause that unfairly bound players to teams, he took a stand for all players, black and white, at the sacrifice of his own career. McCovey, the last of all these players to break in, was a Hall of Famer whose career illustrated that by 1959 it was possible to be a black ballplayer in the majors, who was cheered for his accomplishments—without regard to skin color.

The stories of these black ballplayers should provide detailed information for the young baseball fans who have not heard of some of these stars, and whose upbringing so many years removed from the occurrences shielded them from the knowledge of the Negro Leagues and the sociology of their own country.

If the United States is a more egalitarian society today, men like this contributed to making it so. Today, black players, white players, and Spanish-speaking Latin American players are all equal in the eyes of Major League baseball, its teams, players, and fans. There is no second-class citizenry in baseball in the 2000s the way there was before 1947. The medal posthumously presented to Robinson was a medal of war, honorably earned in the service of his country.

In the 2000s, as youngsters view the equality of the sport, it is important to aging black stars that their early history and the history of those who were born too soon be preserved. That is the inspiration behind and reason for the existence of the Negro Leagues Baseball Museum in Kansas City. Its purpose is to tell it like it was.

"The mission is to research, preserve and disseminate a history of African-American baseball in general and the Negro Leagues in particular," said Raymond Doswell, the museum's curator, who has worked for the organization since 1995. "A research library is in the works. We hope to have documents and manuscripts available."[2]

The museum houses bats, balls, and gloves, and some authentic uniform jerseys used by African American players in the defunct Negro Leagues. "The museum receives numerous calls for public appearances from former players to talk to schoolchildren," Doswell said. "You don't want to squelch any enthusiasm."[3]

The top Negro Leagues teams like the Kansas City Monarchs, the Pittsburgh Crawfords, and the Homestead Grays featured many of the biggest stars, but the stories behind barnstorming teams and less-famous clubs also represent the life of players who were good enough to compete, but not good enough to be All Stars. Many teams employed the name of a community in their title, but rarely played home games in that city.

"We used to go all over the country," said Carl Long of Kinston, North Carolina, recalling play and bus travel with the Nashville Stars and the Birmingham Black Barons in the early 1950s. "Sometimes we'd play in Nashville at night and in Kansas City the next night. When I was a kid I used to sit by the radio and listen to [Major League] games with my dad. You could be the black Ted Williams and they just were not ready [to sign blacks]. One time when I was a boy in Rock Hill, I came home crying to my father, who they called 'Big Bill,' and said, 'A man just called me a nigger.' He said, 'Carl, don't you never forget it, but you keep playin'.' "[4]

Long said he played one game in Bluefield, West Virginia. Most of the men on the other team were white coal miners. Long's team won and he said afterwards an opposing player said, " 'Man you all are good.' I said, 'We just want to play the game.' "[5]

Hard-earned respect is part of the common thread in stories told by old black ballplayers. Hard times, low salaries, bumpy bus rides, and discrimination everywhere are others.

Charles Johnson was ninety-six, only months before his death in June 2006, when he recalled trying to survive as a ballplayer during the Depression. He said he grew up on the south side of Chicago, near the White Sox park, and played sandlot ball with the famous Ted "Double Duty" Radcliffe, a player who both pitched and caught. Johnson came by the nickname "Goulash" because he was always prepared to eat at a 25-cent smorgasbord when it opened at 11 A.M.

Johnson said he never had a regular team contract, but joined any team that asked him to barnstorm. He said he played as an outfielder for the Chicago American Giants in Benton Harbor, Michigan, against the famous House of David touring team, played in Hartford, Connecticut, and in Texas.

"I always could play baseball," Johnson said. "I played wherever anyone offered money to go. I moved a lot. I didn't have nothing else to do. I was hungry. Once, in 1932, we got stranded in Minnesota, fourteen of us, because we ran out of money." Johnson spent fifteen years playing ball and then after getting married retired in 1943 to a life of making kitchen furniture, serving as a train porter, and working for a local police department.[6]

Johnson said he was on teams that played exhibitions against white Major League All Stars from the Philadelphia Athletics of 1929 to Tigers' Hall of Famer Charles Gehringer. "We won some games and they won some games," Johnson said.[7]

That was long before African Americans broke into the majors on their own. When Jackie Robinson was invited into the club and other stars followed, black players who were aging or fell short of stardom knew that the Negro Leagues would fade out. Buck O'Neil, the player-manager institution of the Kansas City Monarchs, played a significant role in the founding of the Negro Baseball Museum. And by making public appearances and appearing in the Ken Burns documentary *Baseball*, O'Neil kept alive memories of the leagues, the teams, and the players he knew.

The story of pre-1947 black baseball is told in the Negro Leagues Baseball Museum, at 18th and Vine Streets, where Kansas City's swingingest jazz players ruled the night scene and the players partied until dawn. There are statues of many great Negro Leagues stars, and exhibits that outline their joys and sorrows. Many times O'Neil lent his name to fundraising efforts, from events where fans could meet him, to the selling of bobble-head dolls with his likeness.

"Buck is one of the most popular people in Kansas City," Doswell said before O'Neil passed away.[8] Those who shared the common cause of African American base-ball—until it became just baseball—share space under the same roof at the museum. But no one is as revered as Jackie Robinson because no one is owed a greater debt. "He was carrying on his shoulders the burden of twenty-one million black Americans," said Joe Black, a Dodger pitcher and teammate of Robinson's.[9]

NOTES

1. Barry Bloom, majorleaguebaseball.com, March 2, 2005.
2. Raymond Doswell, personal interview, December 7, 2005.
3. Ibid.
4. Carl Long, personal interview, January 11, 2006.
5. Ibid.
6. Charles Johnson, personal interview, January 10, 2006.
7. Ibid.
8. Doswell, personal interview.
9. Joe Black, Negro Baseball League exhibit.

TIMELINE

1899—Judy Johnson born October 26 in Snow Hill, Maryland.

1903—James "Cool Papa" Bell born May 17 in Starkville, Mississippi.

1906—Satchel Paige born July 7 in Mobile, Alabama.

1907—Walter "Buck" Leonard born September 8 in Rocky Mount, North Carolina.

1911—John "Buck" O'Neil Jr. born November 13 in Carrabelle, Florida.

1911—Josh Gibson born December 21 in Buena Vista, Georgia.

1918—Judy Johnson makes professional black ball debut with Madison Stars.

1919—Jack Roosevelt Robinson is born January 31 in Cairo, Georgia.

1919—Monte Irvin is born February 25 in Haleburg, Alabama.

1921—Roy Campanella is born November 19 in Philadelphia, Pennsylvania.

1922—James "Cool Papa" Bell plays first professional season with the St. Louis Stars.

1922—Minnie Minoso is born November 29 in Cuba.

1923—Judy Johnson bats .391 for the Philadelphia Hilldale Giants of the Eastern Colored League.

1923—Larry Doby born December 13 in Camden, South Carolina.

1926—Don Newcombe born June 14 in Madison, New Jersey.

1926—Satchel Paige pitches his first game for pay with the Chattanooga Black Lookouts.

1929—Elston Howard born February 23 in St. Louis, Missouri.

1930—Josh Gibson breaks in with the Pittsburgh Crawfords, then joins the Homestead Grays.

1931—Ernie Banks born January 31 in Dallas, Texas.

1931—Willie Mays born May 6 in Westfield, Alabama.

1931—Satchel Paige goes 31–4 for the Pittsburgh Crawfords.

1933—According to the count of James "Cool Papa" Bell, Josh Gibson hits 72 home runs.

1934—Hank Aaron is born February 5 in Mobile, Alabama.

1934—John "Buck" O'Neil makes professional debut with the Tampa Bay Smokers.

1934—Walter "Buck" Leonard breaks in with the Homestead Grays.

1935—Frank Robinson is born August 31 in Beaumont, Texas.

1935—Bob Gibson is born November 9 in Omaha, Nebraska.

1936—The *Negro Leagues Baseball Encyclopedia* gives Josh Gibson credit for 84 home runs.

1936—Roy Campanella turns pro at fifteen and begins long association with the Baltimore Elite Giants.

1938—Willie McCovey born January 10 in Mobile, Alabama.

1938—Curt Flood born January 18 in Houston, Texas.

1938—John "Buck" O'Neil Jr. joins the elite Kansas City Monarchs.

1938—Monte Irvin breaks in with the Newark Eagles.

1944—James "Cool Papa" Bell hits .411 for the Pittsburgh Crawfords.

1945—Jackie Robinson signs a contract on October 23 with Branch Rickey and the Brooklyn Dodgers, the first African American given the opportunity to join a Major League organization in the twentieth century.

1945—After leaving Cuba, Minnie Minoso breaks in with the Negro Leagues' New York Cubans team.

1946—Jackie Robinson makes his debut for the Montreal Royals in Jersey City, New Jersey, the first black to play organized baseball in the twentieth century.

1946—Monte Irvin bats .401 for the Newark Eagles.

1947—Josh Gibson dies of a brain tumor January 20 in Pittsburgh.

1947—Jackie Robinson plays his first game for the Brooklyn Dodgers April 15.

1947—Larry Doby breaks the color line in the American League by joining the Cleveland Indians on July 5.

1948—John "Buck" O'Neil Jr. becomes player-manager of the Kansas City Monarchs.

1948—Satchel Paige becomes the oldest rookie in Major League history in July when he pitches for World Series champ Cleveland Indians.

1948—Roy Campanella makes Major League debut with Brooklyn Dodgers.

1949—Monte Irvin makes Major League debut with the New York Giants.

1949—Don Newcombe named National League rookie of the year for the Brooklyn Dodgers.

1951—Willie Mays makes debut with New York Giants.

1951—Minnie Minoso becomes the first African American to play for the Chicago White Sox.

1951—Roy Campanella wins first of three National League Most Valuable Player awards.

1953—Ernie Banks makes Major League debut as first African American player for the Chicago Cubs along with Gene Baker.

1954—Willie Mays makes the most famous catch in baseball history off the bat of Cleveland Indian Vic Wertz in the World Series.

1954—Hank Aaron makes Major League debut with Milwaukee Braves.

1955—Elston Howard becomes the first African American player for the New York Yankees.

1956—John "Buck" O'Neil Jr. begins scouting for the Chicago Cubs.

1956—Don Newcombe goes 27–7 and wins the first Cy Young award.

1958—Roy Campanella paralyzed in automobile accident January 28.

1958—Ernie Banks wins National League Most Valuable Player award, his first of two.

1959—As a late season call up Willie McCovey turns in one of the most sensational debuts in Major League history and is named National League rookie of the year in less than a half season of play.

1962—John "Buck" O'Neil Jr. becomes the first black coach in Major League history for the Chicago Cubs.

1963—Elston Howard becomes the first African American to win the American League Most Valuable Player award.

1965—Satchel Paige pitches three innings for the Kansas City Athletics, giving up one hit versus the Red Sox at age fifty-nine.

1966—Red Sox superstar Ted Williams inducted into the Baseball Hall of Fame and in his acceptance speech urges opening the Hall to African Americans from the Negro Leagues.

1966—Frank Robinson wins the American League Most Valuable Player award for the Baltimore Orioles, following his 1961 award with the Cincinnati Reds, to become the first player to win the MVP award in both leagues.

1968—Monte Irvin joins baseball administration as special assistant to the commissioner and serves for sixteen years under two commissioners.

1968—Bob Gibson's 1.12 earned run average for the St. Louis Cardinals is the best of the modern era.

1969—Roy Campanella inducted into the Baseball Hall of Fame.

1969—Curt Flood is traded from the St. Louis Cardinals to the Philadelphia Phillies and refuses to report. Flood sues Major League baseball in an attempt to overturn the reserve clause binding players to their teams without ever being able to test the free market and carries the case to the U.S. Supreme Court.

1970—Don Newcombe begins work for Dodgers front office, admits he is an alcoholic and campaigns against its use.

1971—Satchel Paige inducted into the Baseball Hall of Fame.

1971—Ernie Banks retires from nineteen-year Major League career with 512 home runs, and is known as "Mr. Cub" for his devotion to the Chicago Cubs.

1972—Walter "Buck" Leonard and Josh Gibson inducted into the Baseball Hall of Fame.

1972—Jackie Robinson dies October 24 in Stamford, Connecticut.

1973—Monte Irvin is inducted into the Baseball Hall of Fame.

1973—Willie Mays retires with 660 home runs, at the time second only to Babe Ruth.

1974—Hank Aaron hits his career 714th home run to tie Babe Ruth for all-time record on April 4 and breaks record on April 8.

1974—James "Cool Papa" Bell inducted into the Baseball Hall of Fame.

1975—Frank Robinson becomes the first African American manager in baseball history with the Cleveland Indians.

1975—Judy Johnson inducted into the Baseball Hall of Fame.

1976—Minnie Minoso makes a few cameo appearances for the Chicago White Sox to become a rare four-decade player.

1976—Hank Aaron retires with a record of 755 home runs.

1977—Ernie Banks is inducted into the Baseball Hall of Fame.

1978—Larry Doby becomes the second African American manager in history on June 30 when he takes over the Chicago White Sox.

1979—Willie Mays inducted into the Baseball Hall of Fame.

1980—Willie McCovey retires after twenty-two Major League seasons with 521 home runs.

1980—Elston Howard dies December 14 in New York.

1981—Bob Gibson inducted into the Baseball Hall of Fame.

1982—Satchel Paige dies June 8 in Kansas City, Missouri.

1982—Hank Aaron and Frank Robinson inducted into the Baseball Hall of Fame.

1986—Willie McCovey inducted into the Baseball Hall of Fame.

1989—Judy Johnson dies June 15 in Wilmington, Delaware.

1991—James "Cool Papa" Bell dies March 7 in St. Louis, Missouri.

1993—Roy Campanella dies June 26 in Woodland Hills, California.

1994—John "Buck" O'Neil Jr. is featured in documentary *Baseball* and generates a new generation of fans.

1997—Curt Flood dies January 20 in Los Angeles, California.

1997—Walter "Buck" Leonard dies November 27 in Rocky Mount, North Carolina.

1998—Larry Doby inducted into the Baseball Hall of Fame.

2003—Larry Doby dies June 18 in Montclair, New Jersey.

2006—Buck O'Neil dies October 6 in Kansas City.

BUCK O'NEIL

November 13, 1911–October 6, 2006

Buck O'Neil was a leading Negro Leagues player and manager with the Kansas City Monarchs, scouted future Baseball Hall of Famers for the Chicago Cubs, and became the first African American coach in organized ball with the Cubs. He was regarded as an eloquent spokesman for black players born too soon to play in the majors, and was a key figure in the founding and later the growth of the Negro Leagues Baseball Museum.

O'Neil was a first baseman for various black teams from 1934 to 1955, but was most closely identified with the Monarchs. He won the Negro League batting title in 1946 with an average of .346. He was Kansas City's player-manager from 1948 to 1955. O'Neil scouted for the Chicago Cubs from 1956 to 1962 and became the majors' first black coach in June 1962.

On the drive from the airport to downtown Kansas City during the last month of 2005, a visitor to the community of what was once the soul of Negro Leagues baseball saw a billboard featuring the message "Stuck on Buck."

The sign heralded one of the Negro Leagues museum's annual fundraisers tied in with a birthday celebration for the man who linked the modern vault of Negro baseball treasures with its vibrant, lively playing days that expired in 1960. The event was all about giving Buck O'Neil the blues, a roast, a night of comedy at the expense of one of the city's legends.

The event had come and gone on the calendar, but the billboard endured, much like its protagonist had for so long. In the center of the city, where the Negro Leagues Baseball Museum thrives at 18th and Vine Streets, then-ninety-four-year-old Buck O'Neil presided in general fashion over a small empire. As chairman of the board of directors and its most visible face to the outside world, O'Neil was the human conduit to a bygone era.

So many of his contemporaries had passed, some decades earlier. O'Neil outlived almost all of them until he took ill in the fall of 2006 and passed away. During his later years he acted as self-appointed guardian of those players' memories, the protector of the past. He served as institution on two feet, offering education to those who did not know details about the Negro Leagues.

When he was a young man, O'Neil was a highly regarded first baseman, in his best years even a star. He became a leader of men as manager of the Kansas City Monarchs' renowned organization in 1948. Later, when he joined the Chicago Cubs, he became the first African American to be named a Major League coach.

O'Neil was prominent in his time; then when he was too old to play, he earned fresh accolades as a coach and scout in the majors. And then for years he disappeared from the public eye, removed from the game. O'Neil's heyday seemed as consigned to the past as Dwight Eisenhower's. In earlier times, before publishing was so prevalent, before radio's

A key organizer of the Negro Leagues Baseball Museum in Kansas City, former Negro Leagues star Buck O'Neil was a slick-fielding first baseman in his prime.

invention and television's existence, when movies were conducted in the mind, people passed on histories by word of mouth. They told stories to preserve family lore and also to save a tribe's or village's past. Society still places a value on storytelling, but stories are received in different ways. They are all written down, videotaped, or recorded.

Those who played for O'Neil remember him possessing a gift as a storyteller and a special delivery, melodious phrasing of his speech, and the delicious way words rolled off his tongue. It was all accompanied by a glint in the eye seen through tinted glasses. To punctuate his tales, O'Neil lifted an eyebrow and offered a crinkle of a smile.

The rest of the world discovered O'Neil's manner of speaking much later, almost too late. Both baseball aficionados and those introduced to O'Neil's reminisces by accident owe thanks to Ken Burns, the documentary maker. In the course of researching and filming his 1994 epic, eighteen-hour masterpiece, *Baseball*, Burns benefited greatly from O'Neil's charm, and the final product earned O'Neil nationwide accolades. Burns called O'Neil a hero and also described him as elegant.[1]

At the same time, Burns enhanced the richness of baseball by providing O'Neil a forum to talk of all the things he had seen and experienced so long before. The performance raised O'Neil out of the shadows, gave him cache, elevated him to a new celebrityhood, and offered a platform to reach younger generations of baseball fans.

The man lived and made a living during the middle of the twentieth century, when America's racial intolerance was at its most extreme. Yet O'Neil's recitations of evil experiences came off more as a thoughtful regret than an indictment. His mind was a storehouse of stories about certifiable greats of the Negro Leagues, from Satchel Paige and Josh Gibson, to Buck Leonard and Judy Johnson. O'Neil became the gatekeeper of not only his own past, but also his league's and his late friends. Suddenly, partially as the result of attrition, O'Neil became the most genuine symbol of Negro Leagues' spirit.

"I love baseball and I love people," O'Neil said to a newspaper columnist when he visited Cooperstown, New York, home of the Baseball Hall of Fame in 1997. "So that makes for a good combination. Who should I be angry at after all this time? At baseball? Why would I be angry at baseball? You have to be angry at society. It wasn't just baseball."[2]

Illustrating O'Neil's lack of bitterness toward the racist society of his youth—and emphasizing his glass-half-full outlook—he titled his 1996 autobiography *I Was Right on Time*. The choice of the phrase reflected the number of times O'Neil had been asked since his return to prominence if he wished he had been born later, ostensibly to have lived a fuller life with better baseball opportunities.

EARLY LIFE

John Jordan O'Neil Jr. was born in 1911 in Carrabelle, Florida, on the West Coast of the state near Sarasota, the grandson of a slave born in Africa who later resided in one of the Carolinas where he picked cotton. O'Neil's father, John Sr., grew up in Georgia and his mother was born in Quincy, Florida, near Tallahassee.

A farm manager at first, and then a sawmill worker, John Sr. was a ballplayer who competed for a local amateur team. John Jr. was the bat boy for his father's team and he enjoyed the attention of the older men. O'Neil said by the time he was seven or eight years old, "I was a ham."[3]

The bat boy role is one of O'Neil's earliest memories. In his nineties, O'Neil walked with a cane for support when prowling the offices and display rooms of the Negro Leagues museum, and the hair he had left was white. His handshake remained powerful and that firm grip called attention to his long fingers and large palms. It would be easy for someone to tease O'Neil and suggest that he never had need for a baseball glove because his own mitts were so large. "I always had good hands and big hands," he said.[4] The strength in those hands enabled him to carry more boxes of fresh produce on the farm his father worked, but both John Sr.'s urging and his own ambition led O'Neil to baseball at an early age. When O'Neil was a kid in the 1920s, he saw New York Giants spring training games in Sarasota and he remembered seeing the bandy-legged manager Miller Huggins, a future Hall of Famer for his leadership with the Yankees, during spring training in Tampa. O'Neil also watched Babe Ruth and Lou Gehrig batter the fences, their slugging with their ash war clubs formidable.

One story O'Neil had told in many forums revolves around the unique thumping sound the force of a bat smacking a ball makes when it is wielded by a very rare and special power hitter. It is a sound that has propelled him running from a clubhouse to a field to see who connected. O'Neil has said repeatedly that he has heard that clubbing noise just three times in his life: with balls swatted by Ruth, by Josh Gibson, and decades later by Bo Jackson, the football-baseball star of the Chicago White Sox and Kansas City Royals forced to retire young because of a degenerative hip condition.

The local Sarasota Tigers sandlot team practiced on a field near O'Neil's home, and one day the squad's first baseman did not show up. The excuse for the man's absence was that he had to work at his real job. The manager asked fourteen-year-old O'Neil to fill in and he stayed with the club. Instead of sleeping at home with the family that included older sister Fanny and younger brother Warren, O'Neil was sometimes tucked in by adult teammates. "I had a natural talent," O'Neil said. "We traveled around Florida. I was just a kid. They would put me to bed."[5]

The all-black team was not always welcome at small-town hotels, but O'Neil said players were housed by the local preacher or undertaker and he loved the chance to get out of his home town and see a little bit of what he knew to be a much larger universe.[6]

As young as he was, and as enticing and enjoyable as life on the road was playing baseball with older men, O'Neil understood the value of education and he kept up his studies. For a man who suffered indignities because of the color of his skin many times during his baseball journeys, called "nigger," refused a room or a meal, facing whites-only water fountains, the major irritant and frustration of O'Neil's life seemed to be the prejudice at home that prevented him from attending and graduating from high-quality Sarasota High School. The local authorities barred African American children from the public school system beyond the eighth grade—there were only four high schools open to black youths in Florida in the late 1920s. "What bothered me most is that I couldn't attend Sarasota High or the University of Florida," O'Neil said when he was in his nineties.[7]

For three years as a teenager, O'Neil carried boxes of celery for $1.25 a day on the farm his father operated. He toted four crates at a time when others could manage just two. Yet the oppressive heat and humidity convinced him something better awaited. Many African Americans in the area obtained circus jobs since Sarasota was the winter home of the circus, but that's not what O'Neil had in mind. His father subscribed to out-of-town black newspapers to read up on Negro Leagues baseball and O'Neil learned about black stars such as Oscar Charleston and John Henry Lloyd, both of whom would much later be enshrined in the Baseball Hall of Fame.

Snubbed by discrimination, O'Neil found himself without a local school. Instead, he enrolled in Edward Waters College, an historically all-black school in Jacksonville in the northeastern section of the state, and one which attracted high school–aged students from all over Florida. Testing placed him in the eleventh grade. One influence there was the baseball coach, Ox Clemons, who taught his pupil the finer points of first base play and hit-and-run batting.

O'Neil played football and baseball for the school—records of his performance are not available—and in summers barnstormed for amateur baseball clubs that traveled the countryside picking up games against local semipro outfits wherever they could. College baseball was not very sophisticated in the 1930s and it was not until decades later that scouts seriously considered that level of play worthy for developing professionals. For O'Neil, summer play served as career foreshadowing and he left college after two years. The O'Neils were neither abjectly poor nor wealthy, but Buck liked the idea of making his own money, and the lifestyle of a professional baseball player was more alluring than school.

PLAYING CAREER

O'Neil did not immediately sign with a top echelon Negro Leagues club. When he started playing for pay in 1934, O'Neil competed for teams like the Tampa Bay Smokers, Miami Giants, and the Shreveport Acme Giants. There were no organized minor leagues of African American teams, so O'Neil caught on with traveling teams to hone his talent.

Touring clubs were the alternative to joining the Homestead Grays or the Kansas City Monarchs. Even O'Neil, a dignified man with Major League skills, signed on with the Zulu Cannibal Giants out of Louisville, Kentucky, for a month in 1937. This was one of the so-called clown teams that played up showmanship as much as baseball ability. It was also one of the teams that to attract audiences played upon distressing stereotypes and blacks' African roots.

O'Neil said he was pretty much a "straight player," meaning one who did not participate in the entertainment acts, but took his baseball seriously. However, he wrote, "I did have to wear the war paint and the skirt."[8] He discussed the hazards of running the bases and sliding into second with bare legs, disclosing hidden sliding trunks under the skirt. But all the same, those men risked the same type of severe bruises as the women wearing skirt uniforms who participated in the All-American Girls Baseball Association, a World War II–period creation.

Such demeaning stereotypical attire and behavior required by owners and promoters was unimaginable for white players and would not be tolerated in the sport at all seventy years later. While playing for Shreveport, O'Neil reported that the team ran short of rent money, escaped out a back window in the middle of the night and was able to make a getaway. The team somehow put eleven guys into a single automobile and onto the running boards. "It was a lot like a circus act," O'Neil said. "I was starting to think I had joined Ringling Brothers, after all."[9]

O'Neil had always been careful to differentiate between the wild things that took place on the road when barnstorming teams rolled from rural town to rural town and what occurred in organized Negro Leagues games in major city stadiums. They were two different worlds.

It has been said that black ballplayers existed in a shadow world until 1947 when Jackie Robinson broke baseball's color barrier with the Brooklyn Dodgers. That image persists because there was limited documentation of what took place on the field. Many game details or box scores were never recorded in newspapers. In some instances, there has been debate over which teams were genuine Negro Leagues material and which ones were not credentialed. Over time much of the dispute has been ironed out, but some elderly players who claim membership in the Negro Leagues fraternity are not accepted by record keepers because their teams were categorized as barnstormers.

Players like O'Neil had it both ways. He was good enough to play at the top level, but took advantage of opportunities to make extra money with traveling teams that sometimes played more than one exhibition in a day. O'Neil said he is disturbed that less than fully informed people think black ball was sufficiently summarized by *The Bingo Long Traveling All-Stars and Motor Kings* movie starring James Earl Jones, Billy Dee Williams, and Richard Pryor.

When the movie was released in 1976 it was well received and it was also one of white America's first glimpses into the world of black baseball. The story is fiction, set in 1939, but much of what is contained in the film rings true, if telescoped. There was an obvious reliance on real-life players. Williams plays a Satchel Paige–like pitcher character. Jones plays a Josh Gibson–like catcher character. Pryor plays Charlie Snow, a ballplayer who is likely a composite, and who is convinced he will soon be playing in the majors.

"I guess you ain't heard, I'll be playing in the white leagues," the Pryor character said. There are cynical laughs all around from his teammates. Pryor also said he was learning Spanish so he could break into the majors masquerading as a Cuban.

The movie combines all elements of barnstorming life, from cramming into big cars, to having them repossessed, to being unable to meet the rent, to making a flashy entrance in a town to pump up the gate. Also true to life: when a young slugger played by Stan Shaw announces he has been signed to play in the bigs, nobody can believe it. Billy Dee thought it would be him. The same reaction permeated the Negro Leagues when the Dodgers inked Robinson to a contract.

"No, that wasn't the Negro Leagues," O'Neil protested about the movie. "We weren't a bunch of tramps traveling all over the country. Hollywood tried to get down something that approached how they thought the Negro Leagues were. They still don't realize how it was. The Negro Leagues were one of the biggest black owned businesses in the country."[10]

The barnstorming teams did often merely hold things together on a shoestring, drifting from payday to payday. Some teams were more solvent than others. Some were very successful, others folded. Similarly, even teams in the Negro National League and the Eastern Colored League, solid franchises during the 1920s, collapsed in the Depression of the 1930s before O'Neil made his debut. The teams and leagues regrouped and regenerated in the late 1930s and throughout the 1940s, and began to unravel as the 1950s dawned. Following the signing of Jackie Robinson, Major League teams raided Negro League rosters. The top players wanted to go, to at last test themselves against the best, and in only a few instances were their former teams compensated financially.

If O'Neil's experience with barnstorming teams was generally a satisfactory one, not all players had the same pleasure. The pitfalls were highlighted in *Bingo Long*. The barnstormers rarely played home games. They were on the road constantly and they didn't always know what type of reception they would receive when they showed up for a scheduled game. Black ballplayers roaming the south were offered little security, either physically or psychologically. The air was warm, but the hospitality was not.

Carl Long, who played with the Philadelphia Stars and the Birmingham Black Barons in the early 1950s before he joined the Pittsburgh Pirates organization and played for their minor league affiliates, said much like scenes in the movie, many times his teams were not allowed to shower at the ballpark and had to climb on the bus sweaty and dirty from a game.

"We would go down to a creek and stop off to wash ourselves off," said Long, who was seventy-one and living in Kinston, North Carolina in the spring of 2006. "We washed our uniforms, too, then we dried them as the bus drove on. Once, I yelled, 'Stop the bus! My uniform just blew out the window!'"[11]

Baltimore, Louisville, Nashville, Kansas City, Dallas, and Norfolk, Virginia were some of the places Long played left field. After playing in front of small crowds, playing in a big stadium could be unnerving. "I was scared to death when I walked out there," Long said.[12]

One of Long's teammates was future music star Charlie Pride, who strummed a guitar as the bus hurtled through the night after games. The other players did not apparently have much of an ear for talent. "We told him to shut up, we were trying to sleep," Long said. "He became a millionaire singing those country and western songs."[13]

During barnstorming tours, Long said he played with or against Hank Aaron, Ernie Banks, Jackie Robinson, Larry Doby, Luke Easter, Don Newcombe, and Jim Gilliam. Those are the pleasant memories. There are bad ones too, nightmarish. "We used to drive the bus down the highway in the south and a guy would be hanging from a tree," Long said.[14] A lynching. The jokes stopped. The bus grew silent and the men retreated into their own thoughts. America in 1952 was not really a land of freedom for a black man.

Even if he didn't bring incidents up without questioning, O'Neil had no blind spot about what white American society did to innocent black men, and the vicious murders committed with impunity in a seemingly lawless south. "Horrible things did happen," O'Neil said. "You've just got a few fools out there thinking this way now. It was just sickening to think this could happen. But they [other Americans] let it happen."[15]

O'Neil reached the top level of black ball in 1937 when he played for the Memphis Red Sox. A year later he joined the Kansas City Monarchs, the dominant black ball team in the west. The next time he had a new employer it was for a position scouting for the Major League Chicago Cubs in 1955. Playing and managing for the Monarchs, O'Neil became a local institution and became a year-round Kansas City resident in 1946. The new Monarchs first baseman was twenty-four when he came to Kansas City, a place he came to call "my town" and he regarded it as "a huge step" in his career. "We had some of the best ballplayers in the world," he said.[16]

Being a Monarch was something special in the African American community; so was being a musician. The worlds of

Closely aligned with the Kansas City Monarchs for years, O'Neil eventually became the club's manager and tutored several young players on their way up, such as Ernie Banks and Elston Howard.

athletes and entertainers overlapped, as they so often do. Blues and jazz were the preferred music of the time and the black club scene was hot. O'Neil took his cuts at the plate and in the social scene. Much later, after he became manager in 1948, he allowed musical great Lionel Hampton to coach first base for a game. Cab Calloway, Billie Holiday, and Bill "Bojangles" Robinson frequented the area. So did heavyweight champion Joe Louis. O'Neil developed a long-standing affinity for the comfort of Cadillacs, the antithesis ride for someone who affixed his rear end to a less-than cushy bus seat for many miles for many years. He also acquired a fondness for slick clothes and in his nineties still wore dapper outfits such as a beige velour vest with tweed pants.

The bars were the hangouts for the popular ballplayers, the sexiest women, the most stirring musical acts, and the late-night boozers. Only O'Neil had a secret that he imparted quietly to the bartenders at his favorite places, the King Fish bar and the Blue Room. "I never did drink," O'Neil said. "What he [the bartender] would do is give me a glass of water and put a lemon in it. I'd sip on that and act the fool like the other people."[17]

The neighborhood was the hub of nighttime play for years—with clubs crammed into the streets between 12th and 18th Streets like the Chocolate Bar, the Hey-Hay Club, Dante's Inferno, and the Stork Club. Only much later did the area fray around the edges. The same hot corner of the 1930s and 1940s is the precise location of the Negro Leagues Baseball Museum today.

When he was young, O'Neil was called "Foots" by friends because of size twelve shoes. By the time O'Neil planted roots on first base for the Monarchs he had shed his birth name and that moniker, as well. How he came to be called "Buck" instead of John was simple, if somewhat silly. When he joined the Miami Giants briefly in 1934, the owner was Buck O'Neal. Same name, different spelling. Whether it was a case of mistaken identity, or a case of why not call them both Buck, O'Neil the younger left town with a new nickname that stuck.

O'Neil was saddled with still another nickname, courtesy of his old teammate Satchel Paige, the legendary hurler who was the first black player in the twentieth century to transcend black ball and intrude into the consciousness of white baseball fans. Paige could be a handful for a manager and owner and even his teammates. He did his own thing and that included wild behavior in his personal life. Once, O'Neil rescued Paige from the potential wrath of his future wife.

As O'Neil related, the Monarchs played an exhibition game on an Indian reservation in Sioux Falls, South Dakota, where Paige became enamored of a "beautiful Indian maiden named Nancy."

Soon after, O'Neil was snacking in the team's Chicago hotel coffee shop and saw a taxi cab discharging Nancy. O'Neil told her that Paige was in his room. Shortly, another taxi cab dropped off Lahoma, Paige's fiancée, who was not expected. O'Neil told her Paige was not in the hotel, but would be back soon, and got her luggage installed in an empty room.

Paige climbed down the fire escape and then walked around to meet Lahoma with great "surprise." Later that night, Paige slipped out of his room and knocked on the door to Nancy's room. Through his door, O'Neil heard Paige whisper loudly, "Nancy!" Lahoma opened the door to investigate. O'Neil flung his door open as Paige improvised saying, "Nancy, there you are!"[18] For the rest of Paige's life he called O'Neil "Nancy."

The first time O'Neil encountered the man destined to become one of his best friends was during an exhibition game in 1936. Paige jumped teams on a whim, or the promise of any type of better payday, and he was in his prime, a fastballer whose speed was blinding and who derived special pleasure from naming his variety of pitches. O'Neil did not fare well.

"He was a pure flame thrower back then," O'Neil said. "Someone once clocked his fastball at 105 mph. I couldn't tell you if he was throwing the bee ball or the hurry-up ball because it went so fast I couldn't see it." O'Neil said he was well aware of Paige's playing reputation because of all the publicity the hurler garnered, but when he introduced himself and shook hands, O'Neil said he was surprised by Paige's friendliness. The duo remained friends for nearly fifty years, sharing road trips and baseball fields and long nights on buses singing together with Satch playing the ukulele.[19]

With the Monarchs, a team O'Neil likened to being as prestigious as the New York Yankees, the tall and slender young player of six-foot-two and 190 pounds, established himself as a good fielder and as he matured he improved as a hitter.

O'Neil spent three years of World War II in the Navy—and missed the 1945 season when he would have been teammates with Jackie Robinson. But when he returned to baseball in 1946 O'Neil batted a career high .350 and led the Negro American League in hitting. He also married Ora Lee Owen, a Memphis teacher, a union with a half century run. O'Neil played in three Negro League East-West All-Star games. Because records are incomplete, it is not possible to place a totally accurate figure on O'Neil's lifetime batting average. But as part of the Cooperstown Winter Cultural Series in February, 2000, it was indicated by the Baseball Hall of Fame Research Library that O'Neil likely hit .288 during his nineteen seasons in the Negro Leagues. O'Neil made significant playing contributions to Monarchs teams he played on that won three Negro Leagues World Series championships. Teams he managed won five pennants.

There are many stories about the hard times and ill treatment of African American ballplayers barnstorming the country, sometimes with teams even turned away from parks they were scheduled to play in. But O'Neil's take on America's divisiveness of the time is an explanation of how the experiences of the lucky ones in the Negro Leagues took the sting out of discrimination and how those players had a bang-up good time. "We ate at some of the best restaurants in the country," he said. "They just happened to be black owned and operated. We stayed at some of the best hotels in the country. They just happened to be black hotels."[20]

LATER LIFE

O'Neil's longevity in baseball, his photographic-type memory, and his observation of the game span the better part of a century. Since O'Neil watched New York Giants and New York Yankees teams in spring training in the 1920s, saw—or knew—virtually every great Negro Leagues player, and then moved into the majors as a scout and coach, and remained a fan, his personal viewpoints were unique. He saw Babe Ruth and Lou Gehrig in person, batted against Satchel Paige, played against Josh Gibson, signed Ernie Banks for the Cubs, and evaluated Alex Rodriguez of the modern Yankees and Ken Griffey Jr. of the Cincinnati Reds as greats of the present.

Invited to make speeches—in Kansas City at fundraisers for the museum, at the Hall of Fame in Cooperstown, and earlier to promote the Ken Burns documentary—O'Neil became a human time machine, shedding light on a past shrouded by lack of publicity and attention.

O'Neil had keen insights on players who could not speak for themselves and for players for whom there was little or no known video. What was Satchel Paige really like? he was asked. How about Josh Gibson? What do you think about Cool Papa Bell? He reveled in the role of using words to paint pictures in hopes of doing justice to his friends whose actions couldn't be seen any other way. "Josh Gibson had great power as a hitter and he was an outstanding human being," O'Neil said.[21] Cool Papa Bell could do everything on the ballfield, O'Neil said. "He could hit, run, field and throw," he said. "He could fly. He was cool under pressure. So he was called 'Cool.' It was like nothing happened, he was always cool."[22] After returning to the public eye following the Burns' 1994 *Baseball* documentary, O'Neil, who said it was great to become an overnight sensation at age eighty-two,[23] projected a similarly cool image.

Once Jackie Robinson signed a contract with the Dodgers organization in the fall of 1945, it quickly became apparent that black baseball was going to disintegrate. African American fans flocked to National League parks to watch Robinson's historic barrier breaking appearances, abandoning virtually overnight the Negro League teams that sustained their race for decades. Attendance dropped precipitously and when the

Dodgers followed up by signing Roy Campanella, Don Newcombe, and others; and the Cleveland Indians made Larry Doby the first black player in the American League and also signed forty-two-year-old rookie Satchel Paige as the first black pitcher in the league; the handwriting on the wall was not in Egyptian hieroglyphics.

Most of the older black players knew their time had passed and they would never be summoned by the majors, regardless of how good they were. O'Neil, pushing forty, and managing his own team, never expected a call. He did not resent the changes sweeping the baseball landscape, but took note of them and reflected on the situation.

Historians argue that World War II was the greatest prod to widespread integration in the United States. The country was fighting fascism overseas, seeking to prevent the spread of a racist Nazi regime in Germany and a racist Japanese regime in Asia. African American soldiers signed up for the battle, yet wondered why they were not granted equality at home and questioned why they fought in segregated units.

When peace returned, the soldiers coming home from the front refused to accept the same old segregation. Times were changing. Baseball was indisputably the national pastime in the mid-1940s, and the sport became the front lines for believers in integration and equality. Martin Luther King Jr. is considered the most important black leader of the twentieth century, but Jackie Robinson, a baseball player, has been ranked high on the list. "That was the beginning the civil rights movement," O'Neil said.[24]

Robinson was a living, breathing symbol of equality, playing out the dream for American blacks everyday for one-hundred-and-fifty-four games a season, right before spectators' eyes at the ballpark, and beamed into their homes on radios. Paige and Gibson expected to be the first African American given the opportunity to play in the majors and when they were not chosen, they gulped hard. Buck Leonard was good enough in his prime, but was forty when Robinson seized his break.

O'Neil, the biggest name with a proud franchise, was in the Philippines with the Navy when he heard of Robinson signing with Brooklyn. His first reaction was that the agreement represented progress for the whole country.[25] O'Neil met Robinson in Cuba in 1947. "I was impressed with him as a human being," O'Neil said. "He had the tools. He had that quickness. He took Negro League ball into the majors. Hit, run, steal, steal home."[26]

Later that year O'Neil had a conversation with Branch Rickey, the Dodgers' president, who pointedly and determinedly aimed at smashing baseball's color line. "I said, 'Is Jackie going to make it?'" O'Neil recalled. "He said, 'We're going to see that he makes it.'"[27] O'Neil watched Robinson interact with Pee Wee Reese and Eddie Stanky in the infield. "I'm looking at two southern boys with Jackie," O'Neil said. "Before, that just wouldn't have happened."[28]

O'Neil knew the personalities of the best players in the Negro Leagues and while no one claimed that Robinson was the best player available, he was mature, had been in the service, attended integrated University of California, Los Angeles (UCLA), and was probably a better fit than almost anyone else who could have been selected by Rickey. "Jackie was the right guy," O'Neil said. "Some of those guys [other players], if they had had a black cat thrown on the field, they wouldn't have taken it. They would have gone into the stands and shoved it down somebody's throat."[29]

In 1950, when it was apparent that the days of the separate Negro Leagues were numbered, O'Neil was still managing the Monarchs. It was different. As a younger man he caroused with his teammates, soaking up the atmosphere and music in the clubs. Now he could not be buddy-buddy with them. "I'm the boss," he said of those days.

In 1955, after the Kansas City Monarchs closed shop, Buck O'Neil joined the Chicago Cubs as a scout—he signed Ernie Banks and Hall of Famer Lou Brock for the team. In 1962, the Cubs made O'Neil the majors' first black coach.

"I could go out, but I couldn't go with them. It was too bad. When you're the manager, you don't go to the same places with the ballplayers."[30]

However, from a business standpoint, O'Neil was blessed with an eighteen-year-old newcomer who obviously had the talent to go far. That is when O'Neil met future Hall of Famer Ernie Banks, who later excelled for two decades at shortstop and first base with the Chicago Cubs. Banks became known for his sunny disposition and constant use of the phrase "Let's play two" to express his enthusiasm for the game. He was routinely referred to as the nicest man in baseball. Banks gives O'Neil credit for his outlook. "He is a role model, a father, a mentor, a teacher, a sensei, a hero, a gentleman, a man," Banks said. "Who do you think I got my 'let's-play-two' attitude from? Buck O'Neil, that's who."[31]

Banks came into O'Neil's life for the first time in June of 1950, a raw talent, eager for coaching, and clearly in the older man's view, a player who would not linger long on his way up. Cool Papa Bell spotted Banks in Texas, where he grew up, and raved about him to O'Neil. Trusting his old friend's judgment, O'Neil drove to Dallas and signed Banks without seeing him play. Once he got him on the roster, O'Neil worked constantly with Banks on the diamond before games. "Buck used to take me out to the field early and stand behind me while one of his coaches hit grounders to me at short," Banks said. "He'd show me how to go into the hole and get the ball. He's a fine instructor and a tremendous leader. He was always saying nice things about me."[32]

By that time O'Neil knew he was grooming young black talent for the white majors, not for long stays with his own soon-to-be floundering Monarchs. O'Neil steered Banks to the Cubs even though the older man would stay with his old team till the end came in 1955. He also guided the New York Yankees to Elston Howard, the first African American to play with the perennial world champions. In 1956, the Cubs, perhaps mindful of the sharp eye for talent that brought them a player who would become the best in team history, hired O'Neil as a full-time scout.

As a scout, O'Neil discovered Lou Brock as an undergraduate at Southern University. Brock became a major leaguer with the Cubs, but was shipped to the St. Louis Cardinals in what has been termed the worst trade in baseball history. There he blossomed into a Hall of Famer. O'Neil and Brock maintained a close friendship. O'Neil also signed Joe Carter, whose greatest professional moments also came in another uniform, leading the Toronto Blue Jays to a World Series title with a dramatic home run. Another player O'Neil dug up for the Cubs was Lee Smith, the relief pitcher who became baseball's all-time saves leader.

Besides scouting, the Cubs sometimes used O'Neil as a troubleshooter to help guide young black players who might be having a tough time in the minors. Probably O'Neil's most conspicuous and valuable save was reaching out to a homesick minor leaguer playing in San Antonio. Billy Williams was from Mobile, Alabama, missed his family, and had lost his confidence. O'Neil spent time with him, boosted his spirits, and talked him into sticking with the team. Soon enough Williams was in the majors and on his way to a Hall-of-Fame outfielding career.

O'Neil had been a spring training assistant, working with young players. But when the perennially losing, desperate Cubs adopted the most exotic and rarest of operations to manage a Major League club, O'Neil received the official big-league title of coach. When named in June of 1962 as part of the Cubs' College of Coaches, a rotating head coach system, O'Neil was one of eleven coaches and didn't think a lot about it. The rest of the world did. O'Neil made national news for becoming the first African American Major League coach. "Suddenly, I was in *Sports Illustrated* and *Ebony* and all the papers," he said. "It [the College of Coaches] was a ridiculous idea, although I was quoted in the *Ebony* article as saying it was 'a wonderful innovation' that would 'be adopted by most teams.' What was I supposed to say? It just had the ballplayers all confused."[33]

Unlike Robinson's landmark breakthrough, O'Neil's historic first does not resonate as readily with the public. Who was the first black Major League coach? It is a trivia question. "A lot of people don't remember it," O'Neil said. "The baseball fan might remember it. And it didn't last."[34]

There was less chance of other teams substituting the college of coaches idea that was the brainchild of Cubs owner Philip K. Wrigley than the team giving away a free 50,000 tickets. The College of Coaches had never been tried before and after it failed to rejuvenate the losing team was never tried again.

During one of his visits to Cooperstown, O'Neil remarked upon his stay with the Cubs in a food-for-thought manner since he never obtained his college degree. "If I had that piece of paper I might have been the first black general manager in baseball," he said.[35]

As scout, coach, and scout again, O'Neil spent thirty-two years with the Cubs, retiring in 1988. He was retired from baseball for about ten minutes before the home Kansas

City Royals contacted him. O'Neil was offered the job of special assignment scout for the Royals. He accepted since he would be obligated to do much less traveling than he had for the Cubs.

O'Neil was working only part-time on the fringes of baseball until his starring role in Burns' *Baseball* documentary. His presence electrified viewers, leading to publication of his autobiography, his role as a spokesman for the Negro Leagues, and his passion for raising enough money to expand a storefront museum into a permanent, sizable, enduring Negro Leagues Baseball Museum. He parlayed the attention into the gleaming building that now stands at 18th and Vine Streets.

The museum exists at least partially because O'Neil would not always. While Baseball Hall of Fame president Dale Petrosky called him the ultimate "ambassador" for the sport, O'Neil knew he wouldn't live forever.[36] "The majority of the people who come in here," O'Neil said of the Negro Leagues Baseball Museum, "are white folks. That's why I wanted the museum here, so what happened would never be forgotten."[37]

O'Neil was asked many times if he was bitter when the majors began siphoning off black talent and finished the Negro Leagues. "When they signed Jackie Robinson, I knew that was the death knell for the Negro Leagues," O'Neil said. "But it didn't hurt me. I was old. Besides, when the major leagues came after black players, that was what we wanted. We wanted it to change. Way back when Rube Foster started the Negro National League in the 1920s, he thought the American League would take a team and the National League would take a team. But Judge Landis, the commissioner, was not going to have that."[38]

Instead, the Major League boycott of African Americans lasted decades longer. Kenesaw Mountain Landis could have eradicated the odious unwritten rule by executive order. It took Happy Chandler, the commissioner who succeeded Landis upon his death in 1944, to open the door. So many players were hurt for so long, unnecessarily.

"To understand man's inhumanity to man, that's been a terrible thing," O'Neil said. "There was nothing fair about it at all. The tough part about it was I could go to Omaha and seventy percent of the fans were white, then when we left the park we couldn't go to a restaurant or a hotel."[39]

Often, when O'Neil did speaking engagements or interviews he was asked if he came along too soon. Never did he suggest the accidental timing of his arrival in this world rankled him. "If I had been born later, I wouldn't have seen Babe Ruth," he said. "I wouldn't have seen Ty Cobb. I wouldn't have played with Cool Papa Bell. We [African Americans] might have been playing the best baseball in this country."[40]

For all of those decades, when his career played out in the shadows, when he made the most of every opportunity, even if some of those barnstorming trips were sideshows, O'Neil said the one thing that truly bugged him was being banned from Sarasota High School. He repeated that lament often enough that the word ultimately reached Sarasota authorities, many of whom saw him in the *Baseball* documentary.

Seeking to make amends, in 1995 Sarasota city fathers did the best they could. In March of that year, O'Neil went home to a drastically different atmosphere. Sarasota threw a luncheon in his honor. It hosted "An Evening with Buck O'Neil" reception. Sarasota named the Baltimore Orioles' training complex after him. And it bestowed an honorary diploma from Sarasota High School on him.

When he spoke, marvelously pleased over the honors and the scene, O'Neil said he had met President Harry Truman and President Bill Clinton, and even hugged Hillary

Clinton, but that this was a very special occasion. "I would rather be right here, right now, talking to you, than doing anything else I've ever done," O'Neil said.[41]

Once the first black Dodger and Indians players moved into the majors and were successful, other teams investigated the new source of talent. They had to, if only to keep up in the standings. Black superstars eventually emerged on every team. Jackie Robinson was not a solo act, though he opened previously locked gates. And that was the whole point for Branch Rickey, the black community leaders who helped, and the African American players. The signing of Robinson was not about an opportunistic fit in the Brooklyn lineup, it was about providing a level playing field for all Americans and integrating both a sport and society. "When Jackie Robinson went into the major leagues, every black kid wanted to be Jackie Robinson," O'Neil said. "To make a living as a professional athlete, everybody played baseball."[42]

Some sixty years later, the American sports universe is far more diversified and scrambled. While baseball remains popular enough to set attendance records, African American athletes in huge numbers have gravitated to pro football and professional basketball. Black athletes have rearranged priorities to excel in golf, tennis, and every other sport available. It is a different form of integration. Baseball has suffered because top black athletes choose other avenues. The roster space so dearly earned in the Forties and Fifties is now filled by Latin American ballplayers. It is a development O'Neil lived to see.

"Now there are so many ways to make a great living," O'Neil said, expressing no sorrow over this unexpected change among young black athletes. "All they need for basketball is tennis shoes and they can shoot all night. It's tougher to play baseball. You need a ball, a glove, a bat. Football is stealing them [the athletes].

"Baseball moved from the inner city to the suburbs. Now they're playing basketball in the inner city. The Latin kids are just like we were. We wanted to play baseball and get out of the ghetto. We've started something called the RBI Program for kids in Kansas City, New York, Chicago, Atlanta, and Los Angeles. Give us seven or eight years and you'll see black kids back and playing in the major leagues."[43]

American society's human relations have changed in measurably better ways since Buck O'Neil was born in Florida in 1911. He never got a chance to play in the major leagues, but he conquered the worlds available to him. And O'Neil, the survivor, who outlasted most of his contemporaries, knows what he and they accomplished for the black baseball players who crashed the color barrier in 1947.

"We did our duty," O'Neil said. "We laid the groundwork for the Jackie Robinsons and the Willie Mays and the guys who are playing now. We did our part and turned it over to the next generation."[44] And all future generations.

In September 2006, O'Neil was hospitalized in Kansas City. The diagnosis was fatigue, but could have been old age. He never left the hospital and died a few weeks later. Baseball people everywhere mourned, no one more than Ernie Banks and Billy Williams, the two Hall of Famers helped so much by O'Neil when they were still teenagers.

Banks, who called O'Neil a "teacher and a leader," said baseball should be ashamed that O'Neil is not in the Hall of Fame. "That was a real travesty and an embarrassment to the game," Banks said.

Williams, who saw O'Neil in Cooperstown a month earlier, said simply, "Baseball has lost a great ambassador."[45]

Those who know baseball, however, feel that O'Neil's accomplishments will only grow in the public mind and that the next time Buck O'Neil's name is mentioned at the

Hall of Fame it will be when he is inducted and takes his place enshrined next to so many of his old friends.

NOTES

1. Buck O'Neil with Steve Wulf and David Conrads, *I Was Right on Time* (New York: Simon & Schuster, 1996), XI.

2. Bud Poliquin, *Syracuse Herald-American*, 1997. Baseball Hall of Fame Archives, n.d.

3. Buck O'Neil, personal interview, Kansas City, December 7, 2005.

4. Ibid.

5. Ibid.

6. Ibid.

7. Ibid.

8. O'Neil with Wulf and Conrads, *I Was Right on Time*, 71.

9. Ibid.

10. O'Neil, personal interview, December 7, 2005.

11. Carl Long, personal interview (telephone), January 11, 2006.

12. Ibid.

13. Ibid.

14. Ibid.

15. O'Neil, personal interview, December 7, 2005.

16. Ibid.

17. Ibid.

18. O'Neil with Wulf and Conrads, *I Was Right on Time*, 13–15.

19. O'Neil, personal interview, December 7, 2005.

20. Bill Francis, *Freeman's Journal*, February 11, 2000.

21. O'Neil, personal interview, December 7, 2005.

22. Ibid.

23. O'Neil with Wulf and Conrads, *I Was Right on Time*, 2.

24. O'Neil, personal interview, December 7, 2005.

25. Ibid.

26. Ibid.

27. Ibid.

28. Ibid.

29. Ibid.

30. Ibid.

31. Steve Wulf, "The Guiding Light," *Sports Illustrated*, September 19, 1994, 150.

32. Bob Smith, *Chicago Daily News*, June 9, 1962.

33. O'Neil with Wulf and Conrads, *I Was Right on Time*, 212–213.

34. O'Neil, personal interview, December 7, 2005.

35. Ibid.

36. Francis, *Freeman's Journal*, February 11, 2000.

37. O'Neil, personal interview, December 7, 2005.

38. Ibid.

39. Ibid.

40. Ibid.

41. Tom Zucco, *St. Petersburg Times*, March 9, 1995.

42. O'Neil, personal interview, December 7, 2005.

43. Ibid.

44. O'Neil's speech at Cooperstown Winter Cultural Series, February 5, 2000. A copy of the speech is available at the Baseball Hall of Fame Library Archives.

45. Fred Mitchell, *Chicago Tribune*, October, 8, 2006.

Further Reading

O'Neil, Buck, with Steve Wulf and David Conrads, *I Was Right on Time.* New York, Simon & Schuster, 1996.

Wulf, Steve, "The Guiding Light," *Sports Illustrated*, Sept. 19, 1994.

JUDY JOHNSON

October 26, 1899–June 15, 1989

Long retired from active play as one of the greatest all-around infielders from the early days of Negro Leagues play, Judy Johnson was nonetheless selected for the Baseball Hall of Fame. He excelled at third base and shortstop, primarily for the Homestead Grays and Pittsburgh Crawfords in a playing career that began in 1918 and did not conclude until 1938. Johnson batted an eye-opening .391 in 1923, .390 in 1929, and .392 in 1935. Not a power hitter, Johnson, a manager of the Grays later, was a fundamentally solid, smart player who did all of the little things well. After Major League doors opened to African Americans, Johnson scouted for the Philadelphia Athletics, Milwaukee Braves, and the Philadelphia Phillies, and entered the Hall of Fame in 1975.

☆   ☆   ☆

He is forever poised in the dim light of the Coors Field of Legends at the Negro Leagues Baseball Museum in Kansas City, prepared to field a ground ball at shortstop. The statue of Judy Johnson is an homage to a baseball great born too soon, overshadowed until too late, but in the end appropriately honored.

The greats in Negro Leagues baseball history are immortalized on an indoor field at 18th and Vine Streets, deployed around the artificial turf by position. Johnson may not be as famous as some of the biggest stars, but he earned his place with a terrifically productive bat and a smooth fielding style. He was older than most of the memorable greats like Satchel Paige and Josh Gibson, but outlasted many of them, too.

A visitor can walk right up to the frozen-in-time Judy Johnson, his facial features smooth and unlined by the passage of decades, his youthful looks captured in his prime of so long ago. There are museum instructions to be followed, however, for those who venture near the statues. "Please don't touch them. You may talk to them if you like."

Any conversation must be one-way. These symbolic statues cannot talk back, to tell the world about their times in their own voices. They cannot relate the stories of how it was in the early days of the Negro Leagues, of how it was when America's fear and loathing over race consigned men of superb talents to a satellite league in order to play baseball. Instead, the museum offers the substitute voice where everyone can listen to the men speak across the years.

EARLY LIFE

William Julius "Judy" Johnson was born in Snow Hill, Maryland, and died nearly ninety years later in Wilmington, Delaware. He was just nineteen when he made his professional baseball debut in 1918 with a team called the Madison Stars, and he was active for twenty years. He was one of the stalwarts of the Pittsburgh Crawfords late in his career when the Crawfords were the best black team around, in the midst of winning nine consecutive pennants.

Like his good friend James "Cool Papa" Bell, Johnson was slightly built at five-foot-eleven and 150 pounds, and made his reputation as a slick fielder and high

Judy Johnson was a star shortstop and third baseman for two decades ending in 1938, and later was selected for the Baseball Hall of Fame.

average hitter rather than a power swinger. Johnson was seen as a "scientific player," a phrase in vogue at the time, meaning he was excellent at playing the angles and plotting strategy. Johnson didn't bludgeon opponents to defeat with a big bat as much as he bled them to death. More recently the style has become known as "small ball."

Johnson developed his game on sandlots in Delaware and he spent most of his career affiliated with Pennsylvania teams in and around Philadelphia and Pittsburgh, while retaining his residence in Delaware. Johnson was adorned with a girl's nickname quite early in his career, and despite two stories claiming the origin of its application, neither seemed to make much sense. Another player, also nicknamed Judy, told Johnson that he reminded him of himself. Another story has it that teammates are the ones who said Johnson resembled Judy Gans closely enough to be his son, so they afflicted him with the same name. The appellation stuck with Johnson for the rest of his life. It was not because he was a so-called "Punch and Judy" hitter—a placement hitter—although he was. "I've had quite a baseball career," Johnson said with matter-of-fact truth in his tone when interviewed for a 1984 Negro Leagues documentary.[1] Johnson first made his playing mark with the Philadelphia Hilldale Giants in the Eastern Colored League when he batted .391 in 1923. A's Johnson matured, he became not only a better hitter, but also a smarter performer doing the little things. And sometimes doing things fans would never notice. These tricks were appreciated by teammates and howled at by opponents.

Johnson fluffed up the long sleeve of his uniform to better wiggle his way into pitched balls, thereby winning himself a hit-by-pitch designation and a free pass to first base without risk of injury. He stole other teams' signals. And in an era when baseballs were replaced on the field of play only rarely compared to the regularity with which they are tossed out today, Johnson made an art form of scarring balls to help his pitchers' ball movement. He looked for every edge.[2] "Judy was just a great ballplayer," said Cool Papa Bell. "He was a student of the game and played it the right way. He could field, he could throw, he could hit. And he was smart. With him at bat you could put on the bunt, the hit-and-run, or the squeeze."[3]

Johnson was born to William Henry Johnson and Annie Lee Johnson in Maryland. His father was a merchant seaman and after moving to Delaware became a ship builder, a factory worker, and then the athletic director of the Negro Settlement House in Wilmington. He was also a boxing coach. Johnson had one brother and one sister. When he dropped out of high school, Johnson worked as a stevedore, factory worker, and made a few bucks as a semipro baseball player, earning at best $5 a game. But he swiftly moved to the Hilldale organization, switching back and forth between the big club and its lower-level affiliated team, the Madison Stars. The purchase price on the final transfer in 1921 was $200, a bargain for the contract of a future Hall of Famer.[4]

Although Johnson was passionate about baseball, his father strove to turn him into a boxer. That was about money. The elder Johnson didn't think there was much profit to be made as a black baseball player. "I loved baseball and always wanted to be a ballplayer," Johnson said. "My daddy always wanted me to be a prize fighter. My father had a license to train boxers."[5]

PLAYING CAREER

Statistics reported for teams Johnson was affiliated with throughout the 1920s and 1930s were kept with varying degrees of reliability, but when Hilldale won three straight Eastern Colored League pennants between 1923 and 1925, Johnson was the club's top hitter. His best season during that stretch was 1925 when he recorded a .392 batting average. Hilldale represented its league against the Kansas City Monarchs of the Negro National League in the first Negro World Series in 1924 and Johnson was the top hitter with a .341 average.

Johnson's personal life was always stable. He pretty much had just one girlfriend his entire life. Anita Irons was his childhood sweetheart and they married in 1923. She had a long career as a school teacher that helped support the family when Johnson's baseball wages were low. They stayed together until Mrs. Johnson's death in 1986. The Johnsons had no children together, but adopted Irons' niece, Loretta. In the 1950s, Johnson scouted a sleek Delaware ballplayer named Bill Bruton. Bruton became a star outfielder for the Milwaukee Braves—and married Johnson's daughter.

Not only did Johnson's former Pittsburgh Crawfords roommate Ted Page compliment Johnson on the longevity of his marriage, but he also said the infielder was a clean living man who "didn't drink, didn't run around, and knew how to handle money."[6]

Johnson was one of the earliest of the Negro Leagues' big stars, and while he overlapped with many other big-name African American stars who endure in baseball lore, he was too far ahead of the times to come close to the opportunity of playing in the white majors. It was only at the tail end of Johnson's playing career that anyone began suggesting publicly that Major League baseball open its doors to African American players. Instead, Johnson excelled in the Negro Leagues, on barnstorming teams, and in Latin American winter leagues. Discrimination against black players was at its peak in the United States during Johnson's prime, and traveling conditions for those who rode from town to town playing exhibitions were frequently awful. The owners of white hotels and restaurants, especially in southern cities, never welcomed black touring teams, and often insulted them.

Life was harsh for players just trying to scrape by and make a living, playing doubleheaders miles apart in different communities. At the end of the long days there was no soft bed waiting, no hot meal, and perhaps nowhere to wash off the sweat. "There was no place between Chicago and St. Louis where we could stop and eat," said Bill Yancey, a member of the New York Black Yankees. "Unless we stopped in a place where they had a colored settlement."[7]

Ted "Double Duty" Radcliffe, who earned his nickname by switching back and forth between the pitcher's mound and catcher's utensils, was a well-known contemporary of Johnson. "We used to play four in one day just about every Fourth of July," Radcliffe said. "I'd pitch two and catch two. The way I made it was to sleep for the thirty-five minutes between each game."[8]

Johnson recalled the hectic pace of his early days of professional baseball when the schedule demanded cramming as many games into daylight hours as possible. "We played three games most every Sunday," he said. "You were as tired as a yard dog. We played all over the East. We played all over the West. We played all over the South. Of course riding was kind of rough. We had a nice bus, but no bus is comfortable riding every day." The bus only had one door, too, not particularly safe in case of emergency. "We'd need a can opener to come out of the bus. Once we drove from Chicago to Philadelphia without stopping or resting and then we played a doubleheader." Fatigue was a real enemy, but pulling on a baseball uniform seemed to serve as a magical elixir. "When you put the suit on you knew that was your job and you'd just go do it."[9]

Any top-notch African American player enduring the tough conditions of the road, the low, few-hundred-dollar-a-month salaries of black baseball, and the snubs of the major leagues had to be especially mentally strong to cope. Those players had an innate confidence, an unshakable belief in their own skills. But if they were thinking men, as Johnson was, they at some point asked just why they were banned from the majors.

Late in his own life, when his hair had turned white and he was being interviewed for a documentary about life in black baseball, Johnson recounted a conversation he had with Connie Mack, the owner of the Philadelphia Athletics and a patriarch of the game. It was in 1926 when Johnson's teams had just won five out of six exhibition games from the A's. He asked Mack, if the black players were good enough to beat the white players, why couldn't they play in the majors?

" 'There's just too many of you boys to go in at once,' " Johnson recalled Mack telling him. "And that's as far as he got. I could play big-league ball. I knew it. I never dreamed of playing in the major leagues. Then it was really a barrier that kept us apart. But they knew we were good enough."[10]

Johnson was fundamentally an outstanding player. He wielded a forty-ounce bat, a ridiculously sized Fred Flintstone club for an average-sized man, but he could control it. Base hits, the philosophy of "hitting 'em where they ain't" as espoused by turn-of-the-century Major League star Wee Willie Keeler, was Johnson's forte. He was not a big fella and he was much better physically equipped to slap singles than crush doubles. "I tried to make contact," Johnson said, "to get a piece of the ball and hit it someplace. I'd hit three or four home runs a year, mostly inside the park, and you could count the number of times I struck out."[11] Meaning on one hand—unlike many free swingers.

Johnson grasped his strengths on the diamond. He knew he was no slugger, but a move-them-over-a-base-at-a-time hitter. He adopted his slick strategic approaches because he knew what would work for his style and he understood it was a tradeoff. Teams are made up of different types of players. The mix, the blend, is what produces winners. A team that has all big swingers in the lineup who strike out often will probably not win a championship. Neither will a team of all disciplined singles hitters who do not drive in many runs. The same is true of the way teams field. Simply adequate fielders who do not cover much ground hurt their pitchers. Superb fielders who make the great play to save runs atone for not knocking them in.

Johnson was always on the lookout to gain every inch. He delighted in telling a story about a situation in a 1930s exhibition game between the Crawfords and a Major League All-Star team. Long before he became a fiery manager with the Dodgers and Giants, Leo Durocher was a fiery shortstop for the St. Louis Cardinals.

Durocher was on third and Johnson believed he might try to steal home plate. The way Johnson tells it, Durocher danced up and down the base line, leading off third, feinting toward home. During a time out Johnson said he went to the mound and exclaimed loudly to his pitcher Leroy Matlock, "If you don't watch out, that guy's gonna steal the cover right off the ball." He knew Durocher heard him. When Johnson returned to the bag, he said to Durocher, "Man, that's the dumbest pitcher we got." Johnson then whistled to catcher Josh Gibson, a pre-arranged signal. On the next pitch, Matlock threw hard, and Durocher ran too far down the line. Still in his crouch, zip, Gibson fired the ball to Johnson, who tagged a desperately sliding Durocher. The umpire called Durocher out, Durocher howled in protest that he was safe, and Johnson laughed.

"What the hell's so funny?" Durocher fumed. Durocher was standing on Johnson's foot, meaning he still hadn't touched the base safely. "He'd made a perfect hook slide right into my ankle," Johnson said.[12]

Well after he retired, Johnson admitted that he was a genius at doctoring the baseball. It caused quite a furor when Hall of Fame pitcher Gaylord Perry admitted that he threw an out-lawed spitball. But decades passed before Johnson spilled his tales. He did the dirty work for his pitchers. Although Johnson said he never performed his little operations on the ball in Negro Leagues play, only in exhibitions against white players, such a statement requires gullibility. Most of ball-manipulating practices weren't banned in the Negro Leagues as they were in the majors.

Johnson cheerfully provided a clinic on just how he made the baseball wiggle and swerve for his pitchers. Johnson used a bottle cap hidden in the thumb portion of his glove to rough up the ball.[13]

Johnson conceded that this was a form of cheating, but only one of many types of cheating that revolved around the type of stuff pitchers hurled, from mud balls to shine balls, to emery balls and spitters.

"That kind of thing was real common," Johnson said. "When we threw the shine ball, we used to load it up with so much Vaseline it would make your eyes blink on a sunny day. On mud balls, the mud on the seams made the ball sink. When you roughed a ball, depending on how the pitcher held it, it did all sorts of crazy things—dropped, broke up or down, everything."[14]

Johnson recorded many of his best-hitting seasons in the 1920s when he played in Philadelphia, but when the Negro National League and the Eastern Colored League folded, in 1930 he joined the Homestead Grays, which was temporarily an independent team. He emerged as the player-manager for the Grays, the first of his managing jobs, and when he needed a replacement for an injured catcher, Johnson brought Hall of Fame catcher Josh Gibson into the big time of black baseball.

Gibson became the most feared slugger in black baseball and was credited as the equal of Babe Ruth in power. But when Gibson joined the Grays, he was still raw, especially as a fielder. Johnson, although not a catcher, was a noted fielder frequently compared in conversation to the Pirates' star Pie Traynor as a young man and later to the Orioles' Brooks Robinson. Johnson drilled Gibson constantly. He was smart enough to leave Gibson's batting swing alone, but had the authority to work him hard enough to improve in the field. Gibson's glaring weakness was settling under foul pop-ups, then misplaying them and giving other teams' hitters extra chances at the plate. "I credit the man who really helped him on foul balls as Judy Johnson," said Negro Leagues outfielder Ted Page.[15]

Johnson the manager recognized two things about Gibson early on. The young man was going to be a fabulous hitter and that he had the desire to become a better fielder.

"Honestly, he was the greatest hitter I've ever seen, but he wasn't a great catcher," Johnson said. "But he wanted to learn. He used to catch batting practice for me and then catch the ballgame. That boy was game. I've seen the time Josh had his finger split and tied a piece of tape around it and played just as though nothing had happened."[16]

Not only did Johnson manage, but he was also one of the great stars on the best black baseball team of all time. From the mid-1930s to the mid-1940s, at one time or another the Crawfords featured Johnson, Gibson, Satchel Paige, Cool Papa Bell, and Oscar Charleston, all of whom were eventually selected for the Baseball Hall of Fame. Johnson jumped around from the Crawfords to the Hilldale Darby Daisies, to the Homestead Grays, and back to the Crawfords from mid-season 1932 until he retired in 1938.

"If you've got Satchel on your team, you can play a team with nine devils on it," Johnson said. He witnessed an angry Satchel (it was understood that it was never a good idea to rile him up) strike out the side on nine pitches with the bases loaded and proclaim, "Now go back to Philadelphia and tell that."[17]

Buck O'Neil, younger than Johnson, but whose career with the Kansas City Monarchs overlapped with the infielder some, said Johnson was a natural manager, exactly the kind of scrappy player teams like to hire to impart their wisdom. "Judy Johnson was a very intelligent player," O'Neil said. "He knew the game very well. He was an outstanding manager because he knew baseball very well."[18]

Johnson enjoyed showing younger players the fine points of baseball. His own role model was John Henry "Pop" Lloyd, another early black star who reached the Hall of Fame as a shortstop. When he was approaching seventy, Johnson recalled Lloyd's greatness, comparing him to Honus Wagner. "One of my first teachers was John Henry Lloyd," Johnson said. "He was a great teacher. He'd make you play your head off. He played against Ty Cobb in Cuba in 1910 and when Cobb slid into him at second, Lloyd almost threw him into center field. Lloyd was never a home-run hitter, he was just a great hitter like Wagner. Connie Mack used to say, 'If you put Lloyd and Wagner in a bag together, whichever one you picked out first, you wouldn't go wrong.' "[19]

When he reflected on the differences between Negro Leagues ball during his playing era and Major League baseball in the late 1960s, there were many things Johnson could not get over. And not merely that the $1.50 a day meal money was a payoff of the distant past and that his old $150 a month salary would be dwarfed. He could not believe how much the sport had come to rely on relief pitchers. In the first half of the twentieth century, black teams and white teams depended on at most a quartet of starting pitchers to take the ball no more than every fourth day and to stay in the game into the late innings. Complete games were not rarities, they were expected. "When I was managing," Johnson said, "I'd give the ball to the pitcher and say, 'This is your game today.' And he went out there and pitched. Now they go five innings and look to the bullpen for help."[20]

Johnson didn't think much of pitchers who couldn't hold runners on base when they feinted a steal. He said he was amazed to watch how little attention the thrower paid to the base runner.

"I used to steal third base a lot, because if you're on second, the pitcher will get into his stretch, look back twice, and then when he turns his head, all you've got to do is start running," Johnson said, "because that's his pattern. I'm seventy years old and I bet I could steal on some of these pitchers they've got now. Just let me practice a few days. They rock way back and when they're rocking, the man is running."[21]

Like many others who saw Bell play, Johnson proclaimed Cool Papa as swift as a lightning bolt from heaven, and a man almost impossible to defense on a slow roller or a high chopper. "We'd have to draw the infield in when Cool Papa was at bat," Johnson remembered. "He'd chop down on the ball and it would make a big hop and you'd just have to hold the ball, just put it in your pocket. No use throwing it to first because you couldn't catch him."[22]

Playing games when nobody took video, nothing was televised, little was heard on radio, and even newspapers did not always carry their team's box scores, Negro Leagues players needed word-of-mouth observations recorded by those who lived and competed alongside the talents of the game. If the historical record is incomplete, at least there is a record of sorts that preserves the memories of players who would otherwise be completely forgotten. Colorful descriptions, with stories to back them up, substitute for unrecoverable numbers.

Johnson didn't mind playing mythmaker when it came to Gibson. For him, Gibson's stupendous, yet tragic career, was personal. Johnson is the one who gave Gibson his first action at the top level of black baseball and he always remembered the player fondly.

It is little known among modern-day baseball fans that night baseball in the Negro Leagues pre-dated the majors by five years, though the story Johnson liked to tell about putting young Gibson on the field is apparently a bit flawed.

"Josh Gibson was the greatest hitter," Johnson said. "The first game Josh ever played, he played for me. He was my boy. I was managing the Homestead Grays in Pittsburgh in 1930 and we were playing a night game, the first night game ever played in Forbes Field. Buck Ewing, our catcher, got mixed up with a ball and split his hand open. The park was jammed, they had to turn people away. I'd seen Josh play with a playground team and he was in the stands. I asked him if he wanted to catch. He said, 'Yes, sir!' and we held the game up while he put on a suit."[23]

However, a later researcher, pulling together material for a biography of Gibson, reported that Gibson's debut did not take place quite like that. Ewing apparently played through his injury in a day game. Then Gibson was signed by owner Cumberland Posey one day later, elsewhere in Pennsylvania, where he had also been on the night of the game Johnson described. Gibson did join the Grays for the first Forbes Field night game, but he was apparently not an on-the-premises savior stepping out of the grandstand.[24]

When Gibson died in 1947, with his formerly formidable body wasted from illness at only thirty-five, Johnson was long retired. But he was terribly saddened. "I heard the news on the radio and I couldn't believe it," Johnson said. "I just hate to think of it because I thought so much of the boy after starting him out."[25]

LATER LIFE

Johnson retired from playing baseball in 1938, nearly a decade before Jackie Robinson's color-line breakthrough with the Brooklyn Dodgers. Johnson never came close to playing in the majors. Settling in Marshallton, Delaware, he operated a general store with his brother, drove a cab and a school bus, and coached semipro baseball and basketball.

However, after African American players began infiltrating the majors in the wake of Robinson's dramatic entrance with the Dodgers, the Philadelphia Athletics called and asked Johnson whether he would like to scout. He began searching for ballplayers in 1951 and said he could have single-handedly kept the A's from moving to Kansas City after the 1954 season if his superiors had listened to him. Johnson said he recommended the signing of both Minnie Minoso and Hank Aaron, ultimately baseball's greatest home-run hitter.

Before Aaron hooked up with the Braves in the National League, he played a short while for the Indianapolis Clowns. That's where Johnson saw the supremely talented, but still young Aaron. Johnson said he could have signed Aaron for $3,500 on the spot.

"I got my boss out of bed and told him I had a good prospect and he wouldn't cost too much," Johnson said. "And he cussed me out for waking him up at one o'clock in the morning. He said, 'Thirty-five hundred! That's too much money.' "[26]

No deal.

In early 1954, the A's brought Johnson to spring training to work with black hitters Bob Trice and Vic Power. Technically, that made Johnson the first African American coach in Major League history. However, because Johnson did not coach during the regular season, the official honor is acknowledged to Buck O'Neil, who coached for the Chicago Cubs.

Johnson scouted for the Braves, and in the late 1950s he signed on as a scout for the Philadelphia Phillies, a team he stayed with into the 1970s. He had a hand in signing the slugging Richie Allen. Johnson wrapped up his scouting career in 1977 after three years with the Los Angeles Dodgers.

A's one of the oldest living stars of Negro Leagues play, Johnson was asked to be part of the Baseball Hall of Fame Committee on the Negro Baseball Leagues when it was appointed by commissioner Bowie Kuhn in 1971. Johnson was thrilled to be part of the effort to rectify the sport's mistakes of the past and honor overlooked players. He also began to harbor hope that he might also be recognized. That dream came true in 1975 when Johnson was selected for the Hall of Fame as the sixth African American from the old black leagues.

At the time of the announcement of Johnson's enshrinement, the issue of whether he could have been a successful boxer or not re-surfaced. Johnson said no way was that career going to materialize despite his father's exhortations.

"Shoot, my sister could lick the pants off me," Johnson said. He also expressed no bitterness for the time he spent locked out of the majors. "I felt I could play in the big leagues, but you just accepted the way things were in those days. It only hurt to know that you had the talent, but couldn't exercise it."[27]

On March 18 of that year, shortly after it was revealed that Johnson was entering the Hall of Fame, the Delaware State Senate approved a resolution praising him. It read in part, "Whereas, Judy Johnson, a modest, soft-spoken man, never once in his life-long baseball career expressed resentment or bitterness about his exclusion from the major leagues, but simply remarked, 'I was born too soon'; and whereas members of the Senate of the 128th General Assembly wish to congratulate Judy Johnson for such an excellent career in baseball, plus the honor of having been the first Delawarean ever to be elected to baseball's Hall of Fame."[28]

Johnson was inducted into the Hall of Fame during the annual ceremony on August 18, 1975, in Cooperstown, New York, and in his speech thanked wife Anita, many relatives, friends from baseball, and took note that a busload of fans drove north from Delaware. While delivering his short speech, Johnson took breaks for tears at least three times.

"I've loved the game up until now," he said, "and I still love it."[29] On another occasion, some years later, Johnson expressed his joy at being able to play baseball for a living. "Those were my happy days, and I don't regret a minute of it," he said.[30]

Many honors were bestowed on Johnson before his death and afterward. He died in 1989 from complications of stroke. A baseball field was named for him in Wilmington, Delaware, and Johnson was chosen as a member of the charter class of the Delaware Sports Hall of Fame. Delaware fans also began an annual tribute to Johnson in the 1990s, establishing a Judy Johnson Night and a gathering for Negro Leagues baseball.

In April 1995, Delaware proved just how much it admired Judy Johnson the baseball player and man when a statue of him was unveiled in front of Frawley Stadium, home of the Wilmington Blue Rocks of the Carolina League. Buck O'Neil offered first-hand testimony about Johnson's ability.

"I'm sorry you didn't get a chance to see Judy Johnson play third base," O'Neil said to 200 spectators, and told them Johnson was a fielder far superior to another area Hall of Famer Mike Schmidt. "I'm just telling you the truth. The man Schmidt is great, but you've never seen anything like Judy. I saw Judy. I was there with Judy."[31]

The statue depicts Johnson in an infielder's crouch. He is ready as always, just as he is shown on that indoor field in Kansas City, to scoop up any grounder hit his way.

NOTES

1. Craig Davidson (producer, writer), *There Was Always Sun Shining Someplace: Life in the Negro Baseball Leagues*, DVD, Refocus Films, Westport, CT, 1984.

2. Jonah Winter, *Fair Ball! 14 Great Stars from Baseball's Negro Leagues* (New York: Scholastic Press, 1999), 22.

3. Izzy Katzman and Gary Soulsman, *Wilmington News-Journal*, June 16, 1989.

4. Baseball Hall of Fame library archives.

5. Katzman and Soulsman, *Wilmington News-Journal*.

6. Ibid.

7. Negro Leagues Baseball Museum wall display.

8. Ibid.

9. Davidson, *There Was Always Sun Shining Someplace*.

10. Ibid.

11. Frederic Kelly, *Sun*, February 1, 1976.
12. Ibid.
13. Ibid.
14. Ibid.
15. John Holway, *Josh and Satch* (Westport, CT: Meckler Publishing, 1991), 25.
16. Holway, *Josh and Satch*, 26.
17. Davidson, *There Was Always Sun Shining Someplace*.
18. Buck O'Neil, personal interview, December 7, 2005.
19. John Holway, interview on file, Baseball Hall of Fame Library Archives, 1969.
20. Ibid.
21. Ibid.
22. Ibid.
23. Ibid.
24. Mark Ribowsky, *The Power and the Darkness* (New York: Simon & Schuster, 1996), 42.
25. Holway, Hall of Fame file interview.
26. Ibid.
27. Jack Lang, *Sporting News*, March 1, 1975.
28. Text of Resolution, Delaware State Senate, March 18, 1975.
29. Judy Johnson, Text of Baseball Hall of Fame induction speech, August 18, 1975.
30. Donn Rogosin, *Invisible Men* (New York: Atheneum, 1987), 66.
31. Clark DeLeon, *Philadelphia Inquirer*, April 15, 1995.

Further Reading

Davidson, Craig, producer, writer, DVD, *There Was Always Sun Shining Someplace: Life in The Negro Baseball Leagues*, Westport, CT: Refocus Films, 1984.
Holway, John, *Josh and Satch*. Westport, CT: Meckler Publishing, 1991.

BUCK LEONARD

September 8, 1907–November 27, 1997

Buck Leonard was one of the greatest hitting stars in the Negro Leagues, forming the "Thunder Twins" combination with Josh Gibson. He was hailed as "the black Lou Gehrig" and was one of the first African American players from the Negro Leagues who never made it into the majors to be selected for the Baseball Hall of Fame in 1972.

A left-handed hitter, Leonard was a feared batter in any lineup during his playing days with the Baltimore Stars, but mainly the Homestead Grays, between 1934 and 1950. Leonard batted .400 as a Negro Leagues rookie, .410 in 1946, and .395 in 1947 and played on nine pennant winners.

☆   ☆   ☆

When he was an old man, Buck Leonard still had an unlined face and a distinguished bearing. His hair was limited to the sides of his head and it had turned white. He wore a mustache that was thick in the middle and thin on the edges.

Of all the great Negro Leagues ballplayers, Leonard was one of the luckiest who did not make it into the majors, for he was remembered and revered anyway, his feats admired and rewarded. His long toil in anonymity was appreciated by enough long-lived eyewitnesses who made a public case for him when it mattered most.

More than thirty years after the occasion of Leonard's being chosen for the Baseball Hall of Fame, those who immerse themselves in baseball history find it more difficult to learn about the skills of Buck Leonard than of Satchel Paige and Josh Gibson. Paige and Gibson are considered to be of legendary caliber. One is the greatest pitcher in Negro Leagues lore, the other the greatest hitter. If so, Leonard may be characterized as the greatest Negro Leagues supporting actor of all time.

Babe Ruth was the kingpin on the fabulous New York Yankees teams of the 1920s and 1930s, but no one fails to pay homage to the outfielder's first-base slugging partner Lou Gehrig. Gehrig earned his own slot in the Hall of Fame. If Leonard was overshadowed by Gibson, no one doubted their dual prowess as a one-two punch for the perennial pennant-winning Homestead Grays of the 1930s and 1940s. The team won nine flags in a row with the twosome working together.

Between 1934, when he broke into the lineup, and 1950, when he retired from Negro Leagues play, while Gibson provided the power, Leonard provided the high average, hitting .300 or better twelve times. Leonard batted third in the order and Gibson batted cleanup. Illustrating how those in the know realized his stardom, Leonard was also a record twelve-time Negro Leagues All Star in the East-West game.

EARLY LIFE

Walter Fenner "Buck" Leonard was born September 8, 1907, in Rocky Mount, North Carolina, and died ninety years later in the same community. Rocky Mount was a tobacco producing area and during Leonard's youth much of the area's commerce revolved around the Atlantic Coast Railroad.

A feared hitter who excelled at first base after patterning his style after the Yankees' Lou Gehrig, Buck Leonard formed a one-two Negro Leagues hitting punch with Josh Gibson, and they were nicknamed the "Thunder Twins."

For all his greatness, the average-sized, five-foot-ten, 185-pound Leonard was born just a few years too early. When the Major Leagues began integrating in 1947, Leonard was already forty years old and realistically assessed that no white club would seriously pursue him.

Leonard was the son of a railroad fireman named John Leonard and one of six children born to his mother Emma. The family nicknamed him "Buddy," but one of his brothers couldn't pronounce the word and called him "Buck." That was the diminutive that stuck. When he was very young, Leonard shined shoes at the nearby railroad station. Leonard was eleven when his father died of influenza and he went to work full-time. When he was seventeen, he was working at the railroad shop and obtained a free ticket for much of the ride to Washington, D.C., Leonard was a baseball fan and a first baseman, and he wanted to see Lou Gehrig play. He traveled alone, and sat alone in Griffith Stadium, studying the form of the tremendous Yankees star. Then he patterned his own game after Gehrig's.

While holding down a full-time railroad job, Leonard played semipro ball. It was not until he was nearly twenty-seven that he hooked on with the Grays. The late start cost Leonard in terms of statistical accomplishment, but is hard to quantify. The numbers show that Leonard was a terrific hitter, one who hit .400 in a brief introduction to the Negro Leagues in 1934, and according to the Baseball Encyclopedia probably had a lifetime average of .324. He had a good glove, as well. "He was a line drive hitter who could wear out the fastball," said Buck O'Neil, a first baseman for the Kansas City Monarchs when Leonard played. "He was a good hitter. Fielder?" O'Neil laughed. "Nobody was better than me."[1]

When O'Neil wrote his autobiography in 1996, the year before Leonard passed away, he had great praise for his former competitor, calling him "the greatest of us still alive. I remember him as a nice, quiet man who would ride the bus or sit in the hotel lobby working crossword puzzles rather than going to the night spots. Buck Leonard was unique. He was probably the most studious man in the Negro Leagues, and all the young ballplayers would come and talk to him."[2]

Leonard was a homebody, fond of his hometown, and he admitted later he probably never would have left if he hadn't been laid off from his railroad job during the Depression. He was a player-manager in North Carolina and was twenty-five before he had to wonder about a steady source of income coming from anywhere else. This topic became more urgent when Leonard married in 1937. He remained with his wife Sarah until she died in 1966.

Leonard already had a first-rate reputation as a man who could handle himself on a ball field when he broke into the top league. "Buck was the best first baseman we had in the Negro Leagues, but I played against him a long time before that, when we were both playing in the sandlots," said Ray Dandridge, the Hall of Fame third baseman, who like Leonard was seen as too old for an opportunity when the majors opened up.[3]

Leonard certainly needed no seasoning, but he did not make the jump directly from those sandlots to the Grays. He linked up with independent teams first, one a bunch called the Portsmouth Firefighters that already included his brother Charlie on the roster pitching, and then the Baltimore Stars. It didn't take much to make Leonard homesick, but making the time worse away from home was the reception blacks received from whites as they arrived to play in new communities. "It wasn't only in the south, it was in the north, too, they called us names," Leonard said.[4]

In a movie about black baseball, *The Bingo Long Traveling All-Stars and Motor Kings*, a slightly surreal scene plays out. The players cannot afford their hotel bill and their cars are confiscated to be auctioned off and cover the debt. Leonard lived through just such an event. He said the Stars were staying in a New York hotel when they heard a commotion through the windows. It was an auction peddling their cars. The Baltimore team disbanded and a little later Leonard found a new team with a bit more stability.

The Grays were seeking a first baseman, but team owner Cum Posey's image of the man to cover that base was someone taller than Leonard. Homestead gave him a tryout nevertheless and despite his not being six feet tall, decided to keep him. "I wouldn't have ever played, except that I could hit," Leonard said. "That was my main point, hitting the ball."[5] He stayed with the Grays for seventeen seasons, until the club broke up in 1950.

Leonard was fortunate to have a job during the Depression. In his time with traveling teams, Leonard made $50 a month. It was not for many years, until 1942, that he reached the munificent sum of $1,000 a month. Leonard never made more than $10,000 in a calendar year, combining Homestead pay and winter ball.[6] Salaries were low, but then, so were costs. Players received 60 cents a day for meal money. A haircut was 15 cents, a shave 10 cents. When meal money reached $1 a day, Leonard said he could even bank some.[7]

Leonard loved playing baseball and being part of a team—any team—but did not profess much ambition. After his sojourn with the defunct Baltimore Stars, he signed on with another independent team, the Brooklyn Royals. One night, drinking in a bar near the park where the team practiced, Leonard bumped into Smokey Joe Williams. Williams, one of the top hurlers of the day, told Leonard he was wasting himself.

"He said, 'Look, Buck, don't you want to get with a good team?'" Leonard was perplexed. "What are you talking about?" he said. Williams said, "The Homestead Grays." "You think I could make that team?" Leonard asked. Williams pledged to call owner Cum Posey on Leonard's behalf. That was Leonard's entre, and Homestead became home. The pay was $125 a month, a considerable upgrade.[8]

Whether O'Neil was just kidding or not about Leonard's fielding, he did become a smooth-fielding first baseman. But Leonard was serious about his hitting prowess. He hit prolifically in Mexico until he was forty-eight. He was a smooth swinger, not a free swinger, a hitter who was disciplined at the plate and could hit a ball where intended. Sticking around the sport made up for Leonard's late start. The only thing that dimmed Leonard's sharp eyes and his bat speed was a stroke suffered in 1986. By then he was about eighty.

PLAYING CAREER

Josh Gibson was the awesome hitter, the one who received the majority of the attention. He was six-foot-one, weighed about 220 pounds, and had a blacksmith's biceps. Sometimes when he discussed his old teammate's strength and power with the bat, Leonard sounded like a youthful fan. Because Gibson died young in 1947, Leonard was often asked to recount some of the legendary hitter's efforts.

"He was the most powerful hitter we had in Negro baseball," Leonard wrote. "I saw him hit one in New York's Polo Grounds between the upper deck and the roof. It hit an elevated train track on the fly. And he came near to hitting one out of Yankee Stadium. But the longest home run I ever saw him hit was in Monessen, Pennsylvania, a little town outside Pittsburgh. It went over the center field fence, over the top of a schoolhouse, 513 feet. The mayor of the town measured it. He stopped the game and had it measured."[9]

Left unremarked upon is just why some of the best ballplayers in the world were playing in such a small town in the middle of nowhere. The answer, of course, had everything to do with their race and the exclusion of the Leonards and Gibsons from the majors. When Leonard referred to Gibson's hottest year, when he was supposed to have hit more than seventy homers, he said, "We counted them up."[10] By "we" he means teammates and by that statement he indicts the record-keeping. It has long been known that Negro Leagues stats were incomplete. Baseball researchers and historians are haunted by the gaps.

Gibson briefly established himself with the Pittsburgh Crawfords, but the Crawfords and Grays engaged in a bidding war for his talents and he landed with the Grays in 1930. Especially when he was young, Gibson was also a good clubhouse companion.

"Gibson was a nice fellow," Leonard said. "He wasn't loud or rowdy. He was a fun fellow. He always wanted to have some fun, and he was always saying funny things. Everybody liked him. Nobody disliked him. He never did fight anybody, molest anybody, never did ride the umpire. Just seemed to be a nice fellow."[11]

Leonard had no single home-run shot on his resume to compare with Gibson's long-distance blast, though in 1942, a season when he hit 42 home runs between league and barnstorming games, he did say he belted one clear out of a park in Newark over the right-field fence. No tape measure was produced, but Leonard said a spectator later told him, "It just kept going and going."[12]

Satchel Paige was in his prime at the same time as Leonard and Gibson. Although Leonard was not a youthful rookie, he had never faced a thrower like Paige and when he played against him for the first time with the Grays, the masterful Satch had his number. Paige was a magician on the mound, mixing speeds in his tosses, but even more confounding for the batter, switching delivery motions and windups. Leonard was so feeble against Paige that he asked the umpire to examine the ball to determine if it was regulation. "You may as well throw 'em all out, 'cause they're all gonna jump like that," Paige shouted to Leonard while standing on the mound 60 feet, 6 inches away.[13]

Leonard was neither flamboyant nor boastful. His bat did his talking and he cut no wide colorful swath through the game, content to allow Gibson garner much of the attention on the winning club. Like so many of the other top Negro Leagues players, he hoped to one day test himself in the white majors. The only opportunity for his generation to do so was to play off-season exhibitions when the superb pitchers like Dizzy Dean and Bob Feller put together touring teams to make extra money after their pennant races concluded. The African American ballplayers of the era were eager to compete in the fall, as well. Certainly, there was the financial incentive, but those otherwise meaningless games offered the chance to go head-to-head with the white players whose exploits dominated big-city newspaper sports sections. Sometimes, entire teams whose seasons ended shy of the World Series were ready to take advantage of continuing pleasant autumn weather and face black teams.

For ballpark owners, typically Major League team executives, any entertainment events where their otherwise fallow buildings could produce income, were a blessing. These games were good box office. The African American players had something to prove. Even if the games were seen as exhibitions with a fraction of the notoriety regular-season Major League games attracted, it was still a chance to bat against white arms, to throw against white batters.

No one in the universe kept accurate track of the outcomes of all such games, nor was the detail of play recorded fastidiously. The results of individual series were noted and overall it is known that black All Stars won their share of the games. Each victory provided satisfaction to black players who were shut out of the big time, who were like children with faces pressed against the glass of a candy store, staring in at goodies just beyond reach. What those triumphs did was soothe souls, act as reminders of the truth of the matter, that blacks belonged on big-show diamonds as surely as did the whites. There did not seem to be justice in the world of baseball for African Americans, but these games provided a reckoning.

Baseball commissioner Kenesaw Mountain Landis assessed the results of these games. In the early 1940s, black sportswriters in their columns were clamoring to open up the sport and cited frequent victories of black over white to support the case that African Americans should be allowed into the majors. Landis, universally regarded as a closet bigot, countenanced no one messing with his fiefdom and showed not an ounce of sympathy for black players. Landis took mean-spirited action. He banned full teams of Major League ballplayers from even playing exhibitions. The All-Star tours headed by a Dean or Feller could continue, but the entire Boston Red Sox or New York Giants could not engage in contests. "They had everything to lose and nothing to gain and we had everything to gain and nothing to lose," Leonard said.[14]

The style of the African American game in the 1940s differed from the white game. Babe Ruth's home runs had juiced up the majors and exhilarated crowds. Black players depended more on manufacturing runs with daring baserunning. Stealing bases had some-what fallen out of fashion in the Major Leagues, but not in the Negro Leagues. The one category of black player who did not enjoy this approach to the game was the catcher. The catcher's arm was challenged constantly and he did not like it one bit if he was always the loser in these exchanges.

Leonard liked to tell a story that he heard in passing. Paige's favorite catcher was a player named Bill Perkins, who enjoyed a good Negro Leagues career, and one enhanced by his reputation as the best man to catch Paige.

Some men are magnets for publicity even without really trying (Gibson), some are magnets for publicity and realize how they can build a valuable image with it (Paige), and some just do their job quietly and will not go out of their way to seek attention (Leonard). Sometimes those types of players are overlooked, but other times they gain a special sort of respect from peers. Within two years of joining the Grays, Leonard was recognized by team owner Cum Posey as someone who was magnificent whether he cultivated the notice of newspapermen or not.

In 1938, an unattributed newspaper headline that Leonard cites in his autobiogra-phy read, "Grays boast new superstar in Buck Leonard." The author had exceptional judgment, but Leonard said such hosannas never fazed him. "I never paid no attention to what they wrote in the newspapers. I was just happy to be playing baseball."[15]

Given that the Negro Leagues suffered from a dearth of reportage of game-by-game information and statistics, it will remain forever impossible to thoroughly document many facts. For that matter, given that the leagues were sustained more by oral history, it is impossible to ascertain the preciseness of lesser stories passed from player to player and observer to observer, never mind factoring in the shading brought about by the passage of time.

Burnishing of legends through word of mouth should not be be discounted, but also are not to be automatically accepted. There is no one to blame for this as it takes place every day in every way even in an age when it can be argued there is too much documen-tation and exposure of players. It makes sense that Negro Leagues players, disrespected for decades, and discriminated against in their primes, should be granted a certain dis-pensation in protecting their reputations. Hearing a story version from a participant's mouth seems more worthy than hearing it solely from a distant successor.

Leon Day was another great of the Negro Leagues, a notable pitcher whose top-level career almost precisely overlapped with Leonard's from 1934 to 1950. As Leonard was to Gibson, Day was the Leonard-like pitching complement to Satchel Paige's rollicking self, a more subdued, yet supremely confident player. Day needed others to speak up for him and pump up the perception of his skills, despite being a seven-time All Star and going 15–0 in 1937.

Born in 1916, Day was another Negro Leagues star who would have benefited from a later birth. During World War II he bested a team of white big leaguers in an exhibi-tion game before 100,000 servicemen, but was at the tail end of his brilliance when Major League owners were searching for black ballplayers in earnest. He saw time on high-level minor league clubs, but never spent a day in the majors. Despite that lid on his career, Day was chosen for the Baseball Hall of Fame in 1995. He died six days after being notified of his selection.

Day and Leonard had a serious rivalry. Leonard respected Day's fastball and other abilities, but resented one of Day's boasts. Day told people he once struck out the great Buck Leonard three times in one game. Leonard insisted that it was not so. Leonard said he never faced a single pitcher who struck him out three times in any game.[16]

The owners of African American baseball teams in the Depression did not have it easy. In Leonard's mind it was a game for young men, players with few obligations living the single life. And that was after he got a raise to $125 a month with the Grays. Typically, players hustled for every dollar they could by playing every game they could. They mixed in exhibition games before, during, and after the regular season. When it at last got too cold to maintain a schedule in the United States, they abandoned their home country for spots on winter league rosters in Cuba, Puerto Rico, Mexico, and Venezuela. They were not the boys of summer, but the boys for all seasons.

The one problem for Leonard, a homebody to start with who never sought the vagabond lifestyle, but shifted into it out of necessity, was that he was married. Leonard's wife Sarah was from Rocky Mount, too. Her family owned a funeral home, but she became a teacher. Her job did not allow for flexibility. She had to be in the classroom, not accompanying her man around the country and the Caribbean. Unlike Paige, who was happy to gallivant around wherever the next game was scheduled, and who heedlessly left girlfriends and wives behind as he roamed, Leonard loved his wife and preferred to spend time with her. Leonard did play winter ball—it was an economic requirement—but he limited his opportunities on the road. The result was that the Leonards were not wealthy, but managed to survive financially.

"Most of the players who were playing ball back then in the thirties weren't married, or, if they were married, they either weren't staying with their wives or their wives were working and helping take care of them," Leonard said. "You couldn't depend on black baseball. If she [Sarah] hadn't been teaching school, I would have had to quit playing baseball."[17]

For many years, the general public did not demand any type of accuracy from Negro Leagues scorekeeping. Black-oriented newspapers like the *Chicago Defender* and the *Pittsburgh Courier* reported games, ran some box scores, and kept track of statistical categories to a point. However, some newspapers were weeklies and did not include all games. Comprehensiveness was out of the question. There was no league clearinghouse, or even more fanciful, no such thing as a statistically omnivorous outfit in operation like those today that can readily inform inquirers of any offbeat number desired.

Much later, historians like John Holway and Robert Peterson, with a devoted sense of allegiance to accuracy and to advancing Negro Leagues baseball in the public consciousness, performed yeoman work in seeking out every scrap of paper providing evidence from games. Chances were that if they could not discover the record of a ballgame, the numbers had evaporated into the mists.

Leonard relates a humorous story about an aborted attempt to bring consistency to scorebook keeping. Once, he said, a newspaper loaned the Grays a reporter to keep the book while insisting the team pay part of his salary so his combined salary would be a survival wage. The so-called record-keeper, however, kept irregular hours and was known to show up after the first pitch was thrown. Sometimes in the third inning, upon his arrival, he would ask players in the dugout what a batter did in the first inning, Leonard said.

And just as frequently, a player asked who had no memory of the at bat, would make something up. Leonard said that when this less-than-enterprising statistician could find no satisfactory answer, he either credited the batsman with a fly out to center field or a single to center field. Hence, he became known to the players not by his own name, but by the teasing nickname of "Single to Center."

In some ways, this was the ultimate insult to the African American ballplayer. Not only was the black player prohibited from trying to reach the big leagues, forced to play outside the frame of reference of most of American society, and not covered by the mass media, but also when it was all over, there were only the bare bones of a historical record. The combined effect was to cruelly turn the African American baseball player into a sort of a ghost. It was merely another way for white society to look right through the proud, talented ballplayers.

By the late 1930s, rumblings began among white people of conscience who believed that black players should be given a chance to play in the majors. Members of the black press, such as Chester Washington with the *Pittsburgh Courier*, had led the campaign for fairness for some time. Washington took the bold and famous step of sending a telegram to Pie Traynor, Pittsburgh Pirates manager, during a winter meeting's gathering of baseball men, urging him to sign black players who played right down the street from his Forbes Field. The message promised that if Traynor hired Josh Gibson, Buck Leonard, Satchel Paige, and Cool Papa Bell, he would guarantee himself a pennant. No recruitment of these stars took place.

Even with Dodgers president Branch Rickey's careful planning and go-slow approach to integration with just one player, Jackie Robinson, in 1947, racial epithets were screamed from the stands, opposing players called him names, and some Dodger teammates at one point threatened to walk out. A mass signing of African Americans by a poor team would have been worth the risk for the Pirates since it has repeatedly been proven in professional sports that winning cures just about anything. There also would have been a safety-in-numbers factor that would have been a buffer for the black players.

Jimmy Powers of the *New York Daily News* emerged in his columns as one of the earliest white journalists backing the cause of integration in baseball, and so did Shirley Povich in the *Washington Post*. In 1938, Powers picked a dream team in print that included blacks. He selected Josh Gibson as his catcher and Buck Leonard as his first baseman. In 1938 or 1939 (he could not remember which), Leonard said that he and Gibson were invited to the office of Washington Senators owner Clark Griffith to discuss playing in the majors.

At that time the Grays played many of their home games in Washington in Griffith's stadium. Griffith saw the players up close and he knew who the best ones were. Leonard reported a strange conversation in the secrecy of Griffith's headquarters. Griffith asked if they would like to play in the majors and if they thought they could. They said yes and yes. But then Griffith made excuses for why it could not happen right then. No owner wanted to be the first, Griffith said, as Leonard recalled. And besides, if all the best black players were signed for the majors the Negro Leagues would break up, Griffith said.[18]

Griffith did not have to invite the players to such a meeting. The Senators were notorious for being a bad baseball team, had been for some time, and would be for some time longer. Griffith needed reinforcements. He was dealing with fully developed players that needed no minor league training. He was discoursing with players who had the goods and who had demonstrated it countless times. And he was conversing with players who would likely come cheap just for the opportunity to compete. Gibson and Leonard would be bargain pickups who might be able to transform his team quickly.

Yet Griffith took no action. Did he hold the meeting just so he could tell those hungry for change that he had? Did he enter the meeting in good faith truly expecting to strike a deal? Did Griffith enter the meeting and then chicken out? Was he fearful that wrath-of-God commissioner Landis would suspend him? Did he fear that other sanctimonious owners would shut him out? Nobody knows. Griffith had a great opportunity to better his team in the standings, enrich his product with what was sure to be an increase in attendance, and be remembered as a leader in social justice. And he frittered away the chance.

One of the greatest champions of Major League reform and backers of African Americans getting an opportunity was the *Daily Worker*, the American Communist Party newspaper located in New York City. Circumstances sometimes create strange bedfellows. It is difficult to imagine any black ballplayer who had been scrapping for every dime he could make in the environment of the Depression, being anything but a hardcore capitalist, but there it was. In its support for the black baseball player, the *Daily Worker* was simply satisfying its theoretical mission of preaching equality for all mankind. To illustrate the economic diversity of opinion of those concerned, it might he said that Satchel Paige, jumping teams with the frequency of a grasshopper when anyone beckoned with a bigger buck, was the greatest capitalist since Adam Smith.

Just about anyone who is recorded having an impression of Buck Leonard on the ball field remarks upon his terrific hitting. Roy Campanella, who played with the Baltimore Elite Giants before he joined the Brooklyn Dodgers as one of the first African Americans in the majors, raved about Leonard's stick handling.

Yet for all the praise about Leonard's style and speed with the bat, it would take a steam shovel in library archives to dig out much in the way of compliments about his speed on the base paths. He was not Rickey Henderson. In recounting one success, Leonard wrote, "I was not noted for my baserunning." But he took off without the manager's steal sign. "I thought I had a good lead and I left," he said. "My wife was at that game and she got at me about that. She told me to quit trying to steal bases because I might get hurt."[19] Somehow, that lecture did not seem like a vote of confidence in Leonard's sprinting ability.

Leonard's credibility was always unquestioned when it came to matters related to hitting. The best black ballplayers were among the best in the world, but they did not labor under the best conditions. The top sluggers in the white majors during the time period when Leonard played, guys like Ted Williams,

Buck Leonard always did swing a mean bat, although he is smiling during a non-game situation with his lumber of choice.

Joe DiMaggio, Jimmie Foxx, and Stan Musial, had to contend with different obstacles. A Dizzy Dean or Bob Feller might throw as fast as any clocking device could measure, and the odd pitcher like Ewell Blackwell, might throw oddly. And there was always the spitter, the outlawed pitch some hurlers cheated with, but never did the big timers face the array and volume of devious creations Negro Leagues pitchers invented. "In the Negro Leagues, anything went," Leonard proclaimed. "They threw a spitball, knuckleball, cut ball, or anything else they could come up with. There were several players in our league who scratched the ball. It was supposed to be illegal, but the ump didn't call it."[20]

Leonard decried the freedom pitchers had to "dust off" batters, sending them diving to the ground by using inside stuff with impunity. Umpires tolerated the brushback throwers, so the hitters just had to get up and set themselves in the box again. Yet despite this so-called headhunter meanness among pitchers, Leonard said he was almost never hit by a pitch during his long pro career. He had either a faulty memory or remarkable dexterity, but Leonard said he was struck by a pitched ball only three times. Only one of those resulted in a notable injury, a broken thumb, that kept him sidelined about ten days.[21]

Black ball differed from the majors in another significant way—the travel. During Leonard's day the majors played a 154-game schedule. Each team played half of its games at home and half on the road. The African American teams in the Negro Leagues, the most organized of black teams, played shorter league seasons and filled in schedules with exhibition games. Sometimes teams played games in two locations in a day. Sometimes teams traveled for weeks. Baseball teams travel by jet plane now and traveled by train in the first several decades of the twentieth century. Yet black teams, skimping on costs, jammed into automobiles, six, eight, ten men to a car. There was wear and tear on the chassis, the tires, and the humans. For all they accomplished, it was apparent that weary pitchers could not be in top form all the time, that worn-down hitters could not see with the sharpness they needed to strike successfully at 90-mph fastballs.

"We played around two hundred or two-hundred-and-ten games that year," Leonard said in reference to 1941, "and traveled about 30,000 or 40,000 miles. Counting winter ball I guess we played about three hundred games year-round. By mid-summer, it seemed like 3,000. Playing in the Negro Leagues was tough. The traveling was tough."[22]

And there were always exhibitions against white players. While Satchel Paige was notorious for organizing such tours, working with Dean and Feller, and chatting with opponents (it was difficult to imagine the voluble Satch keeping his mouth shut for long), Leonard made it sound as if the African American teams he played with had little to do with the white players. Leonard said he could hit 300-game winner Lefty Grove when the lefty got behind in the count, but Leonard did not make a big deal out of reaching the Hall of Famer for base hits.

"He was thinking about how much he was going to make that day rather who was going to win the ball game," Leonard said. "At that time there was no fraternizing between blacks and whites. We came out and played a ball game and they went their way and we went ours. We didn't talk before the game and didn't do much talking during the ball game. We blacks had an inferiority complex. We felt like the only reason they were playing against us was to make money."[23]

Such games were staged for both sides to make money. However, this is a very rare instance of a top African American player committing to any type of public declaration, the statement that Lefty Grove or any white player did not care about the results much. The precious victories compiled in these black-white encounters were always used as evidence to indicate that blacks could play with whites on equal footing. And every victory seemed to be savored. Leonard's comment about black players having an inferiority complex and not bragging about wins does not seem to fit with other written history or statements ascribed to other black players. Other star African American players knew their worth, but were pleased to be able to point to wins over whites. Satchel Paige did so repeatedly.

When Jackie Robinson broke into the majors with the Dodgers, such exhibitions began to fade as novelties. Paying customers came out to Ebbets Field to watch a black man play against white opponents. Soon, white players and black players shared the same fields regularly in Major League cities.

LATER LIFE

Leonard turned forty in 1947, an age at which all but a tiny number of professional baseball players are retired. The phenomenon of Jackie Robinson paving the way for other blacks to make the transition from the shadows to the pinnacle of the sport was clear to him.

"Jackie was an excellent choice because of his intelligence," Leonard said much later. "And put that together with his ability, it made him a natural." Leonard acknowledged there were other good players who could fit because of their ability, but might not have been able to adjust to the name-calling and torment that Robinson weathered. "They wouldn't have taken what Jackie did. He was smart enough to know that it would all work out. I don't know if I could have done it or not. He was the ideal man. The best man."[24]

For some African American players in the Negro Leagues, the signing of Robinson and his promotion to the Dodgers was the same as a fortune-teller reading their palms. They saw themselves in the next wave, ready for the big chance so many of their predecessors had been denied. But this was not so with Leonard. He was much too grounded, knowing where he stood compared to the Buck Leonard of old and that teams did not scout forty-year-olds as prospects.

Still, the estimable Bill Veeck, who had sought to buy the Philadelphia Phillies during World War II with plans to break the color barrier by hiring several black players, the same Bill Veeck who made Larry Doby the first black in the American League with the Cleveland Indians, contacted Leonard in 1952. By then Veeck was running the St. Louis Browns. He invited Leonard to take a chance, to come hit for him, to show him what he still had.

Veeck was known to make grand gestures, but he also had given Satchel Paige a job as a forty-two-year-old rookie with the Indians in 1948. Paige vindicated his judgment with his relief work leading to a World Series appearance. But Paige was a showman who could put fannies in the seats. For Veeck to approach Leonard when he was forty-five was both an offering based on respect for what he had done, and a sign of respect for what Leonard might possibly still accomplish. If Leonard was so great, perhaps he had enough hitting left in him to make a difference. It had worked with Paige, had it not?

After the Negro Leagues fell apart in 1950 and his longtime employer, the Homestead Grays, went under, Leonard took his bat to the Mexican League in 1951 and hit .322 for Torreon. The next year he batted .325 there. So it was not beyond the bounds of credulity for Veeck to think Leonard retained some pop. But when Veeck came calling with the dream-of-a-lifetime offer, Leonard said no.

"I was too old and I knew it," he said. He kept playing in Mexico until 1955. There was a difference. The majors played every day. In Mexico he could muster his strength for a more restful schedule. "Down there we played three games a week and I could still play like the devil for them for three days, although I couldn't have played every day."[25]

Leonard left the audience wanting more. When Leonard did shelve his bat—after playing one season for the Xalapa Hot Peppers—he promptly returned to Rocky Mount. He had left school early for the work force and then left town for a baseball career. There was no place for him to attend high school in Rocky Mount in the 1920s, but in the late 1950s Leonard earned a high school diploma from the American Correspondence School. He was a cofounder of a minor league team in Rocky Mount and served as vice president, opened a real estate agency, and acted as a part-time scout for the Phillies. He married a second time, to Lugenia, three years after Sarah died.

In 1966, in a milestone acceptance speech upon being inducted into the Hall of Fame, Boston Red Sox slugger Ted Williams urged the hall to open its doors to African American players long overlooked. A few years later, Commissioner Bowie Kuhn appointed a committee to investigate the history and records of Negro Leagues players, and in 1971 Paige became the first inductee from that group. A year later, fittingly with his old pal Josh Gibson, Buck Leonard was invited in.

Not long after New Year's in 1972, Leonard got a phone call from his old friend Monte Irvin, who had been a Newark Eagles Negro Leagues star before joining the New York Giants. At the time, Irvin was working for the major league baseball commissioner's office. Determined to keep Leonard's Hall of Fame selection a secret until a press conference, Irvin convinced Leonard to meet him in New York City by lying to him. His fabricated story was that the majors were going to pick a Negro Leagues All-Star team, then shoot a photograph, and have the picture placed on a plaque for the Hall of Fame. Leonard said he would come.

Irvin treated the matter like a surprise birthday party. He had Leonard fly to New York a day earlier than the so-called scheduled meeting on February 8, register at the Americana Hotel, and then meet him the next morning. Even after Leonard saw a room full of people, even after he saw Kuhn, even after he was told that Gibson had been selected to the Hall, he had no idea that he also had been chosen. Irvin manipulated the circumstances masterfully. Every time Leonard had a question, Irvin gave a plausible answer about what was going on. He even lured Leonard to the stage without Leonard getting wise. Kuhn stepped to the podium and announced that Gibson had been selected. Applause was heard. Kuhn paused and said, "The commitee has also seen fit to nominate Buck Leonard to the Baseball Hall of Fame."

Leonard said he was speechless from shock. This was unfortunate, because he was immediately asked to make a speech. He did not have one handy. He said thank you and suggested maybe people should ask some questions instead. The old Homestead Gray leaned over to Larry Doby and said, "I don't want to wake up and realize I just dreamed this."[26]

Leonard delivered his official Hall of Fame induction speech on August 7, 1972, in Cooperstown, New York. He recounted his surprise at being selected and commented thoughtfully on what it felt like being on the outside for years.

"We in the Negro Leagues felt like we were contributing something to baseball, too, when we were playing," Leonard said. "We played with a round ball and we played with a round bat. And we wore baseball shoes and wore baseball uniforms and we thought that we were making a contribution to baseball. We loved the game and we liked to play it. If we didn't, we wouldn't have played because there wasn't any money in it."[27] After the day of honors in upstate New York, Leonard always said, "That was the greatest moment of my life right there."[28]

Leonard returned to his home in North Carolina, a home filled with baseball memorabilia, from bats and balls and jerseys to plaques and awards of recognition. He then knew that he was not the only one who remembered those preserved artifacts and that they represented a story for a wider audience. Once Leonard was selected for the Hall of Fame, it was as if the entire world validated his years of anonymous sweat. Fans wanted autographs. Leonard wrote a book on his life. The North Carolina Sports Hall of Fame recognized him.

Following his Baseball Hall of Fame election, Leonard lived another twenty-five years, until 1997, and the glow of the spotlight that followed him in that quarter of a century made up for the obscurity he suffered when he was at the top of his game.

NOTES

1. Buck O'Neil, personal interview, December 7, 2005.
2. Buck O'Neil with Steve Wulf and David Conrads, *I Was Right on Time* (New York: Simon & Schuster, 1996), 143.
3. Buck Leonard with James A. Riley, *Buck Leonard: The Black Lou Gehrig* (New York: Carroll & Graf, 1995), 17.
4. Craig Davidson (producer, director, and co-writer), *There Was Always Sun Shining Someplace: Life in the Negro Baseball Leagues*, DVD (Westport, CT: Refocus Films, 1984).
5. Leonard with Riley, *Buck Leonard: The Black Lou Gehrig*, 35.
6. Jim O'Brien, *New York Post*, February 9, 1972.
7. Leonard with Riley, *Buck Leonard: The Black Lou Gehrig*, 37.
8. Buck Leonard with John Holway, *Sporting News*, March 4, 1972.
9. Ibid.
10. Ibid.
11. Ibid.
12. Ibid.
13. Mark Ribowsky, *The Power and the Darkness* (New York: Simon & Schuster, 1996), 129.
14. Davidson, *There Was Always Sun Shining Someplace*.
15. Leonard with Riley, *Buck Leonard: The Black Lou Gehrig*, 83.
16. Leonard with Riley, *Buck Leonard: The Black Lou Gehrig*, 90.
17. Leonard with Riley, *Buck Leonard: The Black Lou Gehrig*, 92.
18. Leonard with Riley, *Buck Leonard: The Black Lou Gehrig*, 100.
19. Leonard with Riley, *Buck Leonard: The Black Lou Gehrig*, 117.
20. Leonard with Riley, *Buck Leonard: The Black Lou Gehrig*, 123.
21. Leonard with Riley, *Buck Leonard: The Black Lou Gehrig*, 189.
22. Leonard with Riley, *Buck Leonard: The Black Lou Gehrig*, 126.
23. Leonard with Riley, *Buck Leonard: The Black Lou Gehrig*, 142–143.
24. Davidson, *There Was Always Sun Shining Someplace*.
25. Eric Enders, *The Scribner Encyclopedia of American Lives* (Volume 5, 2000).
26. Leonard with Riley, *Buck Leonard: The Black Lou Gehrig*, 249–252.
27. Buck Leonard, Transcript of Acceptance Speech Upon Induction to the Baseball Hall of Fame, Baseball Hall of Fame Library Archives.
28. Davidson, *There Was Always Sun Shining Someplace*.

Further Reading

Enders, Eric, *The Scribner Encyclopedia of American Lives* (Volume 5). Charles Scribner's Sons, 2000.
Leonard, Buck, with John Holway, *The Sporting News*, March 4, 1972.
Leonard, Buck, with James A. Riley, *Buck Leonard: The Black Lou Gehrig*. New York: Carroll & Graf, 1995.

COOL PAPA BELL
May 17, 1903–March 7, 1991

Cool Papa Bell was one of the superstars of the Negro Leagues and was sometimes compared to Ty Cobb, the legendary Detroit Tiger during his Negro Leagues playing career between 1922 and 1946, mostly as a center fielder. Bell was regarded as the fastest runner on the bases of his time and maybe the fastest in baseball history while playing for the St. Louis Stars, Pittsburgh Crawfords, Kansas City Monarchs, and Homestead Grays, among other teams.

Sketchy reports credit Bell with a .342 lifetime batting average and with averages of .373 in 1945 and .412 in 1946. Bell was too old to play in the majors once the color line was broken, but was selected for the Baseball Hall of Fame in 1974.

☆　　☆　　☆

The old man sat on a metal folding chair in the sports memorabilia store, relaxing in the air-conditioning at the small shop on a hot Las Vegas afternoon. He wore thick-rimmed glasses, one of his trademark bow-ties and carried a cane.

Slender, even bony in old age, he had never been large, heavy, or tall, even in his athletic prime. But in his eighties, his age just shy of the age of the twentieth century, Cool Papa Bell could reflect that he had once been much fleeter afoot.

Bell and Monte Irvin, his companion on this day, had come to sign autographs. Only there was no line of knowledgeable or eager baseball fans. Either word had not been spread sufficiently, or the names of the two former Negro Leagues stars had not resonated with the public at large the way more recent stars might have. It was a rare opportunity to meet Bell, in the twilight of his life, and Irvin, also in retirement, and an even rarer chance to obtain an autograph from a player like Bell who competed for his entire career in near obscurity, but whose skills and talents were greatly admired.

Anyone who did visit was blessed with an autograph and plenty of time to hang out and talk on the slow afternoon. A few years later, with interest in black baseball on an upswing, savvy fans would have mobbed Bell and Irvin. The mainstream white baseball audience realized what had been overlooked. But by then it was too late, for a few years later Cool Papa Bell was dead.

Stories told about this now sedentary man all revolved around speed, of how he could fly around the bases, and of how he disrupted pitchers and fielders when he jitterbugged off first base playing with their heads, during his years with the Grays and other teams. Cool Papa Bell was the fastest man on the diamond, a sprinter par excellence who instead of running in a straight line ran around the bases. His derring-do ranked him with Rickey Henderson, Jackie Robinson, and Ty Cobb as the most effective forces on the base paths in baseball history. They were among the handful who could ruin a foe because they had larceny in their hearts, wings on their feet, and a fierce sense of entitlement to claim the next base. They wrecked pitchers' and fielders' nerves by envisioning first base as a gateway to more. During his playing days, Bell was frequently called "the black Ty Cobb" as a compliment since Cobb was then the greatest recorded base-stealer.

A young and smiling Cool Papa Bell, who, some suggest, was the fastest man ever to play professional baseball, was a legendary center fielder.

Pure speed is measured by stopwatches in track meets. The runner who owns the world record in the 100-meter dash is regarded as the world's fastest human. Speed in team sport is best measured by results. Cool Papa Bell was one of the few guys whose speed scared other teams. Other players spoke his name in awe, told tales in whispers about just how fast he was. Inevitably, they seemed to become tall tales, yet the number of witnesses who would swear to the truth of them was long and distinguished.

"He [Bell] was the best runner I ever saw," said Buck Leonard, a Bell teammate in Pittsburgh and also a Hall of Famer. "People tell all kinds of stories on him. Some of them are true. He could run. They used to talk about how Cool Papa would run out from under his hat and how he used to go from first to third on an out. But the way he used to go, he would catch the umpire looking at first base and he would cut right across the diamond and go to third base. He would never touch second base. We used to joke him about that."[1] That story sounds like fiction. Opposing players would have screamed. Fans would have howled. Leonard and Bell have both passed away and neither can address the issue.

Bell did perform some incredible baserunning feats. He scored from first base on a bunt more than once. He once hit three inside-the-park home runs in a single game.[2] Buck O'Neil, the old Kansas City Monarchs player and manager, was a great fan of Bell's baserunning acumen and he sometimes traveled with him on barnstorming tours.

"Everywhere he went, everyone would want to know about Cool Papa and how fast he was because there were so many stories of him scoring from first base on a single, or stealing home," O'Neil said. "And Cool would be like a one-man clinic, sitting out on the porch behind the rooming house talking about baseball. Later, when I got to see Cool Papa play, I knew that what everybody said about him was dead-on true."

After Jesse Owens won the gold medal in the Olympic 100-meter dash in Germany in 1936, he came back to the United States and ran exhibitions not only against horses, but also sometimes against baseball players while spotting them a ten-yard head start. "I don't ever remember him racing Cool Papa," O'Neil said. "I don't think he wanted to take that chance. Boy, wouldn't that have been something—Jesse Owens racing against Cool Papa Bell! I'll say this, going from first to home, Jesse wouldn't have beaten Cool Papa."[3]

In a slightly different view of a potential Bell-Owens sprint showdown, a children's book describes the circumstances this way: "Cool Papa Bell was the fastest baseball player ever. During his baseball career he was the fastest man alive. Jesse Owens refused to race him because he knew Bell was the fastest."[4]

True or not, there was no point in Owens taking the risk of racing Bell. He had nothing to gain and everything to lose. And Bell, according to his daughter, and self-described number one fan Connie Brooks, in a document supplied to the Baseball Hall of Fame research library much later, was timed running around the bases in eleven seconds flat. (Bell himself said that it was twelve seconds.)

EARLY LIFE

Cool Papa Bell was born as James Thomas Bell in Starkville, Mississippi, on May 17, 1903, not the best place or time for an African American. He was five-foot-eleven and weighed 150 pounds as a swift and graceful outfielder. Bell never went very far in school because opportunities were limited for black youngsters in Mississippi at the time. There was no high school for Bell to attend as a black youth in Starkville, and he recognized that his best chance for a solid future lay elsewhere, so he began playing semipro baseball by the time he reached high school age. At nineteen he was collecting a paycheck as a professional with the St. Louis Stars.

Bell earned his enduring nickname quite early in his career. When he joined the Stars, Bell said his teammates thought he would be jittery playing in front of big crowds. But he was not.

"I took it so cool they began to call me 'Cool,'" Bell said. "But that wasn't enough, so they added 'Papa' to it."[5] Most likely, in the way these things come about, because it was the opposite of his age. He was also impervious to pressure. So Bell was "Cool" because he really acted cool and he was "Papa" because he was really young.

Before Bell joined the Stars for the start of his twenty-six-year Negro Leagues career, he worked in a meat-packing house. He was well acquainted with racism from an early age, not only because of educational roadblocks, but also because of the separation of the races in bathrooms, swimming pools, and at drinking fountains. And such treatment was not routine only in Mississippi.

"Racism was rampant," Connie Brooks wrote in a summary of her father's life. "He traveled from town to town being denied the right to eat, sleep, or use the bathroom facilities in white-owned hotels, restaurants or public places. Cool Papa knocked on doors trying to find black residences that would take in black baseball players while the team was in town. Many nights he slept on the bus after playing three baseball games in one day, with no place to wash up or eat."[6]

When Bell was elected to the Hall of Fame in 1974, he was asked if he was bitter about the harsh things he experienced and about being excluded from Major League baseball. "Life was that way then," he said. "I lived in that time. It was that way when I was born in Starkville, Mississippi and it was that way when I worked in the packing houses of St. Louis before I played baseball. People lived that life before I did."[7]

Bell sounded philosophical, consistent with his temperament. John Holway, author of several books about Negro Leagues baseball, referred to Bell as "self-effacing" and "as sweet a human being as was ever elected to the Hall of Fame."[8]

Certainly, Brooks admired her father not only for his deeds in baseball, but also because of his personality and the way he treated her. "The legendary James 'Cool Papa' Bell was truly a great athlete, but most of all he was a super human being," she wrote. "I am extremely proud of my father. He was the best dad in the world and I will always love and respect him with all my heart."[9]

Bell is renowned as a great center fielder, a man with a great glove and the speed to cover the territory in the ballpark's widest open spaces. But he actually began as a pitcher, something rarely noted and little remembered. One of Bell's claims to support his talent as a pitcher was striking out the great Oscar Charleston. However, Cool Papa

A slick fielder, here Cool Papa Bell stretches to grab a high throw in the outfield. Bell starred in the Negro Leagues between 1922 and 1946.

earned his renown as a fielder, becoming a regular in the East-West All-Star game when it began in the 1930s. He also had amazing longevity.

PLAYING CAREER

Bell broke in with the Stars in St. Louis and he kept his home in that large Missouri city until he died. His first professional baseball salary was $90 a month and that was not much of a raise from the $21.20 weekly he made as a meat packer. Over the years, Bell also played for the Memphis Red Sox, Kansas City Monarchs, Chicago American Giants, and the Detroit Wolves, as well as the Homestead Grays, where he enjoyed many of his greatest years. For much of his career, Bell doubled by playing winter ball in Latin American countries, a total of twenty-one seasons. If he managed to put together fifty years of baseball by playing year-round, Bell also managed a full life with Clarabelle, his wife of sixty-two years.

His daughter calculates Bell's all seasons lifetime batting average as .419. Other estimates place his Negro Leagues average at .342 for the self-taught switch-hitter who threw left-handed. There is no definitive figure because of poor record-keeping that plagued many teams. However, there are some generally accepted numbers that summarize Bell's best baseball.

Bell always said he stole 175 bases in 1933 with the Crawfords, a year when the team played about 180 games. He hit .379 that season, too. He claims three Negro Leagues batting titles, and it is said that Bell never hit lower than .300 in his black baseball career. But there is evidence he came in under the magic number in some of his winter ball stints. One of Bell's more remarkable seasons was 1946 when he batted .412 for the Grays in 117 at bats at age forty-three. One of his most productive winter ball seasons came in 1940 when he won the Mexican League's batting title with a .437 average in eighty-nine games.

The boycott of African American players was at its zenith among Major League teams when Bell was in his prime. From the standpoint of Major League opportunity, he played at exactly the wrong time. Bell was a spectacular player, flashy, and exciting, so putting his name in the lineup could have aided any weak team at the box office. Moses Fleetwood Walker was the first African American baseball player in the 1880s when the International League was considered a Major League, but no other blacks were invited into the majors until Jackie Robinson broke the color line with the Brooklyn Dodgers in 1947. Robinson was the same type of fan-pleasing player as Bell was, albeit with more power. Robinson electrified crowds with his style on the bases, just as Bell did.

The iron will blockading African Americans from making a living at the top level of baseball belonged to Commissioner Kenesaw Mountain Landis. As long as he ruled—and Landis did rule the sport for nearly a quarter of a century following the Black Sox scandal of 1919—no blacks had a chance. Some owners recognized the fallacy of the policy. Others sought to change it. Most simply shrugged and chose not to cross Landis.

As early as 1935 the acknowledgment of Bell's ability provoked a conversation with Earl Mack, son of the legendary Connie Mack, operator of the Philadelphia Athletics. In an anecdote publicized by the Hall of Fame in 1974 and in a variety of other writings, Bell said the younger Mack approached him and said, "If the door was open, you'd be the first one I'd hire. I'd pay you $75,000 a year. You'd be worth it as drawing power alone." Bell was not even making $7,500 at the time at the tail end of the Depression.

Those who saw Bell play and the way he could take over a game with his swiftness on the base paths knew he was a special player. But compared to other Negro Leagues stars he was not always highly publicized. Many seasons he played in the shadow of colorful pitcher Satchel Paige, long-ball thumper Josh Gibson, and high-average swinger Buck Leonard. Paige's name and flamboyance sold tickets, so the promoters hyped him above all. Gibson's vicious power made fans gasp, so he was a good ticket-seller, as well. By the time Bell's name was listed on the marquee there was only room left for small print, if any at all. Bell did not complain. It was not in his nature to stir things up. He loved being able to play the game, to make a splash on the field, but he was not going to rock the boat by demanding more money and he was not going to jump teams to become a headliner elsewhere.

"When I went to the Crawfords [in 1933] they had [Oscar] Charleston, [Josh] Gibson, [Satchel] Paige," Bell said. "They weren't going to bill anyone over them. They never did advertise you over those guys. The Crawfords advertised Satchel. They just kept dramatizing and dramatizing him, but we had guys who would win more games than him."

"When they billed me, they had those wagons going around saying, 'Bell's going to be here tonight.' But I didn't ask for anything. I only got a cut like the rest of the ballplayers got. I'm not the guy who wants to be praised too much. I never wanted to be a big shot."[10]

Bell's personality was lower key than Paige's for certain. In 1948, 1949, and 1950, when he was approaching fifty, Bell managed the Kansas City Stars, a feeder club for the Monarchs. Buck O'Neil, running the parent franchise at the time, got to know Bell very well.

"He was sweet," O'Neil said. "He's the type of guy everybody liked. Everybody loved Cool. Cool was like your brother. Or if you were a younger player, he was like a father or uncle."[11] It was said that Bell was so nice that he never even bothered himself to argue bad calls with umpires, that he was above it, too dignified.

Although Paige stole the limelight with his crazy pitching motions, his brash predictions, his humorous actions, and his phenomenal results, he was the best press agent Bell ever had. Paige was a renowned raconteur and sometimes his stories focused on Bell. Not surprisingly, they were concocted around Cool Papa's speed. Whenever Paige talked his utterings brought a laugh and were taken with a grain of salt. People believed Paige at the risk of their own gullibility.

One example of Bell's supersonic speed that Paige cited was always taken as a joke, but still made its point. "I saw Bell hit a ground ball and he was declared out because he was hit by his own batted ball while sliding into second base," Paige said.[12]

Paige's signature story about Bell, repeated so often that it is one of the most famous tales in baseball lore, revolves around the days they spent as roommates on the road. Cool Papa Bell was so fast, Paige told the world, that he could turn off the light switch and be in bed under the covers before the room went dark.[13]

Such a feat is impossible. Paige's audience guffawed every time. Paige told the story in public speeches, to interviewers for newspapers, magazines, and books. However, the most remarkable thing about the tale is that it is true. Paige made the world laugh with this apparent fairy tale about Bell's speed, but ironically, Bell had the last laugh.

At a gathering of dozens of former Negro Leagues players in Ashland, Kentucky, in 1981, Bell told the real story—with Paige listening. The light in the hotel room that the two players shared actually had a short circuit. The wiring was faulty, causing a delay of three or four seconds before the light went off. So if Bell hustled after he flicked the switch off, he could be under the covers before the room went dark. That story is related in some papers in the James "Cool Papa" Bell file at the National Baseball Hall of Fame research library. Chief librarian Tim Wiles said that Bell's version of the story is no secret, but that it has been told only a tiny fraction of the number of times that Paige's story is repeated, so comparatively few people recognize the truth. It is an unusual occasion of one-upmanship of Paige by Bell.

In one of his books about Negro Leagues baseball, author John Holway takes the incident a step further. He reports that Cool Papa teased Paige about the faulty switch saying, "See Satch, you been tellin' people that story 'bout me for years, and even you didn't know it was true!"[14]

Monte Irvin, a Negro Leagues star who had a substantial Major League career in the 1950s and then a lengthy run as a special assistant to Commissioner Bowie Kuhn, selected Bell for his all-time Negro Leagues team. Irvin said Bell's nickname aided his name recognition at a time when mainstream newspapers ignored black ball. "Cool Papa Bell is a little better known because he had that magical name," Irvin said. "And he seemed to work a little magic on the field, too. He could run, he could hit, and he could play."[15]

When Bell played baseball year-round, there was nearly as much difficulty authenticating records for English-speaking Americans in Latin American lands as in black leagues. Again, anecdotes established perspective. Judy Johnson, another Hall of Famer from the Negro Leagues, shared foreign-playing time many winters with Bell in Cuba and elsewhere.

"He was so fast that if he hit a ground ball that took more than one hop you couldn't throw him out from the left side of the infield," Johnson said. "Might as well just hold the ball. When he came around second, heading for third, it looked like his feet weren't even touching the ground. Believe it or not, he'd steal second standing up and he'd often score from first on a single, or from second on a deep sacrifice fly."[16]

Players with such speed as to rattle shortstops and third basemen into rushing their throws come along only periodically in the majors. The current speedster that forces that type of left-side-of-the-infield attention is Ichiro Suzuki, the legendary Japanese star batting lead-off for the Seattle Mariners.

One way African American stars of the mid-twentieth century proved they belonged at the highest level of baseball was by excelling during off-season barnstorming tours against white players. Bell was a frequent participant in such games. In an era when players were paid far less than they earn today, even the majors top stars sought extra income. The St. Louis Cardinals' Dizzy Dean, and at different times the Cleveland Indians' Bob Feller and Bob Lemon, were notable for pulling together early autumn swings to play exhibitions against black All-Star teams. Fans were enthusiastic and the players could supplement regular-season salaries with thousands of extra dollars. The documentation of some of these games was more reliable than regular-season Negro Leagues statistics, but it is not possible to know for sure if Bell's daughter's claim of a .391 average against white pitching is precise.

Bell's knack for the spectacular did not fade as he aged. Bell was a member of the Satchel Paige All Stars in a game against the Bob Lemon All-Stars on October 24, 1948, in Los Angeles. Othello "Chico" Renfroe, who later became a well-known sportscaster based in Atlanta, was a Bell teammate for this occasion and he set the scene. "Before the game, Satchel started needling Lemon. 'Hey, Lem,' he said. 'See old man Bell over there? He's forty-seven years old [actually forty-five], but he's still going to make you boys look bad.'"

"Now Lemon wasn't going to let an old man scare him and the first pitch to Cool zipped right under his chin. Didn't seem to bother him much, though. He hit the next pitch for a double and drove in a run. Then, he even stole third base standing up. Boy, was Lemon mad."[17]

Murray Dickson was pitching when Bell next came to the plate. Cool Papa swatted a base hit to center. "I singled and was on first base," Bell recounted. "And Satchel Paige bunted the ball. Now the shortstop goes to second base and the second baseman goes to first. The third baseman, the catcher and the pitcher go out [for the ball]. I went to second. Wasn't nobody at third base, so I went on and third base was open. Roy Partee, who's catching, was running over and there wasn't nobody at home, and I just kept running."[18] That's how Cool Papa Bell, a player in his forties, scored from first on a bunt. It sounded like the Abbott and Costello routine "Who's on First?" but was a real-life variation of slapstick fielding.

Over the final three years of his Negro Leagues connection, Bell did more managing than playing. Initially, the assignment was to develop players for the Monarchs, but it became obvious that neither the Monarchs nor the Negro Leagues were going to be around much longer. Bell scouted Elston Howard and Ernie Banks and touted them to the hometown St. Louis Browns and St. Louis Cardinals. Neither nibbled. Neither team was ready for African American players. Howard became the first black player for the New York Yankees and Banks became the first black player for the Chicago Cubs.

After he retired as a player, Cool Papa Bell helped out the Kansas City Monarchs organization as a coach, sometimes with a traveling team that was more of minor league caliber.

Banks was only sixteen when Bell discovered him and he still had high school to finish in Dallas. Eventually, it was Buck O'Neil who scouted Banks for the Cubs. But Banks never forgot Bell's interest. "Cool Papa Bell was a great influence on my career in professional baseball," the future Hall of Famer said. "If he had been able to play in the major leagues he would have been one of its greatest stars. He was truly one of the best baseball players in the history of the game."[19]

When Banks left Kansas City for the majors, Bell provided some basic advice. "If you miss a ball, catch the next one," he said. "If you strike out, hit the next one out of there." Bell cheered Banks from afar during his Chicago career and was thrilled when Banks, also known as Mr. Cub, was tapped for the Hall of Fame in 1977. "His conduct was almost as outstanding as his ability. It'll be a joy to see him inducted."[20]

Bill Veeck, the owner known as the best friend the baseball fan ever had, operated the Cleveland Indians and the St. Louis Browns in the late 1940s and early 1950s before taking over the Chicago White Sox. At the end of World War II, Veeck put in a bid for the Philadelphia Phillies and planned to rejuvenate the perennial National League last-place finisher by hiring top African American players. Veeck would have been forever honored as the man who broke baseball's color line. Unfortunately, he made his intentions known and was outflanked on the purchase of the team. Landis did not have any intention of seeing blacks in the majors and arranged for another buyer.

Although Veeck's actions are lesser known than Branch Rickey's efforts in favor of Jackie Robinson and integration with the Brooklyn Dodgers, he did bring the second African American to the majors when he signed Larry Doby for the Indians. Veeck signed the majors first black pitcher when he brought Satchel Paige to St. Louis. Obscured by time is the fact that Veeck also made an offer to Cool Papa Bell after Paige lobbied for him, suggesting he was better than anyone else the Browns had. Given how weak the Browns were, Paige might not even have been using hyperbole. Veeck, who had enough respect for Bell to compare him to Tris Speaker, Joe DiMaggio, and Willie Mays as a fielder, was prepared to sign Bell for his Browns outfield in 1951 despite his being forty-eight years old.[21]

But Bell just did not think he could hack it as an everyday player at that age. "Sure, I can still hit," Bell said. "But I'm too old. My legs are gone. I can't catch the ball the other fella hits."[22] It sounded as if Bell did not want to tarnish his reputation by failing in a snapshot moment in the majors.

LATER LIFE

When Bell left baseball, African Americans were just starting to make their move into the Major League spotlight. The Dodgers were in the forefront with Robinson, catcher Roy Campanella, and pitcher Don Newcombe. Irvin was on his way to sharing the New York Giants outfield with Willie Mays. Hank Aaron was on his way to the Braves. But many of Bell's contemporaries, the black players who had made careers despite being discriminated against, disappeared from the scene, and faded from public consciousness.

From the time Bell departed Starkville, St. Louis had been his permanent home in the United States. He settled into a brick apartment building he owned and spent more than twenty years on a night watchman's job at St. Louis City Hall. During the 1950s and throughout most of the 1960s, little attention was paid to former Negro Leagues stars. The new wave of black ballplayers was busy establishing itself and baseball nostalgia did not reach out and touch the Josh Gibsons, Buck Leonards, and Cool Papa Bells. Not until retired Boston Red Sox slugger Ted Williams issued a provocative speech at his Hall of Fame induction ceremony in 1966. Williams' declaration that he hoped some day soon baseball would do the right thing and recognize the great African American players of the past served as a prod. He piqued the interest and consciences of baseball officials.

Within a few years a special committee was formed, deliberated, and selected the first players for the Hall of Fame whose careers were either entirely or mostly forged in black baseball. Bell's name was called in 1974 when he was seventy years old. He entered the Hall of Fame that August with Mickey Mantle and Whitey Ford, two of the great New York Yankees stars of the 1950s and 1960s.

A man who made a mission out of staying cool did not blow his cool when informed that he had been chosen for the Baseball Hall of Fame. Newsmen asked Bell if it was his biggest thrill and he said it was not. "No, it's my biggest honor," Bell said. "My biggest thrill was when they opened the door in the majors for the black players."[23]

Bell sat in the stands at Atlanta's Fulton-County Stadium in 1974 when Hank Aaron broke Babe Ruth's career home-run record en route to setting the new lifetime mark of 755. Watching a member of a later generation of African American players establish so momentous a record caused Bell to reflect on the past when he and his fellow black athletes were barred from Major League baseball. "I realized years ago that Hank someday would catch up with Ruth and pass him by," Bell said, "but I never dreamed I would be there when it happened." Bell said he came close to crying when Aaron clouted the big blow.[24]

More honors came Bell's way in his later years. He was selected for other Halls of Fame and had a stadium, a league, and streets named after him. Without moving his residence, Bell found himself living on James Cool Papa Bell Avenue. After Bell appeared on a Wheaties box with other former Negro Leagues stars and had a tree planted in his name in Israel, his daughter Connie took to describing him as "a universal legend."[25]

The appreciation was late in coming, but as Bell said, he was glad he was still alive to smell the roses upon being inducted into the Baseball Hall of Fame. Near the end of his life, there were two sad incidents where Bell made the news. First, his beloved wife Clara died in 1990 after more than six decades of marriage. Then, Bell was scammed out of about $300,000 of memorabilia he kept in his home, from baseball gloves and bats, to uniforms and autographed items. Bell had been weakened by a heart attack and his vision was failing when he was swindled. Two men were arrested and most of Bell's collection was recovered.

By then, Bell was in poor health and about a year later, on March 7, 1991, he died in a St. Louis hospital at the age of eighty-seven. Most of the men Bell shared his playing life with were gone, dead and buried before him, the Paiges, Gibsons, Charlestons. But the funeral that attracted about 200 people to Central Baptist Church in St. Louis was a baseball funeral nonetheless. Pallbearers included Hall of Famer Lou Brock, Roy Sievers, and Ken Reitz, who shared a St. Louis baseball history. Former teammate Lester Lockett spoke directly to Bell, saying, "If it weren't for the demons of time, you'd still be running like the wind."[26]

Brock called it a shame that Bell's base-stealing theories were not written down anywhere because his career was played out without any bright lights focused on it. Then-Baseball Hall of Fame president Ed Stack said that for fifteen years after his election to the Hall, Bell annually came to the traditional induction event dinner. "Cool Papa was the dean of the living Hall of Famers," Stack said. "What he said had a tremendous amount of meaning. It was the sermon of the evening, the inspiration and mood-setting for the whole weekend."[27]

Bell was buried at St. Peter's Cemetery under a notable memorial designed and paid for by his daughter Connie Brooks. The African granite memorial is ten feet, six inches tall and fifty inches wide, and weighs 8,392 pounds. It also contains a long inscription detailing many of Cool Papa's accomplishments. Brooks said she thought that necessary because so many untrue stories had been written about her father.[28]

For all the honors and awards Bell received in the final years of his life, from the world of baseball and his adopted home of St. Louis, Brooks still felt slighted that her dad had not been better recognized by his birth state of Mississippi and Starkville, the community where he began life.

However, after a Mississippi reverend toured the Negro Leagues Baseball Museum in Kansas City and was surprised to discover Bell's roots, action was taken. In 1999, a special ceremony was held to honor Bell in Starkville. The occasion was proclaimed Cool Papa Bell Day. A street was named Cool Papa Bell Drive. And a historical marker was unveiled noting Bell's connection to the community. Bell's family was present. So was old teammate Buck Leonard and famous Mississippi author Willie Morris. "I just wish I could have seen Cool Papa run once," Morris said. "I wish you could have, too," replied Leonard.[29]

In his later years, after the Hall of Fame elected him as a member, Bell was more in the limelight than he had been for years. Sportswriters interviewed him, older baseball fans listened to hear him speak, and younger generations of baseball players, like Brock, sought his wisdom. Inevitably, Bell would be asked a variation of the same question or be presented with the same sad lament revolving around the belief that it was too bad he was born too soon to truly show his stuff.

"So many people say I was born too early," said Bell with a typically cool response. "But that's not true. They opened the doors too late."[30] For a man who was faster than the speed of light, all it would have taken was to open the door a crack and James "Cool Papa" Bell would have darted through.

NOTES

1. Buck Leonard with James A. Riley, *Buck Leonard: The Black Lou Gehrig* (New York: Carroll & Graf Publishers, 1995), 55.

2. Geoffrey C. Ward and Ken Burns, *Baseball, An Illustrated History* (companion to "Baseball" documentary) (New York: Alfred P. Knopf, 1994), 222.

3. Buck O'Neil with Steve Wulf and David Conrads, *I Was Right on Time* (New York: Simon & Schuster, 1996), 49–50.

4. Jonah Winter, *Fair Ball! 14 Great Stars from Baseball's Negro Leagues* (New York: Scholastic Books, 1999), 28.

5. Dave Anderson, *New York Times*, February 14, 1974.

6. Connie Brooks, "The Legendary James Thomas Cool Papa Bell" (summary of Cool Papa Bell Life), Baseball Hall of Fame library archives, June 2002.

7. Anderson, *New York Times*.

8. John Holway, *Josh and Satch* (Westport, CT: Meckler Publishing, 1991), 57.

9. Brooks, "The Legendary James Thomas Cool Papa Bell."

10. Holway, *Josh and Satch*, 57.

11. Buck O'Neil, personal interview, December 7, 2005.

12. Anderson, *New York Times*.

13. Mark Ribowsky, *Don't Look Back: Satchel Paige in the Shadows of Baseball* (New York: Simon & Schuster, 1994), 282.

14. Holway, *Josh and Satch*, 217.

15. Monte Irvin with James A. Riley, *Nice Guys Finish First* (New York: Carroll & Graf, 1996), 233.

16. Brooks, "The Legendary James Thomas Cool Papa Bell."

17. Ibid.

18. Jack Etkin, *Kansas City Times*, May 11, 1985.

19. Anderson, *New York Times*.

20. Bob Broeg, *St. Louis Post-Dispatch*, August 7, 1977.

21. Ibid.

22. James Bankes, Cool Papa Bell essay, Baseball Hall of Fame library archives, April 1982.

23. Anderson, *New York Times*.

24. James "Cool Papa" Bell, *Black Sports Magazine*, June 1974.

25. Brooks, "The Legendary James Thomas Cool Papa Bell."
26. Vahe Gregorian, *St. Louis Post-Dispatch*, March 17, 1991.
27. Ibid.
28. Brooks, "The Legendary James Thomas Cool Papa Bell."
29. Rick Cleveland, *Clarion-Ledger*, Jackson, Mississippi, May 11, 1999.
30. Gregorian, *St. Louis Post-Dispatch*, March 17, 1991.

Further Reading

Bell, James, "Cool Papa." *Black Sports Magazine*, June 1974.

JOSH GIBSON

December 21, 1911–January 20, 1947

Those who watched Negro Leagues ball closely called Josh Gibson "the black Babe Ruth." He was considered the greatest power hitter to play in black ball, but died as a young man and never had the opportunity to play in the majors. Based on his longtime brilliant performance in the Negro Leagues, he was selected for the Baseball Hall of Fame in 1972.

Gibson was a teenager when he began playing professionally with the Pittsburgh Crawfords (though he spent most of his career with the Homestead Grays). He played between 1930 and 1947 and was still active when he died. Between his Negro Leagues play, exhibition games, and barnstorming, some believe Gibson hit 800 or 900 home runs, more than Hank Aaron, Barry Bonds, or Babe Ruth.

There are few pictures of Josh Gibson smiling. In most of the photographs that show up of him in books commemorating his almost mythological baseball career, he always seems somber. It is almost as if he has glimpsed his future and realized how history would treat him—as a man grimly cursed by tragedy.

Many believe that Gibson was one of the greatest baseball players who ever lived. But in a sport that thrives and breathes on numbers, on statistical comparisons to match eras, and uses records to rate humans' performance more avidly than any other sport, there is only sporadic documentation to support Gibson. He played at a time when African Americans were banned from Major League baseball. His terrific play was admired solely by those who followed the Negro Leagues. And just when the majors began opening their doors to the best black ballplayers, Gibson died at the sorrowfully young age of thirty-five.

A man who was favorably compared to Babe Ruth for his power as a hitter, who had a lengthy career where he made many friends with his good-hearted outlook on life, but who was also at intervals regarded as a loner, Gibson's achievements endure most vividly in anecdotes. As colossal a figure as he was in Negro Leagues ball—and Gibson rated second only to pitcher Satchel Paige as a nationally revered player—it is almost as if many avenues to truly knowing the all-around man were interred with him when he passed away in 1947. He has become a King Tut individual, prominent in the mind, name known to many, but so many treasures taken to the grave that only the greatest of archeologists, with infinite research, can unlock the key to his personality.

The public record on Gibson describes him as a very strong man physically, almost disproportionately powerful for his formidable six-foot-two, 215-pound frame; as a likeable man who could be moody; and as a clutch batter who hit so many home runs that might as well have left the ballpark on a jet plane, that pitchers quaked at his presence. It is difficult to sort fact from fiction in any discussion of Gibson's life, genuine accomplishment from fairy tale, astonishing baseball feats ascribed to him from actual ones achieved. Many of his contemporaries regard Gibson with great affection, and tell

The legendary Josh Gibson, known for his power and home runs, was compared to Babe Ruth during the career cut short by illness and alcoholism, costing him his life at age thirty-five.

stories about him that enhance his glory—and he is not around to speak for himself. That he was special to them is easily recognizable and perhaps fearing time obscuring just how real his impact was, there is no hesitation in perpetuating what everyone wants to hear—tales of remarkable human endeavor. Little was written about Gibson during his life. Mainstream newspapers did not cover Negro Leagues baseball games. America's national magazines ignored African Americans, regarding them as an invisible people. Radio choices were far more limited and less likely to delve into personalities. TV was a fledgling medium, at best. It was only much later, decades after Gibson's death, that baseball historians, authors, and enterprising journalists began to investigate and piece together write-ups of the bygone Negro Leagues. Gibson's voice could not be heard by then. So, a twenty-first-century explorer into Gibson's stature is left with a character presented as a cross between Paul Bunyan and Hank Aaron.

The stories were presented with the limits on documentation, allowing readers to determine whether Gibson's old friends got carried away, or he was the most extraordinary of hitters; whether Josh Gibson hit more than 900 home runs in his career, or did not; whether Josh Gibson hit 84 home runs in a season, or did not; whether Josh Gibson hit 500-foot home runs, or did not.

Author Mark Ribowsky, who wrote *The Power and the Darkness*, the best researched biography of Gibson, found it challenging to pin down so-called facts about Gibson acknowledged through repetition over the years. "Of all the legends that have sprung from the much-fabled Negro Leagues, Josh Gibson's life and career most closely echo the history and fate of the doomed ship of black baseball," Ribowsky said in his introduction. "Gibson went about as far and as high as any black player could. Yet his fame would be no greater than the tragedy of his demise."[1]

EARLY LIFE

Josh Gibson was born on December 21, 1911 (presumably, since there is no birth certificate), in Buena Vista, Georgia, about 100 miles southwest of Atlanta, where his family tilled crops, but made little money. When Gibson was twelve, the family moved to "The Hill" ghetto neighborhood of Pittsburgh. Mark, Josh's father, took a steel mill job and then sent for his wife Nancy, Josh, and daughter Ann. Josh Gibson had a barrel chest, slim waist, and heavily muscled legs. When he was in high school, he too went to work in the mill, part-time. He was big for his age, reaching his adult dimensions early.

Gibson also began playing baseball. His talents were immediately obvious to club operators and before he turned sixteen Gibson hooked up with the local Pittsburgh Crawfords, then a semipro team. In 1930, Gibson, who earned several mentions in the *Pittsburgh Courier*, a black-oriented newspaper, for prodigious home runs, was borrowed for a game by the more advanced Homestead Grays because of their catcher's injury.

In 1930, Gibson was a hot commodity and the object of interest not only to the Crawfords, expanding into a more serious team, but also to the now rival Grays. Gibson shifted to the Grays and much of his legend was forged with this club, teaming with Buck Leonard and other greats to win nine straight Negro National League pennants between the mid-1930s and mid-1940s.

Players marveled at Gibson's right-handed sock, but at first grimaced at his catching. "He couldn't catch a sack of baseballs," said outfielder Ted Page. "We called him 'boxer' because he'd catch like he was wearing boxing gloves. On foul balls [popups] he was terrible. He said they made him drunk,"[2] meaning dizzy.

Gibson had a naturally strong right throwing arm, so killing off base runners was not a worry—the rest of his fielding was. Future Hall of Fame infielder Judy Johnson made Gibson a personal project, tutoring him on those tortuous high ones. "Honestly, he was the greatest hitter I'd ever seen, but he wasn't a great catcher. He wanted to learn."[3] Young Gibson was eager and affable and very much wanted to succeed at this game he loved. If there were doubts about the way he butchered seemingly easy plays behind the plate, there was nothing but awe expressed about his hitting.

Gibson was still only eighteen when the Grays met the New York Lincoln Giants in a postseason game at Yankee Stadium. He had hit just a few home runs for the club when he stepped into the batter's box to face a pitcher named Broadway Connie Rector. On a slightly inside pitch, Gibson hit a rocket to left field that cleared everything man made in its flight until bouncing off the back of the bull pen. The home run was indisputable. The distance was debatable. There were no official measurements, and estimates of long-gone balls were rarely made in those days. Author John Holway, a prestigious historian of Negro Leagues baseball, did his best to reconstruct the shot with accuracy about six decades after the hit. He rounded up a few witnesses with different perspectives, used a map to evaluate the scene, and concluded that the blast was a 505-foot monster.

Gibson was long dead by then, but Holway found an old interview where he briefly noted creaming the ball into the bull pen. "He called it one of the two longest balls he ever hit," Holway said.[4] In some present-day Major League ballparks, it is possible to hit a home run traveling down a foul line going a distance of just 315 feet. A hit of 420 feet will leave just about any area of any park. A home run hit 500 feet might be clubbed once a season. Credit for the all-time longest Major League homer is given to a 565-foot crunch job off the bat of Mickey Mantle at Washington, D.C.'s Griffith Stadium. Gibson, a mere teenager at the time of his swat, was already flirting with immortality.

PLAYING CAREER

Like Hank Aaron, the Braves great, Gibson's power was in his wrists. He would flick at the ball, not take a sweeping swing. He stood flat-footed in the batter's box, had a keen eye, and clobbered many-a-pitcher's fastest stuff. Babe Ruth was known for hitting towering shots that put low-flying airplanes into jeopardy. Lou Gehrig, his power-hitting pal in the Yankee lineup, hit more line drives. That was Gibson. When the ball left his bat it didn't soar toward outer space, it shot on a line, like a bullet headed toward a poor migrating duck being harvested. And Gibson always seemed to be in control of his swing. Many famous power hitters slashed at the ball with wide swings, leaving fans oohing and ahhing, even when they swung and missed, or struck out.

"I never saw Josh take a leaving-the-ground swing," said Newark pitcher Max Manning. "It was always a smooth, quick stroke. A lot of guys would swing, the ground would shake, the air would move, and their hats would fly off. But he'd just take that short, quick stroke, and that ball would leave any ballpark."[5]

Behind the plate there were conflicting accounts about Gibson's behavior. W. Rollo Wilson of the *Pittsburgh Courier* wrote a column indicating Gibson was a talking machine when batters stepped in, going so far as to recreate a scene between Gibson and another great catcher, Biz Mackey. "Aha!" Wilson wrote of Gibson's talk, "So this is Mr. Mackey, the famous catcher and batter. I've been reading a lot about you in the papers. I believe you were in the games in Pittsburgh Friday and yesterday. You didn't do so well, did you? Well, you're going to do worse today." Ribowsky calls this "so much eyewash," that it would have been out of character for Gibson to tease an old pro. There were indications that Gibson, who was shy and did not banter with his teammates when he first joined the Grays in his youth, opened up some a little later.[6] In contrast to many images, Gibson's son, Josh Jr., who played two seasons in the Negro Leagues after his dad's death, said he always remembers his father being "happy go-lucky. Either he was hitting the ball out of the park, or he was laughing."[7]

Judy Johnson, who was much older than Gibson, said Josh Sr. was "the biggest kid you ever saw in your life. Like he was just twelve or thirteen years old. Oh, he was jolly all the time. You just had to love him." Ted Page concurred. "Josh was just a big, overgrown kid," he said. "After a game we'd go to an ice cream parlor. The older fellows would go out drinking or looking for women, but we'd find a field where the kids were playing. He played just as hard with those kids as he had in the two games that afternoon."[8]

Gibson did not chase women because he had a woman. He married Helen Mason, his first sweetheart, when he was only nineteen. If Gibson seemed blissful in his earliest days as a ballplayer in Pittsburgh, he probably was. However, when Helen gave birth to twins in 1930, an undiagnosed kidney ailment was discovered and she died in childbirth. The anguished Gibson was tormented, missed her terribly, and did not know how to be a father. He left Josh Jr. and his sister, Helen, with Rebecca Mason, his wife's sister, and rarely saw them when they were little. Gibson traveled year-round for baseball,

Many of those who knew Josh Gibson said that he was shy and withdrawn, but others said that he frequently clowned around and knew how to have a good time.

also participating in the Latin American winter leagues, and was rarely in Pittsburgh to take charge of his family. He almost never spoke about his deceased wife and seemed to internalize much of the hurt.

"I just thought when Helen died, it looked like it took some of the energy out of him," Rebecca Mason said. "That enthusiasm he had for life was gone. I don't think he was ever the same." Ribowsky said if there were clues, they resided in Gibson's eyes. "Through the years, Josh's face would remain unchanged. His full cheeks and round, unstriated jowls were an effective camouflage for his decaying soul, a dependable mask that Josh fixed into the pose of the eternal phenom. But the eyes would refuse to cooperate with the impersonation. They would look weary, almost lifeless, as if that was where Gibson's pain was being stored."[9]

As Josh Gibson the man receded into his personal thoughts, Josh Gibson the baseball slugger began taking on legendary proportions. Speedster Cool Papa Bell was a teammate of Gibson's with the Grays. He said that during the 1933 season he counted every one of Josh's home runs. Negro Leagues teams played short schedules, but barnstormed around the country playing exhibitions. If their league games were less than 50 percent the length of a Major League schedule, their total number of games possibly exceeded the 154 per season then the norm. Popular teams like the Grays may have played 180 or 200 games in a single year. Double headers were frequent and back-to-back double headers were common. Off days were a rumor. Although once again documentation is missing, Bell said that Gibson hit 72 home runs in 1933. Can it be proven? No. Can it be disproved? No. It is believed that Gibson smashed the longest home run of his career that year. Documentation is vague, but there is little doubt Gibson uncorked a monstrous blast in Monessen, Pennsylvania.[10]

The Grays were playing a Chicago team in an exhibition and Gibson hit a home run that Bell said landed on a passing freight train and went on to other cities, making Gibson's hit a 500-mile home run.[11] He may have been confusing it with another home run in Pennsylvania, or simply exaggerated for the sake of a good story.

There was confusion based on differing verbal accounts whether Gibson might have hit one home run in another part of the state that hitched the ride on the train and another in Monessen that stayed in the neighborhood. Decades later Holway visited Monessen, southwest of Pittsburgh, trying to pin down the truth about the homer hit there. He found that "Old-timers still talk of the blow with an incredulous shake of the head. The site is a cornfield now, but a watchman's old shack still stands beside the railroad tracks beyond what had been the center field fence. It [the swat] cleared the fence and [an apple] tree and landed with a splat on the concrete sidewalk outside the shack and bounded onto the tracks where the watchman ran out and snatched it. The mayor of the town was so amazed that he ordered a tape measure brought immediately and announced that the drive had traveled 512 feet." Gibson called the shot his longest. Holway said that people in Monessen considered it the biggest thing ever to happen in town.[12]

As did many of the leading Negro Leagues players, Gibson turned baseball into a year-round game. With exhibitions in warm-weather climates like the deep South and California, which had no Major League baseball at the time, the United States season lasted into the fall for African Americans. Sometimes they scrimmaged all-white All-Star teams from the majors. Sometimes players put together their own All-Star teams with a headliner like Satchel Paige or Gibson to draw fans in remote areas that had no local big-time baseball. The players would take a brief break and then move on to Mexico, Puerto Rico, Cuba, or Venezuela, places where African Americans might feel more at home than in their true home because they were not discriminated against on the basis of skin color.

Although Paige, the greatest showman in the game's history, and Gibson shared fields as battery mates and were friendly, they had very different personalities. Gibson enjoyed himself, but he was not a showboat. Mostly, in games, he let his hitting do his talking for him. Paige talked all the time, nonstop, leading up to games, during games, after games. He would say anything to hype the gate, to psyche out an opponent, and to get attention. He had fun, but often his gamesmanship had a purpose behind it. For a time, Paige and Gibson were double headliners on a tour.

"What me and Josh did there for a while," Paige said, "was we'd pick up a good glove man for third base and we'd travel around in my station wagon putting on exhibitions. We played all around in here, up in Canada, and all down South. See, we'd recruit six local boys from the town for our team and we'd play anybody. Anybody, anywhere, anytime. See, the folks would come out to see me pitch and Josh hit and they would pack those stands. It didn't matter who we had in the infield and the outfield." The posters advertising the game read, "WORLD'S GREATEST HOME RUN HITTER JOSH GIBSON. GUARANTEED TO HIT THREE HOME RUNS OR YOUR MONEY BACK." It was a bold boast and Paige the promoter came up with the idea, not Gibson the low-keyed slugger. But it sold. Paige added, "I bet we never gave one penny of that money back."[13]

Given Gibson's strength and build highlighted by blacksmith arms, and his general mind-your-own-business pleasant mood, he rarely faced challenges from opposing players. But if a player plays long enough, something will happen on the diamond to ignite his fuse. Gibson may have seemed like Clark Kent, mild-mannered reporter for the *Daily Planet*, most of the time, but brooked no nonsense if situations exploded. In a 1934 exhibition game against white All Stars, a fight broke out.

The Crawfords Vic Harris did not like a call at the plate and yanked on the umpire's mask. The ensuing brouhaha embroiled both teams. Ted Page of the Grays dashed in from the outfield. "Josh and George Susce [a former Detroit Tiger] were the main attraction because they were rolling around," he said, "and Gibson and Susce were down in the corner between the fence and the dugout. Dizzy Dean and I were trying to pull Josh out of there because he was so strong there was no telling what he would do to any man, it didn't matter who, when he got him in a crack like that. We tried to pull him off, but heck, he threw Dean from here to there, just shook him like this and shoved him out of the way, and never let go of Susce with the other hand.

"I can see Josh today, right now, when that was over. He was kind of scratched up and had lost his cap in the scuffle, but he had a big grin on his face, you know, one of those satisfied grins like, 'Well, that was a good one.'"[14]

Gibson's Negro Leagues career was stable, sticking with the Homestead Grays, but he teamed with fresh faces in Latin America every winter. One of the young players off the Newark Eagles franchise who joined him in Puerto Rico was Monte Irvin. Irvin was a younger, up-and-coming five-tool player with Newark, and would become one of the first African American New York Giants in the majors. Irvin got to know the already established star socially when they lived in the same hotel in Puerto Rico and he considered Gibson a player to admire.

"We used to hang out and drink beer together," Irvin recalled more than five decades after the event. "Josh, in his prime, he knew nobody could hit like him. He's the best hitter I've ever seen. He had more power than anyone I've ever seen. He had this great upper body strength. He would muscle the ball over the fence. He would hit a line drive and it would take off. You could never charge one of his line drives. I remember one time in a game back in the States, Josh hit a ball with such force, Willie Wells caught it, but it knocked him backwards. He was incredible. In Mexico and Puerto Rico, he was the man."[15]

Gibson probably was the key man in the lineup wherever he played, but lost in the fog of the past is any accurate way to quantify what he did. At one point, the owner of the Crawfords released statistics indicating Gibson batted .457 with 34 home runs in 190 at bats for a season. There is no proof of the claim. Major city daily newspapers did not print box scores of Negro Leagues games. Newspapers with a primarily African American readership often did, but were not meticulous in making all the news fit all the time. A book called the *Negro League Encyclopedia* gives Gibson credit for 84 home runs in 1936 and 962 in his career, far more than Hank Aaron's Major League record of 755. Another Negro Leagues record book gives Gibson credit for 823 homers. Ribowsky called the Negro League stats a "fantasy."[16] Even if these wild numbers approach the actual record, there is no differentiation between games played in normal league play and games played against touring teams. Gibson probably was not aware of how many home runs he hit in his life. Everyone agrees on one thing: it was a lot.

As Gibson matured from teenager to manhood, the time he put in playing ball around the calendar paid off. Once uneasy behind the plate, those seeing him for the first

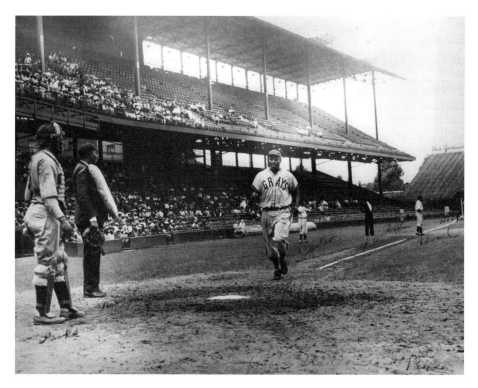

Although Negro Leagues records were sketchy, some claim Josh Gibson—trotting to home plate after a blast—hit more than 800 home runs.

time and those seeing him only in his twenties remarked upon his skill with the glove. He had made the transition from a power hitter with a weak mitt to an overpowering hitter with a superb glove. After his retirement, Walter Johnson, the Washington Senators hurler who was one of the greatest pitchers of all time, saw Gibson catch in Florida and was impressed. His comment reflected the societal situation of the time, too. "That boy is worth $200,000 of anybody's money," Johnson said in 1935. "He can do everything. He hits the ball a mile and he catches so easy he might as well be in a rocking chair. Too bad this Gibson is a colored fellow."[17]

A "too bad" was about all the sympathy the top Negro Leagues stars could expect from white counterparts. There are numerous instances of white managers and players recognizing how terrific black players were and lamenting the unwritten big-league ban of them. Baseball experts knew teaming with black stars would enhance their chance to win. But there was no outcry about the wrongheadedness of discrimination. Appreciative of African Americans abilities or not, players weren't writing the rules. It was their owners who kept African Americans from the majors until 1947. "I've seen a lot of colored players who could make it up here in the big leagues," said Hall of Fame pitcher Carl Hubbell. "First of all, I'd name this big guy Josh Gibson, the catcher. He's one of the greatest backstops in the history of baseball, I think. Boy—how he can throw!"[18]

It was not in Gibson's nature to make many waves—although like Paige he did sometimes jump a contract for better wages. But at least once he was fooled into thinking the Pittsburgh Pirates were sincere about breaking the majors color line. The clamor for the big leagues to hire black ballplayers grew louder during World War II when black soldiers were dying for their country fighting racist regimes in Germany and Japan. Sportswriters on prominent black-oriented newspapers kept the subject in the forefront. The Pirates were a .500 or worse team between 1939 and 1943 and local black journalists pressured the club. The Grays were loaded with All Stars and writers suggested the Pirates could fill their holes and evolve into a pennant winner by hiring them.

President William Benswanger did invite Gibson and Buck Leonard to meet him in his office, but he made no offer and said he didn't want to ruin black ball by helping to hire all the best players.

African American stars in the Negro Leagues got the picture. Despite a lot of talk, they were still not wanted. Friends say that Gibson burned to be accepted in the majors, but there is little public record indicating that he spoke up about the matter. Mostly, the top black players felt that Major League baseball would never change. They thought more about where their next paycheck was coming from in the Negro Leagues or Latin America because they never truly expected to ever draw a check from the Boston Red Sox or the New York Yankees.

"Of course Josh wanted to go to the big leagues, we all did," said player Gene Benson. "But we were satisfied with what we were doin'," he said. "We weren't just pining away for the call to come." Ribowsky concluded that Gibson was eager for that call, but would never show it because he was too proud.[19]

TRAGEDY

Josh Gibson Jr., who came back into his father's life when he was about ten, became a batboy for the Grays and had no doubt at all that his father was the best player around. But if his dad was bitter about never becoming a major leaguer, the younger Gibson knew nothing of it. "He never talked about that," said Josh Jr.[20]

A myth has sprung up around Gibson, that he died from a broken heart when the majors passed over him for Jackie Robinson as the color line breaker. It is a romanticized story since Gibson died a few months before Robinson broke in with the Dodgers. He also suffered from a myriad of health woes that superseded his playing status. The fanciful explanation of a broken heart is out there by those who do not wish Gibson's memory to be sullied by the problems he endured during the final years of his life.

While Major League baseball continued to ignore African American stars, players like Gibson added to their growing legend. The East-West game emerged as a popular annual All-Star festival in Chicago, packing Comiskey Park with fans and putting black stars on display. Paige and Gibson remained the two biggest names in black ball. During all the years they traveled together, they talked about what would happen if they faced one another when it mattered. Paige said of course he would strike out Gibson. Gibson said of course he would homer off Paige. It was good-natured ribbing, but knowing how players jumped teams they might well have been setting the stage for an inevitable confrontation.

That day finally arrived in 1942. Gibson had given a radio interview in which he said he could hit Paige as well as he hit anyone else. A friend of Paige reported the comment to the lanky pitcher. Paige was then affiliated with the Kansas City Monarchs and Gibson with the Grays. As it happened, the teams met in the Negro Leagues World Series. This was the Series when Gibson uttered one of his most famous comments about his hitting. "I don't break 'em," he said of his bats. "I wear 'em out."

Paige was ticked off. He struck Gibson out twice in a row when they first faced off and taunted him in between pitches. "I'm not gonna waste anything on you, get ready to hit," Paige said. "Get ready, I'm gonna throw you one outside and low on the corner. You better swing."[21] After the game Paige was his normal cocky self, boasting of how he overpowered the great Josh Gibson. "Say, you guys," he said to reporters, "don't let me ever hear you ranting about Josh Gibson. Against the Monarchs, he is just another batter who takes his three and then sits down!"[22]

That game turned out to be a warm-up for the drama that followed. Paige itched for the chance to make a more forceful point, one that fans would remember forever. Two days later the Grays and Monarchs met in Pittsburgh. Kansas City led 2–0 in the sixth inning, hardly a safe margin, especially when the Grays leadoff hitter Jerry Benjamin singled. Gibson was three batters away and Paige informed first baseman Buck O'Neil that he was going to walk the next two hitters in order to pitch to Gibson with the bases loaded. O'Neil told Paige he had to be crazy. But Paige walked the two hitters on purpose.

There was such an uproar that Monarchs owner J. L. Wilkinson, the 2006 Baseball Hall of Fame inductee who was the only white owner in the Negro Leagues, and a pioneer himself for introducing night baseball before the majors, marched onto the field to see Paige. "Are you losing your mind?" Wilkinson asked. "What in the world is going on here, you pitching to Josh?" Manager Frank Duncan joined the pow-wow on the mound and said, "Don't you know that's Josh Gibson up there?" Paige told them of Gibson's boast of how it would be "shame on me" because he was going to take Paige deep with men on someday. "So I fixed it like that today." Paige added, "When I told them that, they just laughed." Paige compounded the circumstances by announcing each pitch in advance to Gibson. "I'm not gonna trick you," Paige informed the menacing hitter. He threw a fastball as promised for called strike one, a fastball as promised for called strike two, and then he did fool Gibson, throwing a sidearm curve for strike three. "He was looking for a fastball," Paige said. "Josh threw that bat of his 4,000 feet and stomped off the field."[23]

In his autobiography, Paige said that he and Gibson met in a bar before the game and renewed their teasing about who was better. Paige said they bet $5 on the outcome, but after he struck Gibson out on that highly embarrassing play he said, "I don't think he ever paid me that five dollars."[24]

For O'Neil it was an amazing scene. Paige turned to O'Neil in vindication, smiled, and said, "You know something? Nobody hits Satchel's fastball."[25] The showdown is one of the most enduring legends of Negro League history and in 2006 was immortalized in an art print released by the Baseball Hall of Fame.

No one saw more of Josh Gibson than Buck Leonard, who usually preceded him in the third spot in the Grays batting order. Leonard compared Gibson to Jimmie Foxx, the American League power hitter with the Philadelphia Athletics and the Boston Red Sox who retired with 534 home runs, the second most to Babe Ruth until the 1960s. "Josh was a big, strong, right-handed hitter like Jimmie Foxx," Leonard said. "But he had more power than Foxx. Josh was a good curveball hitter. You could get him out with a fastball, but if you threw him a curveball, he'd hit it a mile."[26]

The flip side of Leonard's observation was how a young Minnie Minoso facing Gibson for the first time reacted to his strength with a bat. Minoso, a future major leaguer who played for the New York Cubans after coming to the United States from Cuba, lined up at third base in a game at the very end of Gibson's career.

"Josh was a big, baby-faced guy," said Minoso, who was a novice at the fielding position. "He was very strong, but not as aggressive as he might have been. Josh had a nice, easy way about him, but he could hit. Boy, could he hit." Gibson came to the plate with a man on first and nobody out and a one-run lead. Minoso was sure Gibson would bunt and planned to charge in, but his manager instructed him to move him way back behind the bag. "Was I surprised! He [Gibson] hit one so hard that it bounced off my glove and into the box seats for an automatic double. I couldn't believe how hard he had hit it. As he ran to second base, he looked over to our pitcher Pat Scarberry and laughed. "Hey, Pat, keep pitching me there and I'll move the right-field bleachers back," he said.[27] If Minoso had obeyed his instincts and come in for the bunt, Gibson might have ripped his head off with the line drive, obliterating any career with the Indians and White Sox.

Paige and Gibson played out their confrontations in front of audiences that were nearly 100 percent black. America moved on, through the Depression, through World War II. Whatever protests originated in the black press to open the gates to black players were ignored. One of the rare white journalists to angrily and repeatedly back the cause of the African American ballplayer was Shirley Povich, a man with a woman's name who wrote columns for the *Washington Post* for more than six decades.

Povich campaigned vigorously to permit black players to join the white majors. In a memorable 1939 column, Povich wrote, "There's a couple of million dollars worth of baseball talent on the loose, ready for the big leagues, yet unsigned by Major League clubs. Only one thing is keeping them out of the big leagues, the pigmentation of their skin. They happen to be colored. That's their crime in the eyes of big league club owners. It's a tight little boycott the majors have set up against colored players." The diatribe was well-thought-out and ignored.[28]

Any hint of a breakthrough brought disappointment rather than joy. Paige, Gibson, and their brethren continued with their lives, continued with their careers. Sympathetic owners would not begin to emerge until nearly a decade after Povich's fusilade. But that was too late for Josh Gibson.

By the mid-1940s, whatever carefully hidden demons plagued Josh Gibson and been guarded with the strictest of imprisoning walls started bursting free. Over a roughly five-year period between 1942 and his death in 1947, Gibson was a man out of control, a victim of dark moods and declining health, seemingly descending into madness under the influence of liquor, and some even said, drugs.

Always regarded as a friendly man, Gibson's on-field persona changed. He snapped at other players. He issued comments that were mean-spirited. He began showing up other players on the field. All of this was contrary to character. His love life was a shambles. He broke up with his longtime girlfriend Hattie Jones and took up with Grace Fournier, who was married. Fournier eventually broke things off and Gibson returned to Hattie. Although he tried to hide it, Gibson had begun drinking heavily. He imagined things, and teammates worried about him. He began having headaches, and finally, he suffered a seizure, blacking out. It was New Year's Day of 1943 when Gibson was rushed to St. Francis Hospital in Pittsburgh.

Later, Annie Gibson Mahaffey said it was at this time her brother was diagnosed with a brain tumor. Doctors wanted to operate, but when he awoke, Gibson forbade it, afraid he might become a "vegetable." Gibson spent ten days in the hospital and got the team to cover for him, saying he had a nervous breakdown. "Had he not gotten to the hospital," Ribowsky wrote, "it is probable he would have died that morning. Josh never spoke about his condition, or the path he took."[29] That path was to continue playing baseball and to continue drinking heavily.

Completely unaware of Gibson's difficulties, *Time* magazine wrote an extensive profile of Gibson. Up until then, only Paige had received such nationally positive treatment from the white mainstream media. But it was too late for Gibson in every way measurable. Also in 1943, Gibson was in and out of St. Elizabeth Hospital in Washington—a mental hospital. Reports of Gibson's health were grim and friends who saw him were alarmed by his drinking. Yet in between hospital stints Gibson showed he could still hit well—batting .521 for the Grays in 190 at bats.

Leonard and Gibson were known as the "Thunder Twins" with the Grays for the devastating way they took apart pitchers the decade they played together. Leonard helplessly watched Gibson fall apart regardless of what help was provided.

"In 1943, Josh was beginning to show signs of problems off the field," Leonard said. "We were close friends, but we didn't go around together because he was a beer drinker and I wasn't. Some people say he was involved with drugs, but I don't know anything about that. I have never known him to do that, but I do know that he drank. Beer tastes good to a ballplayer just like anybody else, and he drank a lot of beer. At that time he had started drinking whiskey, too. He had a whiskey problem when he went in (to St. Elizabeth). He was drinking liquor and that was the reason we sent him out there. But he didn't stop drinking and his problem continued." Leonard said Gibson's off-field running mate was shortstop Sam Bankhead, who also drank heavily. Despite rules against it, Bankhead smuggled beer onto the bus and Gibson helped him finish the bottles, Leonard said. "Three or four times [Gibson] came to the ballfield to catch and he was drunk."[30]

The self-destruction of Josh Gibson continued with only brief interruptions for some medical treatments that didn't take. At first Gibson's body bloated. Photographs of him in games taken near the end of his career show how much heavier he had grown. There were guesses he was up to 235 pounds. Then Gibson began to lose weight precipitately and dropped to around 180 pounds. Twice in January of 1947 Ted Page bumped into Gibson in Pittsburgh. Once he saw him in a bar. Page walked in on an unforgettable scene. One of the greatest power hitters who ever lived held another customer by the collar and shook him. Then, as Gibson spied Page, he shouted, "Tell him who hit the longest ball any place!" A short time later, Page ran into Gibson again, this time outdoors, on a corner, and the two exchanged greetings and teasing banter, including biffs on the arms. Before morning, Gibson was dead. His sister said that Gibson came home drunk, went to bed laughing, and suffered a stroke in the middle of the night that killed him.[31]

Gibson died on January 20, 1947. The coroner ruled that he died from a brain hemorrhage. His old pal Buck O'Neil, whether out of a sense of loyalty, or a belief that admission would diminish the man, always refused to say that alcohol or drugs had anything to do with Gibson's slide. As recently as late 2005 he insisted Gibson's undoing was illness. "Josh wasn't a drunk," O'Neil said. "Josh got sick. He was taking stuff for the pain in his head. If he had been a Major League ballplayer he would have been taken care of in the hospital."[32]

Josh Gibson was mourned throughout black baseball and by African Americans throughout the United States who had seen him play. For a time, during the period when Jackie Robinson broke the color barrier in organized ball and shortly after, when one after another black stars like Paige, Roy Campanella, Willie Mays, and Irvin, who all had roots in the Negro Leagues, received a long-awaited chance in the white majors, Gibson's deeds were overshadowed.

For decades his performances lived on by word of mouth. O'Neil and Cool Papa Bell spoke up for him whenever circumstances offered, but they rarely received a wide audience. Eventually, Major League baseball formed a committee to investigate the credentials of the most worthy past African American candidates for the Hall of Fame. In 1971, Paige was selected. In 1972, the special committee inducted Josh Gibson into the Hall of Fame.

When the announcement was made of Gibson's acceptance, some twenty-four years after his death, his old friend Ted Page expressed a certain satisfaction. "He never got the recognition he deserved," Page said.[33]

No one honor could make up for the slights of a lifetime. No one act by baseball could give back the career Gibson deserved. But for a man whose love of his life died when he was twenty, whose career was consigned to the shadows, and whose own life was snuffed out at thirty-five, it was a beginning. For one day, at least, Josh Gibson got the recognition Page and others said he deserved. And for as long as baseball continues, his placement in the Hall of Fame means that the game will remember him.

NOTES

1. Mark Ribowsky, *The Power and the Darkness* (New York: Simon & Schuster, 1996), 11.
2. John Holway, *Josh and Satch* (Westport, CT: Meckler Publishing, 1991), 25.
3. Holway, *Josh and Satch*, 26.
4. Holway, *Josh and Satch*, 33–34.
5. Holway, *Josh and Satch*, 39–40.
6. Ribowsky, *The Power and the Darkness*, 61.
7. *Pittsburgh Press*, September 23, 1996.
8. Holway, *Josh and Satch*, 44.
9. Ribowsky, *The Power and the Darkness*, 53.
10. Holway, *Josh and Satch*, 53.
11. Ribowsky, *The Power and the Darkness*, 106.
12. Holway, *Josh and Satch*, 53–54.
13. William Price Fox, *Satchel Paige's America* (Tuscaloosa: University of Alabama Press, 2005), 40.
14. Holway, *Josh and Satch*, 68–69.
15. Monte Irvin, personal interview, January 7, 2006.
16. Ribowsky, *The Power and the Darkness*, 108.
17. Holway, *Josh and Satch*, 74.
18. Ribowsky, *The Power and the Darkness*, 195.
19. Ribowsky, *The Power and the Darkness*, 235.
20. *Pittsburgh Press*.
21. Holway, *Josh and Satch*, 159–160.
22. Ribowsky, *The Power and the Darkness*, 240.
23. Holway, *Josh and Satch*, 161–162.
24. Satchel Paige and David Lipman, *Maybe I'll Pitch Forever* (New York: Grove Press, 1962), 134.
25. Buck O'Neil with Steve Wulf and David Conrads, *I Was Right on Time* (New York: Simon & Schuster, 1996), 137.
26. Buck Leonard with James A. Riley, *Buck Leonard: The Black Lou Gehrig* (New York: Carroll & Graf, 1995), 80.
27. Minnie Minoso with Herb Fagen, *Just Call Me Minnie* (Champaign, IL: Sagamore Publishing, 1994), 33.
28. Shirley Povich, *Washington Post*, April 7, 1939.

29. Ribowsky, *The Power and the Darkness*, 252.
30. Leonard with Riley, *Buck Leonard: The Black Lou Gehrig*, 146–148.
31. Holway, *Josh and Satch*, 190.
32. Buck O'Neil, personal interview, December 7, 2005.
33. Dave Anderson, *New York Times*, February 6, 1972.

Further Reading

Fox, William Price, *Satchel Paige's America*. Tuscaloosa, AL: University of Alabama Press, 2005.
Holway, John, *Josh and Satch*. Westport, CT: Meckler Publishing, 1991.
Ribowsky, Mark, *The Power and the Darkness*. New York: Simon & Schuster, 1996.

JACKIE ROBINSON

January 31, 1919–October 24, 1972

The man who broke Major League baseball's color line banning African Americans from participating in organized ball bore the brunt of hatred and discrimination. But Jackie Robinson overcame all obstacles to become a baseball star, a Hall of Famer, and a key figure in American civil rights history.

Robinson played his entire Major League career with the Brooklyn Dodgers after an apprenticeship in the Negro Leagues. In ten seasons, Robinson batted .311. A six-time All Star, Robinson played on six pennant winners and Brooklyn's only World Series championship squad.

☆ ☆ ☆

Few played the game with the fierceness of Jackie Robinson, with the all-out aggression, with such a give-me-an-inch-and-I'll-take-a-mile philosophy. He played baseball like a football player, battling for every yard gained, refusing to be pushed backward. He played with his heart, head, legs, and lungs, giving 100 percent all the time.

Pitcher Satchel Paige may have uttered the phrase, "Don't look back, something might be gaining on you," but Robinson lived it. He played his sport as if his life depended on it. He single-handedly increased the tempo of games, turning languid scenes of a relaxed, pastoral sport into wild, frenzied paced situations.

In some ways, Robinson individually redefined the sport, disrupting its unhurried pace with an urgency rarely seen on the diamond since Ty Cobb retired two decades earlier. Robinson energized the Brooklyn Dodgers lineup and often paralyzed the opposing team's lineup because players did not know what to do about him. Jackie Robinson, the ballplayer, had a phenomenal impact on baseball, because of his style on the field. Jackie Robinson, the man, had a phenomenal impact on baseball, because of the color of his skin.

There are many ways to view someone hailed as a pioneer. All the men of the Negro Leagues who predated Robinson on the field, when Major League baseball shut them out because of discrimination, were pioneers in their own ways. They put up with poor travel conditions, difficult housing arrangements, and the challenge of obtaining their next meal. They were insulted and hated and they persevered in their game because they loved it. Those men lay the foundation for the acceptance of Jackie Robinson in the majors.

What Jackie Robinson did was stand solo in the spotlight, a human barrier breaker, a human being described as an experiment, a symbol of African Americans, and for African Americans. Despite all the star black ballplayers who preceded him, cruelly treated by the passage of time, Robinson became the chosen one because of his character, personality, and talent. He was fortunate enough to be in his prime at the right time, when Americans were beginning to realize the sense of injustice perpetuated on fellow black citizens, when the war to contain Germany's and Japan's imperialistic, racist societies overseas was fresh in their minds.

Dodgers All-Star infielder Jackie Robinson was equally adept playing second base and first base, and his skill and demeanor paved the way for future black players in the major leagues after he broke in with Brooklyn in 1947.

He was available, he was willing, and he was found when a solitary white man named Branch Rickey decided it was time for Major League baseball to overturn injustice. Jackie Robinson was tapped on the shoulder by a man with a plan who stood by him in good and bad times, yet he still needed to throw back his broad shoulders and carry a special burden virtually on his own.

When analyzing statistics, Major League baseball likes to split its history into pre-1900 and the "modern era." In reality, there have been three Major League baseball eras, pre-1900, 1900–1947, and 1947 to the present. The dividing line for the third era is Jackie Robinson. The arrival of Jackie Robinson in the majors, the only black man in the game for months, the only black man in the National League for the entire 1947 season, changed everything.

Baseball was long regarded as the "National Pastime." That phrase may no longer resonate with the younger sports fan, that grew up after pro football became king and a smorgasbord of sports spread across cable television networks almost like a mutating disease. For them it may be difficult to grasp the importance of the game during Jackie's time.

In 1947, baseball was The Sport, the only one that everyone cared about, the only game that everyone loved. The admittance of Robinson to what had been a closed and guarded fortress was a move so significant that it basically reordered society. The majors had been a private white club. Now it was opening its membership roster to black players. This was a powerful symbol. This made blacks eligible to compete for the best jobs available in their field. It meant that blacks and whites would change clothes in the same locker room. They would travel together. They would become teammates. Baseball was not merely a game on playgrounds, it was deeply imbedded in the American soul. It had always been said that part of the American dream was that any youngster could grow up to become president. Now any youngster could grow up to become an outfielder for the Yankees, the Giants, the Dodgers, the Tigers, or the White Sox.

"More even than either Abraham Lincoln and the Civil War, or Martin Luther King Jr. and the Civil Rights movement, Jackie Robinson graphically symbolized and personi-fied the challenge to the vicious legacy and ideology of white supremacy in American history," wrote Cornel West of Harvard University in the foreword to a Robinson auto-biography. "In 1947, Jackie Robinson not only symbolized all of black America on trial in the eyes of white America and the expansion of the ideals of democracy, he also rep-resented the best of a traditional black quest for dignity, excellence and integrity. This quest was primarily a moral effort to preserve black sanity and spirituality in the face of white-supremacist barbarity and bestiality. It was a human attempt to hold on to dreams deferred and hopes dashed, owing mainly to slavery and Jim Crow in America."[1]

Hank Aaron, the all-time Major League home-run hitter, was young enough to be an admirer of Robinson and old enough to be a contemporary in the majors. Aaron was still living in his boyhood home of Mobile, Alabama, when Robinson and the Dodgers passed through for an exhibition game. "I've always looked at Jackie as some kind of icon," Aaron said. "He was a pillar of strength, and he gave me a lot of inner strength. I knew some of the things he had gone through. So when I looked at him, I thought, not only is this man a great athlete, but he's a great man for people like me off the field."[2]

Jackie Robinson was thrust into a crossroads of history. But he was as prepared as it was possible to be for an African American in unique circumstances in post–World War II America. Several of the top stars in the Negro Leagues felt change was coming and often talked among themselves about who would be called to the majors. There is little evidence to suggest that they envisioned the scenario which enveloped Robinson, where he was the only black playing with all whites. Players like Satchel Paige, Josh Gibson, and Buck Leonard were doubtful the doors would ever be opened to the sixteen Major League teams, but they believed if it happened several blacks would be hired simultane-ously. Not one of them foresaw any likelihood that Jackie Robinson, whom they hardly knew during his year with the Kansas City Monarchs, would be invited to the big show before any of them.

Robinson was discharged from the Army in 1944 and then played with the Monarchs for one season while the team's mainstay Buck O'Neil was still in the service. The announcement of Robinson's signing with the Dodgers organization occurred October 23, 1945, and he played with the Dodgers AAA minor league team in 1946. O'Neil said he did not meet Robinson until 1947 during Dodger spring training in Cuba. "He had the tools," O'Neil said. "He had that quickness. He took Negro Leagues baseball to the majors with his hitting and running and base stealing. He would steal home."[3]

EARLY LIFE

Robinson is always associated with California, growing up, in college, and in most references to his life. However, Jack Roosevelt Robinson was born in Cairo, Georgia, in 1919. He was the youngest of five children born to mother Mallie and father Jerry.

His father made a meager living as a sharecropper and deserted the family in 1920 when Robinson was still a baby. His mother thought opportunities would be better in California and moved the clan to Pasadena. She had a brother living in the area and received some assistance from him, but basically supported the family by washing and ironing and accepting government welfare.

The Robinsons were so poor that the baseball player later recalled many days with just two meals, some of them consisting of bread and "sweet water." Robinson said in adulthood he realized all the sacrifices his mother made. "I often thought about the courage it took for my mother to break away from the South," he said. "When she left the South, she also left most of her relatives and friends. I remember, even as a small boy, having a lot of pride in my mother. I thought she must have some kind of magic to be able to do all of the things she did, to work so hard and to never complain and to make us all feel happy."[4]

As a youngster, Robinson was often unruly, joining up with a multiethnic street gang of poor kids that stole golf balls and produce from fruit stands. But it was a group far more benign than the gangs of today that are often implicated in drug dealing and murder.

After high school, Robinson attended Pasadena Junior College and then University of California, Los Angeles (UCLA). He became a football and track star and met his future wife Rachel. Robinson was a gifted all-around athlete, and it ran in the family. His elder brother Mack was an Olympic silver medallist in the 200 meters, second to Jesse Owens in Germany in 1936, and excelled in the long jump.

Jackie Robinson joined the Army and in 1943 became a lieutenant. Some of Robinson's encounters with prejudice in the Army are the common experiences of black men who served. There were segregated units and many black officers were not given much responsibility. Robinson called it the "Jim Crow" Army, almost as if the branch of the service was an additional state in the South. At one point, as morale officer, Robinson intervened on behalf of black soldiers who were being forced to wait for seats in the post exchange snack area at Fort Riley, Kansas, while more than enough seats were provided for whites. His efforts forced a policy change.

However, one major racial incident occurred that led to Robinson being mustered out of the Army early. He was riding on an Army bus, near a white woman who was the wife of someone he knew. When the driver ordered Robinson to move to the back of the vehicle, he refused. He argued with the driver, and the driver summoned help, Robinson got into more trouble arguing with a superior officer, and he was arrested. Ultimately, Robinson was court-martialed, but he was cleared at trial. He was released from the Army with an honorable discharge in November 1944 and was greeted with a $400-a-month offer to play baseball with the Monarchs.[5]

PLAYING CAREER

Robinson was a sturdy five-foot-eleven and weighed 200 pounds, large for a second baseman. He did not know what he wanted to do with his life, so being paid to play a professional sport seemed appealing as a career start. Robinson recalled Negro Leagues travel as brutal and enduring the travails of the road on gas-spewing buses as his brethren had done for much of the twentieth century as not being his favorite time in sports.[6] His experience mirrored the general African American baseball experience of those preceding him. Robinson had no inkling that his life would change and his baseball career would change the lives of all black players who followed him.

Brooklyn Dodgers president and general manager Branch Rickey was nicknamed "The Brain" by some for his intelligence. He was called "The Mahatma" after Gandhi by others. He was a religious man with legal training and a baseball background and by the 1940s he was determined to open the major leagues to black players. He knew that African Americans were a source of untapped talent and while Rickey also believed in social justice, he was aware that superior talent translated into victories, which translated into World Series appearances, which translated into big box office. He had built winning teams with the St. Louis Cardinals, and moved to the Dodgers in 1943. Judge Kenesaw Mountain Landis was still baseball's commissioner. He ruled with absolute power and there were no edicts from his office encouraging anyone to break the color line. But Landis died in 1944. And the mood of the country was shifting—especially in northern cities. More sportswriters wrote columns urging owners to sign blacks.

Wesley Branch Rickey was born in Ohio in 1881. His Christian family was very religious and his mother did not approve of his devotion to baseball. When Rickey left home as a young man he promised his mother he would always observe the Sunday Sabbath and not muddy up the day playing baseball. Despite a short, comparatively unproductive Major League career as a catcher with the St. Louis Browns and the New York Highlanders of the American League sprinkled over four seasons between 1905 and 1914, and time spent managing in the majors, he maintained that oath for the rest of his life.

Rickey was not always a participant at the top of the sport (he also played in the minors), but he stayed connected to baseball. In 1910, he was coaching the Ohio Wesleyan college team. Arriving in South Bend, Indiana, for a game, Rickey became embroiled in a rooming dispute with the hotel manager over his refusal to house a black player named Charley Thomas. Rickey retorted that he would pull the whole team out. A compromise was reached when Rickey suggested putting a cot in with him and to share the room with Thomas.

This was not a story Rickey spread during his younger days, but when he signed Robinson and was asked about his motivation he recounted the sad experience with Thomas. Later that night in the hotel room, Rickey said, Thomas sat crying on his bed, despairing of the discrimination around him. "His whole body shook with emotion," Rickey said. "I sat and watched him, not knowing what to do until he began tearing at one hand with the other—just as if he were trying to scratch the skin off his hands with his fingernails. I was alarmed. I asked him what he was trying to do to himself. 'It's my hands,' he sobbed. 'They're black. If only I were white I'd be as good as anybody then, wouldn't I, Mr. Rickey? If only they were white.'"[7]

Rickey, who wore bowties, and in certain ways resembled Groucho Marx, with his thick eyebrows and his cigars, said right then he vowed to break down the walls of prejudice if he ever got a chance. That story is the signature motivation ascribed to Rickey for going out of his way to seek out a black man for Major League baseball. It is repeated in any lengthy treatise on Rickey and he regularly referred to it when asked why he did what he did. When Rickey got angry, his most profane comment was, "Judas Priest!" While helping Robinson adjust to Major League ball, he had many occasions to utter the pseudo-expletive.

During the 1930s, running the infamous "Gas House Gang" St. Louis Cardinals, featuring the brother-pitching act of Dizzy (Jay Hanna) and Daffy (Paul) Dean and slugger Joe Medwick, Rickey established a reputation as a sharp judge of talent. He invented the farm system, gobbling up large numbers of players to stock minor league teams and develop them into future major leaguers. The idea helped build winners. Rickey also returned to the notion that there were many terrific players in the land who were not in the majors simply because of the color of their skin. He went to Negro Leagues games and took copious notes about players he saw, the way they handled themselves on the field, and the way they behaved. Rickey desperately wanted to uncover the right man. He knew he was skating on ice so thin that any misstep might set back the cause of black ballplayers rather than advance it.

Rickey operated in near secrecy, with few confidantes. He saw what happened when Bill Veeck made it known that he planned to buy the Philadelphia Phillies and stock the roster with top African American players. Before Veeck could blink, the team was sold out from under him. There were no Phillies for Bill and no jobs for blacks. Rickey was too well known to appear at too many ballparks where Negro Leagues teams played without causing a sensation. Rickey floated a false rumor, indicating that he was scouting black players for a new "Brown Dodgers" team in another African American League. Then he ordered some of his scouts to survey the talent. His key operative was Clyde Sukeforth, a future Dodgers coach. Sukeforth followed Robinson, met him, talked to him, and sized him up for Rickey.

Sukeforth approached the player in August of 1945 when Robinson was in Chicago for a game at Comiskey Park. He introduced himself and told Robinson he represented Branch Rickey and the Dodgers. There had been so many false alarms and misleading hints given to black players over the years that few African American players became excited by such a contact. Robinson figured this to be another such circumstance and thought that he was being sought for the rumored Brown Dodgers.

"Blacks have had to learn to protect themselves by being cynical, but not cynical enough to slam the door on potential opportunities," Robinson said of his reaction. "We go through life walking a tightrope to prevent too much disillusionment. 'Here we go, I thought, another time-wasting experience.'" But Robinson met Sukeforth at a hotel later and agreed to rendezvous with Rickey in Brooklyn a few days later.

Rickey knew far more about Robinson than Robinson knew about Rickey when they met in the Dodgers team offices. And Rickey startled Robinson several times, not only with the breadth of his knowledge about his life, but also in the manner in which he challenged him. It became obvious to Robinson fairly quickly that this was not a routine job interview. When Rickey admitted he was not talking to Robinson about playing for the Brown Dodgers, but for the Brooklyn Dodgers organization, the player was almost shell-shocked.

"My reactions seemed like some kind of weird mixture churning in a blender," Robinson said. "I was thrilled, scared, and excited. I was incredulous. Most of all, I was speechless."[8] Robinson, who was then twenty-six years old, would have been less than human if he had reacted in any other manner. This was the first time in the twentieth century a white man who had the authority to sign baseball players for his Major League team was making a serious proposal to a black man.

Rickey followed up his thunderbolt suggestion with a brutally frank assessment of what Robinson would face, how Rickey wanted him to act, and what the stakes were. He understood from background checks that Robinson had a volatile temper. If someone hurt him, he struck back. If someone insulted him, he gave back double. That was his nature. It was fine with Rickey. But with the eyes of the universe on the first black player in white baseball, Rickey said Robinson could not afford to be provoked into incidents and fighting back would be forbidden.

"I know you're a good ballplayer," Rickey said. "What I don't know is whether you have the guts."[9] This was precisely the sort of verbal challenge Robinson bristled over, and he became angry with Rickey. But Rickey explained that the first African American player had to turn the other cheek to insult, that sadly, but unfortunately true, the debut of the first black player was not solely going to be measured by hits, runs, and errors, but by a high-and-mighty standard of behavior set by others. Then followed what was later a widely reported exchange. Robinson, who bonded with Rickey that day and said until the day he died he appreciated the way the older man supported him, said to the Dodgers boss, "Mr. Rickey, are you looking for a Negro who is afraid to fight back?" And Rickey replied, "Robinson, I'm looking for a ballplayer with the guts not to fight back."[10]

It was a milestone moment in American sport—in American history—and Sukeforth witnessed it, quietly on the side of the room. From that moment forward, Rickey and Robinson were partners. Rickey told Robinson to temporarily keep the agreement a secret. About two months later the news was revealed publicly—Robinson's contract was with the Montreal Royals, the Dodgers AAA affiliate. The city was chosen because it seemed likely to be a more hospitable place than some of the southern minor league towns available.

The news that Robinson was going to be the first black in white organized ball was agitating to some, exciting to others, and eye-opening to most. There was cheering in Harlem. There was satisfaction—to a degree—among Negro Leaguers. "I'm afraid Jackie's in for a whole lot of trouble," said black star Buck Leonard, one of the most accomplished hitters of his time. Monte Irvin, who made it big with the Giants, admitted there was "a certain amount of jealousy. I knew it would give us all a chance to possibly make it, but there was a certain amount of envy that he had been picked."[11]

Buck O'Neil recognized instantly what Robinson's signing meant to the future of the leagues that had sustained blacks for decades. "When they signed Jackie Robinson I knew that was the death knell for the Negro Leagues," O'Neil said. "It didn't hurt me. I was too old. It was good for twenty-eight-year-old guys. But that was the end."[12]

In accordance with his plan, and consistent with the announcement that Robinson would begin play with Montreal, Rickey held the introductory press conference in that Canadian city. Robinson was very nervous and very focused on trying to say the right thing. He did not want to blurt out something that would haunt him. Although reporters said he looked cool and calm, Robinson said that was just a good act. When the sports-writers asked what his signing meant to him, Robinson did not obfuscate. Rickey had told him to be himself, and to Robinson, being himself meant telling it as it was. "Of course, I can't begin to tell you how happy I am that I am the first member of my race in organized ball," Robinson said. "I realize how much it means to me, my race, and to baseball. I can only say I'll do my best to come through in every manner."[13]

Rickey signed Robinson in the off-season. That gave Rickey, Robinson, Montreal, Brooklyn, baseball, and the rest of the world time to get used to the idea that a black man would be at spring training the following March. Othello "Chico" Renfroe, a Negro Leagues player who later became a prominent sports broadcaster, said, "They picked [Robinson] for his intelligence, but we had a lot of ballplayers we thought were better ballplayers. Jackie had only played one year in our league."[14] Renfroe was speaking for many Negro Leagues players, but one thing the delay between announcement and reporting date accomplished was to provide Robinson with preparation time to work on his game in the Venezuelan winter league.

Gene Benson, a Negro Leagues player then with the Philadelphia Stars, roomed with Robinson in Venezuela and tutored him. He discovered a Robinson who did not drink or smoke, knew he had to work hard, and who was very edgy about what faced him in the spring. "He used to ask me all of the time, 'Why did they pick me? Why did they pick me?'" Benson said. The men talked baseball constantly and Benson assured Robinson over and over "You'll make it" even if the older man was not sure it was true.[15]

After marrying Rachel in February 1946, and enduring a difficult racial climate at spring training in Florida, Jackie Robinson's first game for Montreal in the International League was played in Jersey City, New Jersey, on April 18, 1946, before a standing room only crowd of 25,000-plus. The Montreal Royals won 14–1 and Robinson's debut was a keeper. He had four hits in five at bats, including a home run, and scored four runs.

Soon after, the Baltimore team threatened to boycott a game if Robinson played, but International League commissioner Frank Shaughnessy was firm. His telegram informed players, "If you don't take the field … you will be suspended from baseball for the rest of your life."[16] The game was played.

As the man chosen to break baseball's color line, Jackie Robinson took a great deal of abuse from opposing players and fans during his early seasons, but emerged as an All Star with a career batting average of .311 and a spot in baseball's Hall of Fame.

The cosmopolitan French-Canadian city of Montreal applauded Robinson's diamond feats, and acted oblivious to his race. However, after the Royals won their pennant, on a road trip to Louisville, Kentucky, in the Little World Series, Robinson was treated shabbily by fans. Shouts of "Hey, nigger, go on back to Montreal where you belong and take your coon fans along," were heard. Royals fans were outraged. When Louisville players came north Royals fans spoke up for Robinson by booing and haranguing them at bat and in the field.[17]

Robinson proved himself on the field, but he also handled the hard part of the job, turning away from taunts and trouble, sublimating his urge to fight. All his life Robinson had met force with force and believed in shoving back when shoved. The strain of putting up with all the malarkey built up inside him that year in Montreal and near the end of the season he showed it. "My nerves were pretty ragged," he said. "I couldn't sleep, and often I couldn't eat. I guess I hadn't realized I wanted to make good so badly. I sort of went to pieces."[18]

Although this was not the kind of topic he dwelled on with sportswriters, and shared only with wife Rachel, the toll Robinson paid as a pioneer mounted on his body. One Montreal doctor suggested Robinson had had a nervous breakdown and needed rest. Robinson ignored that diagnosis and continued to play. Years later, Benson concluded that Robinson's "high-strung" nature contributed to the problems he had coping with all the pressures. "It caused him an early death because he just blew up inside," Benson said. "But Jackie was a man who would do anything to help one of his own. That was his secret, you understand? He went out and gave his life for black athletes."[19]

That was some time in the future. But there was never any step along the way in his early years of organized ball that was an easy one for Robinson. He promised Rickey there would be no incidents, that he would ignore things when they happened on the diamond. Neither man really believed the process of acceptance would be as difficult as it was. Rickey was sure that as soon as Dodgers players saw how terrific Robinson was in spring training they would welcome him enthusiastically. They were more lukewarm. Rickey knew there would be tensions on the field, but he did not know what form they would take. Players, especially southern ballplayers, resented Robinson's arrival more than anticipated.

There was talk of a rebellion on the Dodgers. Rickey said he would happily trade away anyone who felt he could not play with Robinson. Most of the players retreated, but not all, and some players did change teams. It leaked out (though has never been confirmed unequivocally) that the St. Louis Cardinals—the southernmost team in baseball—planned to boycott Dodgers games if Robinson played. National League president Ford Frick adopted a brick-wall stance on the issue. He produced a firm statement informing players where the league stood. "If you do this, you will be suspended from the league," Frick wrote. "You will find that the friends that you think you have in the press box will not support you, that you will be outcasts. I do not care if half the league strikes. Those who do it will encounter quick retribution. They will be suspended, and I do not care if it wrecks the National League for five years. This is the United States of America and one citizen has as much right to play as another."[20]

Frick did not have a particularly admired administration as league president, or tenure as commissioner and his sweeping, powerful statement on behalf of Robinson may have been his finest moment. There was no negotiating room, so as a statement of diplomacy it was more of a fiat, but the declaration terminated boycott threats.

Robinson had to endure other problems: Players laying for him on the base paths with sharpened spikes, pitchers throwing brushback tosses to test him, and vituperative insults fired his way from fans in the stands and from opposing bench jockeys or fielders. The worst example of riding Robinson is attributed to the Philadelphia Phillies and their Alabama-born manager Ben Chapman. The language used was hateful. Lines were zinging at Robinson from Phillies almost like machine-gun bullets. "They're waiting for you in the jungles, black boy!" someone yelled. "Hey, nigger, why don't you go back to the cotton field where you belong?" someone else shouted. "Hey snowflake! Which one of those white boys' wives are you dating tonight?" The viciousness of the comments was so off the charts that team officials became involved, and then Frick, Commissioner Happy Chandler, and the press. There was pressure on the Phillies to fire Chapman and he yielded to an arranged truce. Chapman and Robinson, neither embracing the notion, were pressed into posing for a picture together to present a peaceful front to the public.[21]

That was not Robinson's low point. Hate mail excoriating the Dodgers for playing Robinson, plus letters attacking him personally, piled up in the team offices. Mixed in with the nasty comments were some death threats. Dodgers officials tried to shield Robinson from the hate mail. Road secretary Harold Parrott screened it. "Usually I didn't show Robbie the hate mail," he said, "most of which was scrawled and scribbled like the smut you see on toilet walls."[22]

One death threat centering on a road trip to Cincinnati seemed more serious. The letter was turned over to the FBI and agents searched surrounding buildings and rooftops for a potential sniper. Robinson was notified, but nothing happened.

Duke Snider, the Dodgers Hall of Fame center fielder, could not believe the ordeal Robinson was put through. He was amazed at the vicious reaction to Robinson's playing and how he stood up under the onslaught. "Branch Rickey had to select someone who could take it and Jackie could take it," Snider said. "He dished it out just by ignoring what was hollered at him and done to him. It takes a special type of person, a cocky type who can brush off the things done to him."[23] It became clear later that whatever demeanor Robinson projected, he had not likely brushed off anything. He had only temporarily shelved his anger for Rickey's "noble experiment," and coped with the insults with a burning stomach.

Despite the unprecedented pressures, and scrutiny from white fans, black fans, and reporters, as well as other ballplayers, Robinson distinguished himself with better play than many of his Negro Leagues contemporaries expected. Robinson batted .297, hit 12 home runs, and led the National League in stolen bases with 29. He was selected *The Sporting News* rookie of the year. It was a tangible vindication. Robinson survived and thrived. The baseball world had not collapsed because a black player infiltrated the ranks. Before the end of the 1947 season, Larry Doby, the first black in the American League, joined Robinson by breaking the color line with the Cleveland Indians.

Near the end of the season, the Dodgers threw a special day for Robinson, an unusual reward for a rookie. But then, Robinson had not been the usual rookie. He was presented with a white Cadillac and his friend Bojangles Robinson handed over a gold watch. "I'm sixty-nine years old," said the famous dancer, "and I never thought I'd live to see the day when I'd stand face to face with Ty Cobb in technicolor."[24]

Tim Cohane, the sports editor of *Look* magazine, summarized Robinson's debut season succinctly in the fall of 1947. "Jackie Robinson, first baseman of the Brooklyn Dodgers, had some nasty experiences during his first season in the National League. As the first Negro in modern organized baseball history, he expected them. He wanted

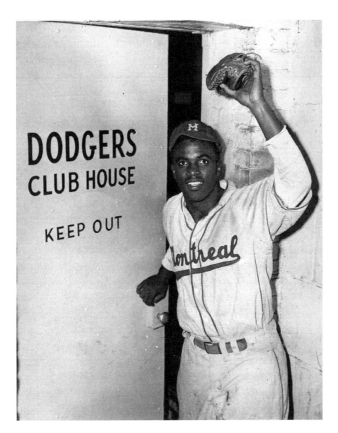

After Jackie Robinson left the Kansas City Monarchs for the Dodgers' organization, he played one season with the Montreal Royals in 1946. Robinson opened doors for African Americans wherever he played.

to be judged as just another ballplayer. He knew, of course, that he couldn't be. He made good as a ballplayer. He proved a Negro could take his place in baseball, as he has in other sports, with the respect, and—in the majority of cases—the goodwill of his fellow players."

The more Robinson played, the more his presence was taken for granted—in a good way. Additional African Americans were promoted to the team, players of great talent like catcher Roy Campanella and pitcher Don Newcombe. And although it took until 1959 when the Boston Red Sox were the last club to hire a black player when they brought up Pumpsie Green to play second base, one by one teams followed the Dodgers and signed the best black talent available. By 1949, Robinson was clearly one of the best players in the National League. He led the league in batting with a .342 average and stole a league-high 37 bases.

The flip side of being detested by racists was being adored by black fans, who considered Robinson a veritable god. The demand for him to make appearances, to sign autographs, and to speak at dinners was relentless. Rickey kept a strict limit on these, though he allowed Robinson to visit children in the hospital. Robinson's play had overcome the odds and in 1947 he was voted the second most popular man in America to Bing Crosby. After two seasons, after it had been established that there was no going back, Rickey lifted the wraps. Robinson was free to respond as he saw fit to any act of on-field intimidation. And he did what he had to do. Fiery by nature, Robinson no longer held back, he answered back. If the situation warranted running over a fielder, he did so.

The racial incidents subsided, but during the height of Robinson's attention in his first years, no one had been a better friend, or more supportive, than Hall of Fame shortstop Pee Wee Reese. Although he played second base and even first, Robinson had been signed as a shortstop. Fresh out of the Navy, the incumbent at the position, and a born-and-bred southerner from Kentucky, Reese paused when he learned of Robinson's acquisition. Then he figured the competition chips would fall as they may, with the best man getting the job. It did not bother him that Robinson was black, it bothered him he might lose his starting spot. Instead Reese and Robinson forged a double-play combination and once, when things were at their worst, when fans were booing Robinson and others were taunting him, Reese wandered toward second base and put his arm around Robinson. It was a very public gesture of friendship and compassion, and a very vivid statement to others that he and Robinson were a team and were teammates. Within a couple of years an in-depth feature story was written about the two men's relationship. "A really nice man is a rare man and the crowd always spots him," Robinson said of Reese's popularity. "They sure guessed right about Pee Wee."[25]

As the years passed, and Robinson, then other blacks, became fixtures in the Dodgers lineup and fresh black stars appeared on the scene like Willie Mays and Hank Aaron, Robinson became less of a phenomenon and more of an established veteran player. He had not been a young rookie, breaking into the Dodgers at the advanced age of twenty-eight. Robinson played ten years in the majors between the 1947 and 1956 seasons and batted .311 lifetime. He played in six All-Star games. During his time with the team, the Dodgers won six pennants. Although his statistics in all categories were good, the way Robinson made his most dramatic impact was by running wild on the bases, either stealing, taking the extra base on a hit, or bunting. Robinson made opposing pitchers jittery and did the little things that revved up his own teammates.

At times Robinson and his renowned teammate and fellow Hall of Famer Campanella disagreed—their personalities were so different—but Campanella always admired what Robinson accomplished and the flair he brought to the game. "Jackie could beat you every way there was to beat you," Campanella said. "I have never seen a ballplayer that could do all of the things Jackie could do."[26]

When Campanella and Robinson played for Brooklyn it was the height of the National League rivalry between the Dodgers and Giants. Fans, as siblings often do, believed in one-upmanship. The teams were stable, with many of the same familiar players on rosters year after year, and the two National League teams always seemed to be contending for the same flag. Robinson had made up his mind to retire after the 1956 season and made a cash deal for the exclusive announcement in a national magazine. The Dodgers, who were no longer run by Rickey, did not know of Robinson's plans and in a move that startled the baseball world, traded him to the Giants. The combination of the controversial trade and the magazine scoop had fans, reporters, and players abuzz. Robinson was accused of using the magazine story to hold the Giants up for more money. The Dodgers were angry at him and he was angry at the Dodgers. In the end, Robinson stuck to his retirement plan. He never swung a bat for the Giants.

LATER LIFE

A celebrity, whose name carried weight not only in the sporting world, but also in the world at large, increasingly so in the political field, Robinson threw himself into the next phase of his life. He became a major figure with the National Association for the Advancement of Colored People (NAACP), campaigning for civil rights. He worked for a number of businesses and helped found a black-owned bank in Harlem. For a period, he acted as an advisor to President Richard Nixon on civil rights issues, but realized too late when Nixon did little to support black causes that he had invested in the wrong stock. Robinson then became more influential with New York governor Nelson Rockefeller.

In a highly publicized tragedy, his oldest son Jack Jr. was hospitalized with a drug addiction, and then when he seemingly had conquered the problem, was killed in an automobile accident at the age of twenty-four. The loss shattered Robinson and wife Rachel. Robinson had just turned thirty-eight when he retired as an active player, but he developed health problems prematurely, notably diabetes, and the disease accelerated his aging.

With the exception of campaigning for baseball to eradicate the next barrier and hire the first African American manager, Robinson was basically divorced from the sport for some time. He was active in charitable and political causes and continuously sought to make a difference at a time when civil rights was a front-burner issue in American society. Yet as the 1960s ended and the 1970s began, he lost some of his vigor, partially attributed to a heart attack in 1968. His hair turned grayish-white and he began losing his eyesight. In the first half of 1972, Robinson's worsening blindness was noted by Campanella and another old friend, Mal Goode. When Goode met up with Robinson in New York, the former player could recognize Goode only by the sound of his voice. "I was about a foot away from him," Goode said. "You talk about something tearing you up."[27]

Robinson had one more grand baseball appearance in him. Before a World Series game between the Cincinnati Reds and the Oakland Athletics in Cincinnati on October 15, 1972, the sport paid tribute to Robinson and he threw out the first pitch. The occasion was the silver anniversary of his color-line breaking first season. During his farewell speech, Robinson once again pushed the idea of baseball hiring a black manager. During conversations with old teammates like Pee Wee Reese and pitcher Joe Black, Robinson said not only were his eyes bad, but also because of the diabetes he was going into the hospital to have a leg amputated.

That never happened. Only nine days after the mini-reunion with some of his closest teammates, Robinson suffered a second heart attack in his Connecticut home and died. It was October 24, 1972 and he was a worn-out fifty-three-year old. Monte Irvin, one of the pallbearers at the funeral, was asked to reflect on Robinson. Irvin said Robinson once confided in him that he had stomach pains for his entire career and that they went away only when he retired. "Maybe they were psychosomatic, or maybe he was so full of nervous tension," Irvin said, "but he always had that pain in his gut and look what he was able to do despite it."[28]

Buck Leonard said many Negro Leagues players thought Robinson was the wrong man to break the color barrier because he was not a good enough player. Leonard said he thought owners would contend that Robinson failed and that would set the idea of taking blacks into the majors back for five or ten years. Leonard later admitted he was wrong all of the way around. "He was what we needed," Leonard said. "He was a college man and he knew how to take charge of his weaknesses. At UCLA, he had played with white players and had played against white players. He grew up with it [integrated teams] so he knew how to cope with the condition. I think Jackie was the right man—the ideal man. I don't know if anyone else could have taken the pressure that Jackie Robinson did."[29]

President Nixon, who never disavowed a friendship with Robinson, even though Robinson drifted away from him politically, called the star the greatest athlete he ever saw. "His courage and sense of brotherhood and his brilliance on the playing field brought a new human dimension not only to the game of baseball, but to every area of American life where black and white people work side by side," Nixon said in a statement upon Robinson's death. "This nation, to which he gave so much in his lifetime, will miss Jackie Robinson, but his example will continue to inspire us for years to come."[30]

The *New York Times*' obituary credited Robinson with not only providing opportunity for African Americans in baseball, but also in other sports such as basketball and football. "He became the pioneer for a generation of blacks in the major professional sports after World War II," the story read.[31]

Robinson's body lay in an open casket for thousands of visitors in Harlem and those paying their respects at the service in New York filled a 2,500-seat church and a 1,000-seat overflow auditorium. It might be said that Robinson was interred, but never buried. Ten years after his death, the visage of Robinson, in baseball cap and uniform, was unveiled on a U.S. postage stamp. The first day of issue was in Cooperstown, New York, home of the Baseball Hall of Fame.

When anniversaries approached—of Robinson's Dodger signing, of his first Montreal game, of his first Major League game—sportswriters wrote lengthy educational stories, informing younger generations just what America was like in 1947 and just what types of indignities Robinson endured. On the fortieth anniversary of Robinson's Dodger debut, each park in the majors painted his number forty-two on second base for a game.

In 1997, fifty years after Robinson broke the color barrier, Major League baseball took the unique step of retiring Robinson's number from the game for all teams for all time. Number forty-two, honored by being worn on Robinson's back for a decade with the Dodgers, would be worn no more by any baseball player. It is a tribute that reminds fans about Robinson on any trip to any ballpark where retired jersey numbers are displayed. For those who attend Major League baseball games and see number forty-two displayed, the gesture from the sport is a simple but permanent history lesson. It is one way to recognize the immortality of Jackie Robinson.

NOTES

1. See Foreword by Cornel West in Jackie Robinson, *I Never Had It Made* (Hopewell, NJ: The Ecco Press, 1995), ix–xi.
2. See Introduction by Hank Aaron, in Jackie Robinson, *I Never Had It Made*, xiii.
3. Buck O'Neil, personal interview, December 7, 2005.
4. Robinson, *I Never Had It Made*, 4–6.
5. Robinson, *I Never Had It Made*, 19, 21.
6. Robinson, *I Never Had It Made*, 24.
7. Robinson, *I Never Had It Made*, 27.
8. Robinson, *I Never Had It Made*, 31.
9. Ibid.
10. Robinson, *I Never Had It Made*, 34.

11. Harvey Frommer, *Rickey & Robinson* (New York: Macmillan Publishing, 1982), 113.

12. O'Neil, personal interview.

13. David Falkner, *Great Time Coming* (New York: Touchstone Books, 1995), 116.

14. Falkner, *Great Time Coming*, 120.

15. Falkner, *Great Time Coming*, 121.

16. Frommer, *Rickey & Robinson*, 120–121.

17. Frommer, *Rickey & Robinson*, 122.

18. Ibid.

19. Falkner, *Great Time Coming*, 124.

20. Frommer, *Rickey & Robinson*, 138.

21. Falkner, *Great Time Coming*, 164–165.

22. Falkner, *Great Time Coming*, 166.

23. Frommer, *Rickey & Robinson*, 140.

24. Bob Cooke, *Brooklyn Eagle*, September 23, 1947.

25. John Lardner, *New Yorker*, September 18, 1949.

26. Frommer, *Rickey & Robinson*, 204.

27. Frommer, *Rickey & Robinson*, 224.

28. Falkner, *Great Time Coming*, 334.

29. Buck Leonard with James A. Riley, *Buck Leonard: The Black Lou Gehrig* (New York: Carroll & Graf Publishers, 1995).

30. *San Francisco Chronicle/Associated Press*, October 25, 1972.

31. Dave Anderson, *New York Times*, October 26, 1972.

Further Reading

Falkner, David, *Great Time Coming*. New York: Touchstone Books, 1995.

Frommer, Harvey, *Rickey & Robinson*. New York: Macmillan Publishing, 1982.

Robinson, Jackie, *I Never Had It Made*. Hopewell, NJ: Ecco Press, 1995.

ROY CAMPANELLA
November 19, 1921–June 26, 1993

Some consider Roy Campanella the greatest all-around catcher in the history of base-ball. Campanella began playing professionally in his midteens, was the second African American signed by the Brooklyn Dodgers, and after integrating two minor league teams, became a three-time National League Most Valuable Player (MVP). After he was paralyzed in an automobile accident, Campanella worked tirelessly to help others who suffered similar fates.

Campanella broke into the Negro Leagues when he was fifteen years old in 1936 and spent most of his formative years with the Baltimore Elite Giants until his 1946 signing by the Dodgers. Campanella broke into the majors in 1948 and won the MVP award in 1951, 1953, and 1955, playing on the Dodgers only world championship team before moving to Los Angeles.

He was only fifteen. Too young for traveling baseball, his mother thought. Just fifteen. Too young to spend his days with grown men. A mere fifteen, with his vast potential before him. There was just one thing. Roy Campanella was such a good baseball player at fifteen, his future was now. He could play with the best in the Negro Leagues imme-diately. The Bacharach Giants and then the Baltimore Elite Giants wanted his name on contracts and willingly paid what seemed to be big money to a family that could use the cash just after the Depression.

And so young Roy became a professional as a teenager. And he was again in the right place, catching the eye of the right organization a few years later when the walls of discrimination came tumbling down and the Brooklyn Dodgers looked to sign the best players in the world.

Affable, easygoing, Roy Campanella made friends easily and won admirers just as easily because of his power with the bat and his way with the glove. He was a star as a youth and became one of the greatest catchers in baseball history during the 1950s, win-ning three National League MVP awards before his career was cut short by tragedy.

Campanella could do anything on the diamond. Scouts drooled over his potential. They saw a player so young who could play as well as a player in his prime, a player still learning who could match the best in the sport. It is often said that catcher's equip-ment represents the "tools of ignorance," but in Campanella's possession, they became the tools of genius.

He was graceful and quick in his tasks, powerful with a bat, and had a know-everything awareness of what transpired on the field. Campanella was on the short list for the best-ever Dodger player, if not owner of the crown, and if he had been allowed to play out the final seasons he normally would have been allotted, it is possible some would remember him among the absolute greatest of baseball's great players.

Instead, with a spinal cord damaged in an unlikely and unlucky automobile accident, Campanella's role in American society expanded. As a man who had spent his entire time

The star Dodgers' catcher began playing professional baseball in the Negro Leagues when he was fifteen and became a three-time National League Most Valuable Player for Brooklyn.

in the baseball limelight being open, cooperative, and generous to people, Campanella's public demeanor did not change with adversity. He became a symbol of courage and inspiration to others dealt serious physical blows. Through speeches and a best-selling book, he proved to an uninformed populace that a man could function and do wonderful things even if he lived in a wheelchair.

The way the nation got to know Campanella initially, however, was as a baseball player, in 1948 one of the first African Americans to follow Jackie Robinson across the Major League color barrier. That was a broader unveiling, but by then Campanella already had been playing baseball at a high level for a decade.

EARLY LIFE

Roy Campanella was born in 1921 to an Italian father, John, who owned a vegetable truck, and an African American mother, Ida, and as one of six children spent much of his youth in the Nicetown section of Philadelphia. He picked up baseball on the sandlots, as playgrounds were called then. Other kids called Campanella "half-breed." Originally, he said he did not know what it meant, but when he realized they were insulting him because of his parents' mixed color, Campanella beat up his taunters. "Fortunately, I was a pretty good scrapper," he said.[1]

Campanella joined a boxing club to hone those skills. He also delivered newspapers and shined shoes to make money. His father did not like baseball and wanted him to stop playing, especially after he got hit in the face with a ball while catching without a mask. But Campanella loved the game. A representative of the Bacharach Giants black ballclub saw Campanella on the sandlot when he was still attending high school and convinced his mother Ida he should be allowed to play weekends with the team. The offer was for $35 for the first two games, real money in 1936. He also assured her that Campanella would attend church on Sunday while on the road.

On his first weekend with the team, the Giants rolled into New York and a wide-eyed Campanella could not believe the sights of the metropolis. "We went by way of Broadway," he said. "I'd never seen so many lights and people and excitement in all my life. It looked like the whole world was having a party."[2]

The next day, when Campanella walked out of the hotel lobby he saw a fancy bus parked on Seventh Avenue. Written on the side was "Baltimore Elite Giants." Campanella was impressed. "To me, and I guess to any Negro kid, the Elite Giants were like the New York Yankees. I just sort of drank in the sight of that big, bright-painted bus. That's class with a capital K, ain't it."[3]

Fortuitously, Campanella was introduced to Elite Giants manager Biz Mackey, looking for help at the catcher position for his ballclub. Mackey gave "Campy" his card and told him to call when he returned home to Philadelphia. Campanella played out the weekend with the Bacharach team, went home flushed with pleasure from the experience, and forgot all about Mackey. But Mackey called him, persuaded Campanella to join the Giants, and then sweet-talked his mom into allowing her son to play weekends until the end of school, and full time in the summer. A full-time ballplayer in 1937, Campanella's $60 a month starting salary (lower than the Bacharach Giants paid) was sent directly to Mrs. Campanella. Campanella kept his expense money.

Mackey was one of the best catchers to ever play in the Negro Leagues and he was inducted into the Baseball Hall of Fame in 2006. He was willing to mentor Campanella, especially with fielding techniques. "Biz wasn't satisfied for me to do just one or two things good," Campanella said. "He wanted me to do everything good. There were times when Biz Mackey made me cry with his constant dogging. But no one ever had a better teacher."[4]

There was a lot to learn for a raw kid fresh from high school. The Negro Leagues were men's leagues, with mature players pursuing a livelihood. The travel was long and challenging—Campanella was away from home for two straight months his first summer with the Elite Giants. Players sought any kind of edge, even sometimes resorting to illegal techniques. The rules were lax governing a pitcher's repertoire, and as a catcher Campanella had to learn how to call a game, make older pitchers respect him, and also how to catch a devious, savvy pitcher who knew all of the tricks.

"Anything went in the Negro National League," Campanella said. No one prevented pitchers in the Negro Leagues from tarnishing a ball's horsehide with foreign substances, or from cutting them with razor blades or other tools. The youth who had not yet earned a diploma from everyday high school was immersed in a graduate course in catching.[5]

When young Campy turned sixteen he quit school, obtained working papers and committed to a baseball career. He was off to spring training with the Baltimore Elite Giants in March of 1938. His mother gave Campanella a Bible, dated it March 17, and inscribed his name in it. He kept that Bible the rest of his life.

The team traveled by train to Nashville, Tennessee, and on his first night on the rails Campanella was surrounded by players discussing whether or not the Major League color line would ever be breached. Campanella was excited about this adventure, and never considered he might one day achieve the dream many of these same players would fall short of attaining. Campanella was eased into the Elite Giants lineup, but made an impact with his talent almost immediately. The Negro Leagues represented a small club of organizations and players on different teams got to know one another quite well from league play, traveling teams playing exhibitions, and winter ball in Latin America. Right from the start Campanella began filling his winters with competition in Puerto Rico. He visited Latin America so often he learned to speak Spanish and became a year-around player. Or as he put it, he was "playing the game fifty out of fifty-two weeks" a year. The Elite Giants realized what they had—Campanella's salary quickly jumped to $150 a month.

Buck O'Neil, the legendary Kansas City Monarchs player and manager, met Campanella as a rookie. "They had been telling me about this young phenom," O'Neil said of other players' comments. "When I met him, I said, 'I've heard about you. I'm gonna get on base and I'm gonna steal second on the first pitch.' He was feisty. I got on and I ran and he threw the ball into centerfield. I'm safe at second. I'm laughing. The next month he comes to Kansas City and there we are again. I'm on first. I run. And oh, the sucker, he throws me out when I'm only halfway down. He was an outstanding catcher. You know, if he hadn't been in that crash, he probably would have been the first black manager in Major League baseball. Everybody liked Campy."[6]

During that rookie year Campanella was focused primarily on being accepted by his older teammates, and becoming a better player. Like so many other statistics from the Negro Leagues, the documentation of Campanella's first season has evaporated. Most numbers from his first few years with Baltimore cannot be found. By 1940, though, Campanella was a reliable .300 right-handed hitter over the course of about thirty games each season with the Elite Giants. He actually got many more at bats in Puerto Rico over the winters of 1940–1941 and 1941–1942.

Monte Irvin, the future New York Giants Hall of Famer, was on the San Juan team at the same time Campanella played for Caguas in winter ball. Irvin was not playing well and felt he was in danger of being shipped back to the States for poor performance. Campanella subtlety took pity on Irvin. "Dude, I see you're in a slump," Campy told Irvin when he stepped into the batter's box. And Campanella informed Irvin that as a gesture of camaraderie since the game was not close, he would help him out. Campanella told him a fastball was coming. Irvin did not believe Campy, did not swing, and took a strike. Next pitch, Campanella warned him a curveball was coming. Still, Irvin did not swing. Strike two. Now Irvin understood Campanella was for real. This time Campanella tipped off an approaching fastball and Irvin slugged it for a home run. Campanella acted in the same cooperative manner for Irvin's second at bat, too. When Irvin came up the third time, however, Campanella said, "Well, dude, since the game is close, now you're on your own." Irvin played out the season in Puerto Rico instead of being sent into exile.[7]

One reason Irvin did not believe Campanella's gift offer at first was that Campy was always a chatterbox behind the plate. Many of the best catchers talk incessantly when a batter steps in, saying anything, seeking to disrupt their concentration. Campanella was an expert.

Later that same season when Campanella fell into his own hitting slump, Irvin invited him to San Juan for a night of partying. Campanella drank only Coca-Cola at the time, but every time Campy hit the dance floor Irvin slipped a little bit of rum into his drink to perk him up. Campanella did marvel at how terrific he felt and said he had a good time. At the end of the evening, Campanella said, "You thought you were fooling me [with the rum], but I knew what you were doing. But please invite me back again and do the same thing."[8]

During years of Negro Leagues play, and after his early death, players raved about Josh Gibson as the black Babe Ruth. Gibson's slugging prowess was extraordinary and he was regarded as the best to play his position in the black leagues. Perhaps that was true for all-around play, but Irvin said Campanella was better defensively.[9]

Buck Leonard, the sterling first baseman who was a Gibson teammate with the Homestead Grays, reached the same conclusion. He rated both Campanella and Biz Mackey ahead of Gibson in the field and in taking charge of a game. Fans sometimes forget that catchers not only touch the ball more often than any other fielder, take a regular turn at bat, but also communicate with the pitcher on every throw, frequently calling the game pitch by pitch. The combination of physical and mental effort is what makes catching the most challenging position on the field. "He [Gibson] wasn't as good defensively as Biz Mackey or Campanella," Leonard said.[10]

In school, Campanella was big for his age. He was big-boned and carried a lot of weight. Although the *Baseball Encyclopedia* lists Campy's size as five-foot-eight and 200 pounds, some newspaper stories describe him as slightly taller and contained many references to his gaining weight in the off-season without always reducing enough to satisfy his managers. There is no completely reliable poundage figure, however. Campanella did have a lot of muscle and moved with a cat-like quickness in chasing a foul ball or a wild pitch. He often fooled opponents with his moves. "Roy had that squatty body, but that sucker was strong," Buck O'Neil said.[11]

Campanella, who also suited up in Mexico and Venezuela over the years, was playing winter ball in Puerto Rico when he read about the bombing of Pearl Harbor in December of 1941. At first he thought it had nothing to do with him, but quickly discovered how wrong he was. He was classified 1A by his draft board and had to vacate Puerto Rico for the mainland. Given the United States move into war mode, it was difficult to get out of Puerto Rico and when blocked from flying Campanella spent seven days on a ship that passed through a storm before reaching New York. The boat had a German submarine scare on the way north, too. Because Campanella was married—to Ruthe—and had two children, he was reclassified 3A and given a defense plant job in Philadelphia. After some months, Campanella was allowed to resume his baseball career.

It was during World War II, when there was a shortage of baseball talent in the major leagues with so many players wearing the uniform of their country rather than the uniform of their ballclub, that Campanella became cognizant of serious talk suggesting African Americans would be permitted to play organized ball. By then Campanella was a wary twenty-one-year-old, who had seen discrimination in many cities. He doubted rumors that baseball was going to change overnight and invite in banned blacks.

"I paid no mind to all that idle gossip," Campanella said. "I had little faith that these bars would ever come down, at least in my playing lifetime. The color line in the major leagues did not take a man's talent into account. As far as I was concerned the big leagues were as far away as Siberia." One day a newspaper reporter from the *Daily Worker*, the Communist newspaper that pushed for equality on the playing field, approached Campanella and asked if he would like a tryout with the Pittsburgh Pirates. Soon a letter arrived from William Benswagner, the president of the Pirates. Campanella said the letter was discouraging and full of "buts," but he wrote back anyway, saying all he wanted was a chance. He never heard back from Benswagner and there never was a tryout. At Shibe Park, a little later, Campanella challenged the owner of the Phillies to give him a tryout. No opportunity was offered.[12]

It is ironic that others consider Campanella to be a better catcher than Josh Gibson because Campanella looked to Gibson for assistance when he first joined the Baltimore Elite Giants.

"I had a very erratic arm when I broke in," Campanella said. "It was strong enough, all right, but I never was too sure where the ball was going. I'll always be grateful to him [Gibson] for the help he gave me when I was a skinny little catcher away from home for the first time, and he was the great man of baseball. He tried to show me how to set myself to improve my speed and accuracy. 'You got the arm, that's the important thing,'" he said. He credited Josh Gibson with guidance and reminding him to practice constantly if he wanted to improve.[13]

Before an Elite Giants game in 1948, Campanella was tipped off that a white man in the stands was a baseball scout for the Dodgers. He was again disbelieving. But Clyde Sukeforth, on assignment from Branch Rickey to find the best black talent for Brooklyn, was watching Campanella. Sukeforth was the front man for the Dodgers and he brought Jackie Robinson to Rickey. Before embarking on his annual Latin American pilgrimage, Campanella played in an exhibition series against white players handled by Dodgers manager Charlie Dressen. Dressen took Campanella aside and told him Rickey wanted to meet him in the Dodgers offices.

Campanella went through a long interview with Rickey, but when Rickey said he wanted Campy to play for him, he thought the Dodgers boss meant in a rumored new black league. Campanella, making a good living with the Elite Giants and in winter ball, did not want to jeopardize his security for that. Rickey said they would talk again. A short time later, Robinson confided to Campy that the Dodgers would announce Robinson as the first African American in organized baseball in the twentieth century. Campanella realized he misread the discussion with Rickey and worried the mistake would ruin his prospects for the majors.

"I could have given myself a swift kick," Campanella said. "I really felt bad. What should I do?" At least he had promised Rickey he would not sign with another Major League team without talking to the Dodgers. All winter Campanella waited to hear back from Rickey. On March 1, 1946, "I got a cablegram," Campanella said. "Please report Brooklyn office by March 10. Very important."[14]

Campanella reported. It was a life-altering meeting. Campy signed with the Dodgers organization. He thought he would join Robinson with the Montreal Royals, a northern-based team at the top minor league level where Rickey hoped there would be a comparative minimum of discrimination. Only at Montreal's spring training site in Sanford, Florida, there was some unrest and Rickey decided it was not a good time to add more black players to the roster there. Instead, Campanella, and another important signee, black pitcher Don Newcombe, were sent to a Dodger minor league club in Nashua, New Hampshire. Although it was only the Class B level of play, the Dodgers had a good management team in place. General manager Buzzie Bavasi and manager Walter Alston were both influential in helping Campanella make a smooth adjustment, and became key Dodger figures later on.

Nashua was not roiling with racial animosity. Campanella said it was a pleasant community for him and his family and the only racial overtones during the season stemmed from on-field name-calling. Campanella had been a player-manager in

Venezuela and not thought much about it. One day, Alston told Campanella that if he ever got thrown out of a game he wanted Campanella to run the team.

Alston encouraged Campanella to show his take-charge side, more or less allowing him to be a coach on the field. A few weeks later, Alston protested too loudly about balls and strikes and was ejected from a game in the sixth inning. Campanella managed the rest of the game.[15]

Decades later, in making the argument that Campanella could have been a big-league manager, Buck O'Neil cited that incident. "I wonder if many people know that, in a way, Campy was the first black manager in organized ball," O'Neil said.[16]

Campanella was named the MVP of the New England League. He figured he would be up with the Dodgers the next season. Manager Leo

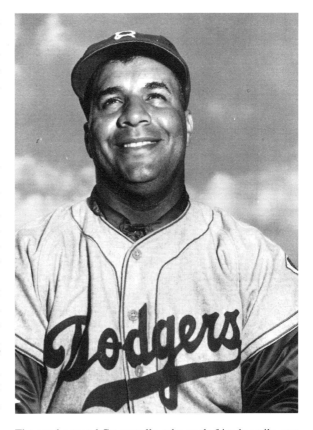

The good-natured Campanella, who made friends easily, was in the first group of African American players on the Dodgers' Nashua, New Hampshire, farm team and also in St. Paul, Minnesota.

Durocher wanted Campanella. Rickey had other plans. After playing well enough to make the team, despite a crowd at catcher, and suiting up with the Dodgers briefly in April of 1948, Campanella was sent to St. Paul in Minnesota. Rickey told Campy that he wanted to integrate another league, the American Association. Campanella was disappointed, but happier when he discovered Alston was managing the Saints. Campanella tore up AAA pitching with a .325 average and in midsummer was recalled to the Dodgers after catcher Bruce Edwards injured his shoulder.

MAJOR LEAGUE CAREER

So many years after leaving home for a weekend's worth of activity with the Bacharach Giants, Campanella made his Major League debut on July 2, 1948. He stroked a double in his first at bat against the Giants and he recorded three hits. Campanella said he had many satisfying games in the big leagues, but playing was "never quite so sweet" as in his first one.[17]

The Dodgers were loaded with catching Campanella's rookie year and he played in just eighty-three games and hit .258 while clouting 9 home runs. He did not become a regular starter until 1949 when he clubbed 22 homers, drove in 82 runs, and batted .287. After that the catcher's job had his name stamped on it for good.

By midsummer of the 1949 season, Brooklyn writers were asking Campanella about his ascension from the Negro Leagues and Sukeforth said it was easy to see Campy as a can't-miss prospect. "Sure I saw him and recommended him," Sukeforth said. "But so did half a dozen other scouts. They all liked him. There never was any question about his ability."[18]

When he was first called up to the majors, Campanella refused to wear a hard shell batting helmet that has long since become mandatory for hitters' safety. Shortstop Pee Wee Reese tried to convince Campanella it was only prudent to wear the protection, but he said he never had been hit in the head. Soon after, Pirates pitcher Bill Werle unleashed a sidearm pitch that Campanella did not see coming. He tried to duck, but was slow, and the pitch conked him. "The ball hit me on the side of the head, dropping me like a felled steer," Campy said. He was taken to the hospital, where he had X-rays, and spent the night. When Campanella returned to the Dodgers he was ready to change hat wear. "From now on," he said, "ain't nobody going to get me to take this off, batting, catching, or running the bases." Then he asked Reese how he looked. "You're a doll," the infielder said.[19]

By 1950, Campanella was a two-time National League All Star. After a long career in the Negro Leagues and in winter ball, Campanella enjoyed many trappings of success. He had electric trains, tropical fish, liked to golf, went fishing and boating, and lived in Glen Cove, Long Island, a well-to-do neighborhood.

In early 1951, during a winter cold spell, the hot-water heater went out in the house and the repair job produced frightening results. Campanella and Ruthe attempted to fix it themselves. Campanella tried to light the pilot, but things went horribly wrong. "There was a muffled explosion, then a blinding flash," Campanella said. "The water heater had exploded and blew both of us clear across the basement." Campanella was burned in the face and he could not see. Both of his corneas were blistered. His head was bandaged and his eyes were covered with patches. For four days, Campanella wondered if he was blind. But when the doctor removed the bandages, Campanella's vision returned first in blurry fashion and shortly in fine order.

Always concerned that Campanella might go flabby, the Dodgers ordered him to go on a diet that emphasized nutrition and de-emphasized beer. The 1951 season turned out to be Campanella's greatest to date. He moved into the realm of superstar with a spectacular performance. Campy cranked 33 home runs, drove in 108 runs, and batted .325. The statistics led to his selection as the MVP of the National League.

That was about as individually fulfilling as a full season could be. Except for one thing. That was the year of the Miracle Giants, the year the apparently doomed-by-August Giants rallied to win the pennant and eliminate the Dodgers in a playoff on Bobby Thomson's famous home run. Campanella watched the ball fly off Thomson's bat and willed it to be caught. "Sink, you devil, sink!" he said. But the ball soared into the stands over left-fielder Andy Pafko's head. And the Giants, not the Dodgers, advanced to the World Series.[20]

When Campanella was notified later in the fall that he had won the MVP award, his manager, then Charlie Dressen, sent a telegram of congratulations. One thing the diet-authoring Dressen sneaked into the note was "Weight 200. Ha. Ha."[21]

Campanella's next season was not as formidable, but in 1953 he turned in one of the greatest hitting seasons ever compiled by a catcher. Campy led the league with 142

RBIs, smashed 41 home runs, and averaged .312. He also won a second MVP award. Later, he said, "I feel proudest of my 1953 season."[22]

Campanella never let his outstanding hitting overshadow his outstanding fielding. Campy was particularly close to Reese and years later Reese still remembered the big catcher's skill behind the plate even more than at the plate. "Campy was the best I ever saw at keeping the ball in front of him," Reese said.[23]

Campanella was a good-humored man. He could get angry on the field if he felt he had been wronged, but those occasions were rare. He tried to get along with everyone and generally succeeded. *New York Times* Pulitzer Prize–winning sports columnist Arthur Daley once called Campanella "The jolly, round man." Reaching the majors a couple of years after Robinson, playing with northern minor league teams, Campanella did not suffer nearly as much torment as Robinson, nor did he let what he did experience sear him as deeply. He rarely referred to racial incidents during his ballplaying days and usually kept a smile on his face. He was not oblivious to matters of black and white and he felt that he was part of a brotherhood as one of the early African Americans in the majors.

The first two black players to make the roster of the Chicago Cubs were future Hall of Famer Ernie Banks and second baseman Gene Baker. After a losing game in Brooklyn in 1955, just two years into their careers, the down-hearted players were walking through the streets. A Cadillac pulled alongside and a voice urged them to get in. It was Campanella. Banks said that Campanella drove them to their hotel, but along the way told them about his early days with the Dodgers, and imparted some advice.

"It wasn't a lecture," Banks said, "just an expression of his sincere interest in our success. I don't remember hearing anybody express himself better than Campy did that day. He stressed the opportunities baseball had given him, as well as us, and the responsibility we all owed to the game in return. No one in baseball has earned more respect than Campy."[24]

By the early 1950s, Campanella had become a nationally known figure who transcended sport. On October 2, 1953, Campanella was famed broadcaster Edward R. Murrow's first guest on his new *Person-to-Person* show. "Now, Roy, all you have to do is hit a home run in the ninth inning," Murrow said to Campanella. "That will make the show a success." Campanella homered in the eighth inning. Close enough.[25]

In 1955, Campanella met the aging Ty Cobb, regarded by some as the greatest baseball player of all time. Cobb was known as an irascible man when he played and considered a racist by some. There were no racial overtones from either man when they crossed paths, only compliments flowing from Cobb. "He was quoted as saying that I would be remembered more than any other player of my time; that someday I would be rated with the greatest catchers of all time. I appreciated that coming from such a man," Campanella said.[26]

The Dodgers were a National League dynasty during Campanella's playing career. Their main problem was that the New York Yankees, just over the bridge in Manhattan, were baseball's overall dynasty. The Dodgers won five pennants during Campanella's ten seasons with the club in Brooklyn. The Yankees won ten World Series in twelve years during much of the same time period.

During the winter of 1954, Campanella attended a banquet sponsored by the B'Nai B'rith Association. He was presented with a plaque for "High Principle and Achievement in Sports" during 1953. This was an award rewarding brotherhood and excellence, both things Campanella represented. At that dinner Campanella uttered the most famous quote attributed to him and one of baseball's most enduring statements. In his thank-you, he said, "You have to be a man to be a big leaguer, but you have to have a lot of little boy in you, too."[27] It is doubtful that any story of substance written about Campanella from then on omitted that observation.

The season of 1955 was the finally-did-it campaign for the Dodgers. For the first time in Brooklyn franchise history the team won the World Series, beating the hated Yankees to boot. It was the culmination of a quest for a great team that would otherwise have been destined to be remembered as the close-but-no-cigar team. It was the apex of the Dodgers life in Brooklyn. After clinching the championship, the Dodgers celebrated in the clubhouse, as expected. But then they adjourned to the Brossert Hotel, where owner Walter O'Malley sponsored a victory party.

Campanella was impressed by the scope of the party. Fans took to the streets to celebrate as if the Dodgers victory was emblematic of their own personal holiday. They partied as loudly and as vigorously as if it was the end of the Millenium bash.[28]

It was unfathomable to believe on that glorious night that within a few years it would all be over, the devoted fans abandoned, the Dodgers on their way to Los Angeles, and Campanella in a fight for his life.

Not long before the Dodgers had at last outlasted the Yankees, Campanella's growing celebrityhood was on display in another way. In August of that season he was the subject of a lengthy *Time* magazine profile. The entire cover consisted of a portrait of Campy surrounded by bats, balls, and gloves. *Time* described Campanella as the "cocoa colored catcher" who was the heart of the Dodgers and who had the best aptitude in America for handling the demanding catcher's job.[29]

To capitalize on his name, Campanella established his own business, a liquor store in Harlem, and spent his free time tutoring kids on baseball fundamentals. Campy's contract for 1956 was the highest in Dodgers history to that time at $50,000. Although after the World Series Campanella had become a three-time MVP, putting him in exclusive company, he had also experienced arm numbness and injuries that periodically slowed him. Campy had already devoted twenty years to baseball, but because of his early start Campanella was only thirty-four entering the 1956 season. Around this time he had to undergo hand surgery and also broke his leg. It was possible Campanella was wearing out playing the most demanding position on the field day everyday.

Between bouts in hospitals and appearances on the field, Campanella became embroiled in a minor feud with Robinson. Their personalities were dramatically different, but the two men had been friendly for a decade. Robinson decided he was going to retire at the end of the 1956 season. However, he had signed an exclusive deal with a national magazine to be paid for such an announcement when the time came. As a result, when the Dodgers abruptly traded Robinson to the despised Giants, he did not return phone calls from his longtime employer. The way the entire matter played out, Robinson appeared to be a money-grubber. Robinson stuck to his retirement plan, but there were hard feelings all around, and the duo spouted off about one another.

Campanella criticized Robinson for the manner of his departure from the game. Robinson implied that because of his injuries, Campanella was all through, too. Campanella said he would retire when he felt like it. "When it's my turn to bow out of baseball, I certainly don't want to go out like he did," Campanella said. "It just wasn't the dignified way to do it."[30] Robinson fired back once more. "He has always been envious of me, that I was the first Negro in baseball," Robinson said.[31]

It was after the 1957 season when O'Malley, the Dodgers owner, uprooted the franchise and exited Ebbets Field and Brooklyn, leaving fans broken-hearted and accusing him of being a mercenary. Deeply entrenched in New York, Campanella had no desire to leave the East, but he was not about to retire, either. He was fully prepared to play in Los Angeles in 1958. During the off-season, in preparation for the arrival of the team, a Los Angeles newspaper did a series of interviews with Dodger players about to move West.

The story on Campanella included such descriptions as, "Campanella is considered by many as the greatest catcher of all time." Campanella was also referred to as a "human backstop" and noted that he was often called "the nice guy from Nicetown." Harkening back to that long-ago present of a Bible from his mother, Campanella said he told her he would read it regularly and said, "I haven't missed a day since." Also cited was the gospel according to Campanella the catcher. In an oft-told story, pitcher Don Newcombe once crossed up Campanella by throwing a curve when he had signaled for a fastball. Campanella hustled to the mound, and said to Newcombe, "How come you give me a local when I signal for the express?"[32]

Also in that newspaper story, the writer mentioned that Campanella was due in town for a clinic on February 8 and would begin California househunting on the trip. That never happened. Only two days after the story appeared in print, on January 28, 1958, Campanella lay near death in a hospital on Long Island, his athletic body battered by a violent one-car crash. Not only would Campanella never play an inning for the Los Angeles Dodgers, but also he would never play baseball again, and was fortunate to survive.

LATER LIFE

On the night he was injured, Campanella was scheduled to tape a radio promotion in New York for a charitable cause. It was postponed and instead Campanella worked late at his liquor store. Only a short distance from his Long Island home on his usual driving route, Campanella hit a patch of ice on a winding part of the road and crashed head-on into a telephone pole. Campanella thought he was going no more than 35 mph on the S curve, if that, and he did not hit the pole that forcefully. But the accident's result was devastating.

"I just did hit it [the pole], the right front fender crashing against it," Campanella said. "The car bounced off and turned completely over, landing on its right side. I felt the car turning over and the force of it tore my hands from the wheel. The collision knocked me forward and down onto the floor on the passenger's

Campanella's baseball career was cut short by an automobile accident in 1958 that left him in a wheelchair for the rest of his life. Friend and former teammate Don Newcombe shares time with his old catcher.

side of the front seat. I guess my neck hit the dashboard as I plunged. Anyway, my body jackknifed, and I was wedged in under the dash and on the floor. I could feel no pain. In fact, I couldn't feel a thing." Still in the car, Campanella thought, "I'm paralyzed."[33]

Campanella passed out and was taken by ambulance to the hospital. In the middle of the night doctors reviewed X-rays and it became apparent that Campy was paralyzed. The dreadful diagnosis of a broken neck and the fracture and dislocation of two vertebrae caused paralysis from just below Campanella's shoulders to his toes. He underwent immediate surgery to relieve pressure on his spinal cord. The four-hour operation saved Campanella's life.

Doctors did not immediately rule out the possibility of Campanella walking again, but said it might be two months to two years before it was known. "Those first hundred days after the accident were the worst of my life," Campanella said. "I was strapped in bed, unable to move any part of my body except my arms—and those only a little." Three days after the operation, he caught pneumonia and underwent a tracheotomy and his concern shifted from the ability to move to the ability to breathe. "God was good to me. He spared me. I beat the pneumonia and pulled through," he said.[34]

Time dragged in the hospital. As almost anyone in his situation would be, Campanella battled depression during every waking moment. He could not imagine a future and despaired over how swiftly his life had changed. He cried frequently, then turned to the Bible seeking peace. He needed help to find the right place, but sought comfort in the 23rd Psalm.[35]

For months, until April, Campanella's only visitor was his wife. Then he allowed his children to visit. His mother and father came from Philadelphia a day later. Slowly, over three months in that hospital, Campanella made incremental improvements. He would never walk again, but he gradually regained strength, became more mobile in a wheelchair. Ultimately, he became a visible personality again. *Life* magazine, complemented by many photographs, wrote a story about Campy. So did the *Saturday Evening Post*.

Walter O'Malley, known as Scrooge to Brooklyn fans, promised Campanella that he would remain on the Dodgers payroll for life, as a coach if he could walk, in the front office if he could not. When Campanella returned home he was reenergized by an exciting offer. He began broadcasting a radio show called *Campy's Corner* with famous sports announcer Chris Schenkel.

In late winter of 1959, Campanella joined the Dodgers in Vero Beach, Florida, flown by private team plane from New York. His assignment was specific—teach young catcher John Roseboro all that he knew. It was good, useful work, and Campanella played the role of mentor, much as Biz Mackey (with an assist from Josh Gibson) had done for him years before. Later, the Dodgers held a tribute day for Campanella at their temporary new home, the Los Angeles Coliseum, and 93,103 fans attended, still the record turnout for a Major League game. The lights were turned off and spectators held up candles in Campanella's honor. The Dodgers retired his number thirty-nine uniform jersey.

Although Campanella regained some of his strength, additional gloomy times were ahead. Campanella split up with his wife and moved to an apartment in New York City, which he shared with many of his favorite tropical fish. He had a paid attendant, but by 1962 he had given up on the hope of walking again. "I know the score," he said. "My problem is mastering this thing [an electric wheelchair] and I feel I've done a good job. I don't think I can ever be hurt anymore." The pace of get-well cards trickled to near invisibility and the same was true of well-wishers. "Any mature person knows these things can be expected," he said. "It's part of living. Nothing disturbs me anymore. I've got to keep going, not only for my sake, but I know if I keep going it will enourage others like me to keep going, too."[36]

A year later Campanella was sharing his apartment with two of his teenaged children, not only still managing his liquor store, but also managing a seventeen-unit apartment complex he owned. When he had the chance, Campy attended American League games at Yankee Stadium. He said he did not see National League games because the ramps were better for wheelchair users at the stadium than they were at the Polo Grounds. Campanella ended up with his own TV show and traveled when he could, making speeches to boost the attitude of those who suffered similar debilitating injuries. "My big goal is to help others like myself realize they have something to live for," Campanella said. "I feel an example is the best teacher. I want to be a good example."[37]

What was perplexing to many was the delay in enshrining Campanella in the Baseball Hall of Fame. Given his accomplishments, and the widespread view of his abilities, it seemed likely that he would be elected as soon as he became eligible. That did not occur, though. Many questioned any reasoning why. Campanella's final stats were 242 home runs, 856 RBIs, and a .276 lifetime batting average. Worry turned to joy in 1969 when Campy was at last called, selected for residence in Cooperstown along with Stan Musial.

"Nothing could be more satisfying to a diamond devotee than the election of Campy," it was written in the *New York Times*. "The happiest of the Dodgers had been waiting on the threshold for so long that the fear began to grow that he might never make it."[38] About the time of his election, Campanella was chosen to serve on the special baseball committee created to recommend worthy candidates for the hall who had starred in the Negro Leagues.

Campanella remarried. He and wife Roxie moved to Hartsdale in Westchester County. By 1972 he was also working as a bank official and that spring son Roy Jr. graduated from Harvard. Once robust, Campanella's body lost muscle mass and he shrank. Also that year, Campanella was stricken by a pulmonary embolism, a blood clot in the lungs, and was rushed to the hospital unconscious. His life was in jeopardy for a period of time, but by midyear he was traveling again. Before Jackie Robinson died, the two old teammates made peace.

In 1974, a made-for-TV movie was aired based on Campanella's *It's Good to Be Alive* best-selling autobiography. Actor Paul Winfield played Campanella and Lou Gossett played the therapist who helped him most. At the time, Campanella said it was okay with him if people cried when they watched the movie. He said watching it did not disturb him, but reflecting back on many real-life events during the most troubled time of his life did affect him. "I can't say I felt pain when I saw the movie," he said. "But going back and looking at some of the things that happened, well, there were a few tears."[39]

Later, Campanella and Roxie relocated to California, setting up a household in Woodland Hills. Campanella became a regular once more at Dodgers home games and went to work for the team's Community Services Department making speeches. "Like everybody else, I have good days and bad days," Campy said in 1985. "But most of them are good, and if I'm going to a game I almost never have a bad day. Baseball does something for me."[40]

Baseball was the link to his early life, the sport that provided him with a good livelihood, the game that made him nationally known. Baseball played a major role in Campanella's life right up until the moment he died of a heart attack at age seventy-one in his Woodland Hills home on June 26, 1993. The Dodgers flew the American flag at half staff at Chavez Ravine, the ballpark that replaced the Coliseum.

The saddened Dodgers were dealt another blow when Hall of Fame pitcher Don Drysdale also died suddenly soon after. That summer, the team printed a tribute section in a program, announcing that for the rest of the season players would wear a commemorative patch featuring the numbers of both Campanella and Drysdale. A picture of Campanella in his wheelchair, wearing a Dodgers cap and jersey while talking baseball with first baseman Steve Garvey, accompanied comments from current and past Dodgers about the men.

"It's a real loss to baseball and to the world itself," said former Dodger infielder Jim Lefebvre when Campanella died. "It touches all of us. He was one of the finest human beings who ever walked the earth. He was a man who had a lot of respect from a lot of people. He was a real treasure to the game."[41]

During the final years of his life, Campanella visited victims of paralyzing injuries like the one he incurred. After he died, his widow started the Roy and Roxie Campanella Foundation and in its initial years the organization provided $169,000 worth of physical therapy scholarships to needy patients. Roxie's health began to falter from cancer, and she sold the Hall of Famer's sports memorabilia collection. That raised $600,000 more for the foundation before she passed away in 2004.[42] The foundation ensured that long after his death, Roy Campanella, who like Will Rogers never seemed to meet a man he did not like, was still making new friends.

NOTES

1. Roy Campanella, *It's Good to Be Alive* (Boston: Little, Brown and Company, 1959), 36.

2. Campanella, *It's Good to Be Alive*, 55.

3. Campanella, *It's Good to Be Alive*, 57.

4. Campanella, *It's Good to Be Alive*, 65.

5. Ibid.

6. Buck O'Neil, personal interview, December 7, 2005.

7. Monte Irvin with James A. Riley, *Nice Guys Finish First* (New York: Carroll & Graf Publishers, 1996), 87.

8. Ibid.

9. Monte Irvin, personal interview, January 7, 2006.

10. Buck Leonard with James A. Riley, *Buck Leonard: The Black Lou Gehrig* (New York: Carroll & Graf, 1995), 190.

11. Buck O'Neil with Steve Wulf and David Conrads, *I Was Right on Time* (New York: Simon & Schuster, 1996), 153.

12. Campanella, *It's Good to Be Alive*, 94–95.

13. Campanella, *It's Good to Be Alive*, 99.

14. Campanella, *It's Good to Be Alive*, 114.

15. Campanella, *It's Good to Be Alive*, 120–121.

16. O'Neil with Wulf and Conrads, *I Was Right on Time*, 153.

17. Campanella, *It's Good to Be Alive*, 139.

18. Tommy Holmes, *Brooklyn Eagle*, June 27, 1949.

19. Campanella, *It's Good to Be Alive*, 142.

20. Campanella, *It's Good to Be Alive*, 162.

21. Campanella, *It's Good to Be Alive*, 164.

22. Campanella, *It's Good to Be Alive*, 170.

23. Roger Kahn, *The Boys of Summer* (New York: Harper and Row, 1971), 293.

24. Ernie Banks and Jim Enright, *Mr. Cub* (Chicago: Follett Publishing Company, 1971), 90–91.

25. Campanella, *It's Good to Be Alive*, 171.
26. Campanella, *It's Good to Be Alive*, 170.
27. Campanella, *It's Good to Be Alive*, 172–173.
28. Campanella, *It's Good to Be Alive*, 182.
29. *Time*, August 8, 1955.
30. *New York World-Telegram*, January 26, 1957.
31. *St. Louis Globe-Democrat*, January 27, 1957.
32. Vincent X. Flaherty, *Los Angeles Examiner*, January 26, 1958.
33. Campanella, *It's Good to Be Alive*, 21–22.
34. Campanella, *It's Good to Be Alive*, 191.
35. Campanella, *It's Good to Be Alive*, 194, 195.
36. Melvin Durslag, *Los Angeles Examiner*, March 20, 1962.
37. John Brogan, *Philadelphia Bulletin*, March 10, 1964.
38. Arthur Daley, *New York Times*, January 22, 1969.
39. Tony Kornheiser, *Newsday*, February 19, 1974.
40. Bob Oates, *Los Angeles Times*, July 8, 1985.
41. *Associated Press*, June 28, 1993.
42. Bill Shaikin, *Los Angeles Times*, March 15, 2004.

Further Reading

Campanella, Roy, *It's Good To Be Alive*. Boston: Little, Brown and Company, 1959.
Kahn, Roger, *The Boys of Summer*. New York: Harper and Row, 1971.

DON NEWCOMBE
June 14, 1926–

After the Brooklyn Dodgers signed Jackie Robinson, the team went searching for more African American talent. Don Newcombe was the first star black pitcher in the National League and when the Cy Young Award was created in 1956 honoring the best pitcher of each season, Newcombe was the first recipient.

Newcombe was a phenomenal 27–7 one season and in compiling 149 career victories he won 62.3 percent of his games. Newcombe was able to star both in the Negro Leagues and the majors. After retirement, Newcombe became an eloquent spokesman against alcohol consumption and was a very visible community ambassador for the Dodgers in Los Angeles.

☆   ☆   ☆

Many years after Don Newcombe earned the highest honor a pitcher can receive, he was asked what it meant to win the first Cy Young Award ever bestowed. "It was very gratifying," Newcombe said from Los Angeles, where he was a longtime member of the Dodgers community relations staff.[1]

Newcombe was the third African American signed by a Major League team when he put his John Hancock on a contract with the Brooklyn Dodgers and joined their minor league Nashua, New Hampshire affiliate in 1946. Not long afterward, he became the first dominant black starting pitcher in the majors, claiming the National League rookie of the year award and in 1956 the Cy Young Award. Later, it was determined appropriate to give the paramount individual award for pitchers to one hurler in each league, but in the beginning there was just the solo presentation. That in effect meant that the winner of the award named for the winningest pitcher in baseball history was being chosen the best pitcher in the entire sport for that season.

By that 27–7 season, Newcombe was well established in the Dodgers rotation and had become one of the most feared fastball pitchers in the league. The award was a validation and a culmination of a challenging life's journey, a trophy toasting both Newcombe's physical ability and rewarding the triumph of his spirit. He had overcome poverty and discrimination and achieved at a high athletic level despite an addiction to alcohol that disrupted his career and likely wore him out before his time.

EARLY LIFE

Don Newcombe was born in Madison, New Jersey. He grew up in poor circumstances and by the age of eighteen sought a way to make a living in professional baseball. Major League doors were still bolted against black athletes and Newcombe, who had a blistering fastball, and whose six-foot-four, 220-pound size gave him an intimidating presence, broke in with the Newark Eagles of the Negro National League.

A provocative painting on display in the Baseball Hall of Fame in 2006 illustrates a scene the artist claims is the wooing of Newcombe by Eagles owner Effa Manley. She

A one-time Negro Leagues star pitcher, Don Newcombe helped integrate minor league teams along with future Dodger teammate Roy
Campanella, and was a rookie of the year and won the first Cy Young
award in 1956, then given to the top pitcher in the entire game.

is portrayed walking down a staircase into her parlor wearing a red gown slashed thigh
high. The young athlete waiting at a table is a teenaged Newcombe, no match for her
wiles in contract negotiations.

With his muscled bulk and an accompanying scowl, Newcombe possessed a manner that wilted batters even before he threw a 90 mph fastball in their direction. Almost
as a supplemental insult, Newcombe was an extraordinarily fine hitter for a pitcher.
Newcombe made his mark with owner Manley's club very quickly and before he was
out of his teens he had compiled a record of 14–4. Dodger general manager Branch
Rickey was committed to integrating his team and while he spent countless man hours
searching the country for the one man to break through first, Rickey had his minions
follow up with other top African American players they studied. Jackie Robinson broke
the Major League color barrier with the Dodgers, but catcher Roy Campanella and
Newcombe, usually called "Newk" by friends, were on deck.

Newcombe was lucky to be born late enough to make the transition from the Negro
Leagues to the majors, but he did not come along late enough to avoid second-class
citizenship in the game completely. His career straddled the near-end days of the Negro
Leagues and the pioneering days of African Americans in the majors.

Later in life, Newcombe was candid in recognizing his good fortune in coming
along at just the right time to be offered the critical chance as baseball moved toward

integration. "The Negro Leagues were a beginning," Newcombe said, "a chance for a poor kid to get out of the ghetto and a chance to become famous. Even in the Negro Leagues you were famous if you were playing on a Negro League team. It turned out okay for me because I got a chance to play Major League baseball with the Dodgers."[2]

Being a black player anywhere in organized baseball in the late 1940s meant you were not going to slip under the radar. Rickey made it clear he wished to integrate all of baseball and so he sent Newcombe and Campanella to Class B Nashua in the New England League together. The two became roommates and friends, shared experiences—good times and hard times—in the minors, in winter ball in Latin America, and with the Dodgers, for more than a decade.

The Nashua team was managed by Walter Alston, who was just starting what would turn out to be a Hall of Fame managing career over more than twenty seasons in charge of the Dodgers. One game, Alston was ejected in the sixth inning and he turned over the bench duties to Campanella. Nashua trailed by two runs and had a man on base when Campanella told Newcombe to grab a bat and pinch hit.

Laughing at taking orders from his roommate, Newcombe turned to Campanella and said, "Any instructions, Mr. Manager?" Campanella stared back and said, "Yeah, hit one out of here." Newcombe promptly hit a home run to tie the game and Nashua eventually won. There was a lot of teasing and celebrating in the locker room. Alston joked that he would never get thrown out of a game again because he did not want to risk his job. Campanella said, "Aw, Newk did it, not me." And Newcombe responded, "What are you talking about? I would have bunted if you hadn't ordered me to hit one out of the park."[3]

Even while still in the minors Newcombe and Campanella gathered some attention from New York writers because it was apparent that they would soon be members of the Brooklyn club. Newcombe won fourteen games for Nashua in 1946. He won nineteen games for the team in 1947 and then won seventeen games for AAA Montreal in 1948.

The time that Newcombe and Campanella spent in New Hampshire was both pleasant and surprising. At the same time Jackie Robinson was experiencing widespread discrimination and that Negro Leagues players faced racism everyday, the duo was warmly welcomed. The first time Newcombe and Campanella took the field for Nashua as a pitching battery, they were given a standing ovation. They could not believe the reception. Campanella rose from his catcher's squat and visited Newcombe on the mound. "Do you see what I see?" Campy said. "Roy, I'm standing here with you. I see and hear," Newcombe replied. A half century later, Newcombe returned to Nashua for the first time since his two-season stay to be honored during an emotional reunion.[4]

While some newspaper reports of the forties indicate Newcombe had a dangerous curveball and sharp control, others suggested that it took some time for him to harness the accuracy of his throws. Carl Long, who played with the Birmingham Black Barons at the tail end of the Negro Leagues existence, and faced Newcombe in nonprofessional games, said Newk was "loud, big and wild. Newcombe was good, but I would jump on his fastball."[5]

Monte Irvin, another former Newark Eagle who went on to stardom with the New York Giants and reached the Hall of Fame, said the two became friends in New Jersey and shared playing time in Cuba, but Newcombe was still feeling his way as a pitcher.

"He threw very hard, but he was very wild," Irvin said. "But there was a game in Cuba during the winter of 1948–1949 with 40,000 people when he pitched a two-hitter and lost 2–1. He gained his confidence and he gained his control. From then on he became a Major League prospect."[6]

In his earliest minor league seasons, Newcombe thrived on potential. Then he became a pitcher. It was a career track not so different from current day star southpaw Randy Johnson's beginnings.

MAJOR LEAGUE CAREER

In 1949, Newcombe became a regular member of the Dodgers pitching rotation. He was not brought up from the minors until mid-May and was batted around pretty good in his debut relief appearance. Greeted by a standing ovation from many of the black fans in attendance, Newcombe surrendered four hits following a single strikeout and said goodnight early. But when Newcombe took the mound as a starter, he threw a five-hit shutout and flourished from then on, completing the season with a 17–8 record and the rookie of the year award on his resume.

The splendid won-loss record and the nice award made Newcombe quite popular. After the season, he approached a publicist named Irving Rudd, who was known both for his brashness and offbeat schemes, and asked him to become his agent. Rudd was a genius at drumming up attention for sports figures and teams, but was at the beginning of his career. He later made headlines by purposely having the construction crew raise the "Y" in Yonkers Raceway backward, acting as public relations man for the Brooklyn Dodgers boys of summer, and later outfitting middleweight boxer Caveman Lee with a plastic, Flintstones-like club when he battled Marvin Hagler for the title. Initially, Rudd did not know what to do for Newcombe.

Newcombe had been hired as a greeter for a couple of weeks at a clothing store and Rudd's first task was to publicize this. Newcombe, who for some unknown reason called Rudd "Meat," then asked him to become his manager for a 10 percent cut.

"I thought, 'Ten percent of what?' " Rudd said. "Black guys and gals weren't even on television much back then. He was the hottest rookie around, but he wasn't in great demand. He really wanted me as a screener to fend off characters and maybe get him a few bucks for a speaking engagement here and there. I got Newk some endorsements—Jeris hair tonic, Champ hats, some black insurance company—some $10,000 worth of endorsements, which was staggering back then, and then I was approached to book him into a series of exhibitions as a wrestling referee." That did not last long. Rickey pulled the plug on the tour after a short while, ostensibly because he did not like the Dodgers image involved.[7]

Newk's prime Dodger years were from 1949 to 1956. After the rookie of the year campaign, Newcombe had an even better sophomore year, going 19–11. In 1950, the hard-throwing right-hander finished 20–9. It was a great start to what promised to be a long career. However, Newcombe was drafted to serve with the U.S. Army during the Korean War and missed the next two seasons. When he returned to the Dodgers in 1954 he finished only 9–8. Periodically bothered by a sore arm and attempting to regain his rhythm, Newcombe did not regain top form until 1955. He went 20–5 and the Dodgers won their only World Series in Brooklyn. One regular-season Newcombe gem was a one-hitter in a 3–0 shutout of the Chicago Cubs at Wrigley Field. Newcombe faced the minimum of twenty-seven batters and polished off the hosts in less than two hours. The only disappointing aspect of the outing was a pathetically small crowd of 6,686 fans.

The next season was Newcombe's best. His 27–7 record was astonishing and the performance put him in special company. Not only did Newcombe win the National League Most Valuable Player award, but that was also the year baseball decided to honor the late Cy Young by naming its premier pitching award after him. Young had been retired for four decades, but died the year before. Enough time had passed since his playing days for historians to realize Young's feat of winning 511 Major League games would never be approached. Fifty years later that observation is still set in concrete.

Newcombe was not a student of baseball history as a young man and when he won the Cy Young award he said he knew little about the player besides his exceptional capacity for winning. "I knew he won 500 games," Newcombe said. "That seems to be two baseball careers. It's pretty hard to get to 300."[8]

Minnie Minoso, the first black player with the Chicago White Sox, who traveled a different route to the majors from his native Cuba, first saw Newcombe pitch on the tropical island. He added his voice to the chorus that noted how erratic Newcombe could be in those days, but Minoso also said Newcombe posed challenges at the plate.

"Newk gave me lots of trouble," Minoso said. "I couldn't follow the rotation on his pitches. When a hitter cannot follow the rotation, he is in trouble. Newcombe's big problem when he pitched in Cuba was that he was wild. Because of that, few people thought he would ever be the dominant pitcher he later became with the Dodgers."[9]

During the 1950s, with the Dodgers qualifying for the World Series about every other year, Newcombe had the misfortune to go 0–4 in postseason games. Some critics charged that he could not win the big one and that he was someone who choked under pressure. Alston defended Newcombe with emphatic statements like, "Every manager in the majors should have a twenty-seven game winner who chokes up like Newk."[10]

Newcombe had a lot on his plate and even more on his mind during his stay with the Dodgers. Not only did he frequently experience arm miseries that he generally overcame—Campanella referred to Newcombe's "usual sore arm he suffered in the spring"[11]—but also discrimination in many forms still followed black members of the club. This was especially true during spring training in Florida when African American players were housed separately from their white teammates and even in St. Louis during the regular season.

During one spring training trip to Florida, Newcombe feared for his life. He had a dispute going with Fermin Garcia, Newcombe's white Cuban manager from the winter before who had sent him home early. They bumped into one another again in Vero Beach.

"I was still angry," Newcombe said. "Here was a black man arguing with a white man in front of all these people. We were standing by a picket fence, and one guy in the crowd grabbed a picket off that fence, threw it to Garcia and told him to kill me with it. Sam Lacy, a writer for the Baltimore *Afro-American*, grabbed me and got me out of there, and it's a good thing he did. Who knows what that crowd would have done? After that they almost had to spirit me out of town. There was talk that I was going to be lynched and nobody took it lightly." Newcombe said that in the middle of the night a meeting was held involving him, Jackie Robinson, Campanella, Rickey, the mayor, the sheriff, and other Dodger officials, to settle the matter. It was decided that Newcombe would just stay inside the training complex and not venture into town, but he insisted that while the discussions were taking place a plane was waiting on the runway in case the decision went the other way to ship him out.[12]

Even after he had been in the majors for several years, Newcombe said the Dodgers African American players had to stay in the black-only, air-conditioning deprived Adams Hotel in St. Louis for Cardinals' road trips, instead of with the rest of the team in the more modern Chase Hotel. Newcombe had just returned from the army in 1954 and he felt the arrangements had to be challenged.

"Look, I just got back from serving my country for two years," Newcombe said to Robinson, "and I'll be damned if I'm going to put up with this." Newcombe and Robinson took a cab from their hotel to the Chase and met with the manager, asking why the African American players could not board there. "The only reason you men can't stay here is that we don't want you using the swimming pool," the man said. Newcombe said Robinson almost fell out of his chair and replied, "Mister, I don't even know how to swim."

Newcombe said he thought Robinson was fibbing about that because he could do anything athletically. From then on, however, the black Dodgers stayed with the white Dodgers at the Chase. "None of us ever got a room on the side of the pool, though," Newcombe said. "That bigot didn't want us looking at those pretty women in their bikinis. But what he didn't know was that I had women in my room all of the time. Black women, white women, all kinds. That bigot should have come to my room one night and seen what was going on."[13]

The prejudice occasionally got to Newcombe and years later he reflected on how simply trying to play a sport on equal footing with white guys was a constant topic of conversation among the early black players.

"We talked about what our state was from 1947 to 1954," Newcombe said. "What we were going to do about things that were important to us. What we could do as a team or a group. We made significant strides in getting other civil rights people involved and interested in what we were doing."[14]

Some newspapermen, and even other players, formed the opinion that Newcombe was wild off the field even after he had tamed the wildness in his pitching delivery. There was an unease, usually unspoken, often unprinted, that he was troubled. It came out later that Newcombe was an alcoholic, but even decades later Monte Irvin did not think that was Newcombe's flaw.

"Newk didn't have a drinking problem," Irvin said. "He needed a very stern manager. You had to hit him over the head to get his attention. Newk had these moods. He would be asked, 'Why don't you show up on time?' and 'Why don't you follow your roommate's [Campanella] example?' Newk would get a little boisterous, but he only drank beer."[15]

Whatever problems Newcombe faced during the 1940s and 1950s with the Dodgers, he usually brought his A game to the field. He was an anchor in the rotation and in an era when starting pitchers were handed the ball every fourth day and planned to stick around for nine innings, Newk was an above-average mainstay. Once, Newcombe pitched all nine innings in a victory over the Philadelphia Phillies in a double header and then went seven innings more in the second game. Such a performance would be unimaginable these days. "Guys today don't want to pitch seven innings, never mind a double header," Newcombe said.[16]

For all of the good times in Brooklyn—and there were many—Newcombe's many actions off the field left people cold and seemed unexplainable. In hindsight, realizing he was battling the demons of alcoholism, explanations seem more obvious.

Newcombe's showpiece 1956 season, when he notched that brilliant 27–7 throwing record, was not followed up by any other seasonal mark of such substance. A year later he was just 11–12. And in June of 1958, when his record had tumbled to 0–6 with a horrific 7.93 earned run average, the Dodgers traded Newcombe to the Cincinnati Reds. Columnists expressed their sadness, frustration and listed many shoulda-coulda-wouldas in summing up the big guy's decade in Brooklyn with less than the kindest of farewells.

"Don Newcombe has been a man of strange behavior," one scribe wrote. "At times he has displayed pitching ability equaled by few athletes of our time. But he has been a chronic complainer of injury, even the many miseries suspected to exist only in his mind. Most teammates finally despaired of building up his ego."[17]

Another columnist wrote, "One of the top pitchers of the last decade, he has steered a stormy course marked by swiftly changing moments of glory, despondency and quarrels. Don is a moody creature, but basically generous and well-meaning. Never a gladhander, nor unduly diplomatic, he didn't enjoy the popularity he deserved in Brooklyn, not even the year he won twenty-seven games. The gods conspired somehow to get Newk loused up. He gets knocked out of the box in the World Series, walks despondently to his car—and a brash character in the parking lot calls him gutless. Newk shakes him up and the guy sues him for $25,000."[18]

Newcombe was not sure he wanted to report to Cincinnati. A letter from the retired Jackie Robinson encouraged him and suggested it might be for the best. Many athletes of great talent whose time has run its course in one city, revive their careers in another. Such a scenario seemed likely for Newcombe who was only thirty-two and still seemed savvy enough to become a double-figure winner. His new team enjoyed the way Newcombe looked when he made his debut for the Reds against the Cardinals only a few days after the trade. Newcombe stopped the Cards on six hits, winning 6–1. It was his first victory of the season, but Newcombe was undefeated in new surroundings. "As far as I'm concerned, mister," he said to a postgame questioner, "I'm 1–0. The records might say 1–6, but I'm 1–0, wiping the books clean."[19]

The fact that Robinson's letter played so well with Newcombe may have marked a new stage of friendship. The two had not always been the best of friends while teammates. Newcombe and Campanella were always tight, but there was a standoffishness in the relationship between Newcombe and Robinson, although Newcombe greatly respected Robinson for the trials he endured as the first African American in the majors. If there was tension, Newcombe never let it interfere with their roles as teammates, always responding as a protector when Robinson or any other black player needed it.

During one game in the 1950s against the Phillies, opposition players rained insults and slurs on Robinson, who was stationed on third base near their dugout, and on Newcombe as well, using the word "nigger" repeatedly. Robinson traipsed to the mound and said, "Newk, did you hear what that man's saying in the dugout, the guy over there hiding behind the water cooler?" Newcombe replied, "I hear that sonuvabitch, Jack." Robinson said, "Well, what are you gonna do about it?" What Newcombe did was wait until Del Ennis, an above-average hitter, stepped in next. The first pitch fastball plunged Ennis into the dirt and he figured out quite quickly what might be coming next. Instead of charging the mound, however, to start a fight with Newcombe, Ennis called time, went back to the dugout, and had a little chat with someone. The derogatory remarks ceased and years later Ennis informed Newcombe why that still-unnamed guy shut up. "Newk, I said to that SOB if he didn't leave you alone, I was gonna pull his tongue out of his head. I told him that he didn't have to hit off you, I did."[20]

Newcombe played well for the Reds, if not terrifically, going 7–7 over the remainder of that summer. He definitely seemed reinvigorated in 1959, showing a lot of his good stuff in a 13–8 season. It was to be Newcombe's last notable year, however. In 1960, Newcombe was just 4–6 with the Reds and 2–3 with the Cleveland Indians in an American League cameo. And that was it. His big-league career was over after ten seasons and five All-Star games. Newcombe's final won-loss total was 149–90.

LATER LIFE

Long after he retired from baseball, and several years after Newcombe began work-ing for the Dodgers front office in Los Angeles in 1970, he went public about his alcohol addiction. He said he did not even admit how much of a problem he had to himself until 1966. Newcombe used to throw himself into binge drinking of vodka and grape juice, then return home in a rage, yelling, swearing, even hitting his wife. His children cow-ered. One day his wife Billie told him she was taking the children and leaving. At that moment, Newcombe saw the light in a way he had never been able to before. He fell to his knees as if praying, put one hand on son Don Jr.'s head, and took an oath. He swore he would never again take a drink. "I was ashamed," Newcombe said. "I was ashamed where I had allowed alcohol to lead me."[21]

Once reticent to admit or discuss his problem, Newcombe stayed sober and worked for the National Institute on Alcohol Abuse and Alcoholism and the National Clearinghouse for Alcohol Information. He worked with professional athletes who had drinking problems, such as former Dodgers pitcher Bob Welch, and told stories about his own difficulties. Because of alcohol, he said, he lost his house and a business and went into debt. Once, Newcombe said, he passed out in a New York alley with $3,000 in cash on him, content to spend the night on the ground until a teammate found him.[22]

Newcombe, who later admitted to being an alcoholic and spent decades working with the Dodgers' community service department, was friendly with New York Yankee star pitcher Whitey Ford.

Newcombe went public with a vengeance. He preached about the evils of alcohol to hundreds of thousands of young people. In his candor he admitted that alcohol, not any other obstacle, cost him years of playing time. "Alcohol shortened my career by at least five or six years," Newcombe said in 1976. "It ended my desire to get in shape and stay in shape. When I was young, I'd run three hours a day. Then it was down to one hour. Then a half an hour. Finally, I didn't want to run at all. What fastball can a pitcher pitch when he's out of shape? I never drank the night before I pitched, but I drank every other night."[23]

Although Newcombe kept his drinking under wraps as a player, his weight did fluctuate mightily, in the end going up on the charts like a good stretch in the stock market. He broke in at 220 pounds, played successfully at 230 pounds, then inched up to 240 pounds, and finally at retirement was carrying 250 pounds. From his own description about lack of training, it was logical that Newcombe was unable to pitch as well as he approached thirty-five.

Newcombe said he began drinking more heavily in the 1950s because he was scared of flying. He smuggled whiskey on board planes to soothe his nerves. After retiring from the majors and going back to New Jersey following a one-year stint playing professionally in Japan, Newcombe bought a night club. It was a big mistake. He used to drink regularly with the customers. Once he set himself straight Newcombe felt he had to make up for lost years. He felt a need to inform the unsuspecting that alcohol is "poison. I owe something to society. I shortchanged society. I'm trying to repay it as though I were a damned criminal. I've never been scared of anything in my life except one thing: alcohol. You can be given a second chance if you give life a second chance."[24]

As a young man, Newcombe said he pitched with anger. It was his answer to the racism directed at players in a harsh world, but he harmed himself with his drinking. After Newcombe gave up liquor, he also seemed to gain a clearer perspective on life. Besides working with the Dodgers to promote the team and baseball, Newcombe worked as a vice president of a savings and loan association, directed the National Alliance of Businessmen's youth programs, and served on the vice president's task force on youth motivation. Newcombe always remembered the old days shared with Campanella and Robinson, however, and how as the first blacks with the Dodger organization they sat around late at night talking about what they might face in the majors. They knew there would be provocations, but they pledged to ignore what negative incidents might occur with the best dignity they could muster.

Years later, Hank Aaron, the all-time home-run leader, who followed the trio into the big leagues by a few seasons, called them his heroes. "My little contributions could never compare with those of Jackie and Don and the other pioneers," Aaron said. Only a few weeks before he was assassinated in Memphis, civil rights leader Martin Luther King Jr. visited Newcombe's house and said something Newcombe had always hoped was true. Aaron reported that King said, "Don, you and Jackie and Roy will never know how easy you made it to do my job." Newcombe always wanted to believe that his efforts had made a difference and King's comment must have been a special blessing. "I'm sure," Aaron said, "that hearing those words made it all seem worthwhile to Don a thousand times over."[25]

In 1994, Newcombe, who criticized many big-name athletes for taking beer sponsorship money, actually sued Adolph Coors Brewing Co. for $100 million, claiming the manufacturer used an old baseball photograph of him in a magazine ad to make it seem as if he endorsed the product. Coors said its advertising agency told the company it was original art.

When Newcombe returned to Nashua and the community that had treated him so well as a young man for the special tribute in 1997, he was in his seventies. Robinson had long since passed away and Campanella had been dead for four years. But Newcombe did not overlook them on his day. "I'm proud to say, 'I'm part of your legacy, Jackie Robinson,' " Newcombe said. "I'm proud to say, 'I'll never forget you, Roy, wherever you are.' "[26] And the big man who acted so tough when he confronted discrimination in society and when he pitched against savvy hitters, let the tears run down his face.

NOTES

1. Lew Freedman, personal interview with Don Newcombe, *Anchorage Daily News*, November 11, 1992.

2. Ross Forman, *Sports Collectors Digest*, June 3, 1994.

3. Roy Campanella, *It's Good to Be Alive* (Boston: Little, Brown and Company, 1959), 121–122.

4. Lois Shea, *Boston Globe*, April 15, 1997.

5. Carl Long, personal interview, January 11, 2006.

6. Monte Irvin, personal interview, January 7, 2006.

7. Harvey Frommer, *Rickey & Robinson: The Men Who Broke Baseball's Color Barrier* (New York: Macmillan Publishing, 1982), 169–170.

8. Freedman, Newcombe, personal interview, *Anchorage Daily News*.

9. Minnie Minoso with Herb Fagen, *Just Call Me Minnie* (Champaign, IL: Sagamore Publishing, 1994), 36.

10. Jimmy Powers, *New York Daily News*, October 18, 1956.

11. Campanella, *It's Good to Be Alive*, 12.

12. Hank Aaron with Lonnie Wheeler, *I Had a Hammer: The Hank Aaron Story* (New York: HarperPaperbacks, 1992), 137–138.

13. Aaron with Wheeler, *I Had a Hammer*, 123–124.

14. Charlie Vascellaro, *Hank Aaron: A Biography* (Westport, CT: Greenwood Press, 2005), 51.

15. Irvin, personal interview.

16. Freedman, Newcombe, personal interview, *Anchorage Daily News*.

17. Dave Condon, *Chicago Tribune*, June 18, 1958.

18. Melvin Durslag, *Los Angeles Examiner*, June 17, 1958.

19. Bob Broeg, *St. Louis Post-Dispatch*, July 19, 1958.

20. David Falkner, *Great Time Coming* (New York: Touchstone, 1996), 225–226.

21. Rodney Foo, *Gannett News Service*, July 22, 1981.

22. Ibid.

23. Dan Coughlin, *Cleveland Press*, January 30, 1976.

24. Ibid.

25. Aaron with Wheeler, *I Had A Hammer*.

26. Shea, *Boston Globe*.

Further Reading

Falkner, David, *Great Time Coming*. New York: Touchstone Books, 1995.
Forman, Ross, *Sports Collectors Digest*, June 3, 1994.

LARRY DOBY
December 13, 1923–June 18, 2003

Larry Doby became the first African American player in the American League when he broke in with the Cleveland Indians in 1947 and also became the second black manager in baseball history when he took over the Chicago White Sox for part of the 1977 season.

Doby began playing baseball professionally in 1943 for the Newark Eagles and made an impact with his skills in the Negro Leagues before owner Bill Veeck brought him to the Indians in 1947 as the second black in the majors and first in the American League. Doby was hitting .458 with Newark when he went straight to the Indians' outfield. Doby was a seven-time All Star for Cleveland and led the league in home runs twice.

☆   ☆   ☆

It was one step behind. That was Larry Doby's baseball career. He might have been the first twice, but both times he was the second. Americans have always had difficulty assimilating seconds in their minds. They know how to celebrate firsts, know how to praise breakthroughs, know how to treat men who achieve a barrier-breaking feat as somebody special.

The second one through the ring of fire? They're not sure. Well, some-one has already done it, what's the big deal? It's great to make it to the World Series, but only the winners are feted with a parade. The runner-up is seen as first among also-rans. Americans simply have a much larger degree of trouble with rarity than they do uniqueness. The "only" appeals to them. The "second" bores them.

Jackie Robinson, the first African American in the major leagues in the twentieth century, is remembered by all. Larry Doby, the second black player in the major leagues, is over-looked by many. Only a tiny percent-age of the fans who know that Frank

The first African American player in the American League with the Cleveland Indians in 1947, Doby swung a big bat and was a seven-time All Star.

Robinson was the first black manager realize that Doby was the second. There has been a certain cruelty of fate toying with Doby's baseball legacy. He was the second banana on the movie marquee. He was the next of many to widen the tunnel through which the famous firsts wiggled through. It is a strange place in history to occupy, looking over the shoulder of a pioneer not once, but twice.

Yet Doby, too, was a pioneer. He was the first black player in the American League. At a time when no one knew how common African Americans would become as managers, he ascended to that top management level with the White Sox. A man very different in personality than Jackie Robinson, Doby's determination was quieter, more innerly directed. If Jackie Robinson wore his ferocity on his sleeve, then Doby wore his commitment under his cap. There was no easy path for black ballplayers in the 1940s and 1950s, but it seemed as if it was tougher for Doby than for many of the rest of his generation.

While Indians owner Bill Veeck had his heart in the right place, wishing to give black players an opportunity in the majors, integration moved at a slower pace than anticipated. And unlike Branch Rickey, the Dodgers president and general manager who signed Jackie Robinson, and who also paved the way for acceptance with employees, newspapermen, and the public, Veeck pretty much just suited Doby up and inserted him into the lineup. Robinson was more mature, had seen more of life. Doby was younger, still uncertain of his abilities. Rickey ran interference for Robinson. Veeck counseled Doby, but left him more on his own.

Mustering his inner resolve, Doby still emerged as a Hall of Fame player. He put up with a lot, endured much, but conquered all. His entree to the Hall of Fame was delayed by decades, however. Doby was not selected as a member until long after his retirement. When the moment came, Doby did reflect on being second to Jackie Robinson. "It's not bad being in the background I'm in," Doby said. "Being second ain't all that bad, baby."[1]

EARLY LIFE

Lawrence Eugene Doby was born in Camden, South Carolina, the only child of Etta and David (who drowned when Larry was eight) Doby, and although baseball fans seem to forget, he actually lived in the town until he was fifteen, developing a southern accent in his speech. The neighborhood was known as the "Black Bottom." Many identify Doby as being from New Jersey, but throughout his life he corrected those making the assumption. The family moved to Paterson, New Jersey in 1938 and that is where his athletic skills evolved.

The Doby family had deep roots in the South, but much of the detail was obscured because earlier generations grew into adulthood as slaves. In a biography of Doby it was speculated that his ancestors were taken from West Africa sometime between 1619 and 1808. One Doby emerged as a free man in the years after the Civil War. The ballplaying Doby attended integrated Eastside High School in Paterson, an industrialized city much different from South Carolina. Doby was a superb athlete, winning eleven varsity letters in football, basketball, baseball, and track at a high school that had a sterling academic reputation. Near the end of high school, Doby was playing baseball on three semipro teams at once. He spent some time studying at Virginia Union college, where he hoped to train as a teacher and coach.

Doby made his debut with the Newark Eagles of the Negro Leagues in 1943, but was drafted and assigned to the Navy. There was much to question when recruits were

LARRY DOBY   111

separated by race from the start. Doby was serving in the Navy when he heard a radio broadcast announce the Dodgers 1945 signing of Jackie Robinson. The implications were obvious to him immediately. "Then I felt I had a chance to play Major League baseball," Doby said. "Everybody had said to me that I could. I forgot about going back to college."[2]

When Doby was released from the Navy after two-and-a-half years, he rejoined the Eagles, where one of his teammates was the outstanding outfielder Monte Irvin. Doby was still in his early twenties and had not clearly defined a position on the diamond for himself.

In his Newark rookie year, Doby, then playing second base, faced the Homestead Grays and coped with a big Homestead catcher chattering away to disrupt concentration at the plate. After Doby hit safely in his first at bat, Josh Gibson peered from his mask and said, "Well, you hit that fastball pretty good kid. Now let's see how you do with the curve." Doby got another hit. His third time up, Gibson made more chit-chat, asking him where he was from. Doby replied, " 'None of your damn business! Just call for the pitches!' That shut him up, but it was also the last time Josh told me what was coming."[3]

Such outbursts were out of character for Doby, who was soft-spoken and was not a troublemaker. Indeed, one writer called him "normally a meek" man.[4] Doby was a raw talent, and as baseball changed, opening its rosters to black players, he was also well positioned. Doby was not too old, yet had a Newark track record to show off to potential big-league scouts.

"Larry Doby was a kid playing second base," said Buck O'Neil, then managing the Kansas City Monarchs. "He was kind of timid, but the tools were there. What he could do was hit, throw, field and run. He would have been a top second baseman if he hadn't moved to the outfield."[5]

Much later, after completing his Major League career, Doby reenvisioned his younger self, fresh out of the Navy, hopeful of a chance at the big-time. He was optimistic, a player on the way up, and someone whose idealism was still strong. There was something pure about the Newark experience. "I had the most fun," Doby said. "I played for all the right reasons. I loved the game and I will never forget those days."[6]

Irvin, who would also be selected for the Hall of Fame after a career that featured a World Series championship with the New York Giants, was an admirer of Doby and spotted him as a can't-miss player. Irvin happened to see Doby in an Eastside game and said, "When I saw that swing I knew all the stories about this kid did not exaggerate. He was going to be a star, somewhere, some day. He had competitive fire. He was big and he was strong and he could hit the ball a ton. He was the American League's first black and he had a very, very tough road to travel."[7]

Minnie Minoso, who broke the color line with the Chicago White Sox, also had an early glimpse of Doby in Newark. Doby, said Minoso, was notable for his presentation on and off the field, an interesting mix that did not always endear him to opposing players. "He played the game so aggressively," Minoso said, describing Doby as a friend. "On the bases he was such an aggressive slider. He was a rough, tough guy who wouldn't let anyone push him around. If you didn't mess with Larry, he was just a quiet, elegant man who could play baseball well. If you overstepped your bounds with him, he could let you have it.

"Larry also had lots of style. Good looking, well dressed, he seemed to tower over everyone. When you looked at him you would say to yourself that this is a guy who belongs on a poster board. No one ever looked better in a baseball uniform."[8]

MAJOR LEAGUE CAREER

Doby was six feet tall and weighed about 180 pounds as a player. When Bill Veeck bought the Indians and tried to turn them into a pennant winner quickly, he saw Jackie Robinson generate big crowds for Brooklyn and make a difference on the field. Veeck knew that the Negro Leagues were loaded with players who could achieve in the majors if given a chance. Veeck went after Doby as his first hire. Veeck was even gracious enough to pay Newark owner Effa Manley $10,000 for Doby's services with a bonus of $10,000 if he made it. Most of the white owners ignored black players' connections and stole them from their former teams.

Robinson spent a season with Montreal, the Dodgers' AAA farm team. He spent spring training with the Dodgers and then went north with the club. Veeck signed Doby about three months after Robinson made good with Brooklyn and brought Doby directly to the majors. At a press conference, Veeck told reporters, "Robinson has proved to be a real big leaguer. So I wanted to get the best of the available Negro boys while the grabbing was good. Why wait? Within ten years Negro players will be in regular service with big league teams, for there are many colored players with sufficient capabilities to make the majors."[9]

The rushed circumstances made Doby nervous. He did not know anyone with the Indians except Lou Jones, the scout who brought him to the team, but he did appreciate Veeck's backing. Veeck told manager Lou Boudreau to find a place for Doby, and Veeck let Boudreau, Doby, and the players work out the racial dynamics. Not, though, before making one clubhouse speech. Veeck gathered his players and let them know where he stood. There would be no racial slurs, he said and if anyone used the word "nigger, well, you can leave this room right now because Larry Doby is going to be a bigger star than any of you."[10]

There was one problem. Boudreau, the player-manager, did not know how to use Doby, even if the guy had been hitting over .400 in Newark. Doby arrived as a second baseman, but All-Star Joe Gordon held down that spot. Perhaps in the outfield? Maybe at first base? Doby did not have a background at first and when Boudreau decided to start him there one game, Doby had to scramble for a mitt. Neither of the team's first basemen would lend him a glove.

The locker room and dugout were cold places for Doby. The introductory handshakes were less than enthusiastic. Doby said later some players refused to shake hands. Several players looked at the floor when they met him. Some worried about job security. Some, it was obvious, were not liberals on race mixing. At that introductory press conference, Boudreau said, "race, creed and color are not factors in baseball success."[11] However, no one took Boudreau seriously when he called Doby's acquisition "a routine baseball purchase."[12] Such nonchalance was farfetched.

The local Cleveland newspapers editorialized in favor of Veeck's move, but the owner also received about 20,000 racist hate letters, not something that much bothered the showman promoter who had for years been interested in integrating baseball. Doby said he sat down with Veeck before meeting the other Indians for a pep talk. Veeck told him to be careful, not to become embroiled in disputes on the field with umpires or other players. If this was not as formal a rule as Rickey laid on Robinson, it was close. Don't rock the boat was the message, since, after all, Doby's mere presence was guiding the ship into heavy weather. When Doby first met Veeck, the usually informal owner insisted he call him Bill. Doby said Veeck always called him Lawrence and he called Veeck William.

"He made it very comfortable for me," Doby said of Veeck. "He sat and talked with me and told me things, you know a list of things you could and couldn't do—and most things on the list were things you could not do."[13]

Veeck later said that Rickey was lucky to be affiliated with a team in Brooklyn, a cosmopolitan northern community attached to New York City that was not racially explosive. Veeck did not know what the reception to Doby would be in Cleveland. "If Jackie Robinson was the ideal man to break the color line, Brooklyn was also the ideal place," Veeck said. "I wasn't that sure about Cleveland." That was one reason why Veeck announced Doby's signing on a road trip to Chicago.[14]

Veeck, who said he was as close to Doby as any player who played on his Major League teams, said he later decided—too late—that Doby was not the right person to integrate the American League. Doby's upbringing in New Jersey had shielded him from much prejudice and Veeck wondered if he did Doby a disservice by putting him into controversial circumstances.

"Prejudice was something he knew existed, something which he had accommo-dated himself to in his youth if only in the knowledge that it was going to keep him out of organized baseball," Veeck said. "He had not been bruised as a human being, though.

Larry Doby looks for a fly ball in the bright sunshine. After starting his career in the Negro Leagues, the outfielder made his mark with the Indians and Chicago White Sox and also became the second black manager with the White Sox in 1977.

He had not had his nose rubbed in it. It hit him late in life. It hit him at a time he thought he had it licked. And it hit him hard."[15]

Not only did Doby feel unwelcome among his teammates, but also frequently wondered where he stood with Boudreau. He could not eat with or stay with his teammates on the road in many locations. During exhibitions against minor league teams the next season, Doby was booed. In Houston, he had difficulty getting a cab to the ballpark.

"Larry was not a man to shake off those earlier slights and insults easily," Veeck said. "He was always very sensitive. With all of that, his inner turmoil was such a constant drain on him that he was never able to realize his full potential. Not to my mind, at any rate. If Larry had come up just a little later, when things were just a little better, he might very well have become one of the greatest players of all time."[16]

Veeck said that some teammates behaved poorly toward Doby, but that he sent them to faraway places in trades. Joe Gordon, the star second baseman who could have been most threatened by Doby's arrival, was the friendliest. When things were uncomfortably strained in the clubhouse early on, Gordon broke the ice and invited Doby to play catch with him. It was both a gesture of camaraderie to the new guy—saying he was just like anyone else—and a symbolic gesture to the rest of the Indians. There is an oft-repeated story that Doby struck out in poor fashion soon after joining the team, returned to the dugout and lowered his head into his hands in despair. And that only a few minutes later his disappointment was interrupted by a grinning Gordon saying that he, too, had struck out. Another indication of solidarity. Veeck perpetuated the story, saying it was the nicest thing he ever heard of in sports, yet there really was never any on-the-record proof that Gordon had struck out on purpose to make Doby feel better, as Veeck suggested. Veeck said he never asked Gordon directly if he did so.

Doby was hardly used in 1947, participating in only twenty-nine games and batting only thirty-two times. However, Veeck did quickly turn the Indians into winners and Doby was a key member of the team in 1948 when the Tribe captured the World Series. He batted .301 that season and also launched a home run that won game four in the Series.

Doby's home run gave the Indians a 2–1 victory and put the decision in the win column for hurler Steve Gromek. When the game ended, Gromek and Doby hugged in celebration. Their picture was taken and flashed around the world. Not merely a good sports photograph capturing the moment, the fact that Gromek was white and Doby was black focused a huge spotlight on the photo. It was the first time black and white baseball players were photographed hugging one another. The action and the photo engendered phenomenal reaction. Some considered it a positive expression of brotherhood, others responded with hate mail.

A half century after the game, Gromek said in his mind the hug was blown out of proportion, he was just reacting naturally. "Color was never an issue with me," Gromek said. "Doby won the game for me. I was happy. I always got along well with him. He won a lot of games for me with his bat and glove."[17]

Doby's thoughts were similar. "It wasn't planned out for us to do," he said. "We were just two happy people fortunate enough to win."[18]

The hug said more about America in 1948 than it did about the participants. Both men did what came naturally in the situation. The rest of the country was busy reacting and overreacting.

Doby played thirteen years in the major leagues, retiring after the 1959 season. He stayed with the Indians through the 1955 season, but then split his remaining years between the White Sox, Tigers, and again the Indians. In all, he batted .283 with 253 home runs and 970 RBIs in 1,533 games, the vast majority of them as an outfielder after those beginnings as a second baseman. During his first spring training with the Indians in 1948, the team arranged to have long-retired centerfielder Tris Speaker work on fielding with Doby. Speaker is regarded as one of the greatest fielding outfielders of all time.

Although at various times it was noted that Doby put up with the same type of prejudicial guff that Jackie Robinson did, author Joseph Thomas Moore, a professor of history at Montclair State College in New Jersey and Doby's biographer, ran into a confounding situation. While doing research and interviews for his Doby book, Moore could find no white men who admitted having any prejudice. "Therefore they could not talk about how they had changed over the years," Moore said, "or how they had tried to change. If nobody was racially prejudiced, then there was no problem. And if there was no problem, why did Doby have to break a color line to play in the American League?"[19]

Midway through the 1948 season, Veeck signed legendary Negro Leagues pitcher Satchel Paige. The forty-two-year-old rookie roomed on the road with Doby. Doby had nothing against Paige, but they were different types of men. Doby was more introspective, Paige more outgoing. Paige was also set in his ways. He brought an electric stove into the room and cooked catfish. Doby hated catfish and the smoke and aroma drove him nuts. However, the Indians were a more racially harmonious club in 1948, even sharing songs in the shower with a quartet of Doby, Jim Hegan, Eddie Robinson, and Paige. The activity was "an expression of team unity that no one could have imagined" when Doby first joined the team, Moore wrote.[20]

When the Indians won the World Series, the city partied with 200,000-person viewership along a ten-mile parade route and Doby and his wife Helyn were honored back home in Paterson. Yet Doby was still frequently reminded that he was an African American, not just an American. He had trouble buying a home in the neighborhood he wished to live in without the intervention of the mayor. Teammates watched *Amos 'n Andy* on television and thoughtlessly laughed at racially stereotyped jokes in front of him.

A movie was made to capitalize on the Indians success and Doby had a small part in *The Kid from Cleveland*. One scene mimicked the supposed Doby-Gordon "real-life" strikeout empathy. The relationship between Doby and some teammates may have matured with his acceptance, but Doby was never a party animal who spent his free time in nightclub haunts. He was not a prankster, but a more serious man. Some players were not close to Doby because of who he was, but others kept their distance because of how he was. It was not beyond some sportswriters of the day to call Doby a loner who was sort of estranged from his teammates. He did not like the term.

"I think 'loner' is an unfair word to describe anybody," he said. "I needed my privacy to deal with some of the insults that were directed at me because of my race. That's how I handled the insults, in private. If I had stayed in the clubhouse, and spoken about my feelings, I think the writers would have called me 'militant.' I felt that they had me in a no-win situation."[21]

Doby was a seven-time All Star, who led the American League in home runs twice, in 1952 and 1954, and in RBIs in 1954. He wielded a big bat in the heart of the order, but it was all-around talent, just as Buck O'Neil had noticed years before, that made him a weapon capable of hurting opposing teams even when he was not a hot hitter.

Loner or not, Doby did not always seem to have a wide circle of people to share things with besides his family. Once, in thinking back to that turbulent, breakthrough year of 1947, Willie Mays said that Jackie Robinson seemed to have more aid from white teammates like Pee Wee Reese, Gil Hodges, and Ralph Branca. "But Larry didn't have anybody."[22]

In July of 1954, during a regular-season game against the Washington Senators, Doby made what might have been the greatest catch of his career in Cleveland's vast Municipal Stadium. The Indians led 5–3, and Doby was playing shallow against light-hitting Tom Umphlett. However, Umphlett got hold of one of hurler Art Houtteman's tosses and propelled it toward the wall in deep left-center. Doby ran back, clawed his way up the fence to a secondary five-foot barrier, and thrust his glove out. He caught the ball, bounced off the wall, came down. Teammate Al Smith swiftly grabbed the ball from him and fired to first for a near double play. Broadcaster Dizzy Dean, the one-time fabulous fireballer, was nearly overcome with disbelief by Doby's catch. "That was the greatest catch I ever saw," Dean said, "as a player or as a broadcaster."[23]

The Indians won 111 games in 1954 to beat out the New York Yankees for the pennant, and entered the World Series heavily favored, only to fall to the Giants. This was the World Series Mays made what is often considered the best catch in the history of mankind (Dizzy Dean notwithstanding). Mays tracked down a 460-shot off the bat of Vic Wertz with an over-the-shoulder grab, then turned in a single motion and threw toward the infield. Doby had to double back on the base paths to avoid being thrown out.

When Doby was traded to the Chicago White Sox after the 1955 season, he did not leave behind all friends in Cleveland. Some newspaper reporters were not his biggest fans and were often his critics. Sportswriter Franklin Lewis said Doby never lived up to his potential and that he thought of himself as the symbol of blacks in the American League.

Doby bristled at Lewis' characterizations. "I was looked on as a black man, not as a human being," he said, "a gentleman that would carry himself in a way that people would respect. I did feel a responsibility to the black players who came after me, but that was a responsibility, basically, to people, not just to black people. I never thought of myself as a symbol."[24]

So much of the dispute seemed enmeshed in the word "symbol." But Doby was a symbol for black Americans. It is odd that the word "symbol" was seen as a dirty word rather than one that offered encouragement for African Americans in baseball seeking better opportunities.

LATER LIFE

When Doby retired as a player, he stayed in the game. He worked for the White Sox as a scout, worked for various teams as a coach, then hooked up with the Montreal Expos as a scout. When Veeck bought the White Sox, he was loyal, hiring Doby, and ultimately made him the second black manager.

Doby actually thought he might get his chance to manage with Montreal after he became Gene Mauch's hitting coach in 1971. Mauch became a big fan. Mauch thought Doby was the rare star who could communicate well with players of all capabilities.[25]

In October of 1972, with his eyesight failing, and diabetes ravaging his body, Jackie Robinson threw out the first pitch at a World Series game. Doby hung out with Robinson at the airport before flying home. "He had not lost any spirit," Doby said. "He wasn't looking for sympathy. He still had that toughness in him." Nine days later Robinson died. Doby was one of six pallbearers at the funeral.[26]

The Indians wooed Doby back to Cleveland for the 1974 season. Ken Aspromonte was fizzling as Indians manager, but when he was fired in 1975, Doby, who had managed five seasons of winter ball to beef up his credentials, was stunned when the team chose Frank Robinson to become the new manager and the sport's first African American manager over him. Robinson fired Doby, who went back to the Expos, where he was passed over for the manager's job. Then Doby landed with the White Sox again in 1977 after Veeck bought the team for a second time.

Doby began the season as a coach under Bob Lemon, like Veeck, another compatriot from Cleveland in 1948. But when the White Sox slumped, Veeck fired Lemon on June 30 and replaced him with Doby. Doby had achieved one of his life's ambitions. However, the White Sox did not improve much on his watch and to his deep disappointment Veeck fired him at the end of the year. It was probably the only schism between them in a lifetime of friendship. Veeck said he deeply regretted doing it and said Doby might not have been given a completely fair chance. "I did not think Larry was particularly outstanding, nor did I think he was particularly bad," Veeck said years later.[27]

Doby performed some minor league instructional hitting work, then joined the New Jersey Nets' National Basketball Association franchise front-office staff. He also worked with Major League Properties' Former Player Cross Licensing Program. In 1995, Doby joined the staff of the American League as a special assistant to the president. For many years, Doby was considered a candidate for the Hall of Fame, but he was never selected by the regular writer voters. His case passed on to the Veterans Committee, where he was not immediately embraced either. Then, in March of 1998, it was announced that the Veterans Committee had chosen Doby for the hall. His selection elated Doby. "This is just a tremendous feeling," Doby said. "Fifty-one years ago [when he was a rookie] I never thought this type of situation would come about."[28]

In his later years, Doby received several honors. Being elected to the Baseball Hall of Fame was the big one. However, in July of 1994, the Indians retired Doby's number fourteen playing jersey. In May of 1997, Doby's original hometown of Camden, South Carolina named a baseball field in his honor and held a special day for Doby. He had not visited in twenty-five years. "I've never lost sight of where I came from," Doby said at the event. "I always let people know I come from Camden, South Carolina."[29]

In June of 1997, the Texas Rangers hosted a Larry Doby tribute at The Ballpark at Arlington. Governor George W. Bush, the team's former owner, and on his way to a bigger job as president of the United States, proclaimed it Larry Doby Day across Texas. On that occasion, when they had been married for fifty-one years, Helyn Doby said her husband had rarely explicitly told her how much stress he was under and what types of insults were thrown his way. But she knew. "It was really rough on him," she said. "He didn't say much, but I knew what he had to go through."[30]

Larry Doby had to wait a long time to be fully appreciated, but recognition did come during his lifetime. When Doby died of cancer at age seventy-nine on June 18, 2003, he seemed a fully contented man, aware of his contribution to baseball—and American—history.

"I was told by Veeck what it meant for others who would follow," Doby said in 1994. "My conduct had to be unquestionable. It was part of being a pioneer. I thought more about the historical aspects after I was in the league three or four years. When you don't have hatred or bitterness in yourself, you can defeat those people who do by performing well. Then they have to worry, because you've defeated their thinking in trying to defeat you."[31]

NOTES

1. C. L. Brown, *Cleveland Plain-Dealer*, July 27, 1998.
2. Joseph Thomas Moore, *Pride Against Prejudice* (New York: Praeger Publishers, 1988), 29.
3. Mark Ribowsky, *The Power and the Darkness* (New York: Simon & Schuster, 1996), 267.
4. Ibid.
5. Buck O'Neil, personal interview, December 7, 2005.
6. Jerry Izenberg, *Newark Star-Ledger*, June 19, 2003.
7. Ibid.
8. Minnie Minoso with Herb Fagen, *Just Call Me Minnie: My Six Decades in Baseball* (Champaign, IL: Sagamore Publishing, 1994), 34.
9. United Press International, July 3, 1947.
10. Terry Pluto, *Akron Beacon-Journal*, April 20, 1997.
11. United Press International.
12. Ibid.
13. Gerald Eskenazi, *Bill Veeck: A Baseball Legend* (New York: McGraw-Hill Book Company, 1988), 40.
14. Bill Veeck with Ed Linn, *Veeck—As in Wreck* (Chicago: University of Chicago Press, 1962), 175.
15. Veeck with Linn, *Veeck—As in Wreck*, 177.
16. Veeck with Linn, *Veeck—As in Wreck*, 179.
17. Bob Dolgan, *Cleveland Plain-Dealer*, April 26, 1998.
18. Brown, *Cleveland Plain-Dealer*.
19. Moore, *Pride Against Prejudice*, 54.
20. Moore, *Pride Against Prejudice*, 79.
21. Moore, *Pride Against Prejudice*, 98.
22. Associated Press, June 19, 2003.
23. Moore, *Pride Against Prejudice*, 102–103.
24. Moore, *Pride Against Prejudice*, 110–111.
25. Moore, *Pride Against Prejudice*, 131–132.
26. Moore, *Pride Against Prejudice*, 133.
27. Moore, *Pride Against Prejudice*, 161.
28. Hal Bodley, *USA Today*, March 4, 1998.
29. *USA Today*, May 23, 1997.
30. Kelly D. Patterson, *Arlington Morning News*, June 22, 1997.
31. Rod Allee, *The Record* (Hackensack, NJ), July 14, 1994.

Further Reading

Moore, Joseph Thomas, *Pride Against Prejudice*. New York: Praeger Publishers, 1988.
Pluto, Terry, *Akron Beacon-Journal*, April 20, 1997.
Veeck, Bill, with Ed Linn, *Veeck—As in Wreck: The Autobiography of Bill Veeck*. Chicago, IL: University of Chicago Press, 2001.

SATCHEL PAIGE

July 7, 1906–June 8, 1982

Satchel Paige was a unique character on the American landscape, the most famous player in the Negro Leagues, who with his talent and talkative personality came closest among black stars to transcending the nation's racial divide. When he was past forty, Paige became the first African American pitcher in the majors, and the first to pitch in a World Series. In his mid-forties he made a Major League All-Star team.

Although record-keeping in the Negro Leagues was vague at best, Paige claimed to pitch in about 2,500 games and said he won about 2,000 of them in a pitching career that began in the 1920s and did not conclude until the 1960s. In 1971, he was the first of the black stars kept from the majors in their prime by discrimination to be inducted into the Baseball Hall of Fame.

He was a magician with a baseball, a master of sleight of hand, his motion a baffling combination of three-card monte switcheroos and high kicking chorus line thrusts. Satchel Paige was so mesmerizing before he released the ball that batters had as much difficulty tracking its flight from the mound as they did pinpointing a buzzing mosquito. It was always a challenge to get a hold of either.

Paige was a pitcher, a competitor, and a mixture of trickster wizard and athletic marvel. He was ageless and of the moment and quite possibly the greatest showman who ever played high level baseball in North America. The best hitters could not hit him. The best pitchers could not beat him. He put more miles on his body and arm than an aging Greyhound bus, but never seemed to age himself. He pitched in the big time and in the small time, in steel stadiums, in downtowns, all over the land, and all over Latin America, too. He pitched on sandlot diamonds where the walls were rickety wood and the benches, too. And everywhere he traveled, for more than forty years, Paige proved himself to doubters, pleased audiences seeking to see a legend in the flesh, and struck out men older, younger, and in-between who possessed the temerity to think they could bat safely against old Satch.

He left the hitters swinging at air and stirring up dust. He left the fans oohing and ahhing and laughing. He pitched for semipro nines, traveling All Stars, winter ball clubs, the Negro Leagues best, and finally, in the major leagues. Satchel Paige had the braggadocio of Muhammad Ali and like the heavyweight champ, the wherewithal to back it up. He owned a fastball that some said could move at 100 mph at a time when no machine existed to measure it accurately. When he kicked his left leg improbably high, his big foot looked as if it was coming down on home plate. There is evidence to suggest he was the best pitcher who ever lived and he talked an even better game. Satchel Paige was rolling entertainment on two legs with one very rubbery arm and like the entertainer he was, held the belief the show must go on. He was impossible to pin down with commitments, yet always rose to the occasion. He told whatever story fit the occasion, but always delivered the truth with immediacy from his throwing arm.

A nearly mythological figure in baseball history, Satchel
Paige claimed to pitch 2,500 games and win 2,000 during a
four-decade career. He had more windups than pitches and
more pitches than stories to tell.

Paige won more than 2,000 games—he said—despite there being no way to document
them. But few doubt that it is true the way he breezed through towns like a one-man
circus. His best years were behind him when radio baseball truly took hold, when television spread the gospel of the game, when record-keeping became more meticulous, and
when Major League baseball beckoned to African American baseball players. For the
most part, Satchel Paige's essence was passed on to future generations as a form of tribal
literature, by word of mouth and anecdote.

There was never anyone else like Satchel Paige in baseball. "Satchel," said his dear
friend Buck O'Neil of the Kansas City Monarchs, "was a great pitcher. I had never seen
anything like him. He just had it all. The poise and the speed. He had it all. He had the
greatest control I've ever seen on a pitcher."[1]

Paige might have had more confidence than Ali. Ali predicted in poetry the round
his foe would go down; Paige taunted batters, teased them, and cockily challenged them
from the mound. He used a baseball instead of his fists, but the results were the same as
Ali's. Paige announced to the world, "Let's do it, right now, right here." And he made
the hitters angry enough to lose concentration.

O'Neil remembered playing an exhibition game with Paige in Denver decades ago.
The local club was pretty good. The first batter tapped a slow roller to third and beat it
out. So did the second man. Paige overheard a batter on deck say, "Let's beat him." And
Paige heard a first rumbling that he was overrated. The insults were akin to tugging on

Superman's cape. "Satch said, 'Bring 'em on in,'" O'Neil said. This was Paige at his most outrageous, one of the periodic times he called in his fielders and ordered them to congregate behind him on the mound. It was the ultimate in arrogance, to show another team contempt by telling them he did not even need fielders beyond a catcher for help. "There were seven of us kneeling on the pitching mound," O'Neil said. "Then he struck out the side on nine pitches and yelled, 'Overrated, hey?'"[2]

Paige was never overrated, but was often over the top. A pitcher toiling with that type gall today would be ripped by newspapers coast to coast. If Paige did always rise to the occasion, he also sometimes created the occasion.

EARLY LIFE

Leroy Robert "Satchel" Paige was born in Mobile, Alabama, possibly on July 7, 1906. Paige's actual age was an enduring mystery of the twentieth century, and his birth was barely better documented than that of an orphan foundling left on a police doorstep. It did not help accuracy that off and on for decades Paige juggled his facts with the alacrity of a baton twirler. Sometimes he said he was born in 1908. Sometimes he said he was born earlier. Sometimes he said he was born later. True to the spirit of the myth perpetuated by her son, when a writer once tracked down Paige's mother, Lula Coleman Paige, to ask, she talked circles around the questioner and merely added to the confusion. Although he did his best to obfuscate, for its records Major League baseball officially accepted the 1906 date as Paige's genuine birth date.

Bill Veeck, the maverick baseball owner who administered operations of the Cleveland Indians, St. Louis Browns, and Chicago White Sox twice, was both friend and employer to Paige. Veeck was the man who brought Paige into the majors when it seemed Jackie Robinson's cracking of the color barrier had come too late for him. "Satch's age has always been the subject of lively debate," Veeck wrote in his autobiography, "a debate he did not go out of his way to discourage. It could even be said that he dished out his age the way he dished out his pitches, mixing his figures up nicely and always keeping his interviewers off balance."[3] Somehow, whether they are stories about his pitching prowess, stories of his elusive nature, his private life, the origin of his nickname, or his age, there is always a mist obscuring a completely clear Satchel view.

Paige was one of twelve children. His father John did little to assist with his upbringing and Paige said his clothes were rags and shoes nonexistent at times. Over the years Paige delighted in the guessing game he provoked about his age. He said it helped make him more famous and swore childhood buddy Ted "Double Duty" Radcliffe, the Negro Leagues pitcher-catcher, to secrecy. Radcliffe did not keep the secret, but issued more erroneous age information. Paige, who had a repertoire of more one-liners than a professional standup comic, slyly told yarns about his age. He liked to say that his mother had the important date in her Bible, but unfortunately had never shown him that particular copy of the good book. "Mother always told me if you tell a lie always rehearse it," Paige said. "If it don't sound good to you, it won't sound good to nobody else." Paige left his audience laughing, if short on facts.[4]

Between a certain age and a certain age (perhaps eighteen to fifty-five) Paige's looks did not seem to change much. He had the lanky angularity of Abraham Lincoln, wore a pencil thin mustache, had a long, smooth, dark-skinned face, with full lips, a long neck, and short black hair. He stood about six-foot-three and his weight remained steady at around 190 pounds.

Paige was not much for school as a youth. He skipped out on classes regularly. He wanted to make money and none was to be had at home. So he took a job at the railroad station carrying luggage, or satchels. When he realized he could make a bigger profit by carrying more than one bag at a time Paige invented a wobbly stick support system to balance several suitcases simultaneously. Supposedly, a friend said he looked like a walking "Satchel tree" and his nickname was born. There is also the story that Paige had feet as big as satchels. There was also one about the nickname being bestowed on him when Paige was caught stealing satchels. Whatever the true source, the nickname stuck, and Paige's real first name was used so rarely that the majority of baseball fans might not know it.

Paige was sent to reform school at age twelve, but not for hijacking luggage. He got caught stealing rings from a jewelry store. Paige was incarcerated at the Industrial School for Negro Children in Mount Meigs, Alabama, for five-and-a-half years. He entered a restless boy and emerged a restless young man who hardly ever stopped moving for the next fifty years. For most of his life, Paige was as mobile as the name of his hometown. For those five-plus years, he was forcibly stationary at the "school" in a sense, but Paige cut timber, picked cotton, did woodworking, and played baseball.

When Paige emerged from reform school, he began pitching for the Mobile Tigers semipro team, which listed his brother Wilson on the roster. Paige's nickname temporarily morphed into "Satchelfoot" a neat parallel to his brother's "Paddlefoot." Satchel preferred playing first base to pitching at the time and it was not until his second season with the Tigers that he began developing his mound magic. The Chattanooga Black Lookouts, a professional team, liked his looks and signed him in 1926. Years later, with the Cleveland Indians, when Paige was playing conversational games about his age, he boasted that no one would ever find a box score of him playing a pro game before 1927. He said he would pay $500 to anyone who could prove differently. This was a memory slip, indicating that maybe not even Paige remembered how old he really was. In any case, someone turned up at the Indians office with proof of a 1926 showing.

"A few days later, a guy walked into the office with a clipping from a Memphis paper which showed that Satch had pitched for Chattanooga in 1926," Veeck said. "'Oh yeah,' Satch said, 'that was the other Satchel Paige. Now that I recollect, I did once hear there was a Satchel Paige pitched around Chattanooga when I was just a boy. Spelled his name with two LL's. A local fellow.'"[5] Veeck paid the man.

Paige's friends testified that he possessed phenomenal control even as a youngster when he did not practice much baseball. He threw rocks at pigeons and hit them. In Chattanooga, Paige began winning bets by throwing precisely over a folded handkerchief ten times in a row, knocking down bottles, or throwing pitches through a small hole in a fence. The first time Paige used a rag for home plate he fired the ball over it every time. "I just need a scrap for a target," he said. Another time he arranged soda pop bottles at home plate. His manager predicted he would be lucky to clip half of them. Paige said he would get them all—the older man anted up for dinner.[6]

The pitcher grew up in poverty, was stuck in a reform school for the better part of six years, but developed expensive tastes soon enough. He had lost his inclination for roughing it by the time the Lookouts made their first road trip, eight hours by shabby bus to Memphis. When the bus deposited the team at the ballpark in the dark, Paige demanded to be taken to a hotel. His manager laughed, saying there was no hotel, and the team slept at the field. "I had the miseries in the morning," Paige said. "My back was sore, my arms and legs ached, and my mouth was full of dust." Breakfast was a hot dog and a warm orange drink.[7]

Growing up deprived, then coming into a regular paycheck, Paige immediately lit out on a shopping spree. He bought clothes, a shotgun (he became a serious hunter), a steak, booze, and went searching for female companionship. He was just eighteen, but Paige's spending and entertainment patterns only grew pricier as he aged.

PLAYING CAREER

With Chattanooga, Paige swiftly matured into a first-rate pitcher. Bursting with anger because of an error that cost him runs, he called his fielders into the mound for the first time. He won nearly every game and drew crowds and attention. Some thought he was so good that already he belonged in the major leagues, but when they told him it was a shame he was black, Paige's temper raged. "I got real hotheaded every time someone told me it was too bad I couldn't play in the major leagues because of my color," he said.[8] It was the first of about a million times he would hear that phrase during his professional lifetime. But scouts for the Negro Leagues found him quickly. The Birmingham Black Barons bought Paige from the Lookouts for the 1928 season. It was not the majors, but Paige was about to go big-time in black society.

Paige was not overwhelmingly successful in his first outings for the Black Barons, but improved steadily, perfecting more pitches and naming them as he went. He had a "Bee Ball" and a "Jump Ball" in his repertoire as he eased into stardom by 1929 and added pitches such as his "Trouble Ball" and "Hesitation Pitch" later. He formed an alliance with Barons catcher Bill Perkins, whom he wanted as his personal receiver every time he took the mound. Paige considered himself invincible before he really was, but he gradually talked much of the rest of the world into believing it.[9]

Concurrent with his pitching success, Paige evolved into the biggest prima donna this side of Hollywood. His ego was so large that he felt he could show up for games whenever he pleased, that he could skip games when he felt like it, that he could practice when it suited him, and that he could jump contracts whenever a slightly better offer came over the transom. He drove owners and managers crazy, except when he pitched and won and drew large numbers of fans. And with rare exceptions, he got away with these shenanigans as he pleased for decades. If a rare owner stood up to Paige, he simply moved on to a better deal somewhere else. He exasperated employers, but they could not live without him. He tantalized them with his best stuff and then jumped to another league, another country. Paige was an affable loner, who, ironically, always had a satchel packed.

Jimmie Crutchfield, a top Negro Leagues outfielder with the Black Barons, the Newark Eagles, and other teams, and someone counted as a Paige friend, struggled to get a handle on Paige's personality. "He was an odd guy," Crutchfield said. "He was a one-nighter kind of guy. He didn't take to too many ballplayers as very close buddies. He was a good guy, always full of fun, kidding, joking. But he'd pitch on a Sunday and then we wouldn't see him till next Sunday. Very seldom did he travel with us. He'd get there by himself."[10]

Double Duty Radcliffe, who knew Paige as a youth in Mobile and crossed paths with him year after year in Negro Leagues ball, fled with him to Bismarck, North Dakota, for a spell in 1932 where he said his friend was the king of hell-raisers. Radcliffe, who died in 2004 at the age of 103 in Chicago, said he refused to cover up for Paige. Radcliffe earned his nickname by catching one game of a double header and pitching the other. However, in North Dakota, sometimes he had to perform both duties in the same game.

Radcliffe relieved Paige after four innings because Paige wore out. Paige was living a wild lifestyle in their shared trailer and the home was a "revolving door for the ladies," Radcliffe said. "One would be goin' in as one would be goin' out. I can give him hell because he and I were buddies. I used to tell people, 'He's bigger than the game, man. You can't find him and you can't fire him. What you gonna do with him?' I don't care if he could throw a ball so hard you couldn't see it. If he couldn't take orders, I wouldn't want him, would you?"[11]

But everybody did want Paige. They wanted him for a season, a winter, a weekend, or a single game. Promoters did not care if he had less personal discipline than a kindergarten student, there was that fastball that made the batters blink, and there was that innate promotional quality that always lured the fans. Owners wanted him desperately, even if Paige often caused them heartburn.

Only once during his long career roaming in the baseball world did Paige suffer significant payback. A throwing arm injury put his career in jeopardy. For all his partying, Paige was prudent about exercising his arm. "I always took care of my weight and back muscles," he said. "Those muscles gave me balance. That kept my arm from getting strained, ever. And balance is what you need out there on the hill." However, in the winter of 1938, Paige was pitching in Mexico when he felt a burning sensation in his right arm. He tried to pitch through the ache, but gradually the intensity of the pain worsened and Paige could not even lift his throwing arm. "I just sat there sweating, hurting enough to want to cry, getting sicker in the stomach and getting scared—real scared."[12]

Satchel Paige became a legend touring the United States and Latin America, and pitching everywhere and anywhere promotors were willing to put up a dollar. Baseball's color line kept him out of the majors until he was forty-two, but he still became an American League All Star and pitched in the World Series for the Cleveland Indians.

Doctors in Mexico told Paige he would never pitch again and time passed with no improvement in his condition—a probable slight shoulder separation—he stopped trying to throw through the injury and tried to become a first baseman, stunning news since Paige was regarded as the most feared African American pitcher of the time.

Before he became a major leaguer with the New York Giants, Monte Irvin played against Paige in the Negro Leagues. He said Paige was unreal. "Satchel Paige was the big excitement," Irvin said. "People came out to see Satchel. I never saw a man who said he was gonna do something and did it like him. He would say, 'I'm stingy tonight.' That meant he was going to shut you out. He did a lot of talking, but he backed it up."[13]

Most of the owners in the Negro Leagues, whom Paige had treated with high-handed disregard when he was on top of the world, treated him with similar disdain when the sore-armed version of Paige asked for a job. They held the aces this time. They had no need for a Satchel Paige with no fastball. Paige was turned away, door after door. He had offended many of these owners by jumping ship so often that they felt little sympathy. The owners believed Paige would never be game worthy again and they did not mind taking a little revenge.

"As long as he had his fastball, people were willing to put up with Satchel's demands, his speeding tickets, his tardiness," Buck O'Neil said. "But when he pulled up with a sore arm, well, nobody wanted him." O'Neil gave singular credit to the one owner who saw past the injury and either still believed in the future or was rewarding Paige for what he had done for black ball.[14]

J.L. Wilkinson, the Kansas City Monarchs owner, was the exception. He signed Paige and assigned him to a touring Monarchs subsidiary, the "Little Monarchs." For most of 1938, Paige was out of the limelight. He rested his tired arm. And then one day he tested it. "I kicked my leg up fast and threw," Paige said. "I didn't feel anything." By this he meant that he felt no pain. He threw again and again. It was as if he had purchased a new arm at a medical supply store. Paige was back in business. "It was a miracle," he said, "but my arm was alive."[15] Paige recuperated in time for the 1939 Monarchs season and then returned to the lifestyle he had led before, almost as if there had been no interruption.

Although modern baseball stadiums routinely report the speed of a hurler's pitches on the scoreboard during games through the use of speed "guns" and everyone seems to throw more than 90 mph, there was no such reliable indicator to measure the speed of a Cy Young, a Walter Johnson, a Satchel Paige, or a Bob Feller. It is conceded that in their primes those four were probably among the fastest throwers of the first half of the twentieth century, but despite best efforts to clock the pitchers' speed with weird science, there was no way to know how quick they really were. When the best hitters said they could barely see the blur unleashed, then that was at least anecdotal testimony that a pitcher was doing something impressive. Paige had that going for him.

"He threw fire, that's what he threw," said Hall of Fame first baseman Buck Leonard of Paige's stuff. Leonard said he played against Paige for seventeen seasons in the Negro Leagues and never got a base hit off of him. Cool Papa Bell, another great, said, "Satchel was faster than all of them."[16]

Paige's legend expanded in many ways. Diamond proficiency was merely one piece of the package. When Paige was cornered he had a homespun, humorous way of explaining himself. He told stories about everywhere he had been and everyone he had seen. They all contributed to the myth of Satchel Paige, who somewhere along the way had ceased being a mere man and had evolved into a demigod. In the fall of 1933, Paige was playing in California, but when the temperature dipped, he ventured to Venezuela, saying, "That was because I didn't have a topcoat." There were other hazards in South America. Paige played the outfield when he first arrived and while fielding a ball reached into the grass and faced off with a snake. He said it was a boa constrictor, but he may not have identified the species correctly since they usually hang out in trees. Paige had always demonstrated that self-preservation came first and this time it seemed warranted. But as Paige picked up a stick "and beat the devil out of that snake" the hitter rounded the bases with the winning run. "The crowd chased me right out of the park, and the manager of the club wouldn't pay me for that game," he said.[17]

Paige willingly told such tales on himself where he did not always come off as the fearless winner. But he also had the soul of a gunfighter, a fierce pride that would bubble up if someone challenged his pitching ability. If a gunfighter's squint was what let the world know he was serious, Paige's tone of voice also sometimes broke through to inform the observant that he was not kidding right then.

Once, Paige told a writer friend that he had long before informed a reporter that the great Babe Ruth and the great Lou Gehrig might not have put together such gaudy lifetime statistics with the Yankees if they had to go up against the great Satchel Paige on a regular basis. "'... if [they] had to face me back when they were breaking all of those records I could have knocked a few points off of those big, fat lifetime averages.' And hell, I meant it. I was laughing when I said it, but I was not joking. I meant every word I said. See, hitting the ball is one thing, but hitting against a fastball pitcher who can put it where he wants every time is a whole 'nother story."[18]

Before Paige injured his arm, he and a crew of African American All Stars traveled to the Dominican Republic to participate in a famous tournament that has grown in legend because of the way the American participants described the scene. Dictator Rafael Trujillo hired Paige and Cool Papa Bell, Josh Gibson, and Sam Bankhead, among others, to be his team in the island championships. The president wanted to win the tournament very badly and particularly defeat a political challenger's team from the provinces. The way Paige told the story—a thousand times, at least—the players were informed repeatedly they had better win. Trujillo's army ringed the field and the players felt they might be killed if they did not win the championship on the final night. Their emotions were raw and they were on edge already because they had been rounded up and spent the night in jail before the game. The trip was supposed to be a lucrative lark, but there had been hints of the seriousness with which the head man took things. Periodic firing of army rifles aimed at the sky did not soothe the players.

"I started wishing I was home when all those soldiers started following us around everywhere we went and even stood out in front of our rooms at night," Paige said. At the park before the game the manager told the Americans, "Take my advice and win." Paige said the army was starting to look like "a firing squad." The Trujillo team rallied from one run behind to win the title and Paige said the players made a beeline for the airport. "We never did see Trujillo again," Paige said. "I ain't sorry."[19]

The breathless tale was told over and over again, always with the implication that the players were lucky to escape with their lives. Years later, in a biography of Paige, author Mark Ribowsky contended that the players were actually being protected the entire time they were surrounded by armed men and that misunderstandings likely arose from the players' lack of Spanish skills and knowledge of local custom and politics. Paige, Ribowsky contended, did not even flee with his comrades, but stuck around a little longer because he was then on the outs with Negro Leagues owners for jumping their teams once too often.

Paige was a have-fastball, will-travel, baseball mercenary, always on the prowl for the best deal, but, he was in enough demand to regularly bounce back into the limelight.

When the Negro Leagues conducted their famous East-West All-Star classics in Chicago's Comiskey Park, the fans wanted to see Satchel throw. When the Kansas City Monarchs called, Paige was ready to serve. He may have been in greater need of an appointment book than anyone in the country who did not work out of the Oval Office, but Paige turned up in the right place at the right time at key times. Paige never majored in accounting at any fancy college, but he was smart enough to realize his pitching arm was worth more than other players' arms or bats. Paige saved his press clippings, whenever they appeared—a smart move considering Negro Leagues and barnstorming statistics were often vague. (Paige did claim a record of 31–4 for the Pittsburgh Crawfords in 1933.)

Against the odds in a prejudiced America, what some people were starting to notice was that Paige was as good as anybody out there, white or black. "Paige is one of the phenomenons of the crazy-quilted American sporting scene," one sports reporter wrote. "He is the Negro counterpart of the greatest names in big league baseball."[20]

In some parts of the country, little white boys and little black boys played baseball together on the same fields. In some areas they shared high school teams. But never the professional twain did meet in the 1920s, 1930s, and for half of the 1940s. However there was one major exception. The 2000s are the age of the millionaire ballplayer, with a minimum Major League salary of more than $300,000. Players no longer take on second jobs to make it through the winter. And for supplemental income they are invited to endorse products and make personal appearances. In the first half of the twentieth century, the white major leaguers, as well as the black Negro League stars, were on the alert for extra cash. After the World Series, black teams and white teams toured together, playing exhibitions to earn extra money. Although the games were not televised or often viewed by influential reporters, the black players seized the opportunity to show they belonged. No one was more visible in these contests than Paige. He frequently organized the black All Stars, making plans with white counterparts like All-Star pitchers Dizzy Dean and Bob Feller. And then from the mound, Paige handled the white batting orders with the same ease that he did the black batting orders.

More than once, Dean, the St. Louis Cardinals hurler whose career was cut short by injury before he became a broadcaster, said that Paige was the greatest pitcher he ever saw. He wrote it in his syndicated column and he told Paige to his face. "You're a better pitcher'n I ever hope to be, Satch," Paige said Dean once told him. And Dean wrote for public consumption, "He [Paige] sure is a pistol. It's too bad those colored boys don't play in the big leagues because they sure got some great ballplayers. Anyway, that skinny old Satchel Paige with those long arms is my idea of the pitcher with the greatest stuff I ever saw."[21]

Sportswriters in the African American press and white sportswriters of conscience were beginning to campaign for the all-white majors to open up. Periodically, Paige would be asked about those prospects, but he always expressed skepticism. "I don't believe them owners," he said. "If they wanted to try out colored ballplayers they'd take 'em to spring training camps, same as the white boys. This business of trying us out at the tail end of the season makes me laugh." Paige teased that he was probably not a prospect because he was going on thirty years old. (By then he was really closer to forty.) His cynicism was accurate. There never were any tryouts. "They always like to talk nice," Paige said, "but some of the worst medicine I ever swallowed came in some sweet-tasting candy."[22]

In the early 1940s, Paige lived as settled an existence in Kansas City with the Monarchs as he had anywhere since he was in reform school. He played four straight seasons with the Monarchs without jumping a contract. He fished and hunted and enjoyed the hot jazz scene. Many of the celebrities of the music world, from Louis Armstrong to Bojangles Robinson, from Billie Holiday to Lionel Hampton, were as drawn to Paige as he was to them. He began collecting Chinese artifacts such as vases, met his girlfriend Lahoma, and then married her and had children.

During that period, Paige crossed over into the white mainstream journalism world, being written up in *Time* magazine, the *Saturday Evening Post*, and *Life* magazine. Much of black America, and certainly the Negro Leagues, had been invisible to white society. Paige was deposited in the mailbox. The 1941 *Life* spread was headlined, "Satchel Paige, Negro Ballplayer, Is One Of The Best Pitchers In Game." That was not exactly stop-the-presses news for those in the baseball know, but for the average American it was. Ribowsky, who commented that some of the other major pieces on Paige were riddled with errors, noted the way the *Life* story portrayed Paige. "In an array of day-in-the-life pictures," he wrote, "he was the beau ideal of the black leisure class, not the Watusi tribe."[23]

Throughout their Negro Leagues careers, despite the vast differences in their personalities, Paige and catcher Josh Gibson were rated one-two as the brightest stars in the constellation. Gibson was conceded to be the most feared power hitter and was called the black Babe Ruth. It is notable that while comparisons were made linking Gibson and Ruth, Buck Leonard as the black Lou Gehrig, and (less so) Cool Papa Bell as the black Ty Cobb, rarely and never repeatedly, was heard a Paige comparison. There was no Paige-is-as-to Walter Johnson, Christy Mathewson, or Bob Feller. Either imaginations failed, or Paige, as it has been stated many times, was unique. There really was no one like Paige, not a pitcher, not another player, nor perhaps any star in any sport in American history. His sustained greatness, longevity, style, and character set him apart.

Paige and Gibson were coupled together in conversation, but they did not party together in bars. Whereas Paige courted the spotlight, Gibson often ducked it. Paige talked endlessly, Gibson when talked to. Paige adapted to circumstances, Gibson plowed straight ahead. Paige kept his athletic health longer than anyone could have expected, Gibson flamed out early, dead at thirty-five in 1947 from a combination of strokes, alcoholism, and possibly drug addiction. Gibson's death meant sadness for teammates, foes, and fans alike. Buck Leonard, the other half of the "Thunder Twins," was a pallbearer at Gibson's funeral, which he said was attended only by close family and a few friends. "There's no telling what he could have done in the major leagues in his prime," Leonard said.[24]

It was not easy for Paige to sit still in Kansas City and it was only a matter of time before he began barnstorming more actively again. He always needed the money, but he was also a restless soul, with an innate need to be on the go. Something was stoked inside him when people applauded and the lights were turned up high. "I liked playing games against Negro League teams, but I loved barnstorming," Paige said. "It gave us a chance to go everywhere and let millions of people see what we could do. I just loved it. I'd have played every day of the year if I could."[25]

That passion kept Paige rolling long after contemporaries retired. And he was not just hanging on. Wherever Paige played by the 1940s, he was a legend come to life. When he faced younger black hitters, or those who had never played in the Negro Leagues, but only on barnstorming teams, he was like a piece of history in the flesh.

Hank Presswood, who turned eighty-six in 2006, and who played for the Cleveland Buckeyes and the Monarchs in the final years of the Negro Leagues, was also an infielder before that on a Mississippi team called the Black Cats. In his rookie year with Cleveland,

Presswood got his first glimpse of Paige. "The greatest experience I had in baseball with the Buckeyes was when we went to Kansas City to play the Monarchs," Presswood said. "I heard something in the ballpark and it sounded like they were shooting off fireworks. Over and over again. I yelled to the manager, 'Hey, skipper, what in the world is that? This is not July 4.' He said, 'No, Hank, that's old Satchel Paige warming up.' Satchel was warming up, popping them. In our dugout, you could hear a pin fall."

Presswood said he was a speedy runner and used to bunt for infield hits. When Presswood came to the plate the first time he said Paige yelled to him from the mound. "'Hank,' he said, 'I've been hearing you've been bunting the ball and hitting low line drives. Not today. Boy, I'm gonna give you a whipping you never had before.' I believed in myself, though. Paige smiled, as if to say, 'Not today,' again. He threw one at me, but he couldn't frighten me. I'm still woofing at him. I hit a curve for a long foul. Then he threw a fastball down the middle. He's got some smoke. And then he threw the hesitation pitch, a knuckleball. It was dipping and just floating in there. I swung and missed that ball and pulled a muscle. I couldn't swing a bat for three days. He was a great pitcher."[26]

Carl Long, who played with the Philadelphia Stars and Birmingham Black Barons during the waning days of the Negro Leagues, faced Paige in nonleague play. He said Paige may not have even known younger players' names, but he did not want any of them to go around boasting about how they had taken advantage of him.

"I couldn't hit him," Long said. "With him, it was 'Hey, come up here and take your three and go sit down. You're not going to make your name off Satch unless you earn it.' The first pitch was the fastest ball I ever saw in my life. It was a called strike. And he yelled, 'You're never gonna get a hit off Satch with the bat on your shoulder. I'm gonna throw you one faster than that.' I think I swung when it was already in the mitt. The third pitch was strike three. I looked at it and walked to the dugout. It was, let that be a lesson to me."[27]

Paige loved fast cars, especially Cadillacs, and at one point in his barnstorming heyday actually had a prop plane at his disposal with his name scrawled on the side in order to make it to his many playing engagements. Flying in a storm cured him of using that mode of transportation. "You tryin' to kill me?" Paige shouted at the pilot while surfing the rough air. "Get me out of here!"[28]

Paige was a popular raconteur. He held court for teammates in dugouts and clubhouses. He dazzled sportswriters with stories that may have been true, may not have been true, or may have been partially true. He was irresistible copy. But the story that appeared about Paige in *Collier's* magazine took the grand prize. As Paige well knew, part of his mystique stemmed from the common belief that he was like comedian Jack Benny, perpetually thirty-nine going on a hundred years old. The *Collier's* story explored Paige's secret to longevity and the rules for living healthfully. The rules have been attached to his name evermore, glued more tightly to his persona than Einstein's was to his theory of relativity.

The Rules:
1. "Avoid fried meats which angry up the blood."
2. "If your stomach disputes you, lie down and pacify it with cool thoughts."
3. "Keep the juices flowing by jangling around gently as you move."
4. "Go very light on the vices, such as carrying on in society—the social ramble ain't restful."

  5. "Avoid running at all times."
  6. "Don't look back, something may be gaining on you."[29]

They were catchy lines and lingered in the air like the smoke from the cigarettes Paige inhaled. The reality was this: Paige never met a steak he did not like, was a national champion social rambler, participated in most vices anathema to church goers, and was on the go so much that his movements could not have been all that gentle. Paige's stomach was so mixed up that he often imbibed soothing liquid medicine on the mound by the glass. But he did avoid running as assiduously as possible—his preferred method of approaching the mound was a slow shuffle—and he admitted that "Don't look back" represented his real words to live by. "When you look back, you know how long you've been going and that just might stop you from going any farther," Paige said. "And with me, there was an awful lot to look back on."[30]

Truthful or not, the rules became a calling card, and drummed up more publicity for a man who needed a heavy dose of it as much as he required a minimum daily allotment of calories. In the companion book to the documentary "Baseball" the rules are called "an act. Few players, black or white, have ever had a shrewder sense of how to sell themselves."[31] Not even P.T. Barnum could dispute that statement.

When the news broke that Jackie Robinson had been signed by the Brooklyn Dodgers to break Major League baseball's color barrier, black ballplayers were shocked. They never believed it would happen. They had no inkling that Robinson, who had played only briefly with the Kansas City Monarchs, would be the chosen one, and they felt that many other African American stars were better qualified. Paige was one of those hurt at being overlooked, though his public statements were diplomatic. He knew that his was the biggest name in black baseball and he knew he was still good enough to play.

Robinson was the first, but he was not alone for long. The Cleveland Indians, run by Bill Veeck, brought Larry Doby into the outfield as the barrier breaker in the American League only months after Robinson made his debut in the National League. Veeck, who had great respect for Paige, did not let him dangle anxiously for too long. In 1948, the Indians were a top club, chasing their first pennant in almost three decades. Veeck was wary of upsetting team chemistry, but he needed bullpen help. Abe Saperstein, who founded the Harlem Globetrotters, was also involved in promoting black baseball. Veeck asked Saperstein for his opinion of Paige's current abilities and got a thumbs-up. However, Cleveland player-manager Lou Boudreau was cool to the idea. He thought Paige was too old. Veeck had to employ a pretext even to get Boudreau to the ballpark to watch a brief Paige tryout.

The tryout was conducted on July 7, 1948, what Paige said was his forty-second birthday. At first Boudreau caught sharp pitches from Paige, and then he stood in to hit. Boudreau was leading the league in hitting at the time. Veeck stood behind the plate and later said of the twenty pitches Paige threw, nineteen were strikes. Boudreau hit a single pop-up. "If I'm lying, I'm dying," Paige said of how well the tryout went. Boudreau was sold. He told Veeck to sign Paige.[32]

It was electrifying news for baseball fans. Satchel Paige was in the major leagues. Joy was not universal, however. J.G. Taylor Spink, publisher of *The Sporting News*, editorialized against bringing in the elderly Paige, saying in part, "To bring in a pitching 'rookie' of Paige's age casts a reflection on the entire scheme of operation in the major leagues. To sign a hurler at Paige's age is to demean the standards of baseball in the big circuits." Veeck's comment was simple: "If Satch were white, of course, he would have been in the majors twenty-five years earlier, and the question would not have been before the House."[33]

Paige immediately showed that he still knew how to do what he had always done best. He helped the Indians in relief. He won games as a starter. Every time Paige won, Veeck sent Spink a telegram highlighting Paige's gaudy numbers and he jibed the publisher with comments suggesting "Paige definitely in line for *The Sporting News* award as rookie of the year."[34]

The lanky thrower completed his first Major League year with a record of 6–1 and an earned run average of 2.48. When Paige was scheduled to start, he attracted a Chicago night game record crowd of more than 50,000 (not counting standing room) to Comiskey Park. Soon after, in another advertised start, Paige attracted more than 78,000 fans to a game. Paige was the first African American pitcher in the American League and when he did assist the Indians to the pennant, he became the first black pitcher to compete in the World Series. After the Indians won it all, sportswriters asked Paige if he would be back the next year. Now that he had reached the majors, Paige had no intention of slipping away so quickly.[35]

Paige pitched one more season for the Indians, going 4–7 in 1949, but then was cut loose after Veeck sold the team. Veeck got back into baseball with ownership of the St. Louis Browns, and promptly hired Paige again. Paige played the 1951, 1952, and 1953 seasons for the Browns. The 1952 campaign, with a 12–10 record, was Paige's best in the majors. He was selected for the All-Star team when he was forty-six years old—at least.

It was obvious that Veeck, who shared a sense of showmanship with Paige, and the pitcher, were made for each other. They both loved to milk maximum exposure out of the littlest things. When Veeck offered Paige a contract for his second season with the Browns, they conducted a joint press conference. The duo played up Paige's mysterious age. During the 1953 season, Veeck provided a lounge chair for Paige to recline on in the bullpen until the phone rang requesting him to warm up.

But when Veeck, who was always underfinanced, once more had to sell his team and exit baseball, Paige was out of a job, too. Veeck was fond of Paige and always tried to look out for him. When Veeck briefly took over the minor league Miami Marlins with the assignment of breathing life into it, he immediately signed Paige for the rotation. Paige finished 11–4 with a 1.86 earned run average.

Paige was approached to film a movie in 1958 and signed on to play a sergeant in a Civil War flick called *The Wonderful Country* that starred Robert Mitchum. He was not nominated for an Academy Award and Hollywood did not come knocking again, but Paige said he enjoyed the experience. "You get to sit down a lot," he said, "and the pay is real good."[36]

When Veeck returned to the majors with the purchase of the White Sox, and the team needed extra pitching while pursuing the 1959 pennant, Veeck wanted Paige again. As he had demonstrated with Boudreau, the one thing Veeck would not do was overstep the authority of his manager. Al Lopez said no to Paige. Paige was fifty-three at the time; after that it surely seemed the only way he would see another Major League game was by buying a ticket.

Then along came Charlie Finley. Another offbeat owner like Veeck, who suggested using orange baseballs, and featured a donkey as a team mascot for his Kansas City Athletics, Finley activated Paige when late-season rosters expanded in September 1965. On September 25, Paige was on the mound to pitch against the Boston Red Sox in a meaningless end-of-year game. At fifty-nine, Paige threw three innings of one-hit ball.

The only safety was a double by Carl Yastrzemski, one of the league's top hitters. "He looked awfully good for a man about sixty at the time," Yaz said years later.[37]

Paige went out to the hill and threw a few bonus warm-up pitches at the beginning of the fourth inning, but was removed from the game to a standing ovation. The fans, clearly in the spirit of the moment, sang "The Old Gray Mare" and some other aging-relevant songs. Paige went back out on the road, lining up playing gigs everywhere from Portland, Oregon to Anchorage, Alaska. But he was always open to more enticing suggestions.

The A's appearance was not Paige's final appearance in a Major League uniform. In a goodwill gesture, the Atlanta Braves signed Paige as a player-coach for the 1969 season, enabling him to earn a big-league pension. Paige was 158 days short of the required five-year service provision. Paige actually did pitch an inning for the Braves in April of 1969 at the end of the exhibition season and captured the victory at age sixty-two. Although he wore glasses in daily life, Paige said he found them unnecessary to locate the plate. "I don't need glasses to tell me where the outside or the inside edge is," he said.[38] He also fulfilled the pension requirement at an age when he was just about ready to collect it.

Shortly after the regular season began in 1969, Paige held a press conference announcing his retirement from baseball. He said he was doing it for a good cause—the young players on their way up. "I can still throw harder than most of 'em," he said. "But I don't want to embarrass them. It might have a bad effect on 'em."[39]

LATER LIFE

The last unexpected chapter of Paige's episodic life began slowly in 1966. Ted Williams, the famed Boston Red Sox slugger, chose the occasion of his induction into the Baseball Hall of Fame to issue a plea on behalf of Negro Leagues players who had been shut out of organized ball in their best years. He said the injustice would not be put right until the best African American players of the era were allowed into the Hall. Williams' heartfelt speech, which caught many off-guard, initiated a movement. Baseball formed a research committee and followed through. After great deliberation, the first result of the meetings bore fruit. The first black player who had been denied entry to the game because of the color barrier was selected for induction in 1971. The player was Satchel Paige.

When Paige was introduced as a newly elected member of the Hall in New York in 1971, Commissioner Bowie Kuhn called it "an historic first."[40] Several months later when the ceremony was conducted in Cooperstown, New York, Paige said, "I am the proudest man on the earth today. Since I've been here, I've been called some very nice names. And I can remember when some of the men in (the Hall of Fame) called me some ba-a-d names when I used to pitch against them. They'd make fun about me not running, about being slow to get to the mound. But I never rushed myself. I knew that they couldn't start the game 'til I got out there."[41]

Fans could only wonder what Satch would have been capable of if he had been unchained in the majors in his prime. He would have likely had ten times the lifetime statistics, but with more rules and restrictions on his behavior, turned out to be half the legend.

Paige retired to Kansas City, where he had spent so many years with the Monarchs, but by the time he reached his seventies he was really showing his age. A movie called

Don't Look Back, with actor Lou Gossett playing Paige, was shown on television in early 1981, giving fresh life to his legend.

Only weeks later, Paige was a feeble visitor, in a wheelchair and on oxygen, when attending the Negro Leagues veterans reunion in Ashland, Kentucky. The reunions were supposed to be annual, but this was the third and last, with fifty-seven old-timers who played between 1920 and 1950 in attendance. One of them was Willie Mays, who used his Birmingham Black Barons apprenticeship as a springboard to a Hall of Fame career with the New York and San Francisco Giants. Mays came to pay his respects to the men who opened the door for his acceptance in the majors. "History to us, means surviving," Mays said. "And that's what I did. They made me survive."[42]

The man who said he might pitch forever could neither keep the promise nor live forever. In early June of 1982, his body weakening, Satchel Paige threw out the first ball at a baseball game in a stadium being named after him in Kansas City. A few days later, on June 8, he died, to the best of anyone's knowledge, a month shy of his seventy-sixth birthday.

Tributes from the old days littered the sports pages, everyone from Dizzy Dean, Charles Gehringer, and Bob Feller associating Paige's name with greatness. Comments from long-dead Hall of Famers were recycled. Hack Wilson, the man who set the single-season, Major League RBI record, once said of Paige's fastball, "It starts out like a baseball and when it gets to the plate, it looks like a marble."[43]

Buck O'Neil, who outlived all his contemporary players, and so many that he managed, smiled when he talked about Paige, but he could grow reflective, too, since he knew him better as a multifaceted, deeper man than the public did. "Satchel used to say," noted Buck, "'The past is a long and twisty road.' Well, his road was longer and twistier than most." O'Neil was an honorary pallbearer at Paige's funeral and Paige found his most restful repose in Forest Hill Cemetery in Kansas City. O'Neil and others later contributed to a more impressive headstone for the great player, a joint one with his wife Lahoma. The headstone summarizes Paige's career and reads in part, "And Leroy became Satchel, and Satchel became legend." Also engraved are those iffy Paige rules for living. They followed him all the way to the grave.

NOTES

1. Buck O'Neil, personal interview, December 7, 2005.

2. Ibid.

3. Bill Veeck with Ed Linn, *Veeck—As in Wreck* (Chicago: University of Chicago Press, 1962), 188.

4. Mark Ribowsky, *Don't Look Back* (New York: Simon & Schuster, 1994), 22–23.

5. Veeck with Linn, *Veeck—As in Wreck*, 188.

6. Leroy "Satchel" Paige with David Lipman, *Maybe I'll Pitch Forever* (New York: Doubleday, 1962), 32, 35.

7. Paige with Lipman, *Maybe I'll Pitch Forever*, 35–36.

8. Paige with Lipman, *Maybe I'll Pitch Forever*, 37.

9. Ribowsky, *Don't Look Back*, 57.

10. Ribowsky, *Don't Look Back*, 98.

11. Ribowsky, *Don't Look Back*, 127.

12. Paige with Lipman, *Maybe I'll Pitch Forever*, 107–109.

13. Monte Irvin, personal interview, January 7, 2006.

14. Buck O'Neil with Steve Wulf and David Conrads, *I Was Right on Time* (New York: Simon & Schuster, 1996), 105.

15. Paige with Lipman, *Maybe I'll Pitch Forever*, 117–118.

16. John Holway, *Josh & Satch* (Westport, CT: Meckler Publishing, 1991), 11–12.

17. Holway, *Josh & Satch*, 55.

18. William Price Fox, *Satchel Paige's America* (Tuscaloosa: University of Alabama Press, 2005), 87.

19. Paige with Lipman, *Maybe I'll Pitch Forever*, 103–104.

20. Lyall Smith, *Detroit Free Press*, September 6, 1945.

21. Paige with Lipman, *Maybe I'll Pitch Forever*, 79–80.

22. Paige with Lipman, *Maybe I'll Pitch Forever*, 93–94.

23. Ribowsky, *Don't Look Back*, 196.

24. Negro Leagues Baseball Museum exhibit, Kansas City, Missouri.

25. Buck Leonard with James A. Riley, *Buck Leonard: The Black Lou Gehrig* (New York: Carroll & Graf Publishers, 1995), 187.

26. Hank Presswood, personal interview, January 12, 2006.

27. Carl Long, personal interview, January 11, 2006.

28. Paige with Lipman, *Maybe I'll Pitch Forever*, 155.

29. Paige with Lipman, *Maybe I'll Pitch Forever*, 201.

30. Ibid.

31. Geoffrey C. Ward and Ken Burns, *Baseball: An Illustrated History* (New York: Alfred A. Knopf, 1994), 206.

32. Fox, *Satchel Paige's America*, 101.

33. Veeck with Linn, *Veeck—As In Wreck*, 185.

34. Ibid.

35. Paige with Lipman, *Maybe I'll Pitch Forever*, 198.

36. *Arkansas Gazette*, April 19, 1971.

37. Associated Press, June 13, 1982.

38. Melvin Durslag, *Los Angeles Herald-Examiner*, February 28, 1969.

39. Wayne Minshew, *Sporting News*, April 19, 1969.

40. Arthur Daley, *New York Times*, February 10, 1971.

41. Ribowsky, *Don't Look Back*, 327.

42. John Holway, *Sporting News*, July 18, 1981.

43. Henry Hecht, *New York Post*, June 9, 1982.

Further Reading

Fox, William Price, *Satchel Paige's America*. Tuscaloosa: University of Alabama Press, 2005.

Holway, John, *Josh and Satch*. Westport, CT: Meckler Publishing, 1991.

Paige, Leroy "Satchel," with David Lipman, *Maybe I'll Pitch Forever: A Great Baseball Player Tells the Hilarious Story Behind the Legend*. New York: Doubleday, 1962.

MONTE IRVIN
February 25, 1919–

Monte Irvin was a hitting star in the Negro Leagues, was one of the first players to cross over to stardom in the majors, and played a key role in the implementation of policy in the Major League commissioner's office for sixteen years.

Irvin distinguished himself as a player with the Newark Eagles before World War II and returned from the Army to bat .401 in 1946. Irvin was one of the New York Giants earliest black players and along with Willie Mays and Hank Thompson comprised the majors' first all-black outfield. His lifetime Major League batting average was .293.

☆　☆　☆

Monte Irvin might have been the one. "I was told that I had been selected," Irvin said. "That I was the one to break the color barrier."[1]

Monte Irvin of Orange, New Jersey and the Newark Eagles, not Jackie Robinson of Pasadena, California and the Kansas City Monarchs, was the front-runner.

As far back as the late 1930s, sportswriters for newspapers oriented to African American audiences issued a tsunami of criticism of Major League baseball for keeping rosters sealed against invasion by black ballplayers. Their columns were stinging and bold, drawing appreciative readers among Negro League players and their fans. But there was little response from white ball club owners and none of any substance from Major League officials.

Most of the African American players populating teams in the Negro Leagues also barnstormed around the nation playing exhibition games. Often they faced white-only teams of Major Leaguers and defeated them. The black players knew where they stood. They saw the results on the scoreboard in small towns out of the limelight, away from the big-city crowds and the writers at the New York, Washington, and Boston papers. The black players won more than their share of the contests and that let the white players with any sense of realism know that their black brethren could play on equal footing.

The agitation for integration ebbed and flowed, but reached a crescendo during and just after World War II. If segregation of professional baseball just seemed wrong in the 1930s, then it seemed more of an embarrassment at a time when the United States was supposed to be more united than ever against the dangerous armies of Germany and Japan.

The move to integrate baseball was far from organized. One columnist piped up here, another there. A creative thinker would write a note to the owner of a ball club struggling in the standings and suggest a tryout for top hands from the Negro Leagues. One such proposal reached Pittsburgh Pirates manager Pie Traynor, the Hall of Fame third baseman. Just across town many of the best players in the world competed for the black Homestead Grays and the Pittsburgh Crawfords. Powerhouse hitter Josh Gibson and dangerous slugger Buck Leonard were readily available. The answer to the team's problems was right down the street. Essentially the note dared Traynor to take extraordinary steps in order to win. Then there were stories that the Pirates coveted Gibson.

Commissioner Kennesaw Mountain Landis opposed that idea. "Let them stay in their own league," Landis said.[2] Similarly, a pitch was made to Clark Griffith, owner of the Washington Senators, to hire blacks. For decades following their appearance in the 1925 World Series, the Senators fielded feeble teams. The Senators became the butt of a perpetual joke. It went like this: "Washington, first in war, first in peace, last in the American League." Mr. Griffith demonstrated no interest in altering his circumstances, either, by hiring African Americans to fill the quality gaps on his team.

World War II, as it did for much of the planet earth, disrupted daily life and long-range planning. When the war finally encompassed the United States, baseball executives gave thought to suspending play for the duration. President Franklin Delano Roosevelt said it would be good for the country's morale to keep playing, that the entertainment would be sorely needed by home-front workers. Baseball played on, but many of its brightest stars volunteered for military service or were drafted. Among the greats who invested years fighting for their country, Ted Williams, the man who aspired to be called the greatest hitter who ever lived and might have accomplished this quest in his twenty-one years with the Boston Red Sox, and Bob Feller, the 266-game winner for the Cleveland Indians, had their lifetime statistics most adversely affected.

Baseball soldiered on with patchwork lineups. The normally pathetic St. Louis Browns won a wartime pennant. One-armed Pete Gray became an inspiration, managing to perform a season in the Browns outfield. Rosters were short of first-class players and depth, but still no call went out to African American players instantly signable to correct the talent shortfall. Bill Veeck, the maverick owner who introduced the exploding scoreboard to Comiskey Park when he later operated the Chicago White Sox, and who had spent his entire life in baseball, was as color-blind as any owner in that select club of magnates, and was ready to implement his own two-part plan to blow segregation to smithereens.

Veeck was the outsider at the country club, new money (with a shaky bank balance at that) with new ways, compared to old-money owners locked into old ways. In 1943, the Philadelphia Phillies were for sale. Veeck scrambled to piece together an ownership consortium which he would head as president and lead into the National League.

It was Veeck's intention to stock the woeful Phillies (last in the league in 1938, 1939, 1940, 1941, 1942, and 1944) with the best talent available. If that meant mixing white and black players, fine. If that meant stacking the club with mostly black players, fine.

Veeck grew up in baseball. In his youth, his father was president of the Chicago Cubs. Veeck worked for the team for many years and he is the one who planted the famous ivy on the outfield walls at Wrigley Field. Later, in one of his flashiest stunts, and evidence that he was always an equal-opportunity employer, Veeck sent a midget up to bat, wearing the number "one-eighth" on his uniform jersey. Eddie Gaedel walked.

The future Hall of Fame owner was the polar opposite of a stuffed shirt. He repeatedly said baseball should be fun. He was liable to do anything to achieve that end and the other owners knew it. When Veeck hatched his plan to bring African Americans into baseball with the Phillies he made a fatal error. He informed Commissioner Kenesaw Mountain Landis in advance. Before Veeck realized what was going on, the Phillies had been sold to another buyer. Veeck would have rewritten history. There would have been no barrier-breaking Jackie Robinson, but rather a squadron of barrier breakers.

Sometime later, Veeck, while noting that bringing black players into the game and using them to build a winning team swiftly was the proper thing to do, admitted that the maneuver also appealed to his flamboyant side.

"Showman that I am—promoter, con man, knave—I was grabbing for the quick and easy publicity," Veeck said. "I am not going to suggest that I was innocent on that count."[3]

Baseball never did have a written policy excluding blacks. Publicly, Landis uttered statements pointing out that Major League baseball had no official rule blocking blacks from playing. In reality, it was an understood policy, a backroom law that the iron-willed Landis did not wish to see breached.

Unbeknownst to all the passionate do-gooders who were continuously thwarted, Branch Rickey, then running the St. Louis Cardinals, knew that if given a chance he would carefully and meticulously scout the black leagues and find a candidate to smash the color barrier. As it happened, he would not be able to implement his plan until after World War II when he moved to the Dodgers.

Yet even before the United States became embroiled in the war following the bombing of Pearl Harbor in December 1941, others also expected a change in baseball's stringent policy that had excluded African Americans from the game for nearly sixty years. Leaders of Negro League teams like Effa Manley in Newark (who in 2006 was posthumously elected and became the first female to be enshrined in the Baseball Hall of Fame), Gus Greenlee, who anchored the Crawfords, and Cumberland Posey, who

New York Giants outfielder Monte Irvin was a star in the Negro Leagues, but made a successful transition to the majors by swinging a big bat—though not several at a time except during warm-ups.

ran the Grays, recognized the goal of the disenfranchised players would someday be reached.

Yet time passed, year after year, with players aging, retiring, and never getting those Major League opportunities. The players, as Daniel Okrent, the writer and editor put it, "were left with memories, legends and an endless series of what-ifs."[4]

Black players talked among themselves and commented on who was likely to be the first taken. None gave the issue the depth of thought Rickey had. The players primarily thought in terms of the most skilled. Certainly, Satchel Paige, the colorful showman with the super fastball and the rubber arm would get the call. And Josh Gibson, the slugging catcher acknowledged to be the best hitter among them, would be in demand. Professional sport is basically a meritocracy. Those who play the best, who put up the best statistics, who win the most often, are rewarded the most richly. There are exceptions, but for the most part performance equates to payoff. The stars of the Negro Leagues would have been surprised to learn, as they ultimately did in 1947 when Jackie Robinson was signed to a Brooklyn deal by Rickey, that decision makers thought differently.

A first-class player was needed to be the first. But when Rickey ordered his subtle search he had other things in mind besides pure talent. He wanted one man to carry the flag for African Americans, a pathfinder who could hold his temper when insulted and even assaulted. Rickey was buying temperament as well as baseball expertise.

When Landis died in 1944 and was succeeded by Happy Chandler as commissioner, few thought the new man would initiate change. Chandler had been a U.S. senator from Kentucky. It seemed unlikely a southerner would become the standard bearer for the integration of baseball. But Chandler surprised all.

"If a black boy can make it on Okinawa and Guadalcanal," Chandler said, citing prominent World War II battle sites, "hell, he can make it in baseball."

As history showed, Jackie Robinson was the first African American to play in the majors in the twentieth century, but if not for World War II the man recalled as an American hero today might have been Irvin.

EARLY LIFE

Monte Irvin was born in Haleburg, Alabama, in 1919. It was a small town near the Georgia border and both of Irvin's parents, Cupid Alexander and Mary Eliza, were sharecroppers. Irvin was one of ten surviving children and the large family moved to New Jersey when he was eight.

Although like most boys of the day, Irvin was enamored of baseball, he grew up with no illusions. He realized the majors were for white men and the Negro Leagues were for black men.

"When I was growing up," Irvin said, "you could not even think of making it. The doors were closed. It was almost unbelievable when it changed."[5]

But Irvin had mentally catalogued some of the efforts and arguments made on behalf of African American players. The rumblings of "If they can fight for us, why can't they play for us?" grew louder. "Some free-thinking people like New York Mayor Fiorello LaGuardia and Congressman Adam Clayton Powell stood up for us," Irvin said.[6]

Irvin said he was always a guy with a placid disposition who got along with everyone. That attribute, and his all-around playing ability, might have made him attractive to proponents of integration before the war.

"I didn't know about it at the time," he said. "Then Effa Manley told me. It made me feel good, but I went into the Army in 1942. As a player then I didn't have a weakness."[7]

A natural athlete as a kid, Irvin took to swimming first, but played baseball in a church league, on a semipro team, and a multitown suburban team, and whenever an all-black team like the Jacksonville Red Caps appeared in the area, he was in attendance. Irvin lived in an integrated neighborhood and said relations were good between white and black kids who played sports together on the playgrounds.[8]

The young Irvin, who attended Orange High School, was a superb football player (offered a scholarship to Lincoln University), a slugging baseball player, and a top-notch basketball player, and as a track man he could throw a javelin about as far as he could heave a hardball. At least it seemed so since he set a state record that stood for years. Irvin also dabbled in throwing the shot put and discus. He earned sixteen varsity letters during his high school career. Even before high school, Irvin's prowess was evident on the diamond. As a thirteen-year-old he was picked up by the local semipro outfit, the Orange Triangles. Over time Irvin split his game between pitching and catching, and sometimes played shortstop. "I could hit a baseball farther than anyone," he believed.[9]

Every town features a local stud athlete whose future seems boundless. Reality often sets in when the athlete moves on to tougher competition against a wider pool of athletes. Reality set in for Irvin in a different way, however, in the guise of an illness that threatened not only his future in sports, but also his life.

As a senior at Orange High, Irvin was keeping up his usual hectic, around-the-calendar sports pace. The basketball team was about a half dozen games into its season when Irvin became ill. The first signs that something was amiss struck when he was walking home from school with hoop teammates. Initially, Irvin had a bothersome head-ache. But it was not a familiar pain.

"I had to sit down on the curb and wait until my head cleared before I could continue walking," he remembered. "I told my teammates to go on because I thought I would eventually be okay. I only lived about a mile and a half from the high school, but I had to stop and sit down three or four times before I finally made it home."[10]

The aspirin Irvin's mother treated him with did not make a dent in the pounding in his head and Irvin asked to go to a doctor or the hospital. At first doctors thought he had Rocky Mountain Spotted Fever, but that diagnosis was rejected in favor of an infection. Medical personnel believed that a cut on Irvin's middle finger had become infected and the infection had spread up his arm and into his chest. It took three days to reach this conclusion and the medical professionals did not realize it until a large syringe was thrust into Irvin's chest and removed carrying pus.

Sulfur drugs, used to treat such an illness later, had not yet been invented, so Irvin underwent surgery to drain the pus. He burned with fever, was weak, had no appetite, and was placed on the critical list for two days. He required several blood transfusions. At one point doctors summoned Irvin's mother to ask her if they could amputate his left arm. She refused permission. Irvin spent six weeks in the hospital and by the time he began to feel healthier he had lost thirty pounds. "I was near death," Irvin wrote.[11]

In his playing prime, Irvin stood six-foot-two and weighed 195 pounds. He had not completely filled out by the time of his illness, so he seemed skeletal when he finally went home. His mother believed that home cooking would rebuild his strength, and if that sounded like a naive faith, once Irvin sat down at her table with renewed appetite he did rebound.

"When I got home she cooked candied yams, fried corn, carrots, peas and cobbler," Irvin recalled. "All the things that I liked. I also drank very rich goat's milk and in a month I had gained most of the weight back."[12]

As soon as he was sharp enough, Irvin returned to the baseball diamond. In the summer of 1938, only a few months after his life-threatening hospital stay, he began "traveling" with the Newark Eagles for the first time. Irvin skipped home games because he did not want to be recognized. If he played as a professional he would lose his amateur standing and be ineligible to play ball in college.

In a more innocent time, before mass communication spread every rumor in an instant, before radio was comprehensive, television was ubiquitous and the Internet was all-seeking, players could compete out of the limelight under an assumed name. Unless they bumped into someone who knew them from home, they likely were home free. There were no photographs routinely printed of Negro Leagues games and no reason to think a high schooler from Orange would be recognized on the road in Kansas City, Rochester, New York, or elsewhere. Irvin used the name "Jimmy Nelson" for Eagles games, chosen because he had a friend who was a catcher of the same name.

When he was an all-around star for Orange High, Irvin's coaches told him he would earn a scholarship to the University of Michigan or to Rutgers. Their words sounded like promises, but no one delivered. In the fall of 1938, disappointed that the name schools did not come through, Irvin enrolled at Lincoln, a school located about fifty miles south of Philadelphia, that had just one white student.

Wary of jumping into football so soon after his debilitating health problem, Irvin postponed the start of his gridiron career for a few games. When he suited up he was pleased to discover he had not lost speed or power. He then resumed his school year-round schedule of football in the fall, basketball in the winter, and track and baseball in the spring. But Lincoln proved a letdown and Irvin departed from the school before his sophomore year ended. He felt it was time to chase the dream of playing big-time baseball and this time when Irvin joined the Newark Eagles, he did so under his given name.

Irvin was an intelligent man, with a high school diploma on his resume and some college education in his background. After making the rounds with the Eagles in preceding years he understood the lay of the land. He knew that not every town welcomed an African American baseball team with open arms. He realized the road promised prejudice as much as adventure. He was young, just past twenty, but he was not naive. He was a realist, attuned to the difficulty of making a living in the Negro Leagues and wise enough to take his pleasures where he could. Irvin's Negro Leagues experience was typical of the time, including long bus rides, and encountering segregated eating and sleeping conditions whenever the bus stopped.[13]

In a 1986 Newark *Star-Ledger* article, Irvin discussed the complicated pros and cons of Eagles life. "We stayed in third-rate hotels," he said. "I guess it cost $1.50 The travel was bad, the lighting at the parks was terrible, but we didn't fret too much. We just loved the game and were just glad to be playing somewhere."

As someone who had followed black baseball, Irvin came into the Negro Leagues with some historical knowledge. He idolized Oscar Charleston, one of the greatest of the early big-time black players who was nicknamed "The Hoosier Comet." Charleston, who was born in 1894 and died in 1954, was way too early for the recognition gathered by players born a generation later.

Charleston was fiery, but a sweet swinger, with two .400 seasons and nine straight .350 seasons documented in Negro Leagues play. The five-foot-eleven Charleston was a hitting machine when weighing a lean 175 pounds; he was more of a player-manager for several teams late in his career when he weighed in at about 240 pounds. His career was chronicled as much by word of mouth as anything, but in his autobiography *I Was Right on Time*, former Kansas City Monarchs star Buck O'Neil said that Charleston was the best player he ever saw, Willie Mays and Ty Cobb included. In 1976, more than twenty years after his death, Charleston's reputation was still so impressive that he was elected to the Baseball Hall of Fame.[14] "My hero had been Oscar Charleston," Irvin said. "I saw him play near the end of his career."[15]

Irvin's baseball ability was well established before he graduated from Orange High. At age seventeen, Irvin had his first tryout with a Negro Leagues club, the Homestead Grays. The Grays were soon to embark on one of the greatest runs in sports history, capturing nine straight Negro National League pennants. The team's motto was "The same team that won last night is gonna win again tonight," Irvin recalled.[16]

Irvin said he was in the batting cage, taking his cuts, when catcher Josh Gibson, who was called the black Babe Ruth, and first baseman Buck Leonard, who was called the black Lou Gehrig, sauntered up and began chattering. "Who is this fella?" they said, according to Irvin. "They were well-dressed, great looking. I'll never forget it. We became close friends."[17]

That was a little bit later, after Irvin finished high school and began to make his mark with the Eagles. In 1941, he signed up for winter ball in Puerto Rico and Gibson, stayed at the same hotel.

"I got to know him," Irvin said. "We used to hang out and drink beer together. Josh in his prime, he knew nobody could hit like him. He's the best hitter I've ever seen. He had more power than anyone I've ever seen. He had this great upper body strength. We used to talk about hitting. In the winter leagues, in Mexico and Puerto Rico, he was The Man."[18]

Irvin gradually become one of the top men in Newark's lineup. In 1939, the first season for which there are records of Irvin's Negro Leagues play, he got into twenty-two games and batted .403. The next year in thirty-six games he hit .361. In 1941, he batted .380 in thirty games. And in 1942, Irvin saw action in only eight games for Newark, but hit .531. That summer, in Mexico, representing Vera Cruz, Irvin led the league with a .397 average, 20 home runs, and 79 RBIs in sixty-three games. He won the Triple Crown.[19] And then he went into the service, his baseball career on hold until 1945.

Irvin was standing on second base in Puerto Rico, in the middle of a winter league game, when the news broke of the Japanese bombing of Pearl Harbor. The stampede to return to the mainland tied up transportation and with no commitment that he could leave by plane for weeks, Irvin booked passage on a once-a-week ship with fellow players, including future Hall of Famer Roy Campanella.

Irvin felt he was at the top of his game, in this prime, when World War II intervened and he joined the Army.[20] Irvin was assigned to an all-black engineering unit. President Harry Truman's executive order to desegregate the Armed Services was still a few years in the future. The ship that carried Irvin across the Atlantic took nineteen days to reach England, and Irvin served the war cause in England, France, and Germany. Early on Irvin was shaken up by the German bombing of a supply depot in Plymouth shortly after his crew stopped guarding it. The depot was leveled.

By the time the 1313 General Service Engineers rode into France, it was August 1944, two months past D-Day. The liberated French greeted American soldiers with enthusiasm. The unit made a field trip to Epernay, where champagne is a more popular drink than Coca-Cola. The soldiers took advantage of that when they found a wine cellar.

As Major League baseball moved toward integration in the 1940s, there was talk that Monte Irvin would be the first black player invited into organized ball. World War II intervened and Irvin did not get his chance until after the war. Later, Irvin had a second career as a key assistant in the baseball commissioner's office.

"For several weeks many of us never drank water," Irvin recalled. "We would fill our canteens with champagne."

Treating champagne as if it poured from a faucet was something too good to be true and once officers heard about the scheme, they forbade it.[21]

Soldiers always dream of home. The more danger they are in the more acute the longing. The more distance they are stationed from family and familiarity, the more powerful the urge is to seek normalcy. Irvin was in the Army for three years and most of that time he imagined how he would return to the states and resume his baseball career with the Newark Eagles, just where he had left off in 1942.

PLAYING CAREER

When Irvin got home after being discharged on September 1, 1945, he faced more than one surprise. Branch Rickey had begun his surreptitious search for the ideal African American to introduce to the Major League baseball world. He remembered well a young slugging Monte Irvin who could play infield and outfield, hit for average and power. Rickey invited Irvin to the Brooklyn Dodgers offices at 215 Montague Street for a discreet chat.

This was the impossible becoming reality. What Effa Manley talked of was true. A black man in the majors? It had been unthinkable during the entirety of Irvin's youth. Rickey offered Irvin a contract to start in the minors with the plan of moving up to the Dodgers as soon as he demonstrated success. However, there was one problem: Irvin wasn't ready. The years away from the game in the Army, in the war, and overseas messed with his equilibrium. Irvin was not at ease, did not feel ready to play against high level competition, to become the focus of such attention. He wasn't sure about his reflexes, his bat speed, or if he would again be able to master the sport he played so well before joining the Army.

"When I came back I found my nerves had gone bad on me," Irvin said. "I didn't feel right and I wasn't the same person. It was something that happened to a lot of guys from being away from their lives for so long. It was hard to adjust. I had to start over, to relearn everything."[22]

Reluctantly he told Rickey that as much as he wanted to, he couldn't do it. It was a fleeting chance to become a hero to African Americans nationwide, but he couldn't let down himself, his fellow players, or the fans. It was a discouraging moment. After the meeting, Irvin left immediately for winter ball in Puerto Rico to get in condition. Irvin went about recapturing his swing, his thirst for the game, and his skills. He was playing in Puerto Rico when he heard the Dodgers had signed Jackie Robinson to a contract on October 23 to play the 1946 season with their top Montreal farm club of the International League.

Before the war, Irvin thought he might be the player chosen to break baseball's color barrier and when Robinson was selected, he was briefly wistful about the missed chance.[23]

Fate and Branch Rickey decided differently. Irvin understood that Robinson's selection was both an honor and a fearsome burden. Irvin believed he would have been up to the task of carrying the hopes of all black ballplayers on his shoulders if he was at full strength. Irvin believed his priority had to be restoring his game to its top-shelf, pre-Pearl Harbor level. Only then could Irvin worry anew about trying to make it in the white majors.

Just like a patient recovering from an illness, Irvin took care not to do too much too soon. It took until 1946 for the skills Irvin displayed as a young man to return. That season he batted .401 for Newark and led the league in hits and doubles.

Irvin did not really have a feel for how Robinson would fare on the field. Robinson's college exploits indicated he was a great all-around athlete, but he played just one year with the Monarchs before Rickey scoped him out and scooped him up. While Irvin represented the Eagles in the Negro Leagues World Series, Robinson starred for Montreal in the AAA International League minors. That was one step below the National League. Robinson's success surprised and pleased black ballplayers.

"When Branch Rickey first signed him, we didn't think that much of him as a player," Irvin wrote. "At the time we thought there were better players in our league. But when Jackie reported to Montreal in 1946, he tore up the International League. He hit, ran and played good all-around baseball. And he just constantly improved."[24]

For Irvin it was more restoration than improvement. He batted .317 for Newark in 1947 and .319 for the Eagles in 1948. Within a year or two of his breakthrough, Robinson was joined by other black stars in the majors. Irvin realized what that meant for the long-term prospects of the Eagles and other black clubs.

"We knew the Negro Leagues were not going to last," Irvin said. "The attention was all on the big leagues because all the greats were moving up there. Roy Campanella, Larry Doby—everybody."[25]

Irvin was back to being a star in the Negro Leagues, one of the top choices for the annual East-West All-Star game that was a showcase of African American baseball. Even years later, when he had passed through the majors and was selected to the Baseball Hall of Fame, his accomplishments in his old league lived on in players' memories.

"Irvin's not in the Hall of Fame because of what he did in the majors," said Don Newcombe, one of the other Dodger black pioneers. "He's in there because of what he did in the Negro Leagues. I played with him there and he deserved to come to the majors long before he finally did." "He could really run, but he was best at hitting the ball very hard and very far away. I saw him hit some balls into the centerfield bleachers at the Polo Grounds in New York—some 450 feet from home plate."[26]

The contrast in photographs between the front cover and the back cover of Irvin's autobiography *Nice Guys Finish First*, written with black baseball expert James A. Riley, could not be more vivid. The front shows a young man smiling broadly, with his teeth gleaming, eyes flashing, and with excitement and expectation written across his face. The back cover picture shows a slightly graying, fuller-faced, unsmiling Irvin, broader and more filled out, with the look, on his face, of a man who has seen it all.

Hank Thompson was a younger, up-and-coming Negro Leagues player who batted .375 for the Monarchs in 1948. He packed surprising power into his five-foot-nine and a half, 174-pound frame. Like Irvin and other African American players, in an era of U.S. segregation, he found hospitality playing ball in Cuba during the winter. During the winter following the 1948 campaign, he and Irvin were on a hot streak in Cuba when Giants scout Alex Pompez passed through. Pompez liked what he saw in both men. He told Irvin and Thompson that the Giants were interested in their services. Would they be interested in playing for New York? "Of course," Irvin said. "We both signed and they sent us to Jersey City of the International League in 1949."[27]

Few big-league owners were willing to take the chance of bringing an African American player directly to the majors regardless of credentials. Cautiously, the blacks were assigned to top minor league teams, if not for what could be termed insulting "seasoning," at least for adjustment purposes, testing how they mingled and performed with white teammates and foes. Giants owner Horace Stoneham—perhaps because of his proximity to Newark—was more generous than most others who simply raided the Negro Leagues for their best players with nothing offered in return. Stoneham bought Irvin's contract from Newark for $5,000 and Effa Manley used the cash to buy a mink stole. The plush purchase was not going to fill a hole in her lineup, but at least she would feel good.

Irvin and Thompson began the season in Jersey City. Irvin was hitting .373 after sixty-three games. He had the extra pleasure of playing in front of many of his New Jersey friends and relatives. He even lived at his old house. On July 1, Giants manager Leo Durocher requested their promotion to the big club. "We were really tearing the cover off the ball," Irvin said. "We were having so much fun in the International League we didn't want to go."[28]

It was a moment Irvin had awaited for years, but because he was older, more mature, because he had been through a war and the fright of losing his skills, he was not giddy. He appreciated the call-up, but he was also reflective.

"I was ripe at age nineteen for the big leagues," Irvin said. "I was thirty when the big leagues called, well past my peak."[29]

It was more than three years since Branch Rickey had begun his "great experiment" as he described the signing of Jackie Robinson to break the color barrier, but despite the influx of other black players in big-league locker rooms, Durocher felt it necessary to address the primarily white team when the Giants first black players, Irvin and Thompson, reported.

"Durocher came in and introduced himself," Irvin said. "Then he called a five-minute team meeting. It was the only thing he said about race. He said, 'I think they can help us. I don't care what color you are, if you can play and help us make money. Black, white, yellow, pink, you can play for me.' He set the tone for us."[30]

Irvin said he was struck by how simple it was to just go out and play with white players, how there never should have been a fear among black players that they could not measure up, and how white owners should long ago have just signed the best talent.

"Why didn't you think we could play against major leaguers?" Irvin remembered thinking. He said a Major League owner that he wished to keep anonymous once confessed to him, " 'We were stupid. We were dumb.' It just shows the stupidity of Judge Landis. Clark Griffith had been renting his stadium in Washington, D.C. to the Homestead Grays at the same time his Senators were the worst team in the American League. All he had to do was change their uniforms and they would go from last to first. He was too stupid to do it. Bill Veeck should have just gone ahead with his plan with the Phillies. He could have integrated the team and drawn like crazy."[31]

Monte Irvin and Jackie Robinson—the Dodger player who broke baseball's color line when he signed in 1945 and joined the Major League club in 1947—show some children the markings on a bat.

Contrary to Durocher's optimism and Irvin's wishes, neither he nor Thompson contributed much that season. Irvin was tried at third base, but said his reflexes were not as sharp as they had been. He hit only .224 in thirty-six Giants games. Things turned around the next year. In 1950, Irvin suited up for eighteen Jersey City games and was swatting the ball at a surreal .510 pace when he rejoined the Giants for the season as a periodic first baseman, but mainly an outfielder, where he felt most self-assured.

Buck O'Neil, the elder statesman of Negro Leagues players, said Irvin's self-assessment of his abilities, between the time he first played professionally and the time he joined the Giants, is on the money.

"He could hit, run, field, throw and hit with power," O'Neil said. "He could play. I just wish he could have played earlier. When he was nineteen or twenty he was two steps quicker. His bat was quicker."[32]

Irvin's genial manner helped him integrate into the Giants daily life—although he and Thompson did face discrimination with spring training housing in Florida. They were forced to stay in hotels away from the rest of the team. But that did not faze Irvin much because the long-awaited objective of reaching the majors was met.

The Giants were a team on the rise, a team poised to give the Brooklyn Dodgers a run for the pennant. Irvin moved into the lineup in 1950 and batted .299. The next year, the season of the Giants miracle finish on Bobby Thomson's playoff home run to edge the Dodgers, was probably his best in the majors. He looked as if he had regained all the spark of his youth. Playing in 151 games, Irvin hit .312 with 24 home runs and a league-leading 121 RBIs. He also stole 12 bases. Also notable was the periodic Giants lineup that placed Irvin in left field, Willie Mays in center, and Hank Thompson in right, constituting the first all–African American Major League outfield. In the dramatic final inning of the playoff, Irvin made the only out. Later he joked that his contribution was not hitting into a double play.

The rivalry with the Dodgers was so fierce, the capture of the flag so electrifying, Irvin was actually able to say that playing in a World Series against the New York Yankees was an anticlimax. He did have a memorable moment, though—stealing home in the opener of the 1951 World Series against the Yankees.[33]

In 1952, Irvin hit .310, but his season was cut short by a compound fracture of the right ankle, suffered on a slide running from first to third on a Willie Mays single. He came back strong in 1953, hitting a Major League high .329 with 21 homers and 97 RBIs. At thirty-five Irvin had one additional full-time Major League season left in him. In 1954, when the Giants won another pennant and came into the World Series underdogs to the Cleveland Indians, he hit 19 home runs with 64 RBIs, though he batted only .262.

At his finest, Irvin was a feared hitter and certain pitchers never figured out a way to successfully keep him off the base paths. One hurler Irvin particularly chewed up was the Dodgers Preacher Roe. Roe was a slick pitcher who admitted upon retirement that he sometimes threw an illegal spitter, though nothing helped him when Irvin dug into the batter's box.[34] Roe said that Irvin could hit him any time, even when he was throwing the best stuff up to the plate.

The Indians had won an American League record 111 regular-season games. The Tribe featured a dazzling pitching staff that included Bob Lemon, Mike Garcia, and Early Wynn, and a slugging lineup that depended upon Al Rosen and Larry Doby. In one of the most notable upsets in baseball history, the Giants swept the Indians in four straight games. It did not figure then and if the Series were replayed today, the Indians probably would still be favorites. The key play in the Series was Mays' stunning, back-to-the-plate catch of a Vic Wertz shot in deep, deep Polo Grounds centerfield in the opener. As he made the catch, Mays whirled around and fired the ball to the infield to also prevent baserunners from scoring.

"It was the breaks of the game and we got the breaks and they didn't," Irvin said. Irvin, who roomed with Mays on the road, said he did not think even the brilliant fielder could make the grab 460 feet from home and so Irvin was preparing to play a carom and hopefully hold Wertz to a triple. As he and Mays trotted into the dugout at the end of the inning, Irvin said, "Roomie, I didn't think you were going to get that. And he said, 'Are you kidding? I had it all the way.'" Nobody besides Durocher, who may have been fibbing when he said so, believed that. The Mays catch is shown over and over on baseball highlight shows even today.[35]

Mays' brief involvement with Negro Leagues baseball was more like a season of apprenticeship in the high minors. In some ways he was the Irvin that Irvin never got to show the wide world. He was the five-tool player of O'Neil's description, to many the most magnificent all-around baseball player of all time. Mays was a Durocher favorite and Irvin became his mentor, teaching him what he could, imparting tales of his own experiences, shielding him from accidental controversy. Mays was about twelve years younger and Irvin became a protective big brother.

Irvin said that young Willie Mays reminded him of the young Monte Irvin and he knew he could help the young man develop as a player and in coping with the big-league atmosphere. The men became lifelong friends.[36]

Irvin's final season with the Giants was 1955. It was not a terrific one. He batted just .253 and spent part of the summer with Minneapolis in the minors. The demotion shocked Irvin, though he had to concede he had slowed since the broken ankle. The next year he experienced a mini resurgence in his final Major League season with the Chicago Cubs, hitting .271 with 15 home runs and 50 RBIs. Age was affecting his play and Irvin knew it, but he did not feel ready to retire. He played a few games with Los Angeles in the Pacific Coast League in 1957 and then stored his spikes.

Yet Irvin was far from finished with baseball. If his early playing days with the Newark Eagles represented Act I, and his Major League days represented Act II, Irvin's Act III in the game may have been the most significant.

LATER LIFE

After an interlude working for the Rheinhold Brewing Company, in 1968 Irvin was hired to help then-baseball commissioner Spike Eckert at Major League baseball headquarters. When Eckert was fired by the owners, his successor, Bowie Kuhn, kept Irvin on in 1969 and Irvin stayed with the office for sixteen years as special assistant. He was a troubleshooter sent to handle problems all over the nation and during that era, when baseball changed forever, with players gaining the negotiating upper hand over the owners for the first time, the agenda was always full and heated. With player rights, arbitration, gambling issues, and the admittance of Negro Leaguers to the Hall of Fame, the Kuhn administration was never dull. Irvin was always in the mix, in the thick of disputes, a special emissary sent to patch up differences. He was Kuhn's right-hand man and one of the most visible defenders of the same Major Leagues that would not allow his membership two decades earlier.

"It was a perfect job," Irvin said. "I helped promote baseball all over the country and all over the world.[37]

Irvin represented baseball in Puerto Rico, Mexico, Japan, and Venezuela, at All-Star games, and the World Series. When Richie Allen, the star slugger of the Phillies, had difficulty with his front office, and when Curt Flood filed his landmark lawsuit refusing to accept a trade between the St. Louis Cardinals and the Phillies, Irvin was the behind-the-scenes man dispatched to calm hot tempers.

"When Bowie had a problem with a player he would send me to see him," Irvin said. "I asked Richie Allen if he wanted to meet with him [the commissioner]. I tried to talk Curt Flood out of going to Europe and into staying in baseball. I had a chance to build a rapport and relationships with guys I played with and others. I was able to do some good."[38]

Irvin was temperamentally suited for the position. That would not surprise Jerome Holtzman, the Hall of Fame baseball writer who covered the game for Chicago newspapers for decades. In commenting on Irvin's *Nice Guys Finish First* autobiography in the *Chicago Tribune* in 1996, Holtzman said it was an appropriate title.

"I can't ever remember meeting a nicer guy than Monte Irvin," Holtzman wrote. Although many players praise Irvin in the book as a good guy and easygoing, Holtzman said the compliments could be misleading. "If this sounds like Monte Irvin is a marshmallow, beware: Though he was the antithesis of the Leo Durocher dictum, 'Nice guys finish last,' Irvin was a ferocious competitor." Neither did Irvin pitch softballs in the book, Holtzman noted, but rather offered blunt storytelling.[39]

One of Irvin's greatest contributions before he retired again at age sixty-five in 1984 was serving as a member of Kuhn's Negro Leagues Committee for the Hall of Fame. The group was organized to deliver justice to the forgotten, overlooked, and discriminated-against stars of black baseball, players whose careers were over and who never got the Major League shot they deserved. More than thirty-five years later, despite a steady selection of players, owners, and black baseball pioneers, the Hall of Fame was still attempting to right the wrongs of the past. "It's terrific and it's still growing," Irvin said.[40]

Irvin's own Hall of Fame turn came in 1973. The press conference announcing his selection to the Hall brought him and his wife Dee to the Americana Hotel in New York in February. "My only regret was that I didn't get a chance [in the majors] sooner," Irvin said. "But I hold no bitterness. I'm just happy I finally did get a chance. Baseball has been my whole life and it has been wonderful."[41]

Ballplayers from every corner of the game chimed in with their thoughts on Irvin's greatness. Irvin was an All Star in the National League and was the Most Valuable Player in the Negro National League and in the Mexican and Cuban leagues.

"Monte was the best all-around player I have ever seen," former Dodgers catcher Roy Campanella said. "There wasn't anything Monte couldn't do and there wasn't any position he couldn't play. He was one of the fastest men for his size I ever saw and what most people don't know is what a tremendous arm he had. Oh, what an arm. He threw nothing but strikes."[42]

On August 6, 1973, Irvin was inducted into the Hall of Fame in Cooperstown, New York. It was a grand moment for a man who contributed to the sport in so many ways, experienced so many different facets of it, and spent the better part of a half century in the game. "Being elected for this honor is the highest tribute that can be paid to a player," Irvin said, adding that it was "one day I will never forget. It was a sense of accomplishment. It meant that the long bus rides, the hard training, and all of the unfavorable conditions that I faced had finally paid off. This certainly was the crowning point of my life and I was deeply appreciative."[43]

Bob Broeg, the *St. Louis Post-Dispatch* veteran sportswriter, was on hand when Irvin was inducted into the Hall and used the occasion to compare the changes in baseball's racial outlook over the years.

"Once upon a bashful time in America's race relations, the only way big, handsome Monte Merrill Irvin could have gone into Cooperstown's fashionable Otesaga Hotel would have been through the back door," Broeg wrote. "And the only way he could have entered the Baseball Hall of Fame would have been as a cash customer.

"But in ceremonies this morning under the shade trees near the steps of the Hall of Fame's library, Irvin was inducted into the Hall of Fame as a full-fledged member, no questions asked. And the Otesaga, a lovely place overlooking Lake Otsego, headwaters of the Susquehanna River, welcomed him as a first-class, front-door guest."[44]

Just as baseball and society were so interwoven when Jackie Robinson broke in and Monte Irvin followed, Broeg's commentary linked the two again.

In 1984, with no more need to continue living near the New York City headquarters of baseball, Irvin and his wife settled in Homosassa, Florida. Even as he grayed and aged, Irvin continued to be available for baseball causes. He frequently signed autographs and donated the profits to programs benefiting youth baseball and Negro Leagues players. He spoke out against baseball player union strikes, said Pete Rose was definitely guilty of gambling, and picked up the occasional honor.

On June 6, 1986, the former Grover Street Oval in Orange, New Jersey, where Irvin played baseball as a youngster, was named a national historic site and renamed Monte Irvin Field. "The fact that I was honored in that way made me very grateful," Irvin said. "I hope that by naming this park after me, it will be an inspiration to some of the youngsters coming along today."[45]

When Irvin began playing baseball in the 1930s the checks bore microscopic numbers compared to what Major League players earn today. Yet the value of a dollar was quite different, too.

"Before the war I made $200 a month in the Negro Leagues," he said. "The average person made $10 to $20 a week. We got $1 a day meal money, but you could get a complete meal for 30 cents. You could do pretty well. In the majors, the salary was $5,000 minimum and meal money was $5 a day."[46]

The kind of money paid to professional ballplayers in the 2000s, millions to the stars, hundreds of thousands to bench players, was inconceivable in the 1950s, never mind during Depression days. The minimum for a man carried on the twenty-five-man roster of a Major League team in 2005 was $316,000. "Isn't that something?" reflected Irvin. "There's been a lot of progress. I've seen a lot of change."[47] What Monte Irvin did not say was that he helped much of that progress and change along the way.

NOTES

1. Monte Irvin, personal interview, January 7, 2006.
2. Ken Burns (director, producer), *Baseball* documentary, DVD, Florentine Films, The Baseball Film Project, WETA Washington, DC, 1994.
3. Mark Ribowsky, *Don't Look Back: Satchel Paige in the Shadows of Baseball* (New York: Simon & Schuster, 1994).
4. Burns, *Baseball*.
5. Irvin, personal interview, January 7, 2006.
6. Ibid.
7. Ibid.

8. Monte Irvin with James A. Riley, *Nice Guys Finish First: The Autobiography of Monte Irvin* (New York: Carroll & Graf Publishers, 1996).

9. Irvin with Riley, *Nice Guys Finish First*, 25.

10. Irvin with Riley, *Nice Guys Finish First*, 29.

11. Irvin with Riley, *Nice Guys Finish First*, 31.

12. Ibid.

13. Irvin with Riley, *Nice Guys Finish First*, 67.

14. Thom Loverro, *The Encyclopedia of Negro League Baseball* (New York: Checkmark Books, 2003), 51–53.

15. Irvin, personal interview, January 7, 2006.

16. Ibid.

17. Ibid.

18. Ibid.

19. Dick Clark and Larry Lester (eds.), *The Negro Leagues Book* (Cleveland: Society for American Baseball Research, 1994), 286.

20. Irvin with Riley, *Nice Guys Finish First*, 97.

21. Irvin with Riley, *Nice Guys Finish First*, 101.

22. Jeff Becker, *St. Petersburg Times*, June 20, 1993.

23. Irvin with Riley, *Nice Guys Finish First*, 108–109.

24. Irvin with Riley, *Nice Guys Finish First*, 108.

25. Becker, *St. Petersburg Times*, June 20, 1993.

26. Ibid.

27. Irvin, personal interview, January 7, 2006.

28. Ibid.

29. *Newark Star-Ledger*, 1986.

30. Irvin, personal interview, January 7, 2006.

31. Ibid.

32. Buck O'Neil, personal interview, December 7, 2005.

33. Irvin with Riley, *Nice Guys Finish First*, 163.

34. Irvin with Riley, *Nice Guys Finish First*, 150.

35. Irvin with Riley, *Nice Guys Finish First*, 181.

36. Irvin with Riley, *Nice Guys Finish First*, 129–131.

37. Irvin, personal interview, January 7, 2006.

38. Ibid.

39. Jerome Holtzman, *Chicago Tribune*, May 12, 1996.

40. Irvin, personal interview, January 7, 2006.

41. Jack Lang, *Sporting News*, February 24, 1973.

42. Ibid.

43. Irvin with Riley, *Nice Guys Finish First*, 218.

44. Bob Broeg, *St. Louis Post-Dispatch*, August 6, 1973.

45. Irvin with Riley, *Nice Guys Finish First*, 235.

46. Irvin, personal interview, January 7, 2006.

47. Ibid.

Further Reading

Irvin, Monte, with James A. Riley, *Nice Guys Finish First: The Autobiography of Monte Irvin.* New York: Carroll & Graf, 1996.

Loverro, Thom, *The Encyclopedia of Negro League Baseball.* New York: Checkmark Books, 2003.

WILLIE MAYS

May 6, 1931–

Willie Mays was just old enough to play in the Negro Leagues, and just talented enough to make Americans forget what color he was. Mays was the first true Major League African American superstar of the 1950s with the New York and San Francisco Giants.

Mays dazzled baseball fans with his hitting, fielding, and base running and in a twenty-two-year Major League career he batted .302, hit 660 home runs, fourth most in history, and drove in 1,903 runs. A twenty-time All Star, Mays is often considered the best player of his generation and some call the man who began his pay-for-play baseball career with the Birmingham Black Barons the greatest player of all time.

Willie Mays' presence in the midtown baseball stadium where such teams as the Anchorage Glacier Pilots and the Anchorage Bucs compete in the Alaska Baseball League was like the sighting of an Unidentified Flying Object for many of the hundreds of lunchtime visitors who turned out on a summer afternoon for an autograph. They knew what their eyes told them, but when they went back to work and told coworkers they had just seen Willie Mays, they risked being reported to the government.

It was not really that Mays was the equivalent of a flying saucer, it was that he was too familiar to be real. It was difficult to match Willie Mays to Alaska. As it happened, he was there to make a celebrity appearance to play golf and raise money for charity and the baseball fans from the 49th State who wanted to take advantage of the rare experience came out to touch a legend.

It was 1984 and Mays was out of baseball due to a dramatic commissioner's ruling banning him from the sport because he was serving as a

A mature Willie Mays with the San Francisco Giants, long after his debut with the New York Giants. Mays, who some call the greatest player ever, began his career in 1947 with the Negro Leagues' Birmingham Black Barons.

greeter at an Atlantic City casino. But Mays' exploits were not far removed from active memory. He could run, field, hit, hit with power, and throw. Those are the five skills scouts look at when they jot down notes on young prospects. Mays had it all and did it all. The numbers he compiled in his long Major League career were hard to grasp. Not only did Mays smash 660 home runs, but he also collected 3,283 hits in a sport where 3,000 hits classify a batter as immortal.

Those statistics ensured Mays' place in the Baseball Hall of Fame. But Willie Mays the baseball player was more than the sum of all those dry number parts. The way he mastered the diamond was poetry in motion. He wreaked havoc on the base paths stretching singles to doubles, scoring runs from second base when by all rights he should have camped at third. He was like an antelope in the outfield, patrolling center field with seemingly effortless speedy strides. Invariably, as his body churned toward the struck baseball, May's cap flew off. It was a trademark.

Mays made things happen on offense with abruptness, manufacturing the improbable out of the impossible. He ruined the opposition's hopes by stealing his foes' best hits. And then he spun around, off-balance after making the unlikely grab of a fly ball over his shoulder, and threw with all his might toward home plate. The pegs trapped runners, turned them into outs when they were certain to score a run unmolested, and sent them into the dugout hanging their heads.

"The excitement of Willie Mays is never predictable," an early biography of him noted. "He may turn a game upside down with his bat, his glove, his arm, his legs. And even though we know by now that Mays has all these talents, all these vehicles at his disposal, he still continues to amaze and confound us."[1]

It is difficult to simply summarize all what Willie Mays did so well. He created an aura of perfection. He confronted placid lulls in the game and transformed them into exciting moments. A young man of twenty-eight stood in the long line on the Mulcahy Park grass in Alaska waiting his turn for Mays' autograph. He wore a business suit and the Wilson baseball glove that he used to play softball. Al Whittaker could have been devouring a sandwich, soda and chips, but came to see Mays instead. The look that passed across the man's face was one of confusion, as if reacting to a trick question when he was asked why he was there. "Because he's Willie Mays," Whittaker said.[2]

He was Willie Mays and he is Willie Mays. More than three decades after Mays' retirement from baseball, the pool of witnesses who saw him play in person is diminishing. But the film lives on. And any fan of the game, no matter how young, knows the name. There is always someone around to place an arm about a shoulder, point Mays out in a crowd, and inform a youngster that Mays may be the best there ever was.

EARLY LIFE

Willie Howard Mays was born in Westfield, Alabama, in 1931. His father, also named Willie Howard Mays, was a steel worker and then a train porter. He was only eighteen when his son was born and still playing baseball on local teams himself. The older Mays was a first-rate player who gained the nickname of "Kitty Cat" because of his quickness. Mays' mother, Ann, also a teenager, had been a track star, so young Mays inherited athletic ability from both sides of the family. Mays' parents split when he was three. While his mom remarried, his father took in two older orphan girls to help raise Willie. Mays always referred to them as his aunts.

Kitty Cat had his son fooling around with a baseball when he was barely a year old, and young Willie was attracted to the game in his childhood. Sometimes he played catch with a friend, and Mays pretended to be Joe DiMaggio. Mays made his Major League debut the year DiMaggio retired from the Yankees and Mickey Mantle broke in as his replacement. For most of their careers, especially the years centered in New York, Mantle and Mays would be compared. As great as Mantle was, his plague of injuries lessened his long-term impact and few would argue today that Mantle was a greater player than Mays.

Mays was regarded as big for his age in his early teens. But in his prime baseball days he was not especially large, playing for the Giants at five-foot-eleven and 180 pounds or so. After turning fourteen, Mays pitched for a semipro steel mill team. Kitty Cat did not push his son into the game, but the boy loved the sport. The only thing that his father demanded of Mays was a promise to stay clear of the mills as a profession. "Once you get into the mill, you never get out," the older Mays warned. He broke that mold himself when he went to work for the railroad.[3]

Mays grew up in small-town Alabama in the 1930s. Many southern blacks who achieved success in the old Negro Leagues actually left home to play on traveling teams at young ages because they were shut out of local schooling after finishing junior high school. Buck O'Neil, the famous Kansas City Monarchs manager, had to move from Florida's Gulf Coast to the Jacksonville area to attend high school.

Young black men could obtain an education of sorts where Mays lived. He attended Fairfield Industrial High School, a trade school, where he was trained to become a cleaner and presser. He never used those skills. A star football player, as well as an excellent baseball player, Mays did not pretend to be as devoted to math or Shakespeare as sports. "All the time my algebra teacher was saying, 'X equals how much?' I was thinking about the next ballgame," Mays said.[4]

Mays loved the thrills of football, but breaking a leg in the sport helped him focus on baseball. One day Mays hit a game-winning home run, but when he slid across home plate he suffered a dizzy spell. It was a bout of vertigo and Kitty Cat suggested that Mays might be better off in the outfield instead of pitching. He prospered there and it did not take long for Mays to prove he was too good for local leagues. When he was seventeen, Mays was introduced to Lorenzo "Piper" Davis, manager of the Birmingham Black Barons of the Negro National League. Davis liked the enthusiastic teen's demeanor, but demanded that he finish high school before becoming a full-time member of the team. Similar to Hall of Fame catcher Roy Campanella's arrangement with the Baltimore Elite Giants, Mays attended school part-time until he earned his diploma while playing for the Barons.

Davis was a respected player, but Kitty Cat entrusted his son to Davis in 1948 because he knew the older man could teach Mays the finer points of the game and that the Barons provided tough competition. When he joined the Black Barons, Mays was innocent not only in the ways of the adult world, but also in terms of baseball wisdom. If he was bored by algebra he soaked up Davis' instruction about hitting, fielding, and running the bases.

"In so many ways, Piper was the most important person in my early baseball years," Mays said. "He told you something only once and he expected you to go on from there. That was a big reason why I matured so quickly. I learned fast in the Negro League and I learned hard."[5]

One game Mays hit a home run off prominent pitcher Chet Brewer. The next time up, Brewer fired at Mays, clunking him on the arm and dropping him to the ground in pain. Mays sat on the ground in tears. An irritated Davis came out, ordered Mays to stand up, go to first base, and then steal second and third on Brewer. Davis' lesson did not sink in until Mays was standing safely on second. "Piper had made me show the pitcher that he couldn't hurt me by hitting me on the arm," Mays said. "Not only couldn't he hurt me, but that if he tried, I would show him up."[6]

Although the movie *The Bingo Long Traveling All-Stars and Motor Kings*, about a 1940-ish black ball team's challenges playing exhibition games around the country, was dismissed by some Negro Leagues players as an exaggeration, there were real-life incidents that compared to the generally well-received film. The movie showed that African American teams on the move faced many obstacles, from where their next meal was cooked, to where they laid their heads at night, and to how they actually got around in vehicles on the verge of breakdown.

Mays said the Barons bus was always on the brink. On a short trip to Montgomery for a game, the shaky bus seized up. The team was scheduled for a night game. Davis told the players he would find another bus and be right back. He returned driving an ice-cream truck "Got to play a game fellas," Mays quoted Davis as saying. "Can't go disappointing the people none." The players stood up in the truck for the forty-mile ride "with the door open so we wouldn't freeze," Mays said.[7]

The old bus was in essence Mays' mobile classroom since he did so much studying when the team was traversing the countryside between cities. But the vehicle had more miles on it than a fitness center treadmill, and after being repaired once more, it broke down once more. The Black Barons were riding through the Holland Tunnel, on their way to the Polo Grounds to face the New York Cubans, when the bus caught fire. The players abandoned ship. But with the urgency of a firefighter rushing into a burning building to save a baby, Mays ran back to the bus to salvage his suitcase.

"I had just bought four new suits," Mays said, "and I wasn't going to leave them there. I ran back to my seat and came back with my bag, and everybody was laughing. Five minutes later, the bus blew up. We lost everything—equipment, uniforms, everything except my brand-new suits." The Barons played a doubleheader against the Cubans, using the host team's road uniforms, bats, and gloves.[8]

Roy Campanella was just breaking in with the Brooklyn Dodgers when he saw Mays play for the first time. He immediately urged his club to sign Mays, but the Dodgers overlooked him. In the late 1950s, after Mays was established as a star, Campanella revealed his respect for Mays' by-then obvious talent.

"The guy who can be the greatest all-around player of them all is Willie Mays," Campanella said. "That goes for everybody, past and present. I remember Willie when he was just a kid and the way he has developed is something out of this world. I honestly believe Willie doesn't know how good he really is. And I doubt if some of the other teams know. The Dodgers certainly don't. He keeps belting their brains out, and they keep right on pitching to him. I see where they're still challenging him. They just don't ever learn."[9]

It is extremely rare in baseball for managers to risk walking top hitters intentionally. They usually prefer to play the percentages, figuring that even the greatest of hitters will not hurt them every time up. The most recent variance from this type of thinking occurred in the early 2000s when Giants outfielder Barry Bonds was at his best. He set records for bases on balls in a season and intentional walks because teams followed the old Campanella suggestion of refusing to let him hit. Mays was a teammate on the Giants with Bobby Bonds, Barry's father, and Barry Bonds is his godson.

Buck Leonard, the grizzled first baseman for the Homestead Grays, was nearing the end of his Negro Leagues career when the Grays met the Barons in the Negro World

Series in 1948, Mays' rookie year. Leonard was aware of Mays before the Series, but never forgot him afterward.

Leonard was on first when a teammate rapped a single to center field, but willing to test Mays' throwing arm, he thought he could advance to third. That is the way it has always worked in baseball. A newcomer may bring a reputation, but until the old-timers see the real goods for themselves they do not put much stock in the scouting report. Leonard was compelled to challenge Mays' throwing arm and assumed Mays' inexperience would work against him. "I said to myself, 'That young boy's out there,' " Leonard remembered, " 'and he ain't gonna throw true to third base. I'm going on to third base.' And I went to third base and he threw me out." Nearly fifty years later, whenever the men crossed paths, Mays brought up the play to tease Leonard.[10]

During Mays' formative years, and through most of his playing days, Alabama was regarded as a bellwether of the nation's most prejudiced region, a state that clung tenaciously to the past with a bulldog's bite. Alabama resisted change to allow African American voting rights, worked to keep blacks out of the mainstream of community life, and seemed desperate to preserve the heart of the Confederacy. Rosa Parks' refusal to move to the back of the bus took place in Alabama. Martin Luther King led marches in Alabama. Sheriffs turned firehoses on children in Alabama.

Yet Mays said his youth was reasonably calm, somewhat removed from the disgrace of discrimination. "I never understood why an issue was made of who I played with," Mays said of playing baseball with white children, "and I never felt comfortable, when I grew up, telling other people how to act. Over the years, a lot of organizations have asked me to be their spokesman, or have wanted me to make speeches about my experiences as a black athlete, or to talk to Congressmen about racial issues in sports. But see, I never recall trouble. I believe I had a happy childhood. Besides playing school sports, we'd play football against the white kids. And we thought nothing of it, neither the blacks, nor the whites. It was the grown-ups who got upset. If they saw black kids playing on the same team as white kids, they'd call the cops, and the cops would make us stop. I never got in a fight that started because of racism."[11]

Years later, after the 1955 season ended, Mays led a tour of barnstorming black All Stars through the South. One of his fellow outfielders was Hank Aaron of the Braves who later set the all-time home-run record. Aaron, who grew up in Mobile, Alabama, said he usually rode with Mays in the team leader's Cadillac. One day they were in a men's clothing store in Birmingham—Mays' old stomping ground—when Mays pulled a roll of $100 bills out of his pocket to pay for some items.

"When he did that, the people in the store started to call the police," Aaron said. "Then Willie told them he was Willie Mays and that changed everything. It was OK to be black as long as you were Willie Mays."[12]

Mays played for the Birmingham Black Barons in 1948, 1949, and 1950. These were the seasons directly following Jackie Robinson's cracking of the color barrier. By 1950, it was apparent that the Negro Leagues were on the way out and that top black baseball players would be infiltrating all teams in the majors soon. Mays learned from Davis, smoothed out his rough edges, and at nineteen was a coveted prospect. The Boston Braves, the Chicago Cubs, and the Chicago White Sox pursued Mays, though none with an open checkbook. Their offers were minimal, none exceeding $7,500 to sign. And then along came the New York Giants.

In a biographical sheet the San Francisco Giants prepared after Mays retired in 1973, the team told its version of how Mays came to sign with the club when it paid

Willie Mays was all coiled muscle and explosiveness at the plate and he smashed 660 home runs during his Major League career.

Birmingham $14,000 for his contract. "The Giants sent scout Eddie Montague to inspect a first baseman, Alonzo Perry of the New York Cubans in the Negro League in 1950, in a game against the Birmingham Black Barons," the bio stated. "But Montague quickly spotted Mays, a speedy, agile, nineteen-year-old outfielder, with quick hands, a great arm and a powerful bat. Montague forgot about Perry and arranged a deal with the Barons."

After scouts gushingly recommended Mays, the Giants offered $2,000. With his father's guidance, Mays held out for $6,000. He picked the club because it just felt right to him compared to other prospects. The Giants just felt like the right team to him.[13]

The Giants started the still-young Mays in Trenton, New Jersey, with their Class B farm team in the Interstate League. Mays was restless on the train journey. He had time to wonder about his future. Racism was still prevalent in baseball and even in the north Mays was confronted with fans yelling nasty phrases at him. Mays said that during his first game someone in the stands yelled, "Who's that nigger walking on the field?"[14]

The box score from Mays' first official organized baseball game on June 24, 1950, shows that he was in the lineup in center field and that he went 0-for-3 at bat. He said he was tired from the trip and didn't feel right at the plate. Mays didn't feel right that evening, either, when he discovered he could not stay in the same hotel as his team. Hagerstown, Maryland, was the only city in the league below the Mason-Dixon line, but what befuddled Mays was that he could stay anywhere he wanted in Washington, D.C., and anywhere he wanted in Baltimore, but couldn't stay with whites in a town in between.

"Some of my teammates couldn't understand it, either," Mays said. "About midnight, five of my new teammates knocked on my window to check whether I was OK."[15] Not every black ballplayer who made the transition from the Negro Leagues to the white majors had teammates so solicitous. Many spent nights alone and many endured those lonely stays for whole seasons, not simply a weekend at a time as Mays did. On later road trips, manager Chick Genovese, without saying anything specific, showed up to eat dinner with him. Mays thought highly of his first organized ball manager, both as an instructor and a man.

As a young player, Mays was regarded as a friendly, outgoing guy, but the legend of his memorable nickname, "Say-hey, Willie," took root early on. Mays was thrust into a new situation on a team where everyone was a stranger. He developed the habit of shouting, "Say-hey" when he wanted to get someone's attention. Attached to his infectious smile, and positive demeanor, the call was not taken as rudeness, but simply as one of Mays' endearing traits. Mays never had a facility with names.[16]

Mays' bat and play in the field got everyone else to listen to him. He appeared in eighty-one games for Trenton that summer and although he had not yet developed the home-run stroke that became part of his trademark game later, he batted a wicked .353.

One aspect of traveling with Trenton reminded Mays of his days in the Negro Leagues. Those minor league Giants also rode a beat-up bus on road trips, one that also seemed close to death by explosion. The team had favorite songs and Mays sang the first words of "Clarence The Clocker" for a group sing-along. He had learned how to sleep on buses with the Barons, a mandatory skill for a ballplayer unless he wanted to go up to the plate blurry-eyed every time. "I would pile the duffel bags in the back of the bus, lie down on them, and go to sleep," Mays said.[17]

Mays was earmarked for the Minneapolis Millers in AAA the next season, but in spring training he met Giants manager Leo Durocher. Durocher was regarded as one of the fiercest will-to-win managers of his time. He was a smart baseball man and he had already been briefed on Mays' accomplishments in New Jersey when they met in the spring of 1951. "Heard a lot about you," Durocher said as he shook hands with Mays. "Maybe I'll be seeing you around."[18] Not only would Durocher be seeing Mays around quite a bit, but he would also be seeing him sooner than expected in New York. Durocher became almost a father figure to Mays, his most devoted supporter, even when things were not going well, and his greatest public booster. Durocher was part boss, part mentor, and part press agent for Mays. And always he was the man who placed his greatest faith in the young outfielder's ability.

MAJOR LEAGUE CAREER

Mays lasted only thirty-five games in the American Association. This was not because he couldn't handle the pitching in the top minors, but because he was too good for it. He batted an overwhelming .477 and drove in sixty-eight runs, almost two a game. Although the Giants were thinking of their own welfare and winning games in a pennant race with the Dodgers, they promoted Mays at age twenty before he could completely and thoroughly humiliate the whole league.

There was only one problem. Mays had gone from Birmingham to Trenton to Minneapolis so swiftly that he was not comfortable with making another sudden move to New York. Now that the opportunity was at hand, he developed jitters about hitting Major League pitching. In Minneapolis, when Mays was first told he was going to the big time, instead of celebrating, he actually protested, saying he wanted to stay in Minnesota. Durocher got Mays on the phone and asked, "What do you mean, you're not coming?" "I mean it," Mays said. "I can't play that kind of ball." "What can't you do?" Durocher asked. "I can't hit that kind of pitching," Mays replied. "What are you hitting for Minneapolis now?" Durocher asked, knowing the phenomenal number by heart. "Four-seventy-seven," Mays said. "Do you think you could hit half that for me?" Durocher asked in a more or less rhetorical question.[19]

Mays joined the Giants, and the scary thing was that when he went into the lineup not only could he not hit 50 percent of his Minneapolis average, but he could not hit at all. Mays stroked just one hit in his first twenty-six official at bats and plunged into a depression. He sat down by his locker and cried. Mays had a high-pitched voice and even he said it was squeaky when he told Durocher that he could not hit Major League pitching and he was sure that the Giants were going to send him back to Minneapolis. Durocher, who was nicknamed "The Lip" because he always had something to say, had a legendary response to that comment. "Willie, see what's printed across my jersey?" he said. "It says, 'Giants.' As long as I'm the manager of the Giants, you're my center fielder. You're here to stay. Stop worrying."[20]

The two men bonded in Mays' first weeks with the club, when he needed guidance the most and needed someone to show belief in him. "We were two unalike guys," Mays said, "but we developed a love, a respect, that has never faded."[21] Mays gained some local street credibility, and popularity, being photographed playing stickball in the neighborhoods with youngsters. It reminded fans of just how young he was.

Durocher could display his backing in tangible ways like bucking Mays up with pep talks and keeping him in the lineup while he struggled, but Durocher was an older man who circulated in a different actress/nightclub/celebrity orbit. He also had to keep some distance from his players and he was not an African American. It was fortunate for Mays that Monte Irvin, another future Hall of Famer, was also an outfielder with the Giants at the time. Irvin played ten years in the Negro Leagues before he got his chance in the National League. He had been where Mays came from and he was ahead of him entering the majors. He was a wise soul who could offer pertinent advice. The two men were roommates and became close friends.

"Durocher had a knack for knowing how to handle different players," Irvin said. "He handled Mays just right and that had a lot to do with our success. Willie needed instruction off the field in little things and I helped him in that way. But Leo was like a second father to Willie."[22]

Besides the ostentatious way Mays hit with Minneapolis, the reason Durocher wanted to rush him to the majors was the Giants poor start. They fell far behind the hated Dodgers and did not seem capable of contending for first place. In one of the greatest pennant races of all, the Giants trailed by thirteen-and-a-half games in August, but tied the Dodgers in the standings at season's end. A playoff gave the pennant to New York. One reason the Giants made a run was Mays' addition. Even as a rookie Mays was a superb fielder, and Durocher recognized that. Irvin played left field and Don Mueller played right field. Mays was installed in center.

"Willie Mays was patrolling center field at the Polo Grounds like no one had ever done," Irvin said. "He was simply outstanding. One day we had a meeting and Durocher said, 'Monte, you and Don just give Willie plenty of room. If there's anything he can get to and wants to catch, let him have it. You two just play your position and help Willie whenever you can.' We never did run into each other. Willie was great at coming in on a ball, was great going back, and had a rifle for an arm. He was just outstanding as an outfielder, and he always seemed to rise to the occasion when we needed a big play."[23] Durocher essentially told two professional outfielders, one a future Hall of Famer, to stay out of Mays' way. That encapsulated how much faith Durocher had in Mays and how early he recognized that he was a special, perhaps once-in-a-lifetime, talent.

The New York press had been prepped about Mays, how he had torn up the American Association, and how Durocher loved him. Durocher made it just as clear to the sports-writers as he had to Mays when he slumped, that Mays was his man. At one point Durocher even said he would not trade Mays for anyone else in baseball, Ted Williams, Joe DiMaggio, or Stan Musial, included. In August of that rookie season, right about the time that the Giants looked dead, a New York sportswriter asked Durocher about that declaration of Mays being untouchable.

"He's got it, brother," Durocher said, besides pointing out that Mays was younger than all the others. "He can hit and he can run and he can throw. And he's a ballplayer and he's a kid and some day he'll be a great ballplayer. Why should I trade him? Why should I give him up for any ballplayer in the majors today? I don't care who he is. Why should I give up Willie for him?"[24]

The playoff with the Dodgers ended with third baseman Bobby Thomson hitting one of the most exciting walk-off home runs in baseball lore. The home run to left field finished Brooklyn and propelled the Giants into the World Series against the New York Yankees. At the time of Russ Hodges' famous radio call, "The Giants win the pennant! The Giants win the pennant!" Mays was the on-deck hitter. Mays was part of the party, but less a participant than a wide-eyed observer.[25]

Mays finished his rookie year with 20 home runs, 68 RBIs, and a .274 batting average. The Giants won two of the first three games of the World Series, but the Yankees came back to win the championship in six games. A season begun in the minors for Mays ended in the World Series.

Mays, however, was not able to resume in the same fashion in 1952 because he was drafted into the Army. He appeared in just thirty-four games for the Giants, batting only .236, before being inducted. The Giants were in first place when he was drafted and dropped in the standings fast when he departed. This was the season when Dodgers manager Charlie Dressen cackled at the rival Giants plight, saying ungrammatically, but accurately, "The Giants is dead! The Giants is dead!"[26]

Mays also missed all of the 1953 season in the service. Mays was not sent to Korea and he was not employed in many Army tasks that seemed invaluable for the nation during his twenty-two months under government command. Mostly, he played service baseball, batting .420 and .389 in two years representing Uncle Sam rather than Daddy Durocher. The most troubling thing that happened to Mays while he was in the Army was the death of his mother. There was speculation that Mays might be released early as the primary support of his ten half-brothers and sisters, but it did not happen. The political climate was not right. Citizens were complaining that if an athlete was healthy enough to play his sport he should not be deferred from service.

One unexpected bonus of Mays' service time was how he learned to improve his fielding. Another soldier suggested he try it his way when catching a fly ball and Mays' famous basket catch was born. Instead of plucking balls out of the sky one-handed as virtually all outfielders do, Mays developed a flamboyant style that made fans nervous, but which he pulled off with aplomb. He positioned his glove by his belly and let the ball drop into it. It always seemed he might miss—hence suspense for those watching.

"I tried it and it felt more comfortable," Mays said. "My body was aligned correctly. I adopted that style. What it allowed me to do was to have my hands in the correct position to make a throw instantly. What's wrong with it, though, is that you tend to take your eyes off the ball at the last second. Still, I only dropped a couple of flies in my career that way."[27]

Mays did suffer one minor injury, a slight fracture of the ankle, playing baseball in the Army, and an early biographer who suggested that no one had a softer tour of duty than Mays also said maybe he should have been awarded a purple heart for the wound.[28]

When Mays returned to the Giants for the 1954 season, he was in better shape than when he had left, built up by Army calisthenics. So were the Giants. His talents blossomed and the Giants were the best team in the National League. The promise of his rookie campaign was fulfilled. Mays hit 41 home runs, drove in 110, and batted .345. He also stroked thirteen triples, showing off his baserunning. And he had fourteen assists from center field, meaning runners were still reckless enough to test his arm, much as the confident Buck Leonard had been back in 1948. Mays was named Most Valuable Player of the National League and led New York to the pennant. He also became a much larger public figure, his name and face plastered across newspapers in the nation's media center everyday, his talent appreciated not only by a knowing Durocher who saw the potential, but also by everyone in baseball.

Mays passed from simply being visible in the baseball world, to being a figure transcending sport and erupting into the consciousness of public culture at large. A line noted in the *New York Times* by a Mays' biographer summed it up. "Topic A is either the hydrogen bomb, sex, where-shall-I-go-on-my-vacation, or Willie Mays."[29] These days that would probably mean Mays would be simultaneously written up in *People* magazine and the *Wall Street Journal*.

There were even two songs written about Mays that season. One was called "Amazin' Willie Mays." The other was called, "Say Hey, the Willie Mays Song," written by Jane Douglass and Dick Kleiner. In small part, the lyrics of that one went "He covers center like he has jet shoes; The other batters get the Willie blues; Anything hit his way is out; It just don't pay them boys to clout!"[30]

The Cleveland Indians romped through the American League schedule, winning 111 games, and were heavy favorites going into the World Series. In one of the greatest of upsets, the Giants dominated the Series and took the championship. The signature moment of the confrontation was a play that has passed into baseball lore as the greatest catch of all time. The spectacular play began with Mays turning and running at full speed toward the 460-foot mark in center field at the crack of Indians' first baseman Vic Wertz' bat. Mays lost his cap, reached up over his shoulder to glove the ball, and in one motion spun and threw a perfect strike to the infield to prevent a runner from advancing. It left the crowd gasping, reporters gushing, and vivid video for future generations. Mays would not admit it was his finest catch, but it burnished his reputation. Perhaps because the play was witnessed by so many and was replayed many times and described ad nauseam, it entered into mythology. By any definition it was a stunning catch and is the most clearly remembered play of that World Series.

The play was made in the top of the eighth inning at the Polo Grounds with the game tied 2–2. The Giants went on to win and in the afterglow, when the first ravings about the catch reached Mays' ears (and long before such comment became a crescendo) his first reaction was to suggest the grab was not a big deal to him. He did not consider the catch as impressive as observers did.[31]

Monte Irvin was one of the closest on-the-spot viewers. He was playing in the field next to Mays and he ran to back him up in case he could not make the catch. "Willie caught the ball and had the presence of mind to turn around and throw a strike to second on the dead run. That was a key play in the game and Willie made it."[32]

In 1954, the Associated Press named Mays athlete of the year over Roger Bannister, the British runner who was the first to break the four-minute-mile barrier. Mays was not merely the young guy with potential, he was the leader of the best team in the National League. He was a superstar. In 1955, Mays smacked 51 home runs, drove in 127, and averaged .319. "By common consent, his was the game's most electrifying presence the game had known since the heyday of Babe Ruth," one writer opined.[33]

Up through the 1957 season, New York was populated with three Major League baseball teams, the New York Yankees, the New York Giants, and the Brooklyn Dodgers. Each of those teams was blessed with a Hall of Fame outfielder. The Yanks had Mickey Mantle, the Giants Mays, and the Dodgers featured Duke Snider. Much later a song was written about the trio playing the same position. Partisans of each team claimed their man was better, but a more impartial observer, examining the record book, would likely choose Mays.

Mays was made for New York and the adoration of newsmen who couldn't write nicely enough about him. In a way he grew up there, maturing from timid rookie to confident man. When the Giants moved West for the 1958 season, Mays adjusted, but San Francisco did not seem to embrace him as warmly as New York. He initially had difficulty obtaining housing because he was black, and shockingly, when he was less than perfect, fickle San Francisco fans booed him.

"They boo Willie up in San Francisco pretty regularly," it was written in 1961, "but then they had been told to expect a superman and they only got the best player in the world. San Franciscans, for all of their wit and intelligence, and well-dressed women, and for all of their hometown baseballers such as Lefty O'Doul and Joe DiMaggio, know as much about baseball as Castro does about electric shavers."[34]

In New York, Mays was young and open and played with great joy. In San Francisco he began to withdraw, and certainly after his playing days ended, Mays became a less willing guest at events and did not always warm to the moment. He made many personal appearances seem perfunctory, more chore than pleasure. This attitude was written on his face on a daily basis during his $100,000 payday years working in an Atlantic City casino. Back then, it was observed, "He doesn't pursue people, and he keeps his most important, most personal thoughts to himself."[35]

Mays did not have a great all-around year in 1956, but he did become the first player to hit 30 home runs and steal 30 bases in the same season. He was not voted to the All-Star game, but was selected as an alternate by National League manager Walter Alston and hit a pinch-hit home run. In Mays' final game in the Polo Grounds before the Giants fled to the West Coast, the fans gave Mays a prolonged standing ovation. And then they stampeded onto the field, tore up the turf, and carted away seats and other memorabilia for souvenirs.

In San Francisco, the Mays of the 1950s was every bit the star of the 1960s. He was a veteran, but was still capable of extraordinary feats on the diamond. On April 30, 1961, Mays hit four home runs in a game (he still shares that record) against the Braves

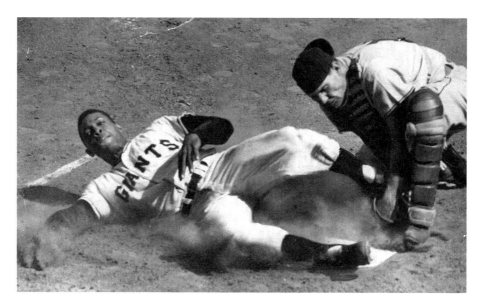

One of Willie Mays' trademarks was the likelihood that his cap would fly off when fielding a fly ball or running the bases. He was as feared on the basepaths as at the plate and here he is shown sliding into home.

in Milwaukee. This was a day Mays awoke sick, thought he had food poisoning, but decided to play at the last minute. Fans reveled in the accomplishment and photographers afterward posed Mays holding four baseballs. The astonishment that greeted the picture stemmed mostly from the fact that Mays grasped all four balls in one hand. Until then few realized the size of the mitts on a man not particularly oversized.

Mays did not even use his own bat that day. He borrowed a bat belonging to infielder Joey Amalfitano, and when it resounded well in batting practice, he decided to swing with it in the game. Mays clubbed the four homers and when the game ended he was on deck, itching to take one more crack at a record fifth homer.

"I'd like to have tried," Mays said. "But you know the truth, I might not have been able to do a thing. I knew what I had done. I never believed I ever could hit four in one game. Never before in my life did I hit more than two in one game. I probably would have pressed, tried to go for the home run and missed. Don't think I'll ever do again what I did yesterday—that's a once in a lifetime."[36]

Mays was always described as a great all-around player, and in a 1966 game against the Dodgers he showed off his throwing arm. He threw out one runner at home, one at third, and one at first. He had another nailed at second, but the tag was missed. "Willie Mays threw for the cycle!" it was trumpeted.[37]

In an eight-team league in the 1950s, the best players in the National League faced each other regularly. They also played together in the All-Star game year after year. Ernie Banks, the Chicago Cubs shortstop, who was a perennial All Star and who perennially predicted that his team would win the pennant only to see it nosedive each season, said he bantered with Mays. "Whenever I tell him the Cubs are going to finish first," Banks said when they were both still active, "he says, 'You'd better find yourself a new league for the Cubs to play in, because they sure aren't going to be first in the National

League. Forget it.' "[38] Years later, Banks called Mays "a great player and a very nice guy. Willie was a tremendous player. He did it all."[39]

Warren Spahn, the winningest left-handed pitcher of all time, was a teammate of Hank Aaron for many years. Aaron ended up surpassing Mays in the major statistics, but spent most of his career in his shadow from a publicity standpoint. Spahn said, "I think he wanted to be a better all-around player than Willie Mays. I never heard Henry say any of this. It's just what I perceived to be the case."[40] Mays played with a more spectacular flair than Aaron, but when experts rate the best player ever, they are usually mentioned in the same paragraph.

Those in the know, who watched Mays perform season after season and perform at an All-Star level, could rarely find the words to match his magical catches and game-winning hits. Los Angeles sports columnist Jim Murray said when Mays' name is mentioned "several things happen [to baseball people], a film comes over their eyes, their cheeks flush, and flecks of foam appear at the corners of their mouths. Listening to them, you half expect to see the Angel Gabriel running around with number twenty-four on his back. Willie Mays is so good other players don't even resent him."[41]

The Giants returned to the World Series in 1962, but could not beat the Yankees. And by 1963, Mays was a $100,000-a-year man, breaking the barrier along with Mantle. It was a long way from $300-a-month paydays with the Birmingham Black Barons.

In August of 1963, Mays made a catch against the Braves that got some journalists thinking he had finally bettered his World Series grab of 1954. He rushed in to nab a sinking line drive off the bat of Lee Maye, did a somersault, and landed on his funny bone. He came up holding his arm, which scared the rest of his teammates, though he was fine when the tingling stopped. "He won't make a more difficult one (catch)," a sportswriter said, "if he stays in the league until Social Security overtakes him."[42]

A different type of stunning moment occurred during the 1963 season. Mays collapsed at home plate during the heat of a day game and had to be helped from the field. Nothing more serious was noted than nervous exhaustion and fatigue, but it may have been symptomatic of how hard Mays played. Dr. E.C. Sailer, the team physician, said as much: "This man plays every game and plays it intensely. He's under constant pressure. He gives 100 percent of himself."[43] Mays bounced back quickly.

Mays provided a revealing interview to syndicated sports columnist Jimmy Cannon the next year. Mays had always been regarded as a fielder who could track down any fly ball as if he possessed radar. He was often sprinting to the unforgiving walls of outfield fences, but was not known to collide with them. Mays told Cannon that he had learned to gauge the distance to the fence by watching Pro Football Hall of Fame receiver Don Hutson work his wizardry with the Green Bay Packers. Cannon pointed out that Hutson retired before Mays had a chance to see him play, but Mays said he watched movies of the split end.

"I always know what I'm doing out there," Mays said. "A friend of mine showed me him [Hutson]. I watched the way he caught a football. He would catch a ball and stop real fast. Go one way, go the other way. I watched what he did. I said if he can do that with a football, why can't I do it with a baseball? I studied what he did. Then I would run hard at the fence and stop. I kept doing it until I could do it good. I twisted just like he did. He'd catch the ball and twist away from a guy going to tackle him. I catch the ball and twist away from the fence." Cannon said it "is a fable that Mays plays the outfield as a fish swims or a bird flies."[44] There was natural ability, but no one suspected as much science was involved.

Further evidence that Mays had become an American icon and not merely a star baseball player was on display when he was a subject of the September 28, 1964, panels of Charles Schultz's famed comic strip "Peanuts." In the strip, Linus is leaning on a stone wall talking to Charlie Brown and he says, "When I get big, I want to become a great doctor. I want to be a doctor among doctors, a physician among physicians." Linus throws his hand in the air and adds, "I want to be the Willie Mays of medicine!" In the last panel, Charlie Brown ruminates, "How ambitious can you get?"

Mays recorded a 47-homer season in 1964 and his all-time high of 52 homers in 1965. It was about then that the first hints of discussion took place suggesting that Mays might be able to match or out-do Babe Ruth's record of 714 home runs. Mays surpassed 500 home runs and he was aware that second place on the all-time list was Jimmie Foxx's 534. But Foxx was an American League player. Mel Ott, the longtime Giant hit 511 and that was the National League record. Mays wanted to hit 512 and break that mark.

"I was intensely aware of where I stood on the all-time homer list," Mays said. "I might not catch Ruth, but I certainly intended to become number one in my league."[45]

Despite making the human mistake of focusing on homers rather than just meeting the ball, the record-setting home run came against the Dodgers in May, off southpaw Claude Osteen. "He threw me a high, outside change-up," Mays said. "I set myself, waited, and then jumped on it and sent it over the fence in right field. Number 512. When I got to the dugout, I heard the fans shouting, 'We want Willie! We want Willie!' I had to come out and tip my cap to them. It was one of my greatest moments."[46]

But Mays displayed a complete lack of sentimentality in any desire to keep a memento of the occasion. A high school kid nabbed the ball and a Giants emissary immediately offered him $100 and another ball for it. The boy's father refused to let him make the deal because he thought the ball was worth more. Mays did not care. "I've never kept souvenirs in my life," he said. "What good do they do? Are you gonna sit home and look at 'em? I give that stuff away as fast as I get it. All it means is something to dust."[47]

By the late 1960s, Mays was slowing down. His seasonal home-run totals dipped into the twenties, his batting average slid below .300, and he developed nagging injuries. Publications from newspapers in Philadelphia, to *Sports Illustrated*, wrote that he was less cooperative with interviews and more remote. Furman Bisher, the star sports columnist in Atlanta, ran into the same kind of roadblock and theorized a reason. "He moves, behaves and responds like a man who's worried," Bisher reported. "Willie Mays wasn't supposed to grow old. He was supposed to go on forever, his cap flying off as he broke the sound barrier on foot, face bright and eyes twinkling like stars. Willie Mays was born for eternal youth. Age is acting in direct violation of the code."[48] Mays had just turned thirty-six.

Mays finished the 1967 season with 564 home runs. He hit twenty-two that year, but his average settled to an un-Mays-like .263. Still, as spring training approached, Mays said his goal was to hit 600 home runs and keep playing several more years. He was on the defensive, being asked if he would retire if he did not play better in 1968. "Maybe four, five more years," he said of his playing future. "And no, I won't quit if I have another bad year. Furthermore, I ain't plannin' on havin' another bad year."[49]

A month after publicizing his attitude, Mays became embroiled in an unlikely argument with Jackie Robinson. After playing under wraps for his first couple of seasons, Robinson began verbalizing his feelings loudly. Mays was more reclusive. After retiring from baseball, Robinson involved himself in African American civil rights causes. Mays kept his thoughts quieter. Just before the start of the 1968 season, Robinson bashed

Mays and his teammates Willie McCovey and Jim Ray Hart as "do nothing" Negroes because they were not outspoken on black issues.

Mays stayed calm and even acknowledged Robinson's huge contribution for all blacks in breaking the color line with the Dodgers. "But that doesn't give him the right to speak for us," Mays said. "Different people do things in different ways. I can't for instance, go out and picket. I can't stand on a soap box and preach. It isn't my nature." Mays said he did many things for his race that he did not take credit for and did not publicize. "I believe understanding is the important thing—making the younger generation understand and realize we're all God's children fighting for the same purpose." Mays said he could not have done what Robinson did. "Great progress has been made since Jackie broke in. Jackie is a great reason behind that progress. I really admire the guy. But I just don't think he should go around pointing fingers at other guys, particularly nice guys like Jimmy Ray and Willie."[50] Before 1960, the Giants spring training hotel in Phoenix, the Adams Hotel, would not let black players sleep there. After the hotel integrated, Mays' response was to refuse to stay there at all. He leaned toward those types of protests.

Near the end of the 1969 season, Mays completed his quest for his 600th home run. The Giants were in San Diego and the home run beat the Padres, 4–2. He had reached 599 twelve days earlier and admitted he was pressing at the plate trying to get the matter over with. "The big thing is that it won the game," Mays said. There were only 4,799 fans present, but they offered a standing ovation. And the entire Giants team met Mays at home plate.[51]

Whether they admit it or not, great players know in their hearts when their skills begin to erode. When doing something becomes difficult after it came so easily, it is impossible not to recognize signs of age. Although Hall of Famer Whitey Ford spent his entire career with the Yankees in the American League, he and Mays met in World Series and All-Star play. Mays hit disproportionately well against Ford. In 1963, when Ford failed to make the All-Star team, he demonstrated a sparkling sense of humor by sending a telegram to Mays reading, "Dear Willie—Sorry—Whitey."[52]

Mays never exhibited the same power to laugh at himself, but the reality was he was coming to the same stage of his career. Mays was ultimately traded by the Giants to the Mets in the middle of the 1972 season. The Mets had replaced the Giants as the National League entry in New York and it was a chance for Mays to return home in the twilight of his career. Mays played in about one third of the games in 1973, his skills clearly eroded, but got the opportunity to appear in one more World Series before retiring at the end of that season.

In his first game as a Met, Mays hit a home run that beat the Giants. In his first game back in San Francisco as a Met, he beat the Giants with another home run. But those were last hurrahs on the field.

LATER LIFE

When Mays retired, U.S. Senator Jacob Javits of New York read remarks into the Congressional Record of September 25, 1973, saying, "His list of vices began and ended with the bedevilment of opposing pitchers."

During the winter leading up to the next spring training, John Holway, an author who wrote voluminously about the Negro Leagues, penned a piece in which he suggested that if Mays had not missed most of two seasons with the Giants because of his Army commitment, he would have surpassed Ruth's home-run record. "How many home runs did he lose in those two missing years?"[53]

After he retired, Mays dabbled in coaching, spring training instruction, and the business world, and worked on his golf game. He traveled the country and made speeches for children's charities, and he made baseball-related appearances. In 1979, the first year he was eligible, Mays was elected to the Baseball Hall of Fame with 94.6 percent of the vote.

Mays cried when he was introduced as a new honoree in New York in January of that year, but he did not hold back answering questions. He tried not to sound too boastful, but was not overly modest when sportswriters asked, "Who in Mays' mind was the greatest?"

"Without being bashful, I thought I was the best baseball player I ever saw," Mays said. "Nobody in the world could do what I could do. I hope I'm not saying anything wrong. If you play ball, you have to believe you're the best. Nothing I did amazed me. When I made great catches, that's what I was supposed to do. When I missed a ball, that was a problem. I couldn't imagine how I missed it. I didn't play for myself. I played for the people who came to the games, so they could go home and say they had enjoyed themselves. What I did, I loved every moment of it."[54]

Mays' Hall of Fame ceremony took place in August, in Cooperstown, New York, and it was an emotional occasion. "I guess maybe tomorrow I'll pinch myself and say, 'Hey, man, I'm in the Hall of Fame.' "[55]

When Mays retired, he had a ten-year contract with the Mets to act as a goodwill ambassador and part-time coach. In the late 1970s, he accepted a promotional job trading on his good name with Bally's, the hotel-casino in Atlantic City. Only three months after his Hall of Fame induction, Commissioner Bowie Kuhn ordered Mays to give up baseball or the casino. Baseball has been extremely sensitive about gambling connections since the Black Sox scandal of 1919 when the Chicago White Sox threw the World Series. In the end, Mays stayed with the casino operation, but he was bitter about this divorce from baseball. Mays did not feel he was doing anything wrong affiliating with Bally's because mostly he visited hospitals, and played golf. When a major boxing match took place at the hotel, Mays was on hand to greet and schmooze with high rollers. He signed baseballs and other items proffered by fans.

"I have nothing to do with gambling," Mays said. "I would never do anything to hurt baseball."[56] Mickey Mantle was caught up in the same ban for much the same reasons. This did not pass quickly. In 1984, Mays was still on the outs and the question of whether he would ever be allowed back into the game he loved was asked at every stop. "I was put out of baseball," Mays said in Alaska. He refused to appeal, refused to beg. "I asked one time. I don't want to be embarrassed again. If he said, 'I'd like to have you come in,' I'd love that."[57]

Kuhn never uttered those words, but when Peter Ueberroth succeeded him as commissioner, the ban was lifted in March of 1985 and Mays was free to work in baseball again. As old age encroached, Mays also began receiving a fresh batch of honors. Various organizations, including *Sports Illustrated*, selected all-time baseball teams and Mays was listed on all of them. Dodgers Hall of Fame pitcher Sandy Koufax said Mays was the best player he competed against. When the Giants opened their new stadium, then called Pac Bell Park, in 2000, the team unveiled a nine-foot-tall bronze statue of Mays gazing after an imaginary ball following one of his big swings. The statue was located at 24 Willie Mays Plaza, the front entrance of the park. "It's scary to me to see a statue of yourself," Mays said after initially tearing up at the idea of the honor. "It's going to be so real that, sometime, you wonder how all this happened to me."[58]

Probably the most surprising ceremony Mays attended took place in Hagerstown, Maryland, the site of his first minor league game at age nineteen and the town where he experienced the worst discrimination his first season in organized ball. Fifty-four years after his debut game, Mays spoke at a $50-per-person dinner, signed autographs for a fee, and participated in a pregame ceremony in Municipal Stadium, the same field where he played. The Hagerstown Suns retired Mays' number, put his name on a street that runs past the park, and presented him with a commemorative plaque.

The headline on the local newspaper story the next day read, "Willie Mays Forgives." Mays had previously turned down invitations to come to Hagerstown, but when he thought about it this time, he said, "You just don't hold that against a town because the town isn't the person who hurt you."[59]

For seventy-three-year-old Willie Mays, life had come full circle.

NOTES

1. Arnold Hano, *The Say-Hey Kid* (New York: Bartholomew House, 1961), 10.
2. Lew Freedman, *Anchorage Daily News*, July 13, 1984.
3. Hano, *The Say-Hey Kid*, 30.
4. Hano, *The Say-Hey Kid*, 31.
5. Willie Mays and Lou Sahedi, *Say Hey: The Autobiography of Willie Mays* (New York: Pocket Books, 1989), 33–34.
6. Mays and Sahedi, *Say Hey*, 34–35.
7. Mays and Sahedi, *Say Hey*, 35.
8. Ibid.
9. Roy Campanella, *Its Good to Be Alive* (Boston: Little, Brown and Company, 1959), 268.
10. Buck Leonard with James A. Riley, *Buck Leonard: The Black Lou Gehrig* (New York: Carroll & Graf Publishers, 1995), 201–202.
11. Mays and Sahedi, *Say Hey*, 11.
12. Hank Aaron with Lonnie Wheeler, *If I Had a Hammer* (New York: HarperPaperbacks, 1992), 147.
13. Hano, *The Say-Hey Kid*, 37.
14. Mays and Sahedi, *Say Hey*, 41–43.
15. Mays and Sahedi, *Say Hey*, 43.
16. Mays and Sahedi, *Say Hey*, 44.
17. Mays and Sahedi, *Say Hey*, 46.
18. Hano, *The Say-Hey Kid*, 44.
19. Hano, *The Say-Hey Kid*, 47.
20. Mays and Sahedi, *Say Hey*, 69.
21. Mays and Sahedi, *Say Hey*, 62.
22. Monte Irvin with James A. Riley, *Nice Guys Finish First* (New York: Carroll & Graf Publishers, 1996), 133.
23. Irvin with Riley, *Nice Guys Finish First*, 152.
24. Frank Graham, *New York Journal-American*, August 16, 1951.
25. Mays and Sahedi, *Say Hey*, 89.
26. Hano, *The Say-Hey Kid*, 77.
27. Mays and Sahedi, *Say Hey*, 102.
28. Hano, *The Say-Hey Kid*, 79.
29. Hano, *The Say-Hey Kid*, 86.
30. Hano, *The Say-Hey Kid*, 98.

31. Hano, *The Say-Hey Kid*, 101.
32. Irvin with Riley, *Nice Guys Finish First,* 181.
33. Charles Einstein, *Willie's Time* (New York: Penguin Books, 1989), 26.
34. Hano, *The Say-Hey Kid*, 121.
35. Hano, *The Say-Hey Kid*, 117.
36. Bob Stevens, *San Francisco Chronicle*, May 2, 1961.
37. Einstein, *Willie's Time*, 62.
38. Ernie Banks and Jim Enright, *Mr. Cub* (Chicago: Follett Publishing Company, 1971), 179.
39. Ernie Banks, personal interview, February 18, 2006.
40. Aaron with Wheeler, *If I Had a Hammer*, 168.
41. Jim Murray, *Los Angeles Times*, May 23, 1962.
42. Dick Friendlich, *San Francisco Chronicle*, August 23, 1963.
43. Curley Grieve, *San Francisco Examiner*, September 3, 1963.
44. Jimmy Cannon, *King Features Syndicate*, April 26, 1964.
45. Mays and Sahedi, *Say Hey*, 240.
46. Mays and Sahedi, *Say Hey*, 243.
47. Melvin Durslag, *Los Angeles Herald-Examiner*, May 20, 1966.
48. Furman Bisher, *Atlanta Journal*, May 17, 1967.
49. Bob Stevens, *Sporting News*, February 17, 1968.
50. Bob Stevens, *Sporting News*, March 30, 1968.
51. Associated Press, September 23, 1969.
52. Einstein, *Willie's Time*, 319.
53. John Holway, *Sporting News*, February 16, 1974.
54. Associated Press, January 24, 1979.
55. Phil Pepe, *New York Daily News*, August 6, 1979.
56. *New York Times*, October 27, 1979.
57. Freedman, *Anchorage Daily News*, July 13, 1984.
58. Richard Weiner, *USA Today*, March 31, 2000.
59. Andrew Schotz, *The (Hagerstown) Herald-Mail*, August 10, 2004.

Further Reading

Einstein, Charles, *Willie's Time.* New York: Penguin Books, 1989.
Hano, Arnold, *The Say-Hey Kid*. New York: Bartholomew House, 1961.
Mays, Willie, and Lou Sahedi, *Say Hey: The Autobiography of Willie Mays*. New York: Pocket Books, 1989.

WILLIE McCOVEY
January 10, 1938–

Willie McCovey straddled an era of change for black players in baseball. When he made his Major League debut in 1959, the last of big-league clubs was still integrating. McCovey was a National League rookie of the year, whose unexpected explosive mid-season debut proved that blacks could receive fair treatment from baseball voters.

McCovey swiftly became one of the team's most popular players in San Francisco partially because he was a homegrown hero, one who came up through the team's farm system after the team moved from New York. McCovey crashed 521 home runs, led his league in home runs thrice and RBIs twice, was a Most Valuable Player (MVP), and was elected to the Baseball Hall of Fame.

It was one of the most magical, out-of-nowhere runs in Major League baseball history. For two months, Willie McCovey ruled the National League, stunning fans, opponents, and teammates with his awesome power, his fabulous batting stroke, and his bolt-from-the-blue arrival.

McCovey left enemy pitchers awed and friendly players in shock. The final months of the 1959 baseball season were Willie's time. Rarely, if ever, has a player made a more dynamic sudden impact when called up from the minor leagues.

Most rookies ease their way into the lineup. McCovey barged into the San Francisco Giants batting order. Most rookies are groomed for a spot on the roster as part of an overall plan hatched over the winter and introduced in spring training. McCovey was summoned from minor league Phoenix in mid-season because he was hot and management thought he might be able to help out a little. McCovey was astounding. He did not just help out with a few timely hits, he put the team on his broad shoulders. His successful appearance indicated to baseball scouts that new generations of African American talent were hidden in out-of-the-way places, and that more than blacks who had been consigned to the Negro Leagues would come along in waves to fill rosters.

It was not as if the Giants did not understand McCovey's strengths and strength. At the start of the 1959 campaign, they just did not know what to do with him. McCovey was a first baseman and the Giants already had 1958 rookie of the year Orlando Cepeda at that position. McCovey was the odd man out, with no regular position. The Giants tried to buy time in order to figure out how to play McCovey, Cepeda, and superstar Willie Mays in the lineup at the same time. Few teams were ever bogged down with the problem of how to sort out use of three future Hall of Famers simultaneously.

McCovey, then just twenty-one, torched AAA minor league pitching in Phoenix. The Giants had signed McCovey to a $175-a-month contract when he was seventeen, and he methodically slugged his way to the brink of the Giants roster in March of 1959. By the time the Giants brain trust thought to call on McCovey, he was clubbing Triple A pitching at a .377 pace. The Giants were in a tight pennant race and were hoping to edge out the Los Angeles Dodgers and Milwaukee Braves for their first trip to the World Series

Nicknamed "Stretch" because of his looks and the way he manned first base, Willie McCovey was the San Francisco Giants' first home-grown hero and his popularity at times eclipsed that of Wille Mays.

since moving west from New York and the Polo Grounds. McCovey received the phone call to pack for the Coast on a Wednesday night. He was so nervous that he did not sleep well, then caught a seven a.m. flight to Frisco, and dressed for that day's game.

The Giants were at home against the Philadelphia Phillies, having lost five of their previous eight games at the end of July, when McCovey was recalled and inserted into the lineup for his Major League debut by manager Bill Rigney. In his first game, McCovey swatted two triples and two singles in a four-for-four start—off future Hall of Famer Robin Roberts. The next day, against the Pittsburgh Pirates, he hit a 390-foot game-winning single.

Les Biederman, a well-known sportswriter of the time, was in San Francisco to cover the Pirates and wrote, "The whole town's talking about Willie. Not Willie Mays, but Willie McCovey, the twenty-one-year-old left-handed slugging first baseman." It is always nice for a position player to get a hit in his first at bat. It is nicer still when it is a home run. But to blast four hits in his first game and win his second game on a big blow, well, that had observers talking already. "I've been around a long time," Rigney said, "but never have I seen a fellow break in like this boy."[1]

Within a few years it would be firmly established that McCovey and Mays were the deadliest hitting African American duo in the sport and one of the greatest twosome hitting partners of all time. In the beginning, Mays was just like the fans, wide eyed and excited by what he saw in McCovey's game-altering swing.

"Nobody ever broke in better than McCovey," Mays said. "We needed somebody to give us a spark and this boy may be our fireman."[2]

McCovey stood six-foot-four and during his playing days weighed about 200 pounds. His power was natural. In an era long before players pumped iron with regularity or ingested steroids or other drug supplements, he did not have the same sculpted physique as would become commonplace later. Around the turn of the nineteenth/twentieth century, one of the most prominent ballplayers was the diminutive Wee Willie Keeler, who made famous a comment indicating he "hit 'em where they ain't." This meant that he placed the ball where there were no fielders. In Keeler's case those were the open spaces on the diamond between fielders. In commenting on his blazing start,

McCovey uttered something similar. But it had an entirely different meaning. "I figure if I hit 'em they're going to take care of themselves," he said. "And I figure I'm strong enough to hit 'em." McCovey was referring to depositing long fly balls in the grandstands, out of the reach of outfielders altogether.[3]

EARLY LIFE

Willie Lee McCovey was born in Mobile, Alabama, not far from where the greatest home-run hitter of all time, Hank Aaron, lived. McCovey wore the number forty-four throughout his Major League career as a tribute to Aaron. The son of railroad worker Frank McCovey and wife Ester, Willie was one of eight boys and two girls. Mobile was a hotbed of great baseball in the first half of the century and sent a disproportionate number of big-name stars into pro ball. Satchel Paige was from Mobile and so was the Chicago Cubs' Billy Williams, another future Hall of Famer.

An All-Star basketball and football player for Central High School, McCovey built a reputation as a hard hitter in the local baseball and softball leagues. The Giants considered him a raw player with potential and paid him no bonus when McCovey joined Sandersville in the Class D Georgia State League in 1955. Actually, McCovey was first noticed by scout Jesse Thomas, who worked for Alex Pompez, the former operator of the New York Cubans of the Negro Leagues. Pompez, who scouted many emerging Latin stars for the Giants and the Pirates, tipped off the Giants. Originally, McCovey was simply sent a train ticket to Melbourne, Florida, for the team's minor league camp, given a travel bag to replace the paper bag he used to carry his shoes, and $1 for a hamburger and soda for lunch on the way. McCovey was signed by the parent club once he demonstrated his hitting talent.

Growing up in Alabama meant that McCovey was hardly ignorant of the racism prevailing in the South. Coming of age in Alabama, playing professionally in Georgia while being away from home for the first extended time period, and then suiting up for Dallas in the Class AA Southern League, McCovey became quickly educated about Jim Crow laws. When the Dallas Giants minor league affiliate played scheduled games in Louisiana, McCovey said local laws prevented his team from fielding a full lineup.

"One of the teams was in Shreveport," McCovey said. "And they didn't allow blacks to play with whites. We had three black players on our team, so when the team traveled to Shreveport, we stayed home in Dallas."[4]

More than a decade had passed since Jackie Robinson broke the color line in the majors, but it was not until 1959 that the last Major League team introduced an African American player into its lineup. While McCovey might have been the youngest and the latest, chronologically, of the period's notable black stars to break into the majors, he still experienced many of the same hurts and insults black players had endured for decades. The main thrust of the American civil rights movement was still ahead in the 1960s. A ballplayer working his way up to the majors was still likely to pass through Confederate thinking southern outposts in the 1950s.

McCovey's breakthrough with the Giants was a revelation. He made headlines coast-to-coast. He was a fresh face in the game. For anyone tired of simple pennant races and the usual stars, McCovey was great fodder for newspaper columns. Better yet, he was not a one-game phenom, a one-week star, or even a month-long flash in the pan. He showed he belonged. Although McCovey could not carry the Giants to the pennant, he did sustain top-level play for the rest of the season.

MAJOR LEAGUE CAREER

McCovey's name and accomplishments swiftly became known to headline writers and fans. Within three weeks of his debut, newspapers were writing series about McCovey's life, telling the story of his beginnings, and yes, even raising the question of whether he could keep up the special hitting and whether he was the genuine article or not. By the time McCovey broke in, mainstream coverage of teams was far less likely to even note the race of a new, hot player and, if mentioned, did not dwell on it.

Dick Young, one of the most prominent baseball writers of the day, had his New York story picked up by San Francisco papers. "It has been almost a month now since Willie McCovey rose like a flaming phoenix from the burning sands of Arizona, picked the collapsed San Francisco ballclub up in his immense claws and carried it into the clouds toward the World Series," Young wrote initially on August 24, 1959. "Most everyone has had a shot at the big bird by now. The vote is in on McCovey. The verdict is virtually unanimous: Willie McCovey is for real, a genuine big-league talent, a superior hitter endowed with the potentialities of greatness."[5] The headline on the San Francisco version of Young's story read, "Tab McCovey for BB Greatness."

McCovey's nickname, applied to the way he fielded at first base in leaning toward his infielders' throws, was "Stretch." McCovey thought that fellow players Willie Kirkland and Leon Wagner gave him the label because he was so thin when they first saw him. However, while every successful first baseman performed the stretching duty, McCovey's elongated body emphasized the maneuver and it was a suitable nickname that stayed with him for the duration of his career.

Day after day during his first week in the majors, McCovey's appearance at the plate signaled that something big was going to happen for the Giants. The fans at Candlestick Park were buzzing before he stepped in to hit. One day McCovey crunched three solid hits. The next day he hit his first homer. On August 5, McCovey boosted the Giants to a 4–1 victory over the Braves with 2 home runs.

"The unending saga of Willie the Stretch continued to stun everyone, including himself yesterday," the *San Francisco Examiner* reported after that game. "Young Willie Lee McCovey tries to assure his questioners that he's only human, but they don't believe him."[6]

The story ridiculed the notion that the sweet lefty swinger could ever fall into a slump, and explained that McCovey hit a low pitch for one homer and a high pitch for the other. "Don't make that much difference when I'm hitting," McCovey said.[7]

Baseball fans periodically swoon from love-at-first-sight infatuation with a phenomenon like McCovey, but there have not been many occasions to match this frenzy. Pitcher Mark Fidrych talked to the baseball before he threw it and endeared himself to fans, but injuries quickly ruined his Detroit Tigers career in the late 1970s. Fernando Valenzuela, who rolled his eyes to the heavens and inspired Mexican-Americans, had more staying power with the Los Angeles Dodgers in the early 1980s. McCovey, however, was the first African American to engender this sort of wild fan mania and, even more notably, his eruption into the forefront of attention in 1959 was prelude to a Hall of Fame career. And at the time, McCovey was being paid $7,500, the rate of the Major League minimum salary, a bargain for the Giants.

About ten days after McCovey's call-up, another San Francisco columnist weighed in on the player's newfound stature. "Something beautiful happened to the San Francisco Candlesticks the other day," the piece began. "His name is Willie McCovey. Willie came into their lives at a time the Candlesticks were flickering and behaving very unlike a team that might win the pennant. In no time at all, he brightened the dark little corners. What kind of superman did San Francisco inherit? How lucky can the Candlesticks get? To catch a character like this at such a critical stage of the pennant race is an unbelievable longshot."[8]

McCovey was almost dizzy from the attention. He had confidence in his ability, knew he could hit, but never expected to emerge as an instant star. "I always dreamed of playing in the big leagues," he said. "But I never expected to start out like this. The reporters, the pictures, the stories. Why, I received more mail in the week I've been here than I did all last year in Phoenix."[9]

In a very unusual rarity, McCovey was voted the National League rookie of the year award even though he played less than half a season with the Giants. But what a stretch it was. McCovey was pencilled into the lineup for only fifty-two games and he batted just 192 times, but he slugged 13 home runs, drove in 38 runs, and his average was .354. McCovey won the rookie vote unanimously, the first time in a decade it was decided that way.

"Next year should really show how I'll do in the big leagues," McCovey said.[10]

McCovey was hitting up a storm and the Giants hovered near first place (though they finished third, four games behind the Dodgers and two behind the Braves), but Orlando Cepeda was shifted to third base part of the time to accommodate all the powerful bats. It was clear that for the 1960 season, room had to be made in the lineup for everyone. McCovey and Cepeda were both too good to leave on the bench. "Watch him go in 1960," Rigney said of McCovey. "He could be baseball's next .400 hitter."[11]

McCovey's 1959 season is one of the most unforgettable individual runs in baseball history. However, in contrast to Rigney's opinion, the big man never did become a .400 hitter, or even come close to fulfilling that prophecy. He only once more hit over .300. Over time—and certainly the way he is best remembered—McCovey evolved into a dangerous home-run hitter with a career total of 521 four-baggers. It is a number equal to the total put up by Hall of Famer Ted Williams. Much like Hank Aaron, McCovey became known as a tremendous wrist hitter.

Bill White, who also became an All-Star first baseman, though

The author of one of the most sensational debut seasons ever in 1959, Willie McCovey won the National League rookie of the year award, hit 521 home runs, and became a Hall of Famer.

mostly with the Cardinals, and later was a barrier breaker as the first African American president of the American League, was a minor league teammate of McCovey in Dallas. McCovey said White passed on some hitting tips that loosened up his swing and the way he held the bat, and the change resulted in his new home-run power.

"White showed me how to grip a bat and how to get good wrist action into my swing," McCovey said. "I had been locking my wrists. The power came gradually, but from the first day, when I hit my first homer, I began to get a lot more wrist freedom."[12]

McCovey hit a career-high 45 homers for the Giants in 1969 and also swatted 44 in 1963. During his twenty-two-season Major League career that also included stops with the San Diego Padres and Oakland A's, McCovey hit more than thirty homers in a year four more times and more than twenty-five two more times. He collected 1,555 RBIs in 2,588 games and batted .270, declining particularly in his last years.

If more sophisticated surgical options had been available and more developed weight training programs in vogue during McCovey's years, his stats would have improved. One thing that burdened McCovey and limited his achievements was weak knees. Even before McCovey reached the majors, he had had an operation on his right knee for torn cartilage and during his excellent start with the Giants, he wore a knee brace.

"I hope to throw the knee brace away next year," McCovey declared after the 1959 season.[13] But given the number of times he suffered knee woes, if he was able to discard that support system it could be only for a brief period.

If 1959 was a fantasy come true, 1960 was a nightmare that was all too real for McCovey. He completed his rookie year on the highest of highs, honored and praised, his swing compared to Ted Williams' in smoothness. But while resting his knee during the off-season, he did not work out. McCovey reported to spring training about 20 pounds overweight. His timing was off. Then his fielding, never as smooth as that hitting, fell off. McCovey made untimely errors. He looked lost in the field and, incredibly, even awkward at the plate. Once the toast of the nation, he was receiving harsh admonishments from team officials.

A prodigy the season before at twenty-one, McCovey came off as a vulnerable youngster at twenty-two. Willie Mays said, "He's shook up, confused. He needs guidance."[14] McCovey needed something. He required a boost in confidence, the recovery of his swagger, and the resurrection of his swing. The unthinkable followed. Roughly a year after McCovey was promoted from the minors to begin his remarkable hitting in the majors, the Giants sent him back to the minors.

Professional athletes have often been labeled victims of a "sophomore slump" if their second season is not as good as their first. Many dismiss that as superstition. But McCovey was the personification of the sophomore slump. A year after tearing up National League pitching, McCovey appeared in 101 games. He batted just 260 times, hit the same number of homers—13—and hit a sad .238 average. The Giants neither rushed him nor ruined him after that disappointing season. Expected to be an everyday ballplayer, McCovey's struggles planted Cepeda back on first base and made his own planned rush into the starting lineup a slower process.

After McCovey's shooting star debut, his assimilation into the Giants regular scheme crept along. In 1961, McCovey hit 18 home runs and batted .271. This was certainly not what had been promised in 1959, but was a marked improvement over 1960. In 1962, when the Giants won the pennant, McCovey hit 20 home runs with a .293 average. One of the most famous plays of McCovey's career occurred at the end of that season, but it is remembered for unfortunate reasons.

The loaded Giants won 103 games in 1962 and needed every one of those victories to edge the Dodgers by a single game in the National League standings. In the World Series, San Francisco carried the New York Yankees into a seventh game. With two outs in the ninth inning, and the tying and winning runs on base, McCovey walked to the plate, taking practice swings with his big lumber, prepared to bomb a pitch out of sight for a Giants triumph. The score was 1–0 and Yankee right-hander Ralph Terry was on the mound. McCovey thought a Terry offering was the pitch to cream. He swung and smashed a hard-line drive toward right field. But Yankee second baseman Bobby Richardson reached out and speared the ball for the final out of the series.

It was the next season, 1963, when McCovey once again showed the big-thumper tendencies he had exhibited during his 1959 stretch. In 1963 McCovey was both healthy and not platooned. He appeared in nearly all the Giants games and led the National League in homers with 44 while driving in more than a hundred (102) runs for the first time in his career. Near the end of the season, McCovey electrified Giants fans with a three-home-run game that was even more special for the way it unfolded.

McCovey homered in three straight plate appearances from the start of the game against the New York Mets. He hit one home run in the first inning off Jay Hook, his second in the second inning off Galen Cisco, and his third in the fourth inning off Grover Powell. He hit three home runs in three at bats. When McCovey came up again in the fifth, Powell was still in the game and the thrower hit McCovey with a pitch that seemed too suspicious to be an accident. The 14,000-plus fans at Candlestick booed that play lustily.[15]

At last, the old Willie McCovey seemed to be back, and better than ever. A year later McCovey reverted to poor form. He hit only .220 and during 1964 and 1965 complained of bad foot pain of unknown origin. Suddenly, Giants managers and coaches were also saying he could not hit left-handed throwers. In his personal life he was going through a divorce. It was a tough time for McCovey. He saw foot specialists. He purchased special shoes to ease pressure on his arches. Nothing he tried allowed him to walk around or play baseball completely pain free. Exasperated, McCovey gave up trying to fix his feet and resigned himself to coping with the problem.

"So I've got bad dogs," he said. "They're mine. There's no way of exchanging them for new ones. I've got to live with the pain."[16]

McCovey ignored the pain and became a better and better ballplayer. He deflected his injuries and improved throughout the rest of the 1960s. By the end of 1965 he had accumulated 39 home runs and the season marked the first year of a splendid five-season run that was the best in McCovey's career. The only fresh aggravation was a lingering hip injury suffered in 1966. In 1968, he led the league in home runs (36) and RBIs (105) and did so again in 1969 (44) and (126), while hitting .320. That was the greatest all-around season of McCovey's career. He was so feared by opposing hurlers that year that he also walked 121 times. This was the first time in twenty-five years that a player had led his league in both homers and RBIs two years in succession.

Despite McCovey's heroics, in the first year Major League baseball adopted a divisional plan for its two leagues, the Giants ninety victories were worth only second place in the NL West to the Atlanta Braves. There were no playoffs or World Series for the Giants. Yet McCovey's monster season was rewarded with the biggest individual honor of his career. He was chosen the National League MVP. It was the topper to an incredible year which additionally included the MVP award in the All-Star game. During this time period McCovey also acquired a reputation as a clutch hitter because he hit grand slams at a pace greater than most players in baseball history. McCovey's prowess paid off with raises that lifted his pay rate far beyond his initial contract—he was making $85,000 a year.

"I'm not afraid of any pitcher," McCovey said in 1969. "But each club has three or four who can be very tough for me on a given day. Guys you've never seen before can cause you a lot of trouble. I'm a better hitter now than I used to be because I'm more knowledgeable."[17]

At the time, McCovey was just past thirty years old. He said he wanted to play another ten years, if possible, but wondered if his nonstop injuries would permit that. He already had arthritis in his knee and calcium deposits in his hip. "I don't drink or smoke and I stay in good shape, so maybe I can play until I'm forty, or close to it," he said."[18]

The best pitchers in the game gave McCovey wary respect when he sauntered to the plate. In his autobiography, St. Louis Cardinals Hall of Fame pitcher Bob Gibson explained his attitude toward McCovey. "The scariest hitter I faced had to be Willie McCovey," Gibson wrote. "As dangerous as he was, I loved pitching to McCovey. He was so long and tall that he liked the ball away from his body so that he could unwrap himself and get his big arms in motion. Once, in St. Louis, I gave him a pitch away that he could handle and Boom!—he crushed it off the left-center field wall so damn hard you could hear the ricochet all over the park. Imagine what that ball would have done to me if he'd hit it back through the box! He was a low-ball hitter, but there wasn't a way to pitch to McCovey without substantial risk."[19]

McCovey and Willie Mays used to hit next to one another in the batting order and that proximity made many opposing pitchers quake. They could not afford to hang a curve or misaim a fastball to either man. Mays and McCovey were friends and roomed together on the road before big stars were given the preferential treatment of single rooms.

They used to take late-night walks in cities the Giants visited and McCovey used to talk Mays into late-night snacks. "Willie was my roommate and used to astound me with the way he could eat so late at night," Mays said. "We passed a take-out joint that specialized in ribs. Willie said we should take some back to our hotel room. He ate most of them." While Willie McCovey's stomach was fine, Willie Mays awoke in the middle of the night throwing up. Mays arrived at the ballpark convinced he was too weak to play and that despite McCovey's good health, sure that his ailment was food poisoning from the ribs. When Mays felt a little better, he decided to suit up. That day he hit a Major League record tying four home runs in a single game.[20]

In 1971, the same year McCovey's appearance at the All-Star game provoked Detroit Tigers skipper Sparky Anderson to suggest that the only thing holding McCovey back from an 80-home-run season was the hesitation of National League hurlers to challenge him without giving up intentional walks; McCovey almost could not walk at all. He damaged his left knee and limped through the entire season, missing more than forty games while putting off surgery until after the season ended.

"He's in pain whenever he goes out there," said Giants manager Charlie Fox. "Some days the pain is greater than other days, but it's always there. The day I saw the tears had to be the worst."[21] Those were tears McCovey tried to hide, but he could not always hide his grimaces or his disappointment while being forced into rests onto the bench.

McCovey was never a super sprinter, but his continuing injury woes slowed his running to turtle-like status and made him seem expendable. In 1973, one of the most popular Giants in franchise history was shipped to the San Diego Padres in a three-player deal. He was thirty-five and when McCovey moved on, the San Francisco reporters who had greatly admired his skills wrote farewells tinged with wistfulness, certain in their belief that he would never pass their way again except for periodic National League regular-season encounters.

"He was really a gentle fellow and one helluva baseball player," it was said in the *San Francisco Chronicle*. "Willie Stretch was counted out dozens of times, but always came back stronger."[22]

McCovey gave the Padres two-plus solid years. He hit more than 20 home runs twice and played in about two-thirds of the team's games. However, in a deal that caught the Bay Area off-guard, Oakland A's owner Charlie Finley maneuvered a waiver trade to obtain McCovey from San Diego and thrust him into the 1976 pennant race. Although McCovey was neither playing much, nor hitting very well, the opportunity to reinvigorate the player's game as a designated hitter in the American League appealed to Finley.

"I'm used hardly at all," McCovey said of his final days in San Diego. "I feel like I've been swept under the rug. All I do is pinch hit and then only when a situation comes up in the eighth or ninth inning. So I go to bat once every other week. You can't build an average, or really hit well in that atmosphere."[23]

McCovey never really got much of a shot at a regular job with the A's either. He did receive a standing ovation for his first Oakland at bat, but was a nonfactor the rest of the season. For all the attention focused on his homecoming, Stretch only got into eleven games before the season ended. It was the next spring, when McCovey's true second act in life—as a member of the Giants again—took place. McCovey played out his option with the A's and attended Giants spring training camp as a nonroster player. But McCovey showed his bat still had some pop. He was signed to the team that had nurtured him since the 1950s and he returned to his station at first base. At age thirty-nine, he also enjoyed a surprisingly productive 1977 season, hitting .280 with 28 homers and 86 RBIs. Once again McCovey was the talk of the game.

"Being a Giant is all I ever wanted to be," McCovey told a reporter on a road trip to Atlanta.[24]

McCovey had not hit as many homers in a season since leaving the Giants after the 1973 campaign, but was described as being a completely "intimidating" batter despite his age. "A more awesome figure at home plate has never been, at least not in this generation of ballplayers. It's something in the way he moves, slow, smooth and confident. As he waits for the pitcher's delivery, he sweeps his bat back and forth, dipping it low in a menacing manner that's his alone. Willie McCovey oozes 'home run' from every pore of his towering frame."[25]

McCovey endured and lasted in a sport where many are finished by thirty. Somehow, he overcame all his injuries, especially the ones to the lower extremities. The knees, feet, and other problems robbed him of considerable playing time, so no wonder he wanted to hang on.

"It's cost me a lot of games, so I guess it's cost me some home runs," McCovey reflected during the 1977 season. "If I hadn't had the injuries, I'd have had 500 home runs by now instead of still going for it. But I can't sit back and feel sorry for myself. I'm not unhappy with my career at all. I'm unhappy about having had so much pain. But I've been fortunate. I've been able to live with it and perform, whereas a lot of guys would have been forced out of the game."[26] McCovey won the National League comeback player of the year award that season.

During the 1979 season, fan debate began on whether a forty-one-year-old McCovey should keep a young, promising hitter named Mike Ivie out of the lineup or not. The newsroom side of the *San Francisco Examiner* took up the issue, inviting letters from fans. The conclusion was ambiguous. The newspaper suggested McCovey consider retirement or becoming a player-coach, but said that he was so beloved that he might be better off declaring his intention to run for governor of California. McCovey stayed out of politics and hit 15 home runs for the Giants that season. He retired during the 1980 season, after fulfilling an ambition to become a rare major leaguer to appear in games in four decades.

LATER LIFE

As his career wound down, McCovey was frustrated. He wanted to play more than Giants manager Dave Bristol wanted to use him. "Willie thinks he can play forever," Bristol said.[27]

Money was not the issue. McCovey had security. When he returned to the Giants for the denouement of his career, he signed a ten-year pact with the team. He was paid $175,000 to play for two years and the remainder represented a personal services contract at a lesser figure. McCovey was tied with Ted Williams for eighth place on the all-time home-run list, but wanted to play a little longer in order to pass Jimmie Foxx (534) and Mickey Mantle (536.)

In the end, McCovey chose not to stick around as a bench warmer and after participating in just forty-eight games in 1980, he retired in mid-season. Immediately, local newspapers ran major retrospectives on his career.

"You think of him like a kind of John Wayne character," said Tom Haller, a former teammate. "He's like a cowboy or a guy in an army movie. He'd go through all kinds of things and to any lengths and not be concerned whether he got the notoriety he deserved. It's his quiet strength that is his strongest characteristic—on and off the field."[28]

Mays, who shared so much time on and off the field with McCovey, said the first baseman's fielding was underrated and it did not matter that he was not a gazelle on the base paths. "He could stretch a long way," Mays said. "I saw him save a bad throw so many times. Besides, we didn't get him to steal bases or whatever else. We got him to hit home runs."[29]

McCovey did that exceptionally well and prolifically (also connecting for a National League record eighteen grand slams). When he reminisced about his long career, he more frequently cited longevity as mattering most to him, not his body of work battering the baseball.

"That is probably the most important thing because of my love for the game and it is the only thing I ever wanted to do," McCovey said. "I had always dreamed and hoped that I would have a long and successful career. The fact that I have been able to play professional baseball for twenty-five years, really, and I include my minor league career, is the most important."[30]

Near the end of the 1980 season, the Giants held a "Willie McCovey Weekend" that trumpeted his service to the club in several ways. The two-day event included an old-timers game and a commemorative poster.

As expected by McCovey and others, when the next baseball season rolled around, he missed playing and being around the team and the clubhouse. Mostly, McCovey made public relations appearances on behalf of the Giants at luncheons and banquets.

Not stepping up to the plate to try to slam another home run was an itch that could not be scratched and it bothered him. But 1981 represented true retirement and he had to get used to it.

McCovey reclaimed the baseball limelight nationwide in 1986, however, when he was elected to the Baseball Hall of Fame in his first year of eligibility. His induction ceremony took place in August of that year and McCovey displayed a smart sense of humor with a joke that surprised his audience in Cooperstown, New York.

"People ask me how I would like to be remembered," said McCovey. "I tell them I'd like to be remembered as the guy who hit the line drive over Bobby Richardson's head."[31] Over, not to. Alas, there are no do-overs in the World Series. It was a season of honors for McCovey. The Giants threw a special day for him in July at Candlestick Park as a warm-up to the Hall of Fame festivities. More than 40,000 fans attended. Former Giants executive and National League president Chub Feeney praised McCovey.

"He's just a lovable guy," Feeney said. "But I think one of the biggest reasons for his great appeal is he broke in here. He didn't come from New York like some of the others. He would play hurt, he would play anywhere. He never complained. He never whined. He was a perfect gentleman"[32]

On the emotional day of his induction into the Hall of Fame, McCovey gave a lengthy speech. "I've been thinking about what a perfect kind of day this is for me to be here on this stage, celebrating the pinnacle of my career and my life," McCovey said. "One reason it seems so right is that it's a warm, summer Sunday afternoon, and, to me, it doesn't matter if you're in Mobile, or San Francisco, or Cooperstown, Sunday afternoons in the summertime have always meant two things—it's a time for baseball and a time for families."[33]

McCovey was such a nice guy and in such a good mood that he even thanked sportswriters he had known. McCovey thanked the family he grew up with and his baseball family, the Giants executives, players, and fans, who treated him so well for so long.

"I've been adopted, too, by all the thousands of great Giants fans everywhere and by the city of San Francisco," McCovey said, "where I've always been welcome and, like the Golden Gate Bridge and the cable cars, I've been made to feel like a landmark, too." In naming so many people whom he appreciated, McCovey wrapped up by saying to the crowd, "I wanted you to know who they are because without them I certainly would not be standing here now. They are the most valuable players in my life. They are the champions of my world. They are the people in my Hall of Fame."[34]

During his years of retirement, McCovey spent some time as a team instructor and a community fund director. He developed arthritis in both his knees and had several surgeries on both of them. Even knee replacements did not produce a completely satisfactory result. Although McCovey's popularity in San Francisco never waned, he lost direct involvement with the Giants for a period in the 1990s.

But that changed in 2000. When the new Giants ballpark opened replacing Candlestick Park, the team named the China Basin Channel beyond the right-field fence "McCovey Cove." As a left-handed slugger, McCovey hit many of his blasts over the right-field wall at Candlestick and at other parks. A special plaque along a twenty-five-foot public walkway, commemorating McCovey's career and explaining the name, was also added. Every time a player hits a home run out of the stadium on the right side, the ball splashes down in the Cove. Occasionally, such as the times when star Barry Bonds was chasing home-run records, entrepreneurs in boats inhabited the area to rescue balls with nets before they sank.

When the construction plan was revealed in late 1999, McCovey said he was honored by the designation. "Let's face it," McCovey said, "to know there's going to be something left behind after you leave with your name on it, it's all you can ask. I thought it was an honor when the Little League field in Woodside was named after me, but this is even better."[35]

Once estranged from the Giants, McCovey developed a new relationship with new owners when the new park opened. He became a special assistant to the president of the club and in 2002 it was announced that when the Giants built a local team theme park adjacent to the ballyard, it would contain a statue of Willie Lee McCovey.

Quite a stretch from Mobile to marble, but the big slugger's love affair with San Francisco was simply taking a new turn. Making the Hall of Fame was one thing, but being preserved as a statue for future generations offered a new kind of immortality. McCovey became a for-real landmark.

NOTES

1. Les Biederman, *San Francisco Chronicle*, August 2, 1959.
2. Ibid.
3. (No byline), *Los Angeles Examiner*, August 4, 1959.
4. Glenn Dickey, *San Francisco Chronicle*, January 30, 2005.
5. Dick Young (*New York Daily News*), *San Francisco Examiner*, September 12, 1959.
6. Art Rosenbaum, *San Francisco Examiner*, August 6, 1959.
7. Ibid.
8. Melvin Durslag, *San Francisco Examiner*, August 9, 1959.
9. Curley Grieve, *San Francisco Examiner*, August 6, 1959.
10. Harold Rosenthal, *New York Herald-Tribune*, November 18, 1959.
11. Ibid.
12. Grieve, *San Francisco Examiner*.
13. Walter Judge, *San Francisco Examiner*, November 18, 1959.
14. Art Rosenbaum, *San Francisco Examiner*, July 19, 1960.
15. Bob Stevens, *San Francisco Chronicle*, September 23, 1963.
16. Bob Stevens, *Sporting News*, June 12, 1965.
17. Pat Frizzell, *Sporting News*, August 9, 1969.
18. Ibid.
19. Bob Gibson with Lonnie Wheeler, *Stranger to the Game: The Autobiography of Bob Gibson* (New York: Viking Penguin, 1994), 177–178.
20. Willie Mays with Lou Sahadi, *Say Hey: The Autobiography of Willie Mays* (New York: Pocket Books, 1989), 173–174.
21. Phil Pepe, *New York Daily News*, August 21, 1971.
22. Art Rosenbaum, *San Francisco Chronicle*, November 1, 1973.
23. Art Rosenbaum, *San Francisco Chronicle*, August 31, 1976.
24. Gary Caruso, *Atlanta Constitution*, June 5, 1977.
25. Ibid.
26. Ibid.
27. Joseph Durso, *New York Times*, June 15, 1980.
28. Stephanie Salter, *San Francisco Examiner*, July 1, 1980.
29. Ibid.
30. Willie McCovey with William Flynn, *San Francisco Examiner/Chronicle*, July 6, 1980.
31. Rich Chere, *Newark Star-Ledger*, August 3, 1986.
32. Ray Ratto, *San Francisco Chronicle*, July 7, 1986.

    33. Willie McCovey, Hall of Fame induction remarks, August 3, 1986, on file Baseball Hall of Fame Library Archives.
    34. Ibid.
    35. Mark Purdy, *San Jose Mercury News*, August 26, 1999.

Further Reading

McCovey, Willie, with William Flynn, "Remembering Willie McCovey," *San Francisco Examiner/ Chronicle*, July 6, 1980.

ERNIE BANKS

January 31, 1931–

One of the greatest National League sluggers of the 1950s and 1960s, Ernie Banks not only won two Most Valuable Player (MVP) awards with the then-lowly Chicago Cubs, but was also that team's first African American player, and remains highly regarded today decades into retirement as one of the sport's most popular ambassadors because of his perpetually upbeat attitude.

Banks' signature phrase was "Let's play two!" a euphemism expressing joy for scheduling doubleheaders everyday. He smacked 512 career home runs and with the nickname "Mr. Cub" is regarded as the face of the franchise. Well into his seventies, Banks aspires to become president of the team and to perform a service so worthwhile for humanity that he would be named winner of the Nobel Peace Prize.

☆ ☆ ☆

A conversation with Ernie Banks will not last more than a minute before the words "wonderful" and "that's great" permeate the discussion. The man who was often

"Mr. Cub," Ernie Banks, the most popular player in Chicago Cubs history, takes a big cut at the plate and is off and running as the ball heads into play.

described as possessing the sunniest disposition in baseball still retains the same positive outlook on life thirty-five years after he retired from active play.

It is a testament to his enduring greatness, popularity, and attitude that the man known as "Mr. Cub" during his nineteen seasons with the Chicago Cubs is still known by that appellation. Hundreds of players have come and gone since, even repeat All Stars like Sammy Sosa, but Banks, the longtime star whose enthusiasm for baseball was eclipsed by no one, retains the title and is greeted by rolled-out red carpets on visits to Chicago.

Banks turned seventy-five in early 2006, but he retains a youthful timber in his voice and seemingly the same amount of energy he did when the late Buck O'Neil, then manager of the Kansas City Monarchs, first heard of him. Cool Papa Bell alerted O'Neil about the teenaged stripling when he was still a high school player in Texas.

"I was playing in Amarillo, Texas with a semi-pro team," said Banks, who attended high school in Dallas. "We played against the Kansas City Monarchs. They had two teams. I guess they were a minor league team and Cool Papa Bell was their manager. Cool Papa Bell saw me. I had a pretty good game and he told me after the game he would recommend me to THE Kansas City Monarchs. And he did. So Buck came down to Dallas and talked to my mother. I wasn't really excited. I was young. I just looked at it that they [well-known baseball players] were coming to my house. But I did end up signing and I did play for him. He was wonderful as a man and to play for. And Cool Papa Bell became a confidant to me, a comforter for me when I arrived in the major leagues."[1]

EARLY LIFE

Jackie Robinson had just broken the color line in Major League baseball, but it was unclear how the long-term integration of the game would play out when Buck O'Neil first saw Ernie Banks play baseball. Cool Papa Bell and O'Neil immediately recognized Banks' talent, but he was still raw. Banks was also still in school. It was not until a little later that the Bell-O'Neil connection paid off for Banks, who in between began traveling with a lesser outfit called the Detroit Colts.

Monarchs representatives came to Banks' house before his senior year in high school, and laid out an offer guaranteeing a job with the team the next summer at $300 a month if he made the club. The offer meant an opportunity for something better in life. Banks grew up in poverty in Texas, and although he could not know his career would soon take him to big cities all over the land and he would become a revered figure with the Cubs, a regular salary of any kind was appealing.

Banks' father Eddie and his mother Essie lived in a segregated neighborhood in Dallas where amenities of the most basic sort were precious commodities. Banks was delivered by a midwife. He is sure that his family could not afford a doctor to attend his childbirth, but is pretty certain there was not even a doctor in the area.

"My father always said I was the smallest baby he had ever seen," said Banks, who grew into a six-foot-one, 180-pound ballplayer from his five-pound, two-ounces beginnings. "We were very poor and my father often worked from dawn till dark seven days a week. I can remember going without lunch and other times when I went to bed hungry. In fact, I never invited friends home to lunch because there just wasn't enough food, and I was never invited to my friends' homes for the same reason."[2]

Banks said a welfare truck dropped off clothing and other items to needy families, and the first job he ever had was picking cotton. He then moved on to a lawn-mowing partnership with a friend. Much of Banks' early diamond training involved high-caliber, fast-pitch softball. One guy he played with, Hank Thompson, became one of the first African Americans in the big leagues, as well. Banks played high school football and basketball, but soon after graduation, at nineteen, he was on a bus to Kansas City.

"Buck got me to Kansas City and I just came out there right away and fielded ground balls before the game that night," Banks said. "Buck was very organized, highly intelligent. He was a playing manager when I was there."[3]

To illustrate the type of fast company Banks suddenly traveled with, in 1950 one of his teammates was Hall of Famer Satchel Paige. Banks became pals with another Monarchs young talent on the rise—Elston Howard, the future New York Yankee. Banks also said that when he made his debut against the Indianapolis Clowns, it was the most nervous he ever was on an athletic field. Ordered to relax by infielder Curt Roberts, a future Pittsburgh Pirate, Banks simply could not.

"It was impossible," he said. "The tension, I found, affected my timing at the plate. I made contact with the ball all three times, but I was swinging late and flied out to right field each time." Afterward, O'Neil told Banks that if he loosened up and increased his bat speed the hits would come.[4] They did. Despite the nerves, Banks showed something because at the end of the season he was invited to join Jackie Robinson's All Stars for a month's tour. Banks was so happy to be noticed that he forgot to ask what he would get paid. It turned out to be $400, plus expenses.

Banks' baseball career was interrupted by a draft notice and he entered the Army. While stationed at Fort Bliss in Texas, Banks played some basketball for the Harlem Globetrotters, even though he knew he was a far better baseball player than Hoopster. Banks was shipped overseas in 1952, but spent much of his service time involved in recreational endeavors. While in the Army, he received letters from the Cleveland Indians and Brooklyn Dodgers inviting him to tryout sessions upon his discharge. But as soon as he mustered out, Banks called O'Neil to ask if he still had a job. Only days later, in March of 1953, he was in spring training with the Monarchs.

However, organized baseball was opening up. More teams were on the lookout for talented, young, black ballplayers. Jackie Robinson paved the way for everyone. The Negro Leagues were fading out and O'Neil saw the future. He told Banks and his other young teammates that the options denied to their predecessors would be there for them and they should think about the major leagues. O'Neil even pointed out Major League scouts sitting in the stands.

Whether it was his naturally optimistic attitude, or Banks was shielded from the worst discrimination traveling black players endured in the early 1950s, he does not speak bitterly about that time in his life. Banks was aware of what was going on, but indicated he may have escaped the worst treatment.

"I wasn't involved in all of that," Banks said. "Buck was planning our trips and where we could stay. There were no hassles. Not with me. I was young, friends with the other guys and we were on the bus and on the go. I got on the bus, got me a sardine sandwich and a peanut butter sandwich and we would go on to the next place. He (O'Neil) handled all that. It was during pre-integrated society. A lot of places were just for blacks and whites and the water fountains and all that kind of stuff. That's the way it is in the world."[5] Banks did not make many waves and preferred seeing the best in other human beings, but he knew that African Americans were not welcome in many places he had to pass through. He chose not to make trouble and was lucky enough to avoid it.

Near the end of the 1953 season, Kansas City, a proud and prominent franchise in the history of Negro Leagues baseball, was approaching the end of its run. O'Neil was too old to become a Major League player, but he knew he could be valuable to big-league clubs hoping to tap black talent.

Cubs General Manager Wid Mathews spoke to O'Neil about the impending demise of Negro Leagues ball, saying, "This is going to be over pretty soon." And he offered O'Neil a scouting job. Then he added, "I want you to sign Ernie Banks to this contract."[6]

The contract was a Major League deal paying Banks $800 a month. That seemed like so much money that he called home and promised to buy his dad Eddie the car he always wanted. The agreement also sent Banks straight to the majors, and he played in ten games in September of 1953 while hitting .314. The brief showing in The Show, as the majors are called, solidified everyone's judgment that Banks was ready to become a big-time player.

Coincidentally, Banks had become a Cubs fan in an odd way. When he traveled with the Monarchs and the team went to Chicago, Banks discovered that the Cubs played all day games and he could kill time until his own night games by watching them on TV. Banks reported to the Cubs with showy yellow laces in his baseball shoes, but Cubs equipment man Yosh Kawano gently suggested trying black ones like the other players. One of Banks' most gracious welcomes came from slugger Ralph Kiner, who urged Banks to call on him for any help needed. Banks, who would soon enough be known as "Mr. Cub," called the reception quite nice for "Mr. Nobody from Dallas." He also noted that from Abe Saperstein of the Globetrotters, to his Cubs bosses, to his teammates, he had never been involved with so many white men and was surprised how well he was treated.[7]

MAJOR LEAGUE CAREER

Banks hit his first Major League home run in his first at bat. He was also joined in the Cubs dugout by Gene Baker, another black shortstop, and they were the club's first black ballplayers. When Baker moved to second base and they played together, Banks and Baker became the first African American Major League double-play combination.

However, their virtually simultaneous arrival on the team also dovetailed with a common practice among Major League teams in the early 1950s—keeping two African American players on the squad instead of one, or three. At a time when players, regardless of stature, still shared hotel rooms with teammates on the road to save the club money, no team was bold enough to force black guys and white guys to room together. Although Banks said the racial atmosphere on the Cubs was positive, he also took note of the separation of the races at road hotels, and when he thinks back to that era of gradual integration, he is very conscious of the fact that it was like Noah's Ark.

"Eight teams in each league, two black players on each team," Banks said. "It was two-by-two. The Dodgers had a few more. The Dodgers were atypical compared to the rest of baseball. I call it the Silent Fifties. Everybody was kind of quiet and we didn't talk very much and everybody was trying to feel their way through and relate to other generations and other ethnic groups and all of that."[8]

Outside the Cubs premises and outside baseball, Banks said it was always possible that a disquieting racial incident might occur. Sometimes it was where players could sleep. Sometimes it involved getting served in a restaurant. It did not seem to matter what part of the country the Cubs were in. The backdrop of Banks' first years in the majors was a country approaching an explosion over race, a United States seeking to come to terms with its own proclaimed identity built upon equality and justice for all. Demonstrations begun in the 1950s spilled into the 1960s. Sides were taken.

"Some people feel that because you are black you will never be treated fairly and that you should voice your opinions, be militant about them," Banks said in 1971. "I don't feel this way. You can't convince a fool against his will. If a man doesn't like me because I'm black, that's fine. I'll just go elsewhere, but I'm not going to let him change my life." "As black athletes, if we speak out on various issues, or wear our hair in certain ways, we are considered militant, in opposition to The Establishment, which puts us in a position of being opposed to what gives us our livelihood. If we don't speak up about racial issues, political matters, or the organization itself, we are called Uncle Toms."[9]

Banks quickly became a top National League player. Most shortstops are prized by their teams for their acrobatic fielding skills. For decades, shortstop was considered the weakest hitting link in the lineup. It was more important to have the good glove than the big bat and generally shortstops who batted .250 with no power could find a job. Banks was the antithesis of that image. He hit home runs that scrawny shortstops could only dream of clubbing.

Banks wielded as potent a bat as any shortstop in history. It was not until later stages of his career, when he slowed a little, that he adjusted to life at first base, a position where long ball hitters are more commonly found.

During his nineteen Major League seasons, all of them with the Cubs, Banks played in 2,528 games, became a member of the exclusive 500-home-run club with his total of

Ernie Banks, who hit 512 Major League home runs, shows off the stance that gave him his power and the lumber that launched so many big hits.

512, drove in 1,636 runs, and batted .274. Banks was known as a wrist hitter. He powdered his long hits with incredible bat speed and the swift follow-through guided by his wrists rather than with brute strength. Although he never played in a World Series—his Cubs were perennial losers during his career—Banks won MVP awards in 1958 and 1959.

A regular All Star, Banks was regarded as one of the best players in the game during his 1953–1971 era, and posted stunning statistics in individual seasons. In 1955, Banks hit 44 home runs and drove in 117. In 1957 he slugged 43 homers, in 1958 it was 47, and in 1959 it was 45. That year he drove in a career-high 143 runs. He made the switch to first base in 1962, but never hit more homers than he did as a shortstop.

When Hy Hurwitz, secretary of the Baseball Writers Association of America, telephoned Banks to inform him for the second year in a row that he had won the National League MVP, Hurwitz said, "This is becoming a habit with you." It is not something as often recalled, but Banks was a good fielding shortstop. He believed fielding helped win him his honors as much as his big batting numbers. Banks committed just twelve errors in 155 games.[10]

When the Bartlett's Quotations of Baseball Comments is published, there will be a place in it for Banks. Quite in keeping with his enthusiasm and image, Banks uttered one of the most famous lines in baseball history many times. Even if the weather was not sunny, Banks was, leading him to say, "Nice day, let's play two." That was Banks, the guy who loved the game so much that he was anxious to play a doubleheader even on lousy days. After he had been around for a few years, one Chicago sportswriter began calling Banks, "Gentleman Ernie." The sportswriter who bestowed Banks' best-known nickname was Jim Enright, who also collaborated on Banks' autobiography with the same name, "Mr. Cub."

It is difficult to find pictures of Banks from his playing days that do not display a broad smile on his face. Exceptions are pictures of Banks concentrating at the plate. Most pictures show a slender looking man with big eyes, a wide smile, a narrow head with pointed jaw, and closely cropped hair. Banks' face lit up when he hung out with children, whether it was signing autographs or visiting them in classrooms or hospitals. Banks met Pope Paul VI during a trip to Rome and visited American troops in Vietnam in 1968.

Also, once during the 1950s, Banks appeared on a television show with Dodgers catcher Roy Campanella and hostess Polly Bergen. When Banks told her that he played shortstop, Bergen asked where the particular base he defended was situated. When he replied that he did not have a base, Bergen joked, "My poor boy, playing without a base. Maybe someday, if you play long enough, you'll end up with a base you can call your very own."[11] And even though the skit was a joke, that is exactly what happened. Banks got a base of his own—first—in 1962 and ceased dropping by shortstop altogether.

One of Banks' best days as a player came during that 1962 season. The Cubs were playing Milwaukee and Hank Aaron was one of the Braves in the lineup. Banks hit home runs in three successive at bats, off three different pitchers. Wrigley Field is known for its fickle winds and after Banks' third blast, Aaron teased him. "Who is the man in the control tower of your friendly windmill?" Aaron said. "Every time you come to the plate, he turns it on and the wind blows a gale toward the outfield fences."[12]

Banks said he was not really a power hitter as a young man and that early scouting reports did not peg him as such. But being tutored by first Hank Thompson, back in Dallas softball days, Ralph Kiner, Jackie Robinson, and Monte Irvin altered Banks' stance, swing, and use of lighter weight bats during the hottest months. "Maturity generates better and deeper concentration, especially when applied to batting practice," Banks said.[13]

After a decade with the Cubs, Banks had embedded himself so deeply into the fans' and the organization's psyches that he was honored with an "Ernie Banks Day" on August 15, 1964. There was no pressing reason for the party at that moment. What made the event even more extraordinary was that never in franchise history had the Cubs feted a player with his own day. "I want it to be such a day in Ernie's life that he'll never forget it," said Cubs owner Phil Wrigley.[14]

Celebrants adopted the theme of "Thanks, Banks" for Ernie's Cubs contributions. Among the presents given to Banks at Wrigley Field that day were a station wagon, savings bonds for his children, a transistor radio, luggage, a TV set, a plaque, and trophies. Banks suggested that all gifts be given to underprivileged children. It was an emotional day, and Banks alternately wiped away a tear and beamed. "Everything I have I owe to baseball," Banks said. "Baseball has been a way of life for me. The game has given me an education, helped me make friends and associations, and established me in athletics and as a big leaguer. And it has helped me reach financial security." And, as Wrigley hoped, when the festivities ended, Banks proclaimed, "This is a day I never will forget."[15]

Banks kept accumulating home runs as a first baseman, but he only once approached the forty-in-a-season level after 1960. Banks was quizzed often about that, and said he gave it a lot of thought since he did not feel he had lost speed in his wrists. "When I was younger, things came easy and I just swung away," he said. "Now, I'm older, and I think about it and I try harder. Maybe a fellow thinks too much."[16]

Occasionally, sportswriters mentioned that Banks seemed too good to be true, but gradually it became universally acknowledged that he was the nicest man in the game. Besides the "let's-play-two" philosophy, Banks was known for predicting a Cubs World Series championship each spring. They never did win it, but Banks was a true believer. Sportswriters wrote tales built around the theme of whether Banks ever got mad at anybody or not.

Banks admitted he got pretty ticked off at Giants pitcher Jack Sanford during the 1959 campaign when the right-hander hit him with a pitch for the third time that season. After the ball struck him in the right shoulder blade, Banks could not swing properly for about two weeks, and among other things lost the National League home run title by one to Eddie Mathews. Banks was interviewed on TV after Sanford's toss and said "I told them Sanford had deliberately thrown at me."[17]

On another occasion—after apologizing to a sportswriter for not being awake when the phone rang—Banks was asked if he ever got mad. "Yes, of course," he said. "At myself. When I take a third strike or make a dumb play. (Being good-natured) "it's just the way I am naturally. I look for the good side of things. Baseball, I love it. I appreciate being part of a great game. I have no real gripes. The game doesn't need me or anyone else. It's just a great game. You get to thinking you're important because people come out to see you. After you're gone, they'll still come out. They come out to see baseball."[18]

Ernie Banks made it impossible not to like him. And those who got to meet him, or to interview him for their newspapers, did their best to spread the word. Pulitzer-Prize winning sports columnist Jim Murray may have been Banks' biggest booster. "Feeling kind of low? Wife not speaking to you? Dogs snap at you when you go by? Boss yelling at you? Worried about the future? The past? The present? Money running low? Feet hurt? Brother-in-law getting on your nerves? I have just the thing for you. Find out where the Chicago Cubs are playing baseball, take a taxi out to the ballpark, and look up number fourteen. This will be Sunshine Ernie Banks, Pollyanna at the plate, the most happy home-run hitter, the last of the great batter's box optimists. Ernie makes Rebecca of Sunnybrook Farm look like an old grouch."[19]

On his tribute day at Wrigley, Banks had said how proud he was to be an American and it made him a logical invitee for the 1968 morale-building trip to visit U.S. troops in Vietnam.

Banks joined pitcher Larry Jackson of the Phillies, pitcher Pete Richert of the Orioles, outfielder Ron Swoboda of the Mets, and some baseball front-office officials on a sixteen-day tour of Vietnam. Banks said he could not get over meeting freshly wounded nineteen-year-olds, or other military men direct from battle who just wanted to talk baseball with him. Soldier after soldier asked who were the toughest pitchers he faced. He did not mention either Jackson or Richert. Bob Gibson, Juan Marichal, Sandy Koufax, and the Reds Jim Maloney got his votes. It seemed to Banks that the fighting troops had been in much tougher circumstances.

"Can you imagine that?" he asked. "These GIs had been in combat. They'd been on the top of a hill, where they'd seen the enemy and had been in battle. And then they ask you, 'Who is the toughest pitcher you ever faced?'"[20]

Banks was also popular with opposing players like Hank Aaron, whom he got to know through years of regular-season showdowns and while sharing a locker room with the National League in All-Star games.

"As far as I'm concerned, there has never been another ballplayer like Ernie Banks," Aaron said. "A guy who could play shortstop as gracefully as he did and who could hit home runs the way he did. Nor has there ever been another ballplayer with Ernie's disposition. It might seem odd that we became good friends, because, in addition to being rivals, we were opposite personalities. He was as outgoing as I wasn't. Ernie was so upbeat and happy all the time that a lot of people thought he was a phony. Well, if Ernie's a phony, he must be a hell of an actor, because he's been fooling me for almost forty years."[21]

Looking back years later, Banks said the 1950s was a great era of baseball with players like Aaron, Willie Mays, and Mickey Mantle making their mark, all nice people, he said. But the country changed considerably in the 1960s and early 1970s and the Vietnam War, student shootings at Kent State, civil rights marches, the assassination of Dr. Martin Luther King, and the riots at the Democratic National Convention in Chicago in 1968 contributed.

"It changed all of that," Banks said referring to the placid 1950s. "I always thought it created a social change for young people, the young people who followed."[22]

One reason fans in Chicago liked Banks so much was because he kept coming through for them on the field. In a 1966 game against the Houston Astros, Banks tied the Major League record for triples in a game with three. Although it was not a major record in the forefront of fan consciousness, Banks got a nice hand. Ron Santo, a long-time teammate as Cubs third baseman, went up to Banks after the game to congratulate him and then asked how many others shared it. When he was told thirty-five, Santo pretended to be unimpressed and said, "That many? Then I take it all back. That wasn't worth congratulations." Banks laughed heartily.[23]

The Cubs of the 1960s, especially those like Banks and Santo who shared the 1969 season, enjoyed an easy and enduring camaraderie. Former Chicago White Sox manager Jimmie Dykes once said of the forever-losing Cubs across town that they would have been doomed to a much worse fate minus Banks in the lineup. "Without Ernie Banks," he said, "the Cubs would finish in Albuquerque."[24]

The constant losing never made Banks gloomy. And as each season began he approached it with the renewed outlook of a farmer anticipating a fresh harvest. "This will be the year the Cubs win the pennant," he always said. The season of 1969 shaped up as the best bet. No one was chuckling at Banks' prognosis that season. For a while he seemed like Nostradomus. The Cubs led the league for much of the summer—one-hundred-and-fifty-six days. Banks was surrounded by talent. The entire infield, with Banks and Santo on the corners, and second baseman Glenn Beckert and shortstop Don Kessinger minding the middle, was an All-Star quartet. In September, as the home stretch of twenty-two games loomed, the Cubs led the National League East by three-and-a-half games. But they could not hold on. The New York Mets played phenomenal baseball, passed the Cubs, and won the division by eight games.

"Who knows what happened then?" Banks said. "Something did. We went into a slump and just couldn't recover. Everything we had been doing right for five months we now did wrong. The fielding, the hitting, and the pitching all went sour together. We just couldn't win for losing."[25] Some suggested that manager Leo Durocher played his starters too much and they ran out of steam, but that was not something easily measured. This was the Cubs best chance for a pennant and a World Series berth during the Banks era.

Decades later, Cubs fans still revere that team and the players who starred on it, even though it did not deliver a championship. The players developed a special bond from their years together and more than most former teammates they stay in touch.

"All the guys," Banks said. "We see each other all the time. It's like a family. They stick together, the children, the grandchildren. You know, we're a close group."[26]

Banks was still a key contributor in 1969, stroking 23 home runs and driving in 106 runs while playing in one-hundred-and-fifty-five games. Two seasons earlier the Cubs had made Banks into a player-coach, a move hinting that retirement was neigh. Witnesses of that Cubs era (such as Hall of Fame sportswriter Jerome Holtzman) felt manager Leo Durocher was a bit jealous of Banks' popularity with management, the town, and the fans and that he wanted to ease Banks out. Durocher put a journeyman named John Boccabella on first and told him he had the job as long as he played well. Not much later, Banks reclaimed it. The Cubs could not keep the good man down. And they sent Boccabella down—to the minors.

By the late 1960s, and by his late thirties, Banks was seen as an elder statesman in the sport. He shrugged publicly when he was benched, simply went about performing better than the next challenger and winning the first baseman's role back. He was asked to speak philosophically about the game. Before Frank Robinson became baseball's first African American manager in 1975, all the major black stars were asked what they thought about the issue and whether they wanted to manage or not. Banks never indicated a desire to manage.

"I definitely believe there will be a Negro manager in the major leagues eventually," Banks said. "It won't happen in the next few years, but perhaps in something like ten to twenty years. It is bound to come because of the great number of Negroes now in the game." Banks said this in 1966. Robinson managed his first game nine years later. Banks said he preferred to coach and he did become a Cubs coach for a while.[27]

Banks hit his 500th career home run on May 12, 1970. At the time he was only the ninth player in baseball history to reach the milestone. His active career was winding down, however, and he hit only twelve additional homers before retiring in 1971, partially because of two arthritic knees.

LATER LIFE

On the last day of the Cubs last home stand of the 1971 season against the Phila-delphia Phillies, Banks sat in the Cubs dugout smiling. "There will be no nostalgia," he said. "Let's just play this one to win. Let's have everyone go home happy except the Phillies, the team that has to lose today." Someone asked Banks about the weather, which was hazy and muggy. "It looks like a great day for baseball," he said.[28]

The Cubs lost 5–1. Mr. Cub reached base once on a single. Banks stayed with the Cubs as a coach and in 1974, when the team was looking for a manager, P.K. Wrigley discussed the job with Banks as a courtesy. Banks reaffirmed his desire to remain a coach and Wrigley issued his famous pronouncement that Banks was too nice a guy to manage. "Why would Ernie want to be a manager?" Wrigley said. "It's the next thing to becoming a kamikaze pilot."[29]

In 1977, Banks was elected to the Baseball Hall of Fame in his first year of eli-gibility. He telephoned Wrigley right after the announcement, important timing since Wrigley died shortly afterward, and before the induction ceremony months later. "I only wish he were here with me," Banks said in Cooperstown, New York, at the event months later, calling Wrigley, "one of the finest gentlemen ever and a man who gave me a lot of confidence."[30]

Banks coached with the Cubs, had his number fourteen jersey retired, and worked with the team's promotional department until 1983, when he and the team had a split. Banks worked in private business, but eventually resumed some connections with the team. In the fall of 2003, Banks underwent two knee replacement surgeries. It helped his mobility and his golf game.

In May of 2006, Banks was at Wrigley Field, his favorite ballpark, to sing "Take Me Out to the Ballgame" during the seventh inning stretch of a game. Banks still loves to talk baseball, but he also stays involved with organizations that help kids and has said he would like to do something to help people around the world who are mired in poverty, something worthy of being acknowledged with the Nobel Prize for Peace.

Jack Rosenberg, formerly sports director of WGN radio in Chicago, once said that Banks is "the most popular athlete ever in Chicago." And in the same newpaper story, Pittsburgh sportswriter Les Biederman took a closer look at Banks. "Banks says the best thing that ever happened to him was baseball. But perhaps one of the finest things that happened to baseball was Ernie Banks."[31]

Playing upon his continuing popularity, Mr. Cub sought to become MR. CUB in early 2006. He met the Tribune Company, the team's owner, probing to see if he could broker a sale to a wealthy group and become a high-profile front-office figure. He was told the team was not for sale.

Ernie Banks was always regarded as a player with grace on the field, who played the game with enthusiasm. At the same time when baseball was debating what a Hall of Famer should be because of individual steroid controversies, a gambling scandal, and players' brushes with the law, Banks was busy aspiring to save the world.

NOTES

1. Ernie Banks, personal interview, February 18, 2006.
2. Ernie Banks and Jim Enright, *Mr. Cub* (Chicago: Follett Publishing Company, 1971), 23.
3. Banks, personal interview, February 18, 2006.

4. Banks and Enright, *Mr. Cub*, 47.
5. Banks, personal interview, February 18, 2006.
6. Buck O'Neil, personal interview, December 7, 2005.
7. Banks and Enright, *Mr. Cub*, 75.
8. Banks, personal interview, February 18, 2006.
9. Banks and Enright, *Mr. Cub*, 84–85.
10. Banks and Enright, *Mr. Cub*, 95.
11. Banks and Enright, *Mr. Cub*, 131.
12. Banks and Enright, *Mr. Cub*, 136.
13. Banks and Enright, *Mr. Cub*, 138.
14. Jim Enright, *Sporting News*, August 22, 1964.
15. Les Biederman, *Pittsburgh Press*, August 16, 1964.
16. Dave Condon, *Chicago Tribune*, August 12, 1964.
17. John Kuenster, *Chicago Daily News*, August 15, 1964.
18. Jimmy Cannon, *New York Journal American*, July 7, 1965.
19. Jim Murray, *Los Angeles Times*, May 18, 1967.
20. Jerome Holtzman, *Chicago Tribune*, December 7, 1968.
21. Hank Aaron with Lonnie Wheeler, *If I Had a Hammer* (New York: HarperPaperbacks, 1992), 190–191.
22. Banks, personal interview, February 18, 2006.
23. *Houston Post*, June 12, 1966.
24. Bill Furlong, *Sport*, August 1967.
25. Banks and Enright, *Mr. Cub*, 149.
26. Banks, personal interview, February 18, 2006.
27. Edgar Munzel, *Chicago Tribune*, May 21, 1966.
28. *Newark Star-Ledger*, September 28, 1971.
29. James Mullen, *Chicago Sun-Times*, August 1, 1974.
30. Bob Broeg, *Sporting News*, August 20, 1977.
31. Les Biederman, *Pittsburgh Press*, July 15, 1968.

Further Reading

Banks, Ernie, with Jim Enright, *Mr. Cub*. Chicago, IL: Follett Publishing Company, 1971.
Enright, Jim, *The Sporting News*, August 22, 1964.
Murray, Jim, *Los Angeles Times*, May 18, 1967.

ELSTON HOWARD

February 23, 1929–December 14, 1980

Elston Howard was the first African American player on the New York Yankees and then served the team as a coach and front office executive at a time when such jobs were scarce for blacks.

Howard broke into the majors in 1955 and played fourteen seasons in the majors. He was a nine-time All Star as a catcher and came to epitomize class with the New York organization. Howard played in a remarkable ten World Series and was the first black Most Valuable Player (MVP) in the American League in 1963. In 1969 he became the first black coach in the league.

☆   ☆   ☆

On a wall at the Negro Leagues Baseball Museum in Kansas City, names of baseball players and teams are displayed. It is a list of African American players who followed Jackie Robinson, first in a trickle, then in a parade, pioneers in their own way, city by city.

The display is in the form of a chart showing the players and the teams they broke in with, marking the debut of the first black player with each American League and National League team. Robinson broke the color barrier for all of baseball, for the National League, and the Brooklyn Dodgers when he played in his first Major League game in 1947. The Dodgers did not lag in adding other African Americans to their roster. Larry Doby's American League debut for the Cleveland Indians followed during the same season. The New York Giants hired men from the Negro Leagues quickly. But Robinson's milestone was not a dam bursting so much as a leak in the dam, a leak, to be sure, that grew larger by the season.

It took twelve full years for the last Major League team, the

Elston Howard was the first African American player on the New York Yankees when he was brought up from the minor leagues in 1955. Many felt the Yankees resisted too long in promoting a black player, and demonstrations were held to prod the team into action.

Boston Red Sox, to integrate in 1959. The proud New York Yankees, the royalty of the sport, with a franchise located just a handful of miles from Brooklyn, managed to offer excuses to not hire a black player for the better part of a decade. The Yankee owners and operators, George Weiss, Del Webb, and Dan Topping, hired no blacks, saying they could not find anyone appropriate. Their argument was not considered plausible and the Yankees were scoffed at. It was not universally believed that the winningest team, with the most resources, could not find a single worthy African American player for eight years. In April 1952, protesters picketed Yankee Stadium to push the process along. Weiss simply responded that as soon as the Yankees found the right guy they would bring him to the Bronx.

New York captured the American League pennant ten seasons out of twelve between 1949 and 1960 and the World Series nearly as frequently. The owners argued, "Why tamper with success?" Those pressuring for a more representative club on the diamond were held off under that guise. As it reads on that museum wall—even the Yankees discovered a player with sufficient skills and appropriate demeanor for their conservative, pin-striped organization. The first African American to dress out for the Yankees was Elston Howard in April of 1955.

Howard made himself impossible to ignore in the minors. Not even the presence of Yogi Berra as the multiple-time MVP and the squad's mainstay behind the plate could keep Howard down by 1955. Berra's talents drove off other catchers hopeful of cracking the roster, but he was not going to catch for the rest of his life. Someone had to be groomed to take over, or to be ready in case of injury. By the time Howard was promoted to the parent club, he was an overdue twenty-six years old. It would have taken a very foolish ownership indeed to overlook what Howard accomplished in 1954 when he was MVP of the International League for Toronto. He crashed 22 home runs, with 108 RBIs, while batting .331.

Yankees manager Casey Stengel simply said that Howard's timing was good. Not everyone agreed even then that the right time had come. The Yankees brought Howard to town, but some thought subtle in-house prejudice still prevailed. Stengel was a fan of Howard, but with the Yankee lineup more or less set and the perennial All Star in Berra to call on behind the plate, he alternated Howard between catcher and outfielder, using him in only ninety-seven games as a rookie. Berra won one of his three league MVP awards that season, and Howard spent much of his time in left field.

The same problem persisted the next season when Howard played in just ninety-eight games. This would not be the first time in baseball history that a player had to wait his turn to become a regular, or the only way a talented player could see action by being switched to a different position. Howard was not a complainer. He was not the type of man to rock the boat, to scream to the newspapers, or to vent in public. He, at all times, preserved his dignity. Others, however, thought more was at issue than the challenge of finding a starting lineup spot for Howard.

The prominent Dodger pitcher Don Newcombe was suspicious of Howard's treatment even after the Yankees brought him up. "I often think back on how it was for Elston when he first joined the Yankees," Newcombe said. "They didn't want a black man on the Yankees even though the Dodgers had Jackie and had broken down the color barrier. The Yankees didn't want Elston because of the innate prejudice at the time on that ballclub and in that organization. And when Elston came, what he had to go through is somewhat the same as what Jackie had to face. I felt for Elston because he was by himself to a degree.

"He was an outstanding baseball player, an outstanding person, and a man who made history. Elston should have been given more publicity in New York, the biggest media market in the world. They seemed to want to hold him down when he first got there. And Elston had to prove himself over and over again."[1] It did take patience to be Elston Howard.

EARLY LIFE

Elston Gene Howard was born in St. Louis. His mother Emmaline was a school teacher who had been spurned by Travis Howard, a scholarly man in Arkansas whose family thought he was too good for her. When she moved to Missouri, Howard's mother became a dietician. He was raised by her, a stepfather, Wayman Hill, and his grandparents.

Howard loved baseball, but was an all-around athlete who excelled at several sports, football, basketball, and track among them, and when Howard graduated from high school, colleges lined up to offer scholarships. The St. Louis Cardinals also provided a baseball tryout. However, in 1948, the Cardinals, the southernmost team in the majors, were not prepared to follow the Dodgers example and hire African American players. Although Howard was scouted heavily by George Sisler Jr., a member of a notable base-ball-playing family, and Sisler reported to officials of the big club that Howard had the goods, Howard never heard back from the Cardinals. The first Cardinals black player— whose name shares the same wall as Howard's in Kansas City—was Tom Alston, and he did not play for St. Louis until 1954.

Illinois, Michigan, and Michigan State, all prominent football powers in the Big Ten, tried to convince Howard his future lay on the gridiron. Many other colleges invited him to matriculate on their campuses with the tempting offers of scholarships for other sports. However, a scout with the same judgment as Sisler, but more support from his team, liked Howard's baseball talent. The Negro Leagues Kansas City Monarchs, the famed team that had once been the home of Satchel Paige and Jackie Robinson and was being managed by Buck O'Neil, came calling. Howard's mother needed some cajoling to allow him to steer away from college, but after he pleaded with her, she decided he could live his own life and take a chance in the sports world.

Although it was getting late in the game for the Negro Leagues, the Monarchs were still a prime attraction. Howard, just nineteen, developed as a player and man at the cen-ter of black culture in Kansas City, eating at the Rose Room, where O'Neil was a star visitor, and shopping at Myers Tailor Shop, where O'Neil purchased his threads.

Howard was never a troublemaker as a child and he was no rollicking teen or out-of-control young man when he moved out from the umbrella of family influence, either. The Monarchs represented class in the Negro Leagues and while no one begrudged a player a good time, it was understood that the carousing had its limits. Howard was so down-to-earth that the team worried very little about him running his train off the tracks.

"Shoot, I never had to worry about Elston off the field," O'Neil said. "He was a fine young man. With Elston it was always baseball, baseball, baseball. He had big hands, he could throw the ball, had some pop in his bat. He wanted to play. All of the guys liked him. In my book, he couldn't miss."[2]

Another young man passing through Kansas City on his way to bigger things was a power-hitting shortstop named Ernie Banks, and he and Howard roomed together. "Elston could handle anything that came his way," said Banks, who became a Hall of Famer after his long career with the Chicago Cubs. "He and I just wanted to play in the major leagues and we had to carry ourselves in the right manner. We had to be impeccable on and off the field."[3]

In terms of baseball, Howard obtained whatever seasoning he really needed to join a big-league club. Then a six-foot-two, 200-pound adult, as a Monarchs rookie in 1948 he hit .283. He was broad-shouldered, with a wide forehead, a square jaw, and a gap-toothed smile because of a missing tooth that later was replaced with a silver tooth, and a physical strength that was never to be underestimated. Many years later, following a minor contretemps in the locker room, then-Yankees coach Howard deposited star hitter Reggie Jackson in a trash can.

In Howard's second Monarchs season his average was .270. Howard's final year with Kansas City was 1950 when he batted .319. During a two-day stretch, once he hit five homers, three in one game, two in the next.

MAJOR LEAGUE CAREER

Yankee scout Tom Greenwade, who made his reputation by discovering Mickey Mantle on an Oklahoma farm, was tipped off by O'Neil that he should grab Howard. Greenwade was responsible for bringing Howard into the New York organization, even though there was an inordinately long wait to bring him up to the major leagues.

While he was in the minors, Howard learned the finer points of catching from Yankee Hall of Famer Bill Dickey, then coaching. The lineage of great Yankee catchers dated back to the 1930s with Dickey followed by Berra, who was followed by Howard. New York virtually owned the position on the American League side in the All-Star game for more than two decades.

During Howard's minor league apprenticeship, he was invited to a Yankee spring training camp in St. Petersburg. While people think of St. Petersburg as a tame community today, catering to retired senior citizens on the shores of Tampa Bay, St. Petersburg was more of a southern backwater in 1953 and 1954 when Howard was forbidden to live with the team because of his black skin. He stayed at a boardinghouse instead of the team quarters. The town still had separate drinking fountains for whites and blacks. Fans had thrown black cats on the grass when Jackie Robinson played at Al Lang Field and seating was segregated. "You can't imagine the rotten times Ellie had in those early days," said Yankee Hall of Fame pitcher Whitey Ford, who became a good friend. "But he took it all without a whimper. He was always a real gentleman."[4]

Black players knew at the time that they would not likely stick around a big-league team if they were the twenty-fifth man on the roster. They had to be better than most to remain. They understood that the magnates of baseball had not overnight become social liberals. In a sense it was worse with the Yankees. Besides Howard, the Yankees also held the rights to Vic Power, a sensational fielding first baseman who was a solid hitter. Power was a black Latin with a fun-loving, flamboyant style, and had a playboy image, even supposedly dating white women. (Buck O'Neil said the particular lady in question who might have gotten Power traded was really a light-skinned black woman, and Power's wife.) That would not do at all for the Yanks. It was not in the cards for Power to become a Yankee in the early 1950s. He did, however, become an All Star for the Kansas City Athletics.

Jackie Robinson, a sensitive man attuned to all slights and a victim of much abuse that was far from slight, ripped the Yankees racial attitude on television. Appearing with youngsters on a New York TV show called *Youth Wants to Know* on November 30, 1952,

Robinson was asked by a girl why the Yankees did not have any black players. "I think the Yankee management is prejudiced," Robinson replied.[5]

Even those who did not oppose him outright in the game recognized that Weiss, the Yankees general manager, was no softie. Those who did not like him thought him mean. Those who worked for him considered him hard. Operating under great pressure, he kept stocking the Yankees with pennant-winning talent. He did not quickly respond to the availability of a fresh pool of black talent. For years, even decades, baseball fans in other cities grew to despise the Yankees as arrogant, resenting their success, and cheering when they hit strained times. The Yankees were identified as the team of rich fans, not the lunch-pail crowd. And the team seemed to enjoy the high-toned clientele and image. Their pin-striped home uniforms represented the bankers' uniforms of baseball.

Weiss was heard at a 1952 cocktail party making his feelings well known about African American ballplayers. "I will never allow a black man to wear a Yankee uniform," Weiss said. "Boxholders from Westchester don't want them. They would be offended to have to sit with niggers."[6]

A professional sports team official uttering such a sentence today would be sitting on the curb in disgrace within twenty-four hours. In the 1950s, the words and attitude were still things a highly placed club leader with power and a history of triumph could get away with.

In 1954 spring training, Casey Stengel trumpeted Howard's talents. Stengel was the king of lineup juggling, a platooning man who sometimes drove his players crazy by shifting them around. But he won and won and won, so there was little credibility to complaints. Stengel was an old-timer, born in 1890 and his last active playing year was 1925. He was a raconteur deluxe, a jokester, and a clever talker who could disguise how he really felt about an issue when he felt compelled to bamboozle the press. Howard was an excellent all-around player with a big bat, but one thing he did not possess was natural speed. One day Stengel startled his adoring listeners by saying of Howard, "When I finally get a nigger, I get the only one that can't run." Yet neither Howard nor his wife Arlene ever felt Stengel was racist, only that he was a product of prior times. They thought he blabbed without thinking and it was "just Casey being Casey."[7]

Although Howard had experience catching, his path to the majors seemed more likely to lie in the outfield. Howard was not happy when the Yankees informed him he was being sent down again in 1954 to perfect his catching ability. Others saw the demotion as simply an excuse to keep a black off the roster. During spring training, Sam Lacy, a legendary sportswriter for the Baltimore *Afro-American*, and one of the longtime campaigners for baseball integration, wrote an inflammatory story blasting the Yankees. The headline over his piece was even more damning: "Vicious Conspiracy Being Conducted."

Rather than remain silent, or flame the controversy by backing Lacy, Howard shocked others by saying he should "punch that guy's head off. There's always someone like that putting words in my mouth misquoting me." Howard's vehemence was uncharacteristic on several fronts.[8]

What not everyone realized was that Howard wanted to make good specifically as a Yankee. It meant something to him to become the first black Yankee. Howard realized he had to put up with certain indignities to do so, but he was determined to make good on his terms. A *Sport* magazine story where Howard was asked to revisit the Lacy incident—and refused—raised the question of whether the Yankees were still holding him back or not. And the story did not appear in print until 1961, years after he made the team. Howard took to Dickey's instruction, working hard to soak up the finer points of catching. He appreciated the older man's commitment to the task and paid close attention to what Dickey taught.[9]

Both the extra year in the AAA minors and Dickey's tutoring polished Howard's catching, and no one could deny he belonged in the majors with the Yankees. Even the Yankees could not deny this. In the 1950s, after the spring training season ended, teams often played their way north. Traveling by train, stopping in cities along the way, they played exhibition games against local teams. The Yankees followed that pattern in 1955. However, their stopovers were in places like New Orleans, Birmingham, and Memphis, southern cities with no history of allowing black and white players to compete on the same field or to stay in the same hotel. As the Yankees headed north, insults to Howard piled up.

In New Orleans, the stadium had segregated seating. The African American section was in left field. Howard started the game in right field. White patrons in that segment of the building shouted curses and called him names. After one inning, left-fielder Hank Bauer urged Stengel to swap Howard and him and the manager did so.[10]

The Yankees did not even try to suit up Howard in Birmingham, simply shipping him ahead to Memphis to avoid trouble with the local law prohibiting whites and blacks from playing together. In Memphis, Howard was with the team, but the Yankees did not play him.

If Stengel was not trusted by some blacks (Jackie Robinson disliked him), he demonstrated his heart was likely in the right place after an early-season road trip. Howard was banned from the team hotel in Kansas City and when the Yankees returned to New York, Stengel confronted traveling secretary Bill McCorry. "Is he on this team or not?" Stengel asserted. "Howard's one of my players, ain't he? If he don't stay there, we don't stay there." On the Yankees next trip to Kansas City, Howard bunked with the team. Unlike the other players, though, he did not have a roommate. Because he was black, Howard gained the benefit of a single room.[11]

That circumstance did not change for years in Major League play. However, on a Yankees exhibition trip to Japan, Howard had company. First baseman Bill Skowron, who grew up in Circero, Illinois, adjacent to Chicago, became his roommate and pronounced himself totally unfazed by the experience. There is no official record keeping of such things, but Skowron speculated that he and Howard might have been baseball's first interracial roommates.[12]

Little gestures from teammates affected Howard hugely. Baseball locker rooms have never been as enlightened as university libraries. No one pretends scholars are plunked down every ten feet. There is a rough camaraderie in sport. When the clubhouse doors are closed, what goes on is supposed to stay private. The watchword is much like the Las Vegas tourist campaign of "What happens in Vegas stays in Vegas." In neither case is that always true, but that is the code.

Teams are thrust together in tense environments for long hours over a period of many months. It is difficult for everyone to be upbeat all the time, to be on perfect behavior, and to not have the occasional explosion or embarrassing moment. Often, on the best of teams, relationships are forged that last a lifetime. Similar personalities get along. Friendships and enmities are made that outlast careers. What can be critical in setting a tone, however, is how a player is accepted from the outset. The smartest teams welcome newcomers with handshakes and pleasant words. In the case of a black player entering an all-white clubhouse, the reception can be critical, both to the new player's well-being and ability to help the team, and the overall atmosphere. Ideally, such a player is greeted warmly.

The Yankee players acted more hospitably than most other players. Repeatedly, Howard was shown little kindnesses such as Skowron driving him to a spring training hotel (without knowing Howard would not be allowed in). On a bus, second baseman Billy Martin went out of his way to sit next to Howard and teased him by saying, "Move over dago." To some that may be offensive, but Martin was a rough-around-the-edges guy who had always uttered that comment to the now-retired Joe DiMaggio. It was a gesture of affection toward Howard.[13]

Yogi Berra could have resented Howard's arrival on the roster. With the highly publicized attention from Dickey, the Yankees seemed to be grooming Howard to steal Berra's job. Instead, the two became close friends. They lived near one another in New Jersey, and the men's wives shopped together and also became great friends.

After Stengel went to bat for Howard for hotel rights, Howard's first night in an all-white hotel was peculiar. He had never stayed in such a place, and he did not really know if he was actually welcome or his presence would create unforeseen problems. He half expected someone to barge through the door to evict him. Later, Howard said he bolted every lock on the door. No maid was getting in for turn-down service that night. It would have taken a sledgehammer and shotgun to get through the door. "I was frightened to death," Howard said.[14]

In 1961, fourteen years after Robinson broke the color line, African American players were still being discriminated against in southern spring training communities. Change came slowly, on a hotel-by-hotel basis with individual teams, but ultimately, black players were obliged to band together and file a complaint with the Major League Players Association.

If the Yankee players were gracious as a whole, none went out of his way more aggressively to court Howard as a teammate than shortstop Phil Rizzuto. Rizzuto was one of the most popular of Yankees, a terrific fielder who won a MVP award and became a longtime Yankee broadcaster whose signature cry for surprising on-field action was "Holy Cow!" Rizzuto did not want Howard to hang around in his room bored, stuck with daytime television leading up to night games. Rizzuto telephoned frequently asking Howard to join him for a day on the town wherever the team and town was. He invited Howard to movies, out for lunch, or to meet people he knew locally.

"Phil Rizzuto, damn, he was great. I will never forget him," Howard said. "He was the type of man I respected, and I give him a lot of credit. I got pretty lonesome at times, and Phil would sense when I hit the real blues."[15]

As talented a player as Howard was, his problems with obtaining enough playing time endured through much of the 1950s. The Yankees did have more depth than any other team, but despite showing up in Stengel's lineup at catcher, left field, right field, and first base (Stengel referring to him as his four-way man), Howard was also often just a pinch hitter, meaning he was on the bench at the start of a number of games.

When given chances, Howard was outstanding. In 1958, Howard was a batting title contender into August. He finished at .314, behind Red Sox superstar Ted Williams. However, under the rules in effect at the time a player had to have 477 plate appearances combining official at bats, walks, sacrifices, and the like. It became obvious Howard was not going to qualify. This was brought to Stengel's attention.

"There's nothin' I'd like to see better, of course, than for him to win it," Stengel said. "He might get up enough yet. [But] I'm not gonna catch him every day and not have him ready for what I want when I need him. I'm still thinkin' about winnin' ballgames and I'm not gonna worry about twistin' everythin' around for one man. I'm not worryin' about that and neither is he." Indeed, when approached on the subject, true to his nature, Howard said he had not given a thought to winning the batting title all season and was only concentrating on winning games and the pennant.[16]

The more Howard played, the more productive he was. When Ralph Houk, a former backup catcher with the Yankees, took over as manager for the 1961 season, he promptly informed Howard his days of rotating through the lineup were over. Howard was his No. 1 catcher from then on. On June 30, 1962, Howard drove in eight runs in a single game against the Kansas City Athletics with two three-run homers and by going four-for-six overall. It was the greatest one-game hitting performance of his career. In 1964, Howard's season-long fielding percentage was a near-perfect .998. He hardly ever

Elston Howard became a stalwart catcher for the Yankees and was the first African American to win the Most Valuble Player award in the American League. Proud to wear pinstripes, Howard was working in the team's front office as a rare black baseball executive when he died at age fifty-one.

made an error anyway, averaging less than three per season during the first ten years of his career, but he outdid himself that summer. Howard also set a Major League record for putouts by a catcher the same season with 931.

Howard hit a career-best .348 in 1961 and batted .313 in 1964. The more active he was, the more apparent how valuable he was. In a famous at bat in the 1967 season, Howard faced Red Sox rookie pitcher Billy Rohr, who was pitching a no-hitter with two outs in the ninth inning. Howard singled cleanly to right field to break it up.

During his fourteen-season Major League career between 1955 and 1968, Howard played in ten World Series and was chosen for nine All-Star teams. In 1963, he became the first African American to win the MVP award in the American League. His big-three category stats were 28 home runs, 85 RBIs, and a .287 average that season.

"Naturally, everywhere I went after the season ended, people would tell me I was a cinch to win it," Howard said. "But I just couldn't bring myself to believe it all of the way."[17]

Usually, it takes bigger numbers for a player to be honored as the best in his league. Howard's statistics were fine, but for someone to be selected MVP often requires more than numerical success. The player must possess intangibles of leadership. Being chosen Most Outstanding Player is one thing. Being voted MVP is quite another. Almost always the winner plays for either a championship team or contender. The honor is a recognition that the team could not have done it without him. The next season newspaper headlines heralded Howard as "the complete catcher."

John Blanchard, who became Howard's backup when Berra moved to the outfield, said, "Ellie gives you 100 percent. He hustles every inning like a guy who hasn't got it made yet."[18]

The one unfortunate aspect of Howard's ascension into first-string catcher and All-Star player was that it came at such a late age. Until recently, baseball was fixated on grabbing its talent young, straight out of high school, rather than waiting for a player to compete a few years for a college. Teams drafted players and the moment after they collected their high school diplomas shipped them out to short-season rookie ball. Then, year by year, the team promoted them through the minor league ranks. Top players would be in the big leagues by the time they were twenty-two. Howard never got his chance until he was twenty-six and he was twenty-eight by the time he played in more than a hundred games in a season. That meant by the time Howard was feted as the best catcher around he was old for the position. Catchers tend to wear out younger than other position players because of all the bending and squatting they do stretching their knees.

Howard pooh-poohed any suggestion that he was getting up there as a method of protective image control. "I may be thirty-five," he said in 1965, "but I'm the youngest thirty-five you ever saw." Actually, at the time he was quoted, Howard was already thirty-six.[19]

Wages were laughable then compared to big-league pay these days when the minimum salary is well into six figures and stars sign multiyear, multimillion-dollar contracts. In 1956, when Howard was rewarded with a $10,000 deal, he and his wife were ecstatic.[20]

As an indicator that players were still not routinely able to solely rely on their baseball salaries year-round, Howard joined Roy Campanella's off-season barnstorming All-Star team to make extra cash. In the tradition of pre-1950s black touring teams, the star Dodger catcher put together his own group to roam the hinterlands. Willie Mays, Hank Aaron, and Don Newcombe were among Howard's teammates.

By 1957, Howard had endorsement contracts for Ballantine beer and Kool cigarettes, making $100 per appearance for the companies. White players made more money for their deals, but getting deals from mainstream businesses at all—even if the commercials were aimed at blacks only—was an improvement over being ignored. The endorsements were signs of respect of an acknowledgement in the biggest city in the country that Howard was a card-carrying, secure, relied-on player for the biggest name team in baseball.

Yet, as the African American players who unified to file a grievance with the Players Association symbolized, it was still the same-old, same-old in spring training. Small Florida towns hosting Major League clubs in spring training still offered reminders to even esteemed visitors like the Yankees that Jim Crow still thrived. Once, Howard and New York outfielder Hector Lopez were not permitted to stay with the team in Fort Myers. Instead, they were put up in a black-owned funeral home with five dead bodies for company. "It was real quiet there. They didn't make much noise," Lopez said.[21]

When Howard earnestly bragged that his fit, healthy body would allow him to catch until he was forty, it was not clear he was completely serious. Since he generally looked trim and sharp, nobody disputed him, though such catching longevity is an uncommon happenstance. Howard had no motivation to step aside. By 1965 he was making $70,000 a year, far more than he ever dreamed and more than Berra or Dickey collected in a season.

"I've got a lot of catching to do before I retire," Howard said. "It's the one position where a day never goes by that you don't learn something new. In many ways, no two ballgames are alike. Not for a catcher, anyway. You squat back there and you are the quarterback. You call the shots and you've got the whole diamond out there in front of you. A catcher has the best seat in the ballpark." "Catching is baseball more than any other position, and I want to be a catcher for as long as I can. If I wake up some morning and find I have to quit, it won't be because of anything I neglected to do. That's for sure."[22]

Howard eased into close relationships with his pitchers. He raved about Whitey Ford's "stuff" and said he was a tremendous clutch pitcher. "He works a game so good, he doesn't need a catcher. He's just chairman of the board."[23]

Howard took young Al Downing under his wing when the southpaw came up to the Yankees and encouraged him to have confidence and not be fearful of shaking off a catcher. They became roommates for seven years. "I used to follow him around like a little puppy," said Downing, who joined the team in 1961, spending seventeen seasons in the majors while winning 123 games. "Every night we would sit in the room and talk about baseball. Talk about pitching, talk about hitters."[24]

Howard had not only earned the confidence of his pitchers, but had also become a Yankee elder statesman. When Howard spoke openly of catching until he turned forty in June of 1965, he was only two months removed from incurring an injury that he had to realize could jeopardize his career. He might have been in denial, but coming out of spring training that year, Howard had bone chips in his right elbow. One of the key fielding attributes of a catcher is an ability to fire to second to nab attempted base stealers. Once it is known that a catcher can not throw, the league will run wild on him stealing bases. A catcher without a strong arm is useless to his club. The injury actually occurred during winter ball in Puerto Rico, making it easier for Howard to hide it at first. Eventually, after the Yankee season got underway, Howard explained what happened during a game played in the rain.

"I went to throw and as I cocked my arm, my feet went out from under me in the mud," Howard said. "That's when I pulled something in my elbow." The prescription was rest, but Howard rushed back. "Believe me, this has nothing to do with my age. I felt better this spring than I did when I was a rookie. This is nothing really."[25]

Howard's confidence sounded typical of what most injured athletes express. To succeed in professional sports, many athletes must consider themselves invulnerable. Their muscular bodies are their livelihood. All along the way, from youth leagues, through high school, sometimes through college, through their professional careers, they progress because their bodies are their strength. They become rich and famous and cash their paychecks because of their bodies' prowess. So when a body part lets them down, an athlete does not want to believe it. Athletes generally put up with much more pain than the average member of the population before agreeing to consult a doctor, spend less time recuperating, and adapt to injuries by often ignoring them. They get paid to play, not lie in bed or on the couch, and they want to play.

Howard's elbow did not heal swiftly as he predicted. The pain lingered, the injury lingered, and his effectiveness was affected. When he woke up one morning after an early-season game and could not bend his arm at the breakfast table, Howard's doctor said he needed surgery to repair the condition. Howard came home from the hospital toting the bone chips in a small glass case, but he did not immediately bounce back. When the Yankees played a game against Kansas City at the end of June in 1965, Athletics pitcher Roland Sheldon, an old Yankee, felt moved by Howard's situation. "I felt sick to the stomach when I saw him throw," Sheldon said. "He used to be so great and now he is in trouble."[26]

Howard spent most of the 1965 season as a pinch hitter and the elbow never got to be 100 percent again despite rest and swimming therapy over the off-season. Howard handled a regular catching load in 1966, but his power numbers and average declined at the plate and halfway through the 1967 season the Yankees surprised the baseball world by trading Howard to the Red Sox for the $20,000 waiver price and two players to be named later. Over the years the team had told Howard he would always be a Yankee and now he was not one.[27]

"When Elston hung up the phone he was visibly shaken, almost to the point of tears," Howard's wife Arlene said. "I thought he was going to tell me there was no way he would go to Boston. Houk said he was doing Elston a favor; the Red Sox were in the thick of the pennant race. Actually, the trade was a rotten thing to do."[28]

The Yankees of the mid-1960s were losers. The great players who had led them to so many World Series triumphs were gone. Upper management had changed. And the Red Sox were indeed in a pennant race, in the middle of their Impossible Dream season. Boston would win the pennant and go on to the World Series for the first time in two decades after finishing ninth in a ten-team league the year before.

Still, Howard was undecided about reporting. With his elbow out of whack and at thirty-eight he wondered if it was time to retire after all. Boston owner Tom Yawkey telephoned and made a personal appeal. It was a good pep talk; Howard made the move and got to play in one bonus World Series. While he played in about a hundred games for both teams combined, however, Howard had his worst offensive year, not reaching a .200 average for either team.

Probably the most satisfying moment of the season occurred on August 28 when the Red Sox invaded the Bronx for a series. Strange as it seemed, Elston Howard was in the lineup for the visiting team. When his name was announced for his first turn at bat, the 27,000 fans in Yankee Stadium welcomed him back by standing and applauding.

Howard stayed with the Red Sox for one more season, playing in seventy-one games. Sometimes his cranky elbow could not even be fully straightened. It was time to retire. Howard batted .274 with 167 home runs and 762 RBIs as a major leaguer, and was recognized as one of the best catchers of his era.

LATER LIFE

A distinguished player who always handled himself with class, Howard was a family man with three children, an esteemed reputation, and a desire to remain in baseball. He had long harbored the notion of becoming a manager—even the first black manager—and he wanted to run the Yankees, his old team. The Yankees promptly offered him the choice of either a minor league managing position or the chance to coach under Ralph Houk with the big club. He liked the idea of staying in the majors. The appointment made him the first African American coach in the American League.

In 1970, Howard predicted that there would be an African American Major League manager within two years. Reading the climate correctly, he was close. He listed

Dodgers Jim Gilliam, John Roseboro, and Maury Wills, and superstars Willie Mays of the Giants, Ernie Banks of the Cubs, and Hank Aaron of the Braves as prospects. He neglected to mention Frank Robinson, who starred for the Reds and Orioles, and who achieved the milestone in 1975 with the Cleveland Indians.

Howard kept learning, patiently, and when Houk left the job in 1973, Howard campaigned vigorously for it. Instead, the Yankees hired ex-Pirates manager Bill Virdon. Howard stayed on as coach and after that began to put out feelers when other teams, notably the Detroit Tigers, sought managers. Nothing materialized and he grew frustrated. Actually, in 1968, Howard came closer to managing than he ever did again. Bill Veeck, the showman owner who operated the Indians, the St. Louis Browns, and Chicago White Sox, put in a bid for the new expansion Washington Senators. It seemed like a done deal and Veeck offered the manager's job to Howard. Then the other owners who nursed old grudges against Veeck because of his flamboyance whisked the team out from under him. Howard lost out, too. "What do I have to do to manage?" Howard asked Arlene. "Why do I have to be better than everyone else?"[29]

New Yankee owner George Steinbrenner asked Howard to join him in the front office, but the catcher preferred to stay on the field and clung to his coaching job. Steinbrenner shuffled managers in and out, never apparently seriously considering Howard as field boss. In early 1979, after ten years as a coach, Howard had a health scare. Retrieving luggage at the airport after a flight home, a few days before his fiftieth birthday, Howard found himself short of breath. After a doctor's examination, he was diagnosed with myocarditis, inflammation of the heart muscle due to a virus.

Howard was ordered to rest. He missed the entire season, although Steinbrenner kept him on the payroll. And when Howard prepared to return to baseball in 1980, a weaker, suddenly aged looking former catcher accepted Steinbrenner's proposal for a front-office job. The duties included visiting the team's farm club teams and making appearances on behalf of the Yankees. "George assured me I wouldn't have to stand in a corner," Howard said at a time when prominent black players were clamoring for more executive office opportunities in the game. "I believe him. I wouldn't take it under such circumstances."[30]

Although Howard handled the job that season he was never truly his old self. He lacked energy and seemed to fade before his friends' and loved ones' eyes. At Thanksgiving dinner late in 1980, he developed shortness of breath. He was in and out of the hospital, but re-entered for what became a last stay on December 4. A doctor said Howard might think about applying for a heart transplant. Just after midnight on December 14, shortly after his wife and family members left Columbia Presbyterian Medical Center for the evening, Howard's heart stopped. The official cause of death was cardiac arrest. Howard, who got a late start in the majors because of prejudice, was dead at the too-young age of fifty-one, his final great ambition of managing unfulfilled.

"Ellie was a permanent fixture in the Yankee picture. He was one of the most popular Yankees of all time," said then-team vice president Cedric Tallis. "He was a humble and unique man."[31]

Steinbrenner was even more effusive in his admiration for Howard. "We have lost a dear friend and a vital part of the organization," the team owner said. "If indeed humility is a trademark of many great men, with that as a measure, Ellie was one of the truly great Yankees."[32]

One of the most memorable speakers at Howard's funeral a few days later at Riverside Church in New York was his old battery mate, Whitey Ford. Upon learning of

Howard's death, Ford said he went to his den and flipped through scrapbooks all night. "Talk about pride in being a Yankee," Ford said. "Nobody exemplified it better. Elston, we love you. We will pray for you always."[33]

Howard's wife Arlene was an energetic defender of his memory. After two decades of reflection, when she coauthored the book *Elston and Me: The Story of the First Black Yankee,* in 2001, she said she believed her husband's life was cut short from the stress of coping with racism and not being able to break through to become a manager. "Baseball killed my husband," she wrote.[34]

One of Howard's children, Karen, who was afflicted with cerebral palsy, also died young. When Howard's father Travis died in 1988, Elston Jr., Howard's only son, attended the funeral. Howard's third child, Cheryl, became a successful singer and was periodically asked to sing the national anthem before home Yankees games.

During the summer of 1984, the New York Yankees held a special ceremony to honor Elston Howard, the first African American to play for the team. Howard's number 32, was retired and a plaque was dedicated to him in center field.

NOTES

1. Don Newcombe, as interviewed by Tom Reed, Members Only Television. Printed as a foreword to Arlene Howard and Ralph Wimbish, *Elston and Me: The Story of the First Black Yankee* (Columbia: University of Missouri Press, 2001).

2. Howard and Wimbish, *Elston and Me*, 20.

3. Howard and Wimbish, *Elston and Me*, 18.

4. Maury Allen, *New York Post*, December 16, 1980.

5. Howard and Wimbish, *Elston and Me*, 27.

6. Howard and Wimbish, *Elston and Me*, 28.

7. Howard and Wimbish, *Elston and Me*, 37.

8. Barry Stainback, *Sport*, December 1961.

9. Howard and Wimbish, *Elston and Me*, 32.

10. Howard and Wimbish, *Elston and Me*, 39.

11. Howard and Wimbish, *Elston and Me*, 41.

12. Ibid.

13. Howard and Wimbish, *Elston and Me*, 41.

14. Howard and Wimbish, *Elston and Me*, 42.

15. Ibid.

16. Stainback, *Sport*, December 1961.

17. Til Ferdenzi, *Sporting News*, November 30, 1963.

18. Til Ferdenzi, *Sporting News*, September 12, 1964.

19. Til Ferdenzi, *Sporting News*, June 5, 1965.

20. Howard and Wimbish, *Elston and Me*, 47.

21. Howard and Wimbish, *Elston and Me*, 99.

22. Ferdenzi, *Sporting News*, June 5, 1965.

23. Howard and Wimbish, *Elston and Me*, 112.

24. Howard and Wimbish, *Elston and Me*, 110.

25. Phil Pepe, *New York Daily News*, April 21, 1965.

26. Joe King, *New York World-Telegram*, June 25, 1965.

27. Howard and Wimbish, *Elston and Me*, 144.

28. Howard and Wimbish, *Elston and Me*, 144.

29. Howard and Wimbish, *Elston and Me*, 175.

30. Will Grimsley, Associated Press, March 16, 1980.

31. Thomas Rogers, *New York Times*, December 15, 1980.

32. Ibid.
33. Murray Schumach, *New York Times*, December 17, 1980.
34. Howard and Wimbish, *Elston and Me*, 196.

Further Reading

Ferdenzi, Til, *The Sporting News,* June 5, 1965.
Howard, Arlene, with Ralph Wimbish, *Elston and Me: The Story of the First Black Yankee*. Columbia: University of Missouri Press, 2001.
Stainback, Barry, *Sport Magazine*, December, 1961.

MINNIE MINOSO

November 29, 1922–

Minnie Minoso, the first black player for the Chicago White Sox, not only overcame prejudice because he was a black Cuban, but also faced dual discrimination because his first language was Spanish. Minoso serves as a symbol of the black Latin American players who had to work doubly hard to achieve in the majors.

Minoso had a colorful, seventeen-year Major League career after making the transition from the Negro Leagues, with a .298 lifetime batting average. A seven-time American League All Star, Minoso led the circuit in triples thrice and led the league in being hit by pitches ten times.

Saturino Orestes Arrieta Armas Minoso was running late, caught up in Chicago's midday traffic. He had difficulty negotiating his Cadillac between expressway cars to reach U.S. Cellular Field on time for lunch. It was an off-season afternoon, but the ballpark was busy. The White Sox were setting up in Arizona for spring training, and opening day of the 2006 season loomed at the Chicago South Side stadium in several weeks.

When Minoso reached his destination, he expressed amazement over the unanticipated gridlock that had sprung up for no reason he could discern, something that happens frequently in the Windy City. Minoso, wearing a beige raincoat and a beret, stepped out from his car in a light rain. When he stripped off the outer garment, Minoso showed off a White Sox jacket heralding the team's 2005 World Series championship. Usually, Minoso wears a suit, or a blazer, tie, and slacks. He said he likes to drive the best and dress accordingly. That has been Minoso's meticulous trademark style since he first appeared in the Major Leagues in 1949 with the Cleveland Indians.

Minoso earned the trappings of his success, and a dapper look is important to him following a childhood steeped in poverty in El Perico, Cuba, a town about a hundred miles north of Havana where many of the residents, including his parents, relied on sugarcane cutting for survival. As Minoso entered the stadium, walked through the business lobby, and took the elevator up a few floors to the employee lunch room, it was challenging to count the number of "Hello, Minnie" greetings. He was either eighty or eighty-three years old, depending on the source, long removed from his active playing days, but Minoso was well known around the baseball park. He answered everyone graciously and flirted with ladies decades younger.

Minoso's regular community appearances on behalf of the team have kept him in the public eye, and he is talked about in tones that suggest he is a beloved individual in Chicago. Minoso is an institution with a long and popular history and he is as readily recognized as a civic signature as Lake Michigan, the Sears Tower, and deep-dish pizza. "I love it," Minoso said of his continuing interaction with the team that won a world championship in 2005 after an eighty-eight-year wait. "I'm having fun."[1]

The nickname "Minnie" stands out for its uniqueness in the sport and for Americans who do not speak Spanish, and is more memorable than his given name. Minoso said he

Minnie Minoso (left) hit for average and got hit by pitches much
more than the average player during his star turn with the Chicago
White Sox during the 1950s and 1960s. A great base runner,
Minoso helped establish the Sox's "Go-Go" running theme. Minoso
remains an ambassador for the club and one of the most popular
players ever to wear the Chicago uniform. Also shown is Minoso's
long-time teammate Luis Aparicio and an unidentified fan.

has no idea how it came to be that sportswriters of the 1950s nicknamed him Minnie.
It was not a childhood nickname that followed him. It was not a name teammates used.
One day, he said, he was reading the newspaper, and there he was being referred to
as Minnie. "They never said anything to me," Minoso said. "I said, 'Where does this
Minnie come from?' If someone gave me a hundred million dollars and asked who was
the first one to call me Minnie, I wouldn't know. I was Orestes Minoso. They just called
me Minnie. Since then I've been Minnie. I don't think there's anything wrong with it.
Now it's legal. So I'm Minnie."

Minoso may have overlooked an obvious contributing factor. His given name was
so long there was no way sports section headline writers could cope. Once in a great
while, Minoso said, he signs his full name as part of an autograph, but he does not do
so with a crowd around him. "Sometimes I do that automatically," he said. "If you are
going to do that to everyone, signing it would take ten days."[2]

In the post–Jackie Robinson breakthrough era of baseball, when African Americans
were first being invited onto the playing field, Minoso was a tweener. Every bit as black
as the American players who had been consigned to the Negro Leagues, Minoso was

also Latino, a black Cuban, not only discriminated against because of his color, but with a second strike against him because his first language was Spanish.

In the preceding decades, light-skinned Latin Americans had played in the major leagues, but the "unwritten" color line that big-league owners adhered to was just as unbreachable a wall for black Latin Americans as it was for blacks raised in New York or Chicago. Breaking in with the Brooklyn Dodgers as a symbol of his race, Jackie Robinson was under tremendous scrutiny and faced immense pressure to succeed. He was called names and treated with contempt by many opposing players and fans. To a lesser extent, virtually all the black players who followed Robinson into the majors in the late 1940s and early 1950s were confronted by the same challenges. They endured scarring minor league experiences, where they had often been taunted and snubbed, forced into secondary housing away from their teams, and required to take meals on the bus instead of at the group table.

The conditions were often demoralizing, and young black men who just wanted to play baseball were surprised and distressed at treatment they felt was almost designed to prevent them from reaching the majors. Frequently, they spent lonely nights in their hotels, only mingling with teammates in the clubhouse. Such a solitary existence was magnified for a black player who was not fluent in English.

EARLY LIFE

Growing up in Cuba, Minoso's family had no electricity. His parents divorced when he was eight years old, his mother died when he was ten, and Minoso grew up with his mother's children from another marriage. As a kid, Minoso was first a pitcher and he had a powerful arm. His baseball hero was Martin Dihigo. Dihigo was a star in winter ball throughout Latin America, and shined in the Negro Leagues in the United States, as well, eventually being selected for the Baseball Hall of Fame. Minoso's upbringing was difficult. Older half-siblings cared for him in the community at first, but then he moved to Havana to live with two sisters. Minoso worked for a cigar factory and a candy factory, but his baseball talent overrode everything else, and by age seventeen he was playing in the Cuban professional league. When Minoso won a batting title, he began to imagine someday playing in the United States.

"There was no dream to play in the big leagues," Minoso said. "That's the way things were then. We never knew we were going to have the opportunity."[3] Minoso's aspiration was to play in the Negro Leagues. He watched the top black players in winter ball and knew they played in a good league.

In the meantime, Minoso was wooed with high-pressure tactics by Mexican League official Jose Pascual, who promised $30,000 for two years' work. Minoso resisted. He said he showed Pascual the $50 in his pocket he had just borrowed and acknowledged it was like two cents compared to the offer. "But money isn't everything to me," Minoso said. "I'm going to America some day." Minoso said, "Pascual grew angry and said because I was black I would be treated like a dog in the United States."[4]

Minoso got his break in 1945 and played third base for the New York Cubans through 1948. It was his long-awaited introduction to the United States and he called it a dream come true. He was surprised and excited by the hubbub of New York, the mix of people of color, and the availability of good music and entertainment.

"In my mind, all of the time, was to come to the United States," Minoso said. Six decades later, when he thought back to refusing the Mexican League offer, he said, "I made the right decision."[5]

Getting paid to play baseball improved Minoso's status in society. He was used to being deprived in Cuba, but now he had spending money. And he knew exactly how he wanted to invest his money. "Buying clothes became a special fancy for me. I had so little in the way of clothes as a boy that now I wanted to compensate. My ambition had always been to dress well and to be a gentleman on and off the field. I bought only the sharpest and most stylish outfits. Some people like to drink, others play golf. I liked buying sharp clothes. Sometimes I'd change outfits two or three times a day. I looked like a man about town, and in certain ways I guess I was."[6]

Minoso played with and against top talent in the Negro Leagues, from Satchel Paige to Josh Gibson, from Larry Doby to Monte Irvin. Although Minoso's Major League career eventually deposited him in the outfield, he held down third base with the Cubans. One day Irvin hit a hard bouncing ball that Minoso missed and it hit him in the lip. He took home six stitches from that game.

Years later, Irvin recalled crossing paths with Minoso, on and off the field. "He was a good player," Irvin said. "And a good teammate. Oh, he loved to dance and he was a snappy dresser."[7] Minoso carried a portable phonograph and at least forty records with him on road trips.

One player Minoso never played against in the Negro Leagues was Jackie Robinson. Robinson was already on his path with the Dodgers' organization that would open up the game. But Minoso said that he and every other black baseball player are indebted to Robinson for the battles he fought on their behalf. "Only through him were so many other black ballplayers able to make the big leagues," Minoso said. "He had such raw courage."[8]

Although general manager Branch Rickey worked to integrate the Dodgers with first Robinson, then players like Roy Campanella and Don Newcombe, when Bill Veeck bought the Cleveland Indians he was right behind Rickey in the search for top black talent. Doby joined Veeck's Indians as the first African American player in the American League. Veeck hired Satchel Paige as the first black pitcher in the American League. And he signed Minnie Minoso. It was the beginning of a beautiful friendship between Veeck and Minoso, lasting the rest of Veeck's life.

Minoso made his Major League debut with the Indians in 1949, but played only nine games, spending most of the season in the minors. Lou Boudreau, Minoso's first manager with Cleveland, praised his personality and his skill, but said Minoso needed more experience after his time with the Cubans. "He was a raw star in the beginning, but in only two years he was a seasoned ballplayer," Boudreau said. "He was a very friendly young man and he had friends all over the place."[9]

Minoso was naturally open and outgoing. But he had heard enough stories, even in Cuba (and not only from Pascual) to realize that being a black baseball player in the United States was not a panacea. "I knew about racism before I came," he said. "I was not surprised. The separate thing. 'You're not supposed to be there or there.' Some places it was a club and you cannot go to the club. Branch Rickey, he opened the door. It's like your house. He opened his ballpark to bring in Mr. Jackie. I talked to Mr. Jackie, sure. That's why I'm here. It is one thing to open the door to your house and another thing to open the door to respect each other in baseball and love each other. We are all human beings. I don't care about color or racism. Every few generations things changed a little bit."[10]

Unlike many young black players shipped to small towns in the lower levels of the minor leagues, Minoso's first minor league stop for the Indians was in nearby

Dayton, Ohio. Dayton of the Class A Central League was more northern than the Sally League with its clubs sprayed around Georgia and the Carolinas, but for the first time Minoso was the only black man on his team and said there were only a handful of blacks in the league.

As so many other black players did, Minoso stayed with black families or at all black hotels rather than with white teammates on road trips. Occasionally, opponents taunted Minoso because of the color of his skin, but they often found themselves eating dirt in the batter's box, courtesy of pitching teammates who retaliated for such attitudes. Minoso did not stay in Dayton long because he crushed league pitching at a shocking .522 pace.

As Minoso's baseball education continued and grew more sophisticated, so did his command of English. Although Minoso still carries a Latino accent in his speech, he experienced language immersion in Dayton from teammate Jose Santiago, a pitcher also on his way to the majors. At the same time Minoso learned English, he learned the team's signs so there would be no mix-ups on the field.

MAJOR LEAGUE CAREER

By the time Minoso reached the majors for good in 1951, he had been traded to the White Sox, his first affiliation with the team that continues to this day. Many other aspects of Minoso's life were already fixed in stone, as well. He wore flashy clothes and drove flashy cars. At one point, he drove a pink Cadillac and drove it right onto the field upon arrival at spring training in Tampa. There, local Cuban residents turned out to fete him. They were known to shout "Viva Minoso!" Also established early on was Minoso's playing style, wielding a mean bat, running the bases with abandon, and fielding with a flourish.

During the 1951 season, after they both advanced to the majors, Minoso was batting against Satchel Paige, then hurling for the St. Louis Browns. Minoso hit a blooper to the left side. The shortstop, the third baseman, and the left-fielder all ran for it, but the ball dropped in safely and Minoso ran all of the way to second for a puny, 120-foot double.

"Satchel yelled, 'Minoso hit the ball right!'" Minoso said. "I said, 'Hey, Satchel, read the paper tomorrow and you'll see Minnie got a double.' I only got one hit off of him in the big leagues. He was a very intelligent guy. A gentleman. He would talk to you all day and I never got tired of listening to him."[11]

Minoso was fond of the Cleveland organization. He enjoyed hanging out with Doby and Luke Easter, another black power hitter. Minoso was completely surprised when he was traded to Chicago in a three-way exchange. The Indians knew Minoso could not supplant Al Rosen at third base, but they did not try to find another home for him in the field.

Minoso was distressed by the trade. He knew Chicago had no black players and did not know what type of reception to expect. In a farewell meeting, Indians teammate Ray Boone told Minoso everything would work out well. Boone was right.

For all his trepidation, Minoso hit it off well in Chicago, literally and figuratively. In his prime, Minoso played at five-foot-ten and 175 pounds, not very big for a big leaguer. He made his White Sox debut on May 1, 1951, against the New York Yankees. And in his first at bat, in the first inning, against premier starter Vic Raschi, Minoso powdered a home run 415 feet to the left-field stands. Minoso further endeared himself to Comiskey Park fans with his speed. He joined outfielder Jim Busby as a base-stealing threat. That season Minoso stole thirty-one bases and Busby stole twenty-six. The thirty-one thefts led the American League. Minoso stroked fourteen triples, another indication of his daring and productive base running. It was the beginning of something special in Chicago, a defining characteristic that more recently has come to be called "small ball." Fans began chanting "Go, Go, Go," when Minoso got on base. Later, after the acquisition of shortstop Luis Aparicio, who routinely led the American League in steals, the White Sox ran to the 1959 pennant and a World Series appearance.

In his full rookie season with the White Sox, Minoso played in 138 games, swatted 10 home runs, accumulated 74 RBIs and batted .324. Whenever Minoso gives talks, he said he is asked by the audience what his best season was and he generally picks his first. "Everything considered I have to go back to my rookie season of 1951," he said. He was also selected American League rookie of the year that season.[12]

The White Sox decided to bestow special gifts on Minoso in September on Minnie Minoso Day. Such days usually take place near the end of a player's career. That kind of tribute in a rookie year is rarer than snow in July. But the White Sox presented Minoso with a car and other presents. It was an electrifying season for him. When he went back to Cuba in the off-season, Minoso was given an automobile there, too, among other gifts. Minoso made the Indians' judgment look bad, and as a White Sox player, he garnered more compliments than a politician who paid off endorsers for their praise.

"I don't believe there is a player in the game today who can give you the thrill that he can," said Bill Veeck, by then the owner of the Browns. "Without him in the lineup it's just another ball game." Yankees manager Casey Stengel remarked on Minoso's swiftness. "Now you see him and then you don't," Stengel said. "You don't suppose he's two guys, do you?" After Minoso darted from first to third safely on a short hit to center field against Detroit, an amazed Tigers shortstop Donie Bush said, "I swear that guy must have cut across the infield. Nobody could get from first to third so fast without taking a short cut."[13]

Minoso exhibited on-field joy and confidence, and success loosened him up more. During his 1951 romp of a season, a story made the rounds about Minoso scoring from third base on a sacrifice fly. The ball seemed to be hit too shallow in center field for him to take the risk and run for the plate. Third base coach Jimmy Adair yelled, "No, no, no." But Minnie had the wheels in those days and the instant the ball nestled into Red Sox center fielder Dom DiMaggio's glove, he took off. At the same time Minoso shouted to Adair, "Too late, I gone." He was also safe.[14]

One notable pattern emerged in Minoso's first Major League season. Pitchers hit him frequently with errant throws. Minoso crowded the plate and hit from a deep crouch. Never backing off in the batter's box, he almost dared hurlers to throw at him. It was just another way to get on base. There was no open suggestion that pitchers threw at him for racial reasons, but at least once, under the guise of a joke, Minoso said to his trainer, "Hey, Doc. You got white paint? They hit me again. Maybe if I am white they no try to kill me so much."[15]

Much later, Minoso said, "It is common knowledge that I had a propensity for being hit by pitches."[16] That was an understatement. Minoso was hit by pitchers 192 times in his Major League career and led the league ten times in that category. In 1956, Minoso was hit twenty-three times, the most for him in a single season. If that happened to a player now, teammates would either riot or the commissioner's office would issue an edict threatening pitcher suspension.

Minoso's worst hit-by-pitch experience occurred during a game against the Yankees in 1955. Bob Grim, a twenty-game-winner the year before, was on the mound. The game was played in fading daylight and when a pitch got away from Grim, Minoso was slow to duck. "Normally, I think I could have gotten out of the way," Minoso said, "but it was getting dark in New York and I couldn't follow the ball well. I felt an explosion in my head and I went down." Minoso, who said he never blamed Grim for the errant pitch, was hospitalized with a hairline fracture of the skull. Later that night Grim and his wife stopped by. Grim apologized and said he never meant to hit Minoso. Minoso absolved him.[17] "I never had it on my mind that he did it on purpose—even though it almost killed me."[18] Minoso was out three weeks with the injury.

A year later, when Grim hit Dave Philley with a pitch, the batter was not as forgiving. Philley charged the mound, still carrying his bat. Grim said he was ready to run, until Philley dropped the club. The two squared off with a couple of roundhouse swings. "I mighta hurt that boy if they hadn't stopped us," Philley said. Still another year later against the Yankees, New York pitcher Al Cicotte fired a fastball that had Minoso eating dirt. He got up yelling and on his next swing, let the bat fly out of his hands toward the mound. The dispute ended there.[19]

In a 1956 game against the Yankees, Minoso was hobbled by a broken toe. He seemed likely to miss several games. But at a critical moment in the eleventh inning, he was sent up to pinch hit. Minoso limped to the plate with a hole cut in his shoe allowing the injured toe to breathe. (He had negotiated with management to pay $25 for new shoes once he performed the leather surgery.) During the back-and-forth discussions about whether Minoso could suit up or not, he said, "Look, I play, but you gotta buy me two pair new shoes." Minoso hit a double and then the White Sox pinch ran for him.[20]

For much of the 1950s, the White Sox-Yankees rivalry was particularly fierce. The Yankees won almost all of the pennants, but the White Sox pursued them vigorously and there were many tense games. Andy Carey, the New York third baseman from 1952 to 1960, said playing against Minoso drove him crazy. Minnie made so many great catches and plays, Carey felt haunted by the outfielder.

"Ol' Minoso, I made a hero out of him," Carey said. "That sucker in left field, it seemed like every time I hit a ball, he would be right there to catch it. I went to an old-timers' game and did the same damn thing, and I told him, 'You son of a bitch, you're still over there.'"[21]

Minoso quickly emerged as one of the prominent players in the American League, becoming a seven-time All Star. Between 1953 and 1957, he hit more than .300 four additional times for the White Sox. He led the league in triples twice more, including a career-high eighteen in 1954, and drove in more than a hundred runs three times. Although Minoso made many errors, he won three Golden Gloves for sometimes spectacular fielding efforts.

Then, before the 1958 season Minoso was traded back to the Indians. It was no accident to Minoso that he was traded from the Indians to the White Sox and back to the Indians because both times he was moved, the manager was Al Lopez. Minoso thought Lopez just did not like him. "Perhaps it was just a bit coincidental," Minoso said, not elaborating.

Minoso was happy in Chicago and mad to be traded. "Things could not have been better," he said. "I was an acknowledged baseball star. I had fame and popularity. I found a real home in Chicago. Everybody knew me there."[22]

It was with a sense of betrayal that Minoso returned to Cleveland. Minoso had shown great promise in Cleveland, and the fans lamented his departure when he played so well in Chicago. Now it was time to show his stuff in his original Major League city.

During two seasons with the Indians, Minoso batted .302 twice. He led the league in being hit by pitches, too. Same old Minnie.

Minoso was nicknamed the "Cuban Comet" for his base running, but he probably should have been called the "Latin Piñata" because he was hit with the baseball so often. Sportswriters asked him how he could take so many hit-by-pitches. "I not afraid," Minoso said. "I no quit. I been hit in the head eight times, but I rather die than stop playing. Is the best game in the world. Sometimes when I am hit I get mad. I get on base and think I slide and cut second baseman. But then I never do it. I change my mind. I think other guy trying to make living just like me. He got wife and kid to support like me."[23]

Later, after his language skills improved, Minoso resented being quoted as speaking English in pidgin fashion.

The main cost to Minoso of spending two years in Cleveland before returning to the White Sox for the 1960 season courtesy of his old friend Bill Veeck, then the owner, was missing out on the team's trip to the 1959 World Series against the Los Angeles Dodgers. Minoso is so identified with the White Sox and spent so much time with the club in the 1950s, that most present-day fans probably do not even realize he missed the World Series hoopla, especially since he came right back one season later and batted .311. The poor timing of Minoso's loan to the Indians meant that he never got the chance to win a World Series ring during his career. It is a hole in his resume, but not a missed opportunity that he broods over.

"I would like to play in a World Series, of course," he said. "But really my ambition was to be able to play in the major leagues."[24] However, because of his close personal connection to the White Sox, Minoso was one of the nonplayers given a 2005 World Series championship ring. He wears the ring on his left hand along with his wedding ring.

If Veeck had been the owner of the Indians longer, or if Veeck had owned the White Sox continuously during the latter stages of Minoso's career, Minnie believes he would never have had a leave of absence from the club. Veeck, though, was always notoriously short of money. He had to sell the club in the early 1960s, reclaimed it in the 1970s, and financial considerations forced him to sell once again. There was a strong rapport between Veeck and Minoso.

"Bill Veeck liked me a lot," Minoso said. "He proved to me he liked and respected me. Some people think that if you are a good friend of the boss, you run to him for everything. My life was to be on the field. I would see him and he said, 'How are you?' and 'See you later.' He wanted me with his team all of the time. If he had a team many more years I would be with him until I die." Later, in retirement, Minoso developed a close relationship with current White Sox owner Jerry Reinsdorf, too. "They [Veeck and Reinsdorf] respect me like I'm one of the ballplayers."[25]

After the 1961 season, Minoso moved on to the St. Louis Cardinals. It was something new playing in the National League. But things did not go particularly well. As always, with his stand-on-the-edge-of-the-plate stance Minoso was a target for pitchers. He was thirty-nine years old (maybe) and might not be as quick at getting out of the way of the inside fastball. That was a worry. But instead, Minoso clobbered himself in a different way by running into an outfield wall in St. Louis in May on a fielding play. He suffered a fractured skull and a broken wrist, and played only thirty-nine games that season.

Prospects of a productive return to baseball were downplayed. Minoso, it was written, "may never play again. To anyone, this would be a brutal blow, to Minnie it would be sheer tragedy because he was born to play."[26] A picture of Minoso lying seemingly unconscious in a hospital bed, his then-wife Edilia's comforting hand on his cast, accompanied an article in the *Pittsburgh Press*. Minoso did not look good.

As it turned out, the supposition about Minoso's future was correct in some respects, and laughably incorrect in another. In the near term, Minoso was nearly finished as a starting outfielder. The next season he drifted to the Washington Senators. In 1964 he showed up in the White Sox training camp for a third go-around. Of all people, Al Lopez gave Minoso a chance to make the club as a pinch hitter. "Minnie always gives 110 percent," Lopez said. "You have to admire him." Grateful for the last chance, Minoso said, "I'm so happy, I'm crazy. Like a boy with a new pair of shoes."[27] As a boy, Minoso would have been happy with any new shoes. As a man he regularly invested in new suede shoes. So it was clear the analogy was heartfelt.

Minoso played in thirty games for the White Sox that season and batted .229. Then he retired with a .298 lifetime average. At the time it was expected to be retirement for good. Minoso was forty-something years old; so, no comebacks in the batter's box loomed. Many years passed. Veeck had to relinquish the White Sox, but in the 1970s he put together a fresh consortium of financiers and bought the team again. For the midwinter 1976 Chicago baseball banquet, Veeck, ever the promoter, announced he was bringing a mystery guest. Veeck kept the secret for a month and then on the night of the dinner introduced Minoso as a new member of the team's coaching staff.

A great deal of emotion flowed that night. Veeck said, "He's always been a fine baseball man, and, anyway, this is where he belongs." Minoso said he was very glad to be back with the White Sox. By then Minoso was in his early fifties, but had been active as a player-manager in Mexico as recently as the season before. Someone wondered if Minoso might find his way into the White Sox lineup, but no such commitment was made. Jerome Holtzman, the longtime sterling Chicago baseball writer, even noted how unlikely that was: "It seems quite doubtful that Minoso, tough old bird that he is, still can hit Major League pitching at the age of fifty-two."[28]

Five baseball players had appeared in games during part of four decades in post-1900 Major League history. Pitcher Bobo Newsom played between 1929 and 1953. Ted Williams played between 1939 and 1960. Mickey Vernon played the same years. Early Wynn pitched between 1939 and 1963. Pitcher Jack Quinn played from 1909 to 1933.

Late in the season of 1976, with the White Sox out of contention for the pennant, the team needing help at the box office, and the rosters expanded from twenty-five to forty players on September 1, Veeck activated Minoso.

"Of course, a lot of people would think it was strictly a publicity stunt," Veeck said. That would be because the circus master of the game never met a publicity stunt he did not embrace. "But that's not true." Presumably he said that with a straight face. Probably the one word in Veeck's first sentence that could be taken issue with was "strictly." Veeck liked to make the establishment squirm, but if he thought Minoso would embarrass himself, he would never put him in the lineup. He had too much regard for the man. Minoso did not take kindly to suggestions that his coming to bat was some kind of joke. "You're damn right I can still hit," he said.[29]

With the season expiring, there was Minnie Minoso on the field again. Minoso got into three games as a designated hitter (helpfully, under the new rules, he did not have to play the field), batted eight times, and stroked one hit. That made him a four-decade ballplayer. Minoso's first at bat at Comiskey Park in twelve years took place on September 11. "Truly, it was a proud and nostalgic moment for me," he said. He struck out and went zero-for-three that day. The next game he cracked a single.[30]

The return to the game at an advanced age gave Minoso notoriety among a new generation of fans. However, that raised the question of just how old Minoso was. The *Baseball Encyclopedia* lists Minoso's date of birth as November 29, 1922. The Indians used that as his date of birth when he played for them. The White Sox listed Minoso's date of birth as 1923 when he played for them. Minoso insists that he was born in 1925, that he is really three years younger than most people have thought all along. "They question how old you are if you're black," Minoso said recently. "Especially if you come from another country."[31]

Most fans and sportswriters thought it was a gimmick when Veeck activated Minoso in 1976. The attitude was "Cool, now he's a four-decade man. No harm, no foul." Four years later, during the 1980 season, the White Sox and Veeck activated Minoso again and he played in two more games. The idea was to have him join Nick Altrock as one of baseball's two five-decade Major Leaguers. Minoso batted twice with no hits.

In the mid-1990s, Minoso claimed he could still hit, as long as he had time to practice and get his timing down. "I believe I can still face big league pitching," he said. "I would do a decent job."[32]

Some people believed him, or at least thought it a good enough idea to give Minoso a chance to prove his boast. The White Sox were ready in 1990, during the last season of old Comiskey Park. Commissioner Fay Vincent stepped in and banned Minoso from active duty. Words like "travesty" were bandied about in the media at the time. Minoso was hurt. "You get that laugh, or disrespect from people," Minoso said. "I would do a thing because I know I could do it. I could swing and run. I could do it. I would not disrespect the game. I love the people."[33] A year later, when the Class A Miami Miracle wanted to allow Minoso to hit, Vincent again refused to permit it.

In 1993, Minoso got a chance to hit live pitching once again. The offer came from the St. Paul Saints of the Independent Northern League in 1993, outside the purview of the commissioner's office. Minoso took his cuts. That made him the first baseball player to ever participate in the sport in parts of six decades.

Ten years later, during the summer of 2003, as part of a Negro Leagues tribute, Minoso was invited back to St. Paul to bat still one more time. He walked. It was no coincidence that the owner of the St. Paul team is Mike Veeck, Bill Veeck's son. And Mike Veeck was the operator of the Miami Miracle, too, when his first attempt to play Minoso was shot down.

"Minnie Minoso was a hero of mine when I was a kid," said the younger Veeck, "and he's an even bigger hero now that I'm a middle-aged fan. Anyone who knows Minnie knows that he is, above all, a professional. He's kept himself in tremendous shape."[34]

Minoso became a seven-decade player with the bases on balls. He now owns a commemorative ring highlighting the accomplishment and it is part of his cache—Minnie Minoso, the only man to play baseball in parts of seven decades.

"I enjoy it myself," Minoso said, "and I enjoy that people know about it. It's beautiful. It's beautiful to be known to the people. I'm happy to do something that people recognize. I'm not ashamed of myself. It's like going to the moon. It's impossible. When you said that before, people said, 'The moon, they must be crazy?' Now, will other people do it? No."[35]

Minoso's Chicago baseball life continues. Sometimes he wears a seven-decades cap to appearances, as if people would not know who he was without it. For those who do have trouble recognizing him, there is a statue of Minoso at bat located in centerfield of

U.S. Cellular Field, the White Sox's home park. When it was unveiled, Minoso hugged the likeness of himself and cried.

Minoso looks younger than his years—whatever they may be—but his face is not unlined and his thinning hair is mostly gray. He has been around the game a long time and he has a long memory about the years gone by, in and out of baseball. It has been decades since Minoso visited his home of Cuba. The loss of freedom under Communist dictator Fidel Castro made it decidedly difficult for players to travel. Minoso said he has never criticized the government and has one living sister still residing in Cuba. But it is not as if he has hopes of imminently vacationing on the island. "My home is Chicago now," Minoso said. "I haven't been there [Cuba] in a long time. I have a lot of relatives here."[36]

Recently, Minoso gained extra attention outside of Chicago in a documentary called *Viva Baseball*, a story about the difficulties Latin players like him faced when trying to break into the majors. "I owe all those people," said Pedro Martinez, the star New York Mets pitcher, of his Latin predecessors.[37]

Minoso was the forerunner of many great Cuban players who made it to the majors before the door was padlocked by Castro. And members of that next generation were big fans of his. "I think everybody loved the way he played hard," said Tony Perez, a Hall of Famer with the Cinncinati Reds. "All the time he goes to the wall and catches the ball. He was aggressive running the bases. He didn't care. He wanted to get on and score runs. Everyone in Cuba loved Minnie." Perez said his uncle took him to games years ago in Cuba and the youngster said, "I'm gonna be like Minnie Minoso."[38]

Vic Power, a phenomenal fielding first baseman from Puerto Rico, who was a colorful player with flamboyant style and became a Major League All Star, said he admired the way Minoso took the hard knocks that came with getting hit by so many pitches. "He was afraid of nothing," Power said. With Minoso, he added, it was "Let's play the game the way it is supposed to be played." Power, however, said Minoso had a few quirks, like taking his bat home to the hotel room on the road and sleeping with it under his pillow. Power called that "some kind of voodoo."[39]

LATER LIFE

Maybe voodoo was Minoso's secret to staying young. If there was ever any doubt that Minoso and Bill Veeck were kindred spirits, when Veeck died in 1986, Minoso dreamed up the best tribute he could think of to the man who meant so much to his career: Minoso wore a White Sox cap and jersey to the funeral. Somehow it figured that Minoso's exit from the church seemed right out of a Veeck script for promotional attention. Minoso walked up to his Cadillac-of-the-moment, and discovered he was locked out of the car. A nun retreated into the church and emerged bearing a coat hanger. As Minoso sought to pry open the lock, funeral attendees, presumably White Sox fans, stood by and cheered him on, yelling, "C'mon, you can do it, Minnie."[40]

Minoso made his Negro Leagues debut with the New York Cubans more than sixty years ago. That seems unreal to him. "It seems like it was yesterday," he said. "That's more than yesterday." One concession to age for Minoso is steering away from pink Cadillacs. "I have to be careful. My wife [Sharon] would say, 'Are you a playboy again?'" Acceptance of racial differences in American society has come a long way from Minoso's earliest days when being black was a bar to entree in big-league baseball. "I can't hide this," he said of his dark skin. "How could I have a birth certificate that said

I was white? I used to go along with the program no matter what words were used and what I was called. I would ignore it and smile. Nobody ever made me lose my control and made me fight."[41]

Still, Minoso said he expects no glory or special credit to accrue for becoming the first black White Sox player. He knows he was a top player and he knows he did many notable things on the diamond. And he revels in his role of a seven-decade player, but Minoso does not single himself out for being a racial barrier breaker. "It happened to be me," he said. "I'm like another guy. If it hadn't been me it would have been another guy. It's not something special or bigger than what other guys did."[42] Others like the Cubans and Latins who followed him into the majors have said differently.

Baseball has been Minoso's life and he has given thought to how he wants his own funeral to play out when he passes on. "I love the game so much," Minoso said. "If I die, please bury me in my uniform."[43] His coffin could also be made in the shape of a new model of his favorite automobile.

When he finished reminiscing about his baseball past, Minoso wrapped his raincoat around his body and placed the beret on his head. He made his way out of U.S. Cellular Field into the soggy afternoon. And then Minoso climbed into his white Cadillac with the Illinois license plate reading, "Minnie," and drove away.

NOTES

1. Minnie Minoso, personal interview, February 17, 2006.
2. Ibid.
3. Ibid.
4. Minnie Minoso with Herb Fagen, *Just Call Me Minnie: My Six Decades in Baseball* (Champaign, IL: Sagamore Publishing, 1994), 26.
5. Minoso, personal interview, February 17, 2006.
6. Minoso with Fagen, *Just Call Me Minnie*, 30.
7. Monte Irvin, personal interview, January 7, 2006.
8. Minoso with Fagen, *Just Call Me Minnie*, 36.
9. Minoso with Fagen, *Just Call Me Minnie*, 38.
10. Minoso, personal interview, February 17, 2006.
11. Minoso, personal interview, February 17, 2006.
12. Minoso with Fagen, *Just Call Me Minnie*, 63.
13. John C. Hoffman, *Collier's*, April 5, 1952.
14. Ibid.
15. Ibid.
16. Minoso with Fagen, *Just Call Me Minnie*, 100.
17. Minoso with Fagen, *Just Call Me Minnie*, 100–101.
18. Bob Vanderberg, *Minnie and the Mick* (South Bend, IN: Diamond Communications, 1996), 195.
19. Vanderberg, *Minnie and the Mick*, 185–186.
20. Vanderberg, *Minnie and the Mick*, 76.
21. Vanderberg, *Minnie and the Mick*, 212.
22. Minoso with Fagen, *Just Call Me Minnie*, 113.
23. Lou Miller, *Cleveland Press*, June 15, 1955.
24. Minoso, personal interview, February 17, 2006.
25. Ibid.
26. Joe Williams, *Pittsburgh Press*, May 20, 1962.
27. Jerome Holtzman, *Chicago Tribune*, March 21, 1964.

28. Jerome Holtzman, *Sporting News*, January 31, 1976.

29. Dave Nightingale, *Chicago Daily News*, August 8, 1976.

30. Minoso with Fagen, *Just Call Me Minnie*, 176.

31. Minoso, personal interview, February 17, 2006.

32. Minoso with Fagen, *Just Call Me Minnie*, 196.

33. Minoso, personal interview, February 17, 2006.

34. Dave Moriah, *Sports Collectors Digest*, August 13, 1993.

35. Minoso, personal interview, February 17, 2006.

36. Ibid.

37. Dan Klores (director and co-producer) and Charles Stuart (writer and co-producer), *Viva Baseball* documentary (New York: Shoot the Moon Productions, 2005).

38. Ibid.

39. Ibid.

40. Gerald Eskenazi, *Bill Veeck: A Baseball Legend* (New York: McGraw-Hill, 1988), XII.

41. Minoso, personal interview, February 17, 2006.

42. Ibid.

43. Klores and Stuart, *Viva Baseball*.

Further Reading

Klores, Dan, director and co-producer, and Charles Stuart, writer and co-producer, *Viva Baseball*, New York, Shoot the Moon Productions, 2005.

Minoso, Minnie, with Herb Fagen, *Just Call Me Minnie: My Six Decades in Baseball.* Champaign, IL: Sagamore Publishing, 1994.

Vanderberg, Bob, *Minnie and the Mick*. South Bend, IN: Diamond Communications, 1996.

FRANK ROBINSON
August 31, 1935–

Not only is Frank Robinson one of two living players to ever win the Triple Crown of hitting in the same season by leading a league in home runs, runs batted in, and average, he won the Most Valuable Player award in both the American and National Leagues and then made history by being named the big leagues first African American manager with the Cleveland Indians in 1975.

Robinson spent twenty-one seasons in the majors between 1956 and 1976, batting .294 with 586 home runs, the fifth most all-time. He also knocked in 1,812 runs while being acknowledged as one of the most feared sluggers of his time.

Frank Robinson sat in the spartan visiting manager's office at Wrigley Field more than three hours before his Washington Nationals were scheduled to play the Chicago

Young Frank Robinson broke in as a slugger and All-Star outfielder with the Cincinnati Reds in 1956 and helped raise the Reds into the status of National League contender.

Cubs, conducting his pregame press briefing. The white cinder block walls behind him were blank. The day's newspapers were arrayed on his desk, for the most part appearing untouched. Resting on a counter, still in its wrapper, was the day's giveaway item to fans—a Snoopy Doll dressed in a Cubs jersey. In Robinson's case it might make a nice souvenir for a grandchild.

Robinson wore his uniform under a blue team jacket with "Nationals" stenciled across the front. His cap was off and his mostly gray, in-parts-going-white, short hair was on view. At the time, halfway through the month of May during the 2006 season, his team was playing poorly, and owned one of the worst records in the National League. One of the Washington reporters accompanying the team on its road trip asked Robinson a question about his bullpen pitchers' performance. It was not about how great they were going.

"You can't just go out there and change the entire bullpen," Robinson said. The way he said it, however, hinted that he might not think that was such a bad suggestion.[1]

Robinson is generally described as a man who does not look his age more than a half century after he broke into organized baseball and more than three decades since he became the first African American manager in Major League history. He was going on seventy-one years old at the time of the Chicago series, but he was in charge of a team that could age any manager. So long after he came up from the minors to break into the Cincinnati Reds lineup in 1956, Robinson was not openly discussing retirement, but as one of the rare septuagenarians to wear big-league colors, he could probably see the end of the road from his clubhouse perch.

When Robinson does retire, does leave the baseball diamond for the last time, it will mark the end of one of the most notable combined playing-managing careers in the sport. Robinson played baseball with a passion that earned him some of the game's top honors. He was National League Most Valuable player with the Reds and he was American League Most Valuable player with the Baltimore Orioles. He is the only player to collect the trophies in both leagues. In 1975, when Robinson became the game's first black manager, he was a barrier breaker almost on the order of another Robinson, Jackie, the first black to play Major League ball in the twentieth century. At the least Frank Robinson was in the right place at the right time to edge out the other highly qualified African American players like Larry Doby, Elston Howard, and others, who sought to become the first black manager.

Robinson joined the Cleveland Indians in 1974, near the end of his playing career, when it seemed unlikely that manager Ken Aspromonte would be invited back for another season. One of the coaches was Doby, who had prepared himself for the task with several seasons of managing in Latin American winter ball. But Cleveland chose Robinson, who also managed in Puerto Rico. With only days left in the 1974 season the *New York Times* speculated that Robinson would be selected.

"I wanted to be ready if a Major League job opens up for me," Robinson said of his winter ball managing. "I wanted to learn what it's like to handle twenty-five different personalities."[2]

The forecast came true barely more than a week later. The Indians named Robinson as the majors first black manager. Robinson understood this was no routine job change, a practice so commonplace in baseball that it is a rarity for a new manager's introduction to break into the paper off the sports pages. In Robinson's case, his appointment was national front-page news, not merely sports section news.

Robinson was not oblivious, but did not assume the job by making civil rights pronouncements. He took the opposite tack, saying he was "born black. That's the color

A savvy player, Frank Robinson built a reputation as a man who knew the game. He apprenticed in Latin America as manager of winter ball teams and in 1975 became the first African American manager in Major League history when he took over the Cleveland Indians.

I am. I'm not a superman. I'm not a miracle worker. Your ballplayers determine how good a team you have."[3] That is probably the key lesson any manager learns on the job and Robinson knew it going in.

Doby, the first black player in the American League, aspired desperately to become the first black manager in baseball. Although he was overlooked (and Robinson soon fired him), Doby was gracious at the time of Robinson's hire. "It should happen," he said, "not for tokenism, or black revolution, but because it's a free country. And God gave us all a certain amount of ability."[4] About two years later, Doby gained the chance to exercise his administrative ability when he was hired to manage the Chicago White Sox.

Robinson was still under contract with the Indians as a player and his salary for doing both jobs was $175,000. He was wrapping up his playing career as a designated hitter in the American League and it was anticipated that he would continue to rely on himself when a right-handed bat was needed off the bench. The precedent of player managers was firmly established decades earlier and one of the most prominent successes was the Indians own Lou Boudreau, shortstop-manager in 1948 when the Tribe won the World Series. At the time of Robinson's hire there had been no player-managers in fifteen years, but he did not shrink from the circumstance.

"I wouldn't mind putting myself in there as the designated hitter a few times a week," said Robinson, who was thirty-nine at the time. "I find I hit better that way, besides. I might take myself out on defense, though."[5] He laughed as he said it, but Robinson had not needed any assistance on defense as a younger man. He was a superb all-around player in his prime.

EARLY LIFE

Frank Robinson was born in Beaumont, Texas, and became a McClymonds High School star athlete in Oakland, California, where he was a basketball teammate of Bill Russell, the future Boston Celtics luminary. Robinson was the tenth and youngest child of his mother Ruth Shaw, who had three husbands, and said he enjoyed living in Oakland even if its image suffered as a place of sophistication in the shadow of San Francisco and Berkeley.

As a youth, Robinson was an avid sports fan and played everything from basketball and football to kick ball and Ping Pong when he was not playing baseball, his favorite. "These other sports were always fill-ins for me, a way to pass the time until we got going on baseball again," he said. "I always favored baseball, the challenge of it, the bat and ball, the fielding part of it. Baseball seemed to bring out my competitive instincts more than anything else, and I was always good at it."[6]

Robinson was a key player on a local American Legion team that won championships. Among his teammates were future major leaguers Vada Pinson and Curt Flood, all of whom signed with the Reds, though Flood had his best years with the St. Louis Cardinals. Flood said that Robinson, who played in the majors at six-foot-one and weighed 195 pounds, "had always been the biggest and most powerful of us."[7]

Robinson spent three seasons in the minors before joining the Reds for the 1956 season. During his first minor league season in Ogden, Utah, Robinson was refused service at a white-run movie theater. It was the first time in his life that he had been confronted by overt prejudice of that nature.

"That was the start of it, and it has touched my life ever since," Robinson said of playing on other teams, being called "nigger," and finding it difficult to purchase housing in a neighborhood he wanted to live in.[8]

However, as a player in his late teens, he did not quite fathom the discriminatory attitude of Ogden. Mostly, he hung around with a Latin player named Chico Terry, who could not speak English well, and his teammates, and said even the long bus rides all over the Rockies were fun. He had a good time traveling and meeting new people, though as a shy transplant from the West Coast that was not his strong suit.

"My trouble was, I couldn't relate to people," Robinson said. "I couldn't go right up and become friendly with people. It's always been tough for me to meet strangers. I was very shy then and I still am to a certain extent, though I talk more than I used to."[9]

After the stopover in Ogden, Robinson was assigned to a Reds farm team in Columbia, South Carolina. Like so many other African American players of the time Robinson found that his skin color was foremost on fans' minds in the South. When the Dodgers Branch Rickey determined to integrate Major League baseball with Jackie Robinson, he was careful to place Robinson with a minor league team in Montreal where Robinson might be shielded from racist attitudes. It worked out well for Robinson. But Robinson was in his mid-twenties, further along in his career. Most other teams that signed young black players knew they needed seasoning in the lower minors. Many of those players suffered in small, rural southern towns where they were either not really welcome on their own team, when the team traveled, or both. The language that peppered them certainly enhanced their vocabularies.

"The home crowd was generally good," Robinson said of his stay in South Carolina with a black roommate named John Jackson. "But when you hit the road, that's when you got it. Those fans in Macon and Augusta, Georgia would give it to us real good. They never let up on us. They always reminded us of the color of our skin. You made an error, or you did something wrong, they'd start hollering—'Nigger, go back to Africa.' Or worse."[10]

MAJOR LEAGUE CAREER

After his minor league apprenticeship, Robinson broke in with Cincinnati with a resounding splash, crashing 38 home runs, driving in 83 runs, and batting .290 in 152 games. Robinson did not spend time on the Reds bench. He was ready to roar upon promotion. Robinson made his Major League debut against the St. Louis Cardinals and the first pitcher he faced was Vinegar Bend Mizell. He took a liking to a Mizell fastball and stroked it for a double in his first at bat. Robinson went two-for-three that day with an intentional walk, a memorable start.

Many years before Robinson made the joke about replacing himself in the field, he was a demon in the outfield, a man so devoted to tracking down fly balls that he routinely barged into the fences. In his rookie year alone, Robinson bruised or stunned himself five times while trying to lasso long blasts. Each time his manager, Birdie Tebbetts, who Robinson described as being like a father to him, trekked to the distant reaches of the outfield to see how his prized pupil was faring. Each time Tebbetts hoped Robinson would not need an ambulance to carry him off the field. Each time Robinson bounded up and stayed in the lineup. Eventually, Tebbetts told Robinson to cut down on his daring because the boss was too old to walk 450 feet from the dugout to check up on him. Soon after, in Pittsburgh, Robinson cracked into an outfield fence yet again. Making the grab, hitting the wall, but holding onto the ball, Robinson dropped to the ground stunned. This time it looked serious and Tebbetts roused himself from his seat. By the time he arrived, however, Robinson had revived somewhat. When Tebbetts leaned over him, Robinson opened his eyes and said, "What took you so long?" Robinson climbed to his feet and went back to his position.[11]

The fleet outfielder made even more noise with his bat and Robinson was chosen for the National League All-Star team, and after the season his rookie-record number of homers helped gain him the National League rookie of the year award. "That kind of capped it all for me," Robinson said. "I felt very pleased about that."[12]

From a playing standpoint, Robinson could hardly have made a greater impact, but as an individual he was not as happy as he might have been. Robinson was only twenty-one and his teammates were older and had different ideas about how to find entertainment after dinner. Many toured the nightclubs, but Robinson was not interested in long drinking bouts. Often he just hunkered down in his hotel room writing letters home. A movie buff, Robinson occasionally sat through triple features to pass the time until night games, especially on the road.

Early in his career, Robinson established that he was a talent with all the tools. He also played the game hard, with a deep-down determination, a fierce pride that announced to onlookers how much he cared about winning. If that meant making the hard slide into second base, so be it. If that meant that opponents did not want to chat him up, he was OK with that. Robinson did not wish to fraternize with other players, he wanted to beat them. He earned a reputation as a player not to cross and he admitted that his intensity was a key weapon in his arsenal.

"Hard-nosed, no-nonsense baseball," he said during the latter stages of his career. "That's the way I've always played the game. That's the way I'll continue to play the game. It has meant personal sacrifice, however. I have, throughout my career, been called all kind of names by opposing ballplayers. One guy said I was 'deliberately vicious.' Another accused me of 'trying to maim people.' A third said, 'I hated his guts when I played against him.' OK, that's their privilege. A lot of this, I think, came because the players didn't know me. I hate, too. I hate all the fellows around the league who are wearing the other uniform. I hate them when we're playing against them, but then it ends."[13]

Of course, Robinson never pretended he was running for the title of Mr. Congeniality, only Mr. Invaluable. Robinson, who was called "F. Robby" by some writers, maintained a distance virtually throughout his Major League career. You were either with him or against him. It used to be this way throughout baseball, two teams taking the field with no love between them. They were opponents out to win and they knew they were scrapping for their jobs. Sensitive to appearances, and a long time recovering from the Black Sox betting scandal of 1919, the commissioner's office frowned on opposing players hanging out together on the field. It was called fraternization and public discourse at the batting cage was discouraged. Over time the outlook has loosened and since it is rare to not play against someone who is an old pal or roommate, common courtesy dictates at least a warm hello.

Robinson never saw it that way, even after he moved on from the Reds to the Baltimore Orioles and had been in the majors for fifteen years. He stayed in the clubhouse longer than his teammates and minimized his time in warm-ups when both clubs might overlap on the field. There were no secret handshakes or hail-fellow-well-met backslaps for him.

"There's too much of it in baseball, especially in the American League," Robinson said in 1971. "Some guys actually show up at the ballpark early so they can get their conversations out of the way. There's no way you can go barreling into second base and dump a guy on a double play, like you should do, when you've been fraternizing with him before the game."[14]

Robinson apparently never heard of Cain and Abel. Robinson's perspective may have seemed sound in theory, but it was open to question just how many players put their competitive instincts on the shelf when playing against someone they knew and liked.

In a Major League career that spanned twenty-one seasons, including the last two with the Indians as a part-timer while managing, Robinson played in 2,808 games, came to bat more than 10,000 times, and slugged 586 home runs, which ranks behind only Hank Aaron, Barry Bonds, Babe Ruth, Willie Mays, and Sammy Sosa.

The Reds won the National League pennant in 1961 and Robinson won the Most Valuable Player award for his 37 home runs, 124 RBIs, and .323 average. He was the best player on the best team in the league that season. After Robinson was traded to the Orioles, he became the only player to win Most Valuable Player honors in both leagues. Inexplicably, the Reds gave up on Robinson during his prime under the guise that he was over-the-hill. "Robinson is an old thirty years of age," said Reds general manager Bill DeWitt at the time of the trade. "He has an old body."[15] The statement infuriated Robinson, not the least because it was not accurate. In his first season in Baltimore,

Robinson swatted 49 home runs, knocked in 122, and hit .316. By leading the American League in all three major categories, Robinson became a rare triple crown winner. That performance won him the Most Valuable Player in his new league.

Robinson had a superstar playing career with the Reds and with the Orioles. In Baltimore, mostly under manager Earl Weaver, Robinson was part of four pennant winners and two World Series champs before being traded to the Los Angeles Dodgers, the California Angels, and the Indians near the end of his active days. He still wielded a powerful bat, however, smacking thirty homers with the Angels in 1973 and twenty-two with the Angels and Indians in 1974.

Robinson poured his body, soul, and energy into winning and when the Reds captured the National League flag in 1961, he was ecstatic. "It's hard for me to explain what that pennant meant to me," Robinson said. "It's a tremendous honor for an individual to play on a championship team, and the first one is the biggest thrill of all. I don't think you can ever recapture the feeling. I don't care how many pennants you win, the first one is always the greatest thrill."[16]

Most players, especially those who enjoy success early in their careers, develop an affinity for the team that first signs them, nurtures them through the minor leagues, puts them in a big-league lineup for the first time, and gives them raises. If that player becomes a star and the team wins, then the relationship usually becomes even closer, with the player becoming a big man in the team's town, often becoming the public face of the club. As years pass, players believe that they will always play in that town, that their entire career will be linked to that team. Any schism is therefore more of a surprise, more hurtful, when a major star and the front office find themselves at odds. Over time, the shy Robinson became more outspoken about conditions when the team traveled and about skewed hotel arrangements. Players came to him with their gripes and asked if he could take them to the management. As such, Robinson said, he "got labeled as a troublemaker."[17]

When Robinson had an off year in 1963, batting only .259 with 21 homers and was asked to take a pay cut, he was shaken up. " 'It was such a bad cut,' I told a writer later, 'I'm going to drop over to the Reds' office and have the stitches taken out.' "[18]

Robinson fit in quickly with the easy-going Orioles who were building a first-rate club. The team was loose in spring training and stayed loose. Sarcasm was prevalent on that team, but the jokes went down well. At one point, Robinson presided over the team's kangaroo court, exacting fines for minor violations. Judge Frank wore the equivalent of a white British judicial wig as he made rulings. At the end of the season $1,000 was contributed to a fund for the education of catcher Pat Corrales' children, whose wife died after childbirth. Robinson enjoyed being with the team and enjoyed playing for manager Hank Bauer, who handled the job before Hall of Famer Weaver.

Boog Powell, the slugging Orioles first baseman who loomed as large as an office building, teased Robinson from the start. He nicknamed him "Pencils" because Robinson had thin legs. Practical jokes were rampant, from hotfoots to wielding of sneezing powder, disappearing ink and rubber snakes. "The joking never stopped," Robinson said. "All of that clowning and joking served a purpose, I think. The mood of a ball club is very important. If you have happy players, they're going to put out extra and do things that a discontented ballplayer won't do."[19]

Robinson said it was a thrill when he won the triple crown of hitting in 1966, but he had much more fun partying with this group of guys when they clinched the pennant. "Oh, what a celebration," he said. "I thought the one I went through in Cincinnati in

1961 was something, but this one was too much. We were in that clubhouse for about three hours with beer and champagne and mustard and cake and mayonnaise and sliced tomatoes splashing over everybody (he did not specify the source of the menu)."

"Somebody smacked me in the mouth with a piece of cake and I stuffed a rubber snake in Luis Aparicio's shoe (who was deathly afraid of snakes). Louie was so jumpy he almost went through the ceiling when he saw that. He let out a scream and kicked the shoe across the clubhouse."[20]

In a season when Emmett Ashford became the Major Leagues first black umpire, the Orioles won their first world title by sweeping the LA Dodgers, four games to none. Robinson homered twice in that Series. After winning 109 games in the regular season, the Orioles were heavy favorites over the New York Mets for their appearance in the 1969 World Series, too.

When the team was in the Big Apple for some of the games, Robinson and his autobiography coauthor Al Silverman of *Sport* magazine and their wives attended the play "Hello, Dolly." Other Orioles players were in the theater and at the end of the show, Pearl Bailey came out and began serenading them: "Hello, Frankie, hello, Frankie, it's so nice to have you Orioles in the house." Then Robinson, pitcher Jim Hardin, and outfielder Don Buford were invited onstage. Bailey joked with the players, and they sang and danced with her. When Robinson returned to his group, he said, "If I don't get a manager's job, I know I can make it in show business." Silverman was struck by the fact that six years before his ambition was realized, Robinson was already thinking about a post-playing career as a field leader.[21]

Just as Branch Rickey did not wake up one day and decide to integrate baseball the next by signing Jackie Robinson, Cleveland Indians general manager Phil Seghi did not wake up and decide, "Hey, I'm going to hire a black manager and be a pioneer." The idea of an African American manager in the big leagues had been discussed for years. Black players and newspaper supporters had talked about it for years. Names of likely candidates were bandied about in print. By the mid-1970s, the time seemed right. There was a surfeit of qualified candidates. It seemed a circumstance almost as much of who as when.

Robinson had pushed himself into the forefront of candidates not only by his stature as a superstar player, but also because he had trained for the job for five seasons running the Santurce ball club in Puerto Rico. In fact, he was the first black American manager in the Caribbean when he succeeded Earl Weaver in the post. Once Weaver became the manager of the Orioles he could not manage in winter ball and recommended that the team hire Robinson to replace him. Robinson won two pennants in five seasons in Puerto Rico.

In 1974, Silverman, as *Sport*'s editor, assigned a story on Robinson to writer Bill Libby, and Robinson made clear he felt it was time for baseball to move. "The time is not only here, but long overdue when a black man should have been made a Major League manager. More than one. They should be hired and fired just like anyone else. They should have their chance."

In 1964, while chowing down on the off-season banquet circuit, the late Elston Howard, an estimable catcher whose knowledge of the game was greatly respected, was asked if baseball would ever accommodate itself to a black manager and if he would want such a job. Howard, who was a coach with the Yankees and aspired to manage that team someday, expressed his desire clearly, predicting there would be an African American manager "relatively soon. Roy Campanella could have managed if he had not been hurt. Jackie Robinson could get a manager's job if he wanted it. I wouldn't hesitate. Baseball is my business."[22]

It is almost as if Frank Robinson had two completely separate baseball careers. He retired as a player so long ago that younger baseball fans do not even realize that he played, never mind played at a Hall of Fame level. They know him now as just one of the many managers in the majors, not as a pioneer. Even if they read about Robinson, teen-agers probably do not recognize that it is the very same Frank Robinson who through the 2006 season handled the Washington Nationals. Thirty years ago might as well be a 100 years ago for them.

LATER LIFE

Three decades after Jackie Robinson cracked baseball's color line as a player, the mood of society was very different for Frank Robinson making his debut writing out lineup cards for the Cleveland Indians. America of the mid-1970s had made much racial progress. Jackie Robinson absorbed amazing verbal abuse. For Frank Robinson, a more aware society would not tolerate the same kind of verbal epithets. The country was in a better place.

There is no way to precisely measure such a thing, but it is likely more Americans were rooting for Frank Robinson to succeed than were rooting for Jackie Robinson to succeed. If the stakes were critical for the future of the game and African Americans that Jackie Robinson succeed, they were high enough when Frank Robinson moved into a position of authority. He had to demonstrate he could handle the job so the next time a team wanted to hire a black manager there would be an antecedent of positive vibes, not the stigma of failure. Even if Frank Robinson was fired by the Indians—and every sportswriter and fan knew he eventually would be because all managers are—he had to succeed well enough for the next black manager to be given an opportunity. It was unlikely that once the dam was breached, there would be any going back, but no one wanted to see white owners handed an excuse not to hire more qualified African American candidates.

Probably the most light-hearted comment made about Robinson ever ascending to the position of manager was uttered by his wife Barbara. She said it in the context of Robinson's managerial skills of their then-two-year-old daughter Nichelle. When Robinson predicted he would be a manager the next year, Barbara said, "You? You can't even manage your own child."[23]

Once introduced as the Indians next manager, Robinson had months to prepare for his debut. Monte Irvin, one of the earliest black stars in the National League and then an assistant to baseball commissioner Bowie Kuhn, said he and Kuhn discussed Robinson's hire. "I told him I thought Frank would do a good job. I was delighted that Cleveland selected him and he did do a good job."[24]

Robinson's historic first day managing a game with a big-league ball club was played out against the so-so backdrop of a northern spring day. It was sunny, but the temperature was in the high thirties for the Indians season opener against the New York Yankees on April 8, 1975. Kuhn attended and so did Rachel Robinson, the widow of Jackie, who died three years previously and who in his final public appearance said he soon hoped to see a black manager in the game.

There were 55,000 paid witnesses to see just that and Robinson provided an extra treat by hitting a home run in his first at bat. "It's just tremendous," Robinson said after the game. "I really can't explain how I feel." The Indians won, 5–3. "I couldn't think of any better way to start my new career."[25]

The day before he managed that first game Robinson granted an interview in which he said he planned to manage only five years "if I last that long, then I'll get out." He said he would then spend the rest of his life with his wife and two kids. The fantasy playing out in his mind involved retirement from all work just shy of his forty-fifth birthday when he would saunter forth to have a good time viewing the Indianapolis 500 and Kentucky Derby and other pleasing spectacles. Robinson said the Baseball Hall of Fame had not requested his first lineup card quite yet and he joked that it would go to the highest bidder. "Do I hear fifty cents? A dollar. Here, take it for nothing."[26]

Once Robinson began managing, he was under a microscope, every move chronicled, every trend reported, every game examined by those who figured anything he did in the role was big news and by those rooting so hard for him to succeed as a symbol to his people. Robinson said he only wanted to be judged as a man, not a black man, in his introductory press conference, and by the job he did as manager. By that standard it was not the best year he ever had. The Indians finished 79–80, fourth in the American League East. Opening-day home-run aside, manager Robinson did not rely much on hitter Robinson. Robinson played in only forty-nine games. His playing days were winding down. The next season he appeared in just thirty-six games. Possibly due to his increased duties as a manager, Robinson retired just short of the milestones of 600 home runs (586) and 3,000 hits (2,943).

He did not cope with defeat managing any better than he had as a player. Maybe not as well. "Sure as hell harder as manager," he said. Robinson admitted to rookie mistakes, but seemed to retain his players' respect. "He doesn't pull any punches," said Buddy Bell, the team's third baseman. "But he's easy to play for. He lets us go out and play. If he sees something he'll correct you and nine times out of ten you deserve it."[27]

The Indians were marginally better in Robinson's second season, finishing 81–78, but in the midst of a 1977 campaign start of 26–31 that would end at 71–90, Robinson was fired. The dream did not last as long as he had hoped. However, Robinson's determination to be a man of leisure after a five-year stretch as Major League manager proved to be as fanciful as a Disney cartoon. In 1978, Robinson managed the Orioles AAA Rochester team in the International League. He returned to the majors with the San Francisco Giants in 1981 and ran that team until 1984.

He became the Orioles manager in 1988, a bad time in the team's history, and suffered through most of the club's 0–21 start. However, in 1989, Robinson's charges finished 87–75, a stunning one-year improvement of thirty-three-and-a-half games in the standings. Robinson was named American League manager of the year for his work.

After 1991, Robinson was out of managing until 2000. The Expos were losing money in Montreal and soon fizzled completely. Major League baseball took over the franchise and eventually moved it to Washington. Despite an uncertain team future, a disappearing fan base, and financial constraints while the sport essentially ran the team, Robinson presided over two straight 83–79 seasons in 2002 and 2003. When the 2006 season began, Robinson was starting his sixteenth season as a Major League manager and was still with the Expos/Nationals. His long-term future was unclear with a new stadium being built and a new management group poised to take over.

There were long gaps between Robinson's managerial tenures, but he was never far removed from the dugout. In 1982, Robinson was elected to the Hall of Fame, along with all-time home-run hitter Hank Aaron, both in their first year of eligibility. In August of that year in Cooperstown, New York, the ceremony was graced by the presence of Rachel Robinson, Jackie's widow, once more. And Frank Robinson directed some of his remarks to her. "Without Jackie, I don't know if that door would have been opened again for a long, long time. I know I couldn't have put up with what he put up with. If that door had not stayed open … I know that for many, many years it would have remained closed to us."[28]

Sometime after Frank Robinson spelled out his plan for a five-year managing career, he turned into a baseball lifer. Between his managerial gigs, he also served five years as assistant general manager of the Orioles, became baseball operations director of the Arizona Fall League, and worked for the commissioner's office. Wherever Robinson worked a pitch was thrown and a bat was swung.

Robinson barely let a bout with prostate cancer interfere with his baseball lifestyle. He was diagnosed in August of 1999, had surgery, and fought back. "Nothing I can do about it," Robinson said. "I can't say, 'Poof, get out of there.' " He spent two weeks in a hospital and then spoke out to focus men's minds on early detection with PSA exams.[29] He returned to Arizona for a second season. That was prelude to a new job in the commissioner's office—vice president of on-field operations—in 2000. That turned Robinson into the sport's king of discipline, the court of last resort, the nun with the ruler who swats wrists. The job also put Robinson at ground zero when the Expos situation expanded into a problem that outgrew its market and became a worry for the entire sport.

Robinson was initially hired as manager to bail out the Expos on a temporary basis while a relocation solution was found. He was supposed to head back to the commissioner's office after one season. Instead, it took several years to direct the Expos to Washington for the 2005 season and Robinson went along for the ride and the job while such strange things occurred as Montreal playing home games in San Juan, Puerto Rico.

Although Robinson left Cincinnati under bitter circumstances, the town never forgot him and his playing triumphs. Those with long memories might have recalled that after he was traded, Robinson still attended an off-season Cincinnati sports banquet and shed tears over his impending shipment to Baltimore. Robinson's number twenty jersey was retired in 1998. And in 2003 the Reds honored him with a statue raised at Crosley Terrace at their new Great American Ball Park. Robinson, who insists that it is not so when anyone uses the word "mellow" about him, was touched. He pumped his right fist and said, "You can come back home. I am home! That was ten wonderful years and I never, never, never, forget that."[30]

It was not revealed immediately, but all that Robinson accomplished after his trade from the Reds came close to never happening at all. Near the end of Robinson's first season with the Orioles, the team threw a swim party. There was a lot of goofing around and Robinson knew he was going to be tossed into the pool despite not knowing how to swim. So he jumped into the shallow end of the pool where the water was only a few feet deep. Robinson bounded up and down, and all of a sudden he slipped into the deep end, over his head.

"I went down a couple of times and kept yelling for help every time I surfaced," he said. "My wife thought I was kidding. And I guess everybody else did, too." However, once Robinson did not come up so quickly and teammate Andy Etchebarren noticed. "I thought he was kidding at first," said the catcher, "but then I decided to do something. When I reached Frank he was just off the bottom and couldn't move up." It took a few tries, but Etchebarren lifted Robinson out of the water, preventing the headline the star feared: "Robinson Drowns At Team Party."[31]

An incident like that would make any man reflective, and a few years later, near the end of his playing career, when Robinson temporarily seemed to have shelved his managerial ambitions, Robinson was asked how he wanted to be remembered. "I would like to be remembered as a man, an outstanding man, who was able in all aspects of life—period," he said. "Not just as a good baseball player … to be a winner. A lot of my teammates in Baltimore have said that I'm a winner. And I think that's one of the highest respects your teammates can pay you."[32]

Robinson was a winner as a player, but entering the 2006 season, one that shaped up with a likely Washington back-of-the-pack finish, his lifetime managing record was 994–1,085. However, in November of 2005, Robinson received one of the greatest awards of his life. And it was an award that measured his life as a whole, not merely as a baseball player. At the White House, President George W. Bush presented Robinson with the Presidential Medal of Freedom. "It doesn't get any better than this," Robinson said.

NOTES

1. Frank Robinson, pre-game Washington Nationals-Chicago Cubs news conference, May 16, 2006.

2. Dave Anderson, *New York Times*, September 26, 1974.

3. *New York Times*, October 4, 1974.

4. Joseph Durso, *New York Times*, October 4, 1974.

5. Gerald Eskenazi, *New York Times*, October 4, 1974.

6. Frank Robinson with Al Silverman, *My Life Is Baseball* (New York: Doubleday & Company, 1968 and 1975), 36.

7. Curt Flood with Richard Carter, *The Way It Is* (New York: Trident Press, 1971), 31.

8. Flood with Carter, *The Way It Is*, 29.

9. Flood with Carter, *The Way It Is*, 57.

10. Flood with Carter, *The Way It Is*, 62.

11. Flood with Carter, *The Way It Is*, 79.

12. Flood with Carter, *The Way It Is*, 82.

13. Flood with Carter, *The Way It Is*, 21.

14. Phil Jackman, *Baltimore Sun*, May 22, 1971.

15. Dave Hirshey, *New York Daily News*, October 4, 1974.

16. Robinson with Silverman, *My Life Is Baseball*, 135.

17. Robinson with Silverman, *My Life Is Baseball*, 156.

18. Robinson with Silverman, *My Life Is Baseball*, 155.

19. Robinson with Silverman, *My Life Is Baseball*, 182.

20. Robinson with Silverman, *My Life Is Baseball*, 199–200.

21. Robinson with Silverman, *My Life Is Baseball*, 227.

22. Arlene Howard with Ralph Wimbish, *Elston and Me: The Story of the First Black Yankee* (Columbia: University of Missouri Press, 2001), 125.

23. Robinson with Silverman, *My Life Is Baseball*, 16.

24. Monte Irvin with James A. Riley, *Nice Guys Finish First* (New York: Carroll & Graf Publishers, 1996), 209.

25. Associated Press, April 9, 1975.

26. Phil Pepe, *New York Daily News*, April 8, 1977.

27. Skip Myslenksi, *Philadelphia Inquirer*, August 3, 1975.

28. Dick Kaegel, *Sporting News*, August 9, 1982.
29. Ken Rosenthal, *Baltimore Sun*, August 30, 1999.
30. John Erardi, *Cincinnati Enquirer*, September 27, 2003.
31. *New York World Journal Tribune*, October 11, 1966.
32. Brad Pye Jr., *Black Sports*, July/August 1972.

Further Reading

Pye, Brad, Jr., *Black Sports* magazine, July/August, 1972.
Robinson, Frank, with Al Silverman, *My Life Is Baseball*. New York: Doubleday, 1968 and 1975.

BOB GIBSON

November 9, 1935–

At a time when there were few African American starting pitchers, Bob Gibson exceled as one of the acknowledged greats of his era. He commanded the national spotlight with dramatic World Series victories and compiled the lowest single-season earned run average in modern baseball history.

Gibson won 251 games in a seventeen-year Hall of Fame career with the St. Louis Cardinals, won twenty games five times in a season (done very rarely by black major leaguers even once), became a member of the elite 3,000-strikeout club by setting down 3,117 batters on strikes, and posted an earned run average of 1.12 for an entire season, an unthinkably low total.

☆　☆　☆

No pitcher threw like the St. Louis Cardinals Bob Gibson. When he completed his windup, and his right arm pointed toward the plate, unleashing the thunder that was his fastball, his body seemed to go all haywire. His follow through made it seem as if he was falling off the mound, plunging sideways, about to topple over. But that was not the reason at all. The man's power carried him away from the hill, but he was not going to fall because Gibson was always in control.

That style was one thing witnesses noticed about Gibson when he pitched, and over the course of his Major League career, they got used to it, even reveled in its uniqueness. Teammates, opposing players, fans, and sportswriters, all drank in the unusual technique, precarious in theory, overpowering in fact. The other thing they all noticed was his face, how hard-bitten, determined, and focused the pitcher's demeanor always was. There was not an ounce of humor in Gibson on the mound. Playfulness was an

Bob Gibson was the heart of the St. Louis pitching staff for seventeen seasons, from 1959 to 1975, winning 251 games and being elected to the Baseball Hall of Fame. Gibson was a flame-throwing fastball pitcher, who intimidated hitters with his speed and his famous scowl.

alien concept. Pitching was all business, all the time. There was no mercy shown to the batter and there were no light moments when it was time to pitch. There was a wall, an invisible shield, erected between Gibson and hitters, never penetrable, because he was always seeking the tiniest edge. Gibson wanted it that way; he wanted no friendships with other teams. Their batters were lined up to hit him, to embarrass him, and to steal his source of making a living, so he saw no point in buddying up. To Gibson, that would be pretense. When it counted, on the field, the guys in the other uniforms were the enemy. Bob Gibson never forgot that and he never let the batters who faced his 90 mph fastballs forget it either. Mostly, Gibson let his normal pitching do the talking, but he also felt that intimidation was a weapon in his repertoire. If the hitters on the other team were scared of him, if he fed doubts in their own ability to hit his best stuff, more the better. He made them even more nervous because they believed he would throw at them without provocation, or worse, hit them with a pitch if they provoked him. Everything about Gibson seemed to shout, "You're going down, mister," if a hitter was brazen enough to do anything he thought was out of order.

Some players can flip a switch, turning their game demeanor off and on. Gibson rarely did. To be successful, he knew what he had to ask of himself. It was not simply the athleticism that he came by as a youth, but the harnessing of the whole package to invent a winner. Gibson fiercely ached to be a winner, and he made himself into one of the most feared pitchers of his era. Subject to many of the same off-field racial incidents as his black contemporaries, Gibson rose above such treatment to excel. In a career that began in 1959 and ended in 1975, Gibson became the first truly great, long-tenured African American starting pitcher of the post–Jackie Robinson era.

Gibson did not tolerate slights stemming from his blackness. He glowered if challenged, verbally attacked if insulted. He was not only a proud man, but was also prepared to fight for his dignity in the sport he loved and in the world he lived. It was no accident that he became inordinately successful and was a cornerstone of the St. Louis franchise for so long. He willed it.

Not only was Gibson a Hall of Fame pitcher based on wins, losses, and longevity, but he also turned in what may have been the greatest one-season pitching performance of all time in 1968 when he recorded a 1.12 earned run average. He barely allowed one run per nine innings. That means over the course of the season almost no team hit Gibson at all. He was also a renowned clutch pitcher, his signature games occurring during the World Series when his team needed him the most.

Gibson carried himself like a warrior and his body language made it clear there was never going to be an easy at bat against him. Reggie Smith, an outstanding outfielder in the 1960s with the Boston Red Sox, and later as a teammate of Gibson's, intuitively understood that when he faced the hurler in the 1967 World Series. "The man was going to war when he pitched," Smith said.[1]

Gibson had cultivated such an intimidating image for so long, that years into his retirement, he felt compelled to explain to sportswriters that he was not really a mean guy. Headlines that read "Gibson Writes Off Nasty Image" and "Gibson Writes off Bad Image" appeared. But when he was pitching, Gibson did not mind personifying a don't-tread-on-me image.

"My arm usually hurt and my grimace might have been mistaken for a glare," Gibson said. "On top of that I didn't wear my glasses when I pitched and I couldn't see very well. I had to squint to get the signs from [catcher Tim] McCarver and that might have been a little unnerving to the guy standing sixty feet away. Of course, my antipathy for the batter might have shown through a little bit, too. The fact is, I didn't feel very charitable to him and his intentions at the plate."[2]

EARLY LIFE

Bob Gibson was born in Omaha, Nebraska, in 1935, and was raised as one of seven children by his mother, Victoria Gibson, a washerwoman. His father, Pack, died from tuberculosis before his son was born. Gibson grew into an athlete, standing six-foot-one and weighing 195 pounds as a player, but always loomed larger. However, as a youngster, Gibson suffered from a variety of health ailments. He had rickets, asthma, pneumonia, and hay fever, and did not at all resemble the robust adult he became. There were long stretches of his early childhood when Gibson could not even leave home.

Although he liked the sport, Gibson was less of a baseball player than basketball player in high school, where he averaged seventeen points a game. And he attended the hometown school of Creighton in Omaha on a basketball scholarship starting in 1953. Gibson did show enough baseball promise at the time, though, to be offered a pitching chance with the Kansas City Monarchs. But the Monarchs were nearing the end of their run and the Creighton educational opportunity looked better to Gibson. Even after Gibson signed a contract with the Cardinals organization in 1957, he kept his hand in basketball. Although it is a lesser known aspect of his professional sports career, Gibson did play for the Harlem Globetrotters, the world-famous touring basketball team, to supplement his income while still in the minors.

Gibson's elder brother Josh instilled a competitive attitude in him. And his high school basketball coach, Neal Mosser, at Omaha Tech, was color blind enough to play five black athletes on the floor at the same time well before it was deemed acceptable or something that would pass without notice.

Many years later, Gibson called Mosser "courageous" and said when five African Americans were introduced as the starters for a high school state semifinal game, fans in the gym were stunned. Gibson admired his coach for being bold enough to start five African Americans at a time when it was just not done and always remembered the crowd's reaction of complete silence when it occurred.[3]

Gibson played against future Boston Celtics great Tommy Heinsohn in college, and completed his eligibility at Creighton as the school's all-time leading scorer, a record that stood for six years, until another future NBA star, Paul Silas, broke it. After his college hoops career, Gibson was contacted by the then-Minneapolis Lakers about joining the franchise, but no contract was ever offered. Ironically, Gibson's college baseball coach was Bill Fitch, a man whose career drifted in the other direction and who many years later coached the Celtics to a world basketball championship.

Unlike so many other baseball future stars who flirted with numerous clubs, Gibson was not in great demand when he finished college. The only serious offer he received was from the Cardinals. At a time when untried high schoolers began commanding upfront payments of $50,000-plus in the first wave of what were termed bonus babies, Gibson's services brought $1,000 on the open market. The Globetrotters promised a $7,000 deal. It would have been easy for Gibson to ignore baseball. He managed to accept both basketball and baseball offers, however. Although he enjoyed handling the ball with his roommate, Meadowlark Lemon, the Globetrotters top showman, and was affronted by his minor league experiences with the Columbus, Georgia Foxes in the Sally League in the American South, Gibson evolved into a full-time baseball player, anyway. For a young black man in the 1950s, life in the South did not resemble a picnic.

"It was a world to which I was unaccustomed and I'm not talking about minor-league baseball," Gibson said. "In many southern towns it was still illegal in 1957 for blacks and whites to play checkers together, much less baseball. Columbus was a long way from the promised land of integration, and as a result, I restricted myself to the black side of town during the few weeks of my Georgia sentence."[4]

MAJOR LEAGUE CAREER

Gibson, who immediately earned the nickname "Hoot" in favor of cowboy actor Hoot Gibson, broke into the majors inauspiciously in 1959 with a 3–5 record and his presence was no more significant in 1960 when he finished 3–6. Gradually, he improved, and by 1963 was a key member of the St. Louis staff. Gibson, whose twenty-four-year-old, post-college start in the majors likely cost him entry to the 300-win club, won 251 big-league games.

Since Gibson spent four years in college and only one-and-a-half years in the minors, he was still a somewhat unfinished product when the Cardinals kept him around for those seasons of limited action. His fastball intrigued management, an attribute that cannot be taught, but comes more or less naturally. However, Gibson did not have ready-made savvy to achieve at the highest level and team managers at first used him only periodically. Still, when he reflected on the issue, Gibson said he thought his development came more rapidly being in a Major League clubhouse than it would have if he had apprenticed longer in the high minors, though it might have come faster yet if he had played in more games.

"You can't learn enough just sitting and looking," Gibson said. "Watching someone make mistakes can't keep you from making mistakes. I've been able to get a much better idea of what to do out there since I've gotten to pitch more. I could throw hard as far back as I can remember."[5]

In 1962, the *St. Louis Post-Dispatch* referred to Gibson as "the good-natured" pitcher.[6] That was unusual. Given his limited number of appearances (thirteen in 1959 with nine starts and twenty-seven in 1960 with a dozen starts), Gibson had not yet struck fear into the hearts of batters. By 1966, though, Gibson's blazing speed was the talk of the league.

"His fastball either sails or sinks, never comes in straight," said Tim McCarver, Gibson's main Cardinals catcher at that point in his career. Dick Groat, the Pittsburgh Pirates shortstop who was the 1960 National League Most Valuable Player, said Gibson made a believer out of him on a couple of occasions. "Twice I've thought he was the fastest pitcher I ever saw," Groat said of performances in 1962 and 1966.[7]

By 1963, Gibson was an eighteen-game winner for the Cards. In 1965 he won twenty games for the first time and in 1966 he won twenty-one. People mentioned Gibson in the same breath as Sandy Koufax as the top pitchers in the game. The refuse-to-lose attitude that infected Gibson's entire personality had something to do with notching win after win. He never took a pitch off, never let a batter off easily. Gibson also brooded over his losses. He took them hard, brought them home with him from the office, and dissected them. He was never a just-let-it-go type of guy. Defeats gnawed at him. You did not want to sidle up to Gibson in front of his locker and make small talk just for kicks after he lost a ballgame.

Bob Gibson put so much power into his throws that his motion
nearly had him falling off the mound every time the right-hander
fired his fastball to the plate. Gibson's 1.12 earned run average
in 1968 endured as the best since the early part of the twentieth
century.

"My teammates—and my wife and children, and even the St. Louis reporters—
knew better than to give me a hard time or even talk to me after a loss," Gibson said.
"Losing made me testy for two or three days, impatient to get back out there and make
up for last time. As soon as my mad wore off, it was time to get my game face on, which
made me grumpy all over again."

Gibson roomed with outfielder Curt Flood on the road and Gibson admitted he
could be a no-fun guy when his turn in the rotation approached. "The night before a
game I'd be so uptight I'd start shouting at the television. After a while, I'd figure Flood
was about to take a punch at me, so I'd leave the room late at night just to be alone and
walk around the city, wherever we were."[8]

Flood echoed Gibson's description of his growing irritability as his starting turn
approached. Flood said Gibson growled at everyone, teammates included, even during
ballgames. "The concentration process began for Bob Gibson the night before the game,
when he would withdraw to his own innermost recesses and snarl at anyone who disturbed him," Flood said. "During the game itself he was at us constantly. 'Get me some
runs, you miserable bastards,' he would mutter in the dugout."[9]

Flood and Gibson shared many similarities. They were black players who came through hard times on southern minor league teams. They were first-class ballplayers frequently selected for the All Star team. And they were both intelligent men who did not speak in cliches in interviews. Flood was an artist who also had the courage to challenge baseball's reserve clause in court, ultimately acting as a stepping stone to eliminate the sport's longstanding contract restriction. Gibson studied current events, and was outspoken about civil rights. But he did not promulgate a hippie, hug-everybody, I-love-the-world outlook from white Americans.

"Love?" Gibson said in a response to a newspaper question once. "No, love isn't the answer. If everybody went around loving everybody else, it would be a weird scene. Respect. That's the word. We must respect one another."[10]

An unlikely confluence of circumstances, teammates, and sport met in the clubhouse of the St. Louis Cardinals in the mid-1960s. America was undergoing upheaval. The civil rights movement was gaining steam, but the turbulence and violence in the South was a disease that often insinuated itself into other settings in other parts of the country. The discrimination was more overt in certain regions, but in subtler forms it was ever present. Despite being located in the center of the country, St. Louis possessed more southern than northern attitudes and was not generally viewed as a hospitable haven for African Americans. But the Cardinals became a symbol of unity for the community, an island of progressiveness, with blacks, whites, and Latin players meshing with a special chemistry to chase a world championship.

Black players like Gibson, Flood, and future Hall of Famer Lou Brock shared the limelight with a white southern catcher like McCarver, who grew up in Memphis and was raised to believe that blacks were inferior. McCarver and Gibson became good friends, and McCarver admits he learned a lot about getting along with different kinds of people by playing for the Cardinals and sharing competition, success, and camaraderie with Gibson.

The dream season of 1964 for St. Louis would have been an impossibility without the sad sack cooperation of the Philadelphia Phillies. Even with a week remaining in the season the Phils seemed to have a stranglehold on the pennant. But a September faltering became a dismal, final weeks collapse as the Phillies lost ten games in a row and the Cardinals squeaked past to win the National League pennant by one game. The World Series against the New York Yankees went the maximum seven games and Gibson was the winning pitcher in the seventh game. Three decades later, former *New York Times* Pulitzer Prize–winning reporter David Halberstam wrote a book about that team's magical ride and highlighted the special relationship between Gibson and McCarver. When the book was released in 1994, *Parade* magazine, the Sunday newspaper supplement read by millions, excerpted it and used the headline "We Were Teammates Because We Had to Be … But Could We Be Friends?" The story was accompanied by a photograph of McCarver and Gibson, then in their fifties, with Gibby's arm wrapped around McCarver's shoulder.

Gibson always resented the high-priced signees favored by management and McCarver was one of them, collecting $75,000 before he played a moment. McCarver was brought to the big club at eighteen and dropped into mixed company the likes of which he had never seen. The son of a policeman, McCarver, who gained even greater fame later in life as a broadcaster, was naive and out of his comfort zone. Gibson tested him immediately, asking for a sip of his soda. Would McCarver drink from the same can as a black man? McCarver told Gibson he would save him some. McCarver lived and learned. Gibson challenged McCarver and changed him.

Gibson credited Hall of Famer Stan Musial, All-Star third baseman Ken Boyer, and general manager Bing Devine, all of them white, for setting a tone on the early-1960s Cardinals that a racial divide would not be tolerated, and said they set the table for the atmosphere of the mid-1960s squad. The cooperative outlook prevailed straight through Gibson's career into the 1970s. Although many of the Cardinals stayed together and played together in harmony for several years, Gibson remembered the 1964 group as special beyond the field.[11]

St. Louis was a baseball-hungry city with a history of success, but the citizens were starved for a champion. The triumph represented the team's first pennant since 1946. The 1964 title represented a beginning, not an isolated accomplishment. The 1967 team was more harmonious, with a greater variety of people, and perhaps a better club with the addition of Orlando Cepeda coming over from the Giants and Roger Maris from the Yankees. If Gibson was still on the upswing in 1964 there was no doubt about his greatness or grit by 1967.

Just after the All-Star break in July, Gibson faced the Pirates. He was pitching a no-hitter into the fourth inning when another future Hall of Famer, Roberto Clemente, blasted a line drive off Gibson's right shin, knocking him down. He was slow to rise and trainer Bob Bauman rushed onto the field to check Gibson's condition. Bauman spritzed Gibson's leg with a healing spray. Gibson at first thought medical attention was being paid to the wrong spot. Then he looked down and saw an indentation in his leg, the size and shape of a baseball. Gibson told Bauman to put a little tape on it and let him resume pitching.

Gibson walked Willie Stargell, popped out Bill Mazeroski, and with a 3–2 count on Donn Clendenon, Gibson reared back for an extra fast fastball. Only when he landed on the leg, the pitcher fell to the ground. This time when help arrived, Gibson left the game.

"The fibula bone had snapped above the ankle," Gibson said. "I was taken to Jewish Hospital, my leg was put in a cast, and I was out of the pennant race for nearly eight weeks."[12]

Gibson had tried to pitch with a broken leg. That only enhanced his legend. Because of the long recuperation period, Gibson's regular-season record was only 13–7. However, he was healthy for the World Series. The Impossible Dream Boston Red Sox had gone from ninth place to first place in a season in one of the wildest, most exciting pennant races ever to win the American League title. Their star player Carl Yastrzemski led the league in home runs, RBIs, and batting average, to win the triple crown, and was voted the Most Valuable Player award. The Red Sox seemed like a team of destiny, zeroing in on their first World Series since 1918. It turned out that overcoming Bob Gibson's best stuff was their biggest obstacle.

Midway through the Series, Yaz was interviewed about Gibson and his focus. "I think he's the best pitcher I ever faced," he said. "I had the feeling it was just Gibson and me with 55,000 people looking on."[13]

Gibson did not try to make friends in the media after games, either. He cooperated with reporters, but not always with a smile.

"Yes, I would rather be left alone after games, but I know that answering questions is a necessary evil," Gibson said. "I know that I make guys mad sometimes, but I can't help it. When I'm out there pitching, I only have to concentrate on my work. But when it's over, I stand around answering the same questions over and over again. I get tired of it."[14]

Boston could not complete its miracle. Gibson brought home the prize for his team instead, winning three of the Cardinals four victories in the Series. The world championship belonged to St. Louis because Gibson bounced back from a broken leg to dominate the Red Sox. Gibson, as was obvious to onlookers, claimed the Most Valuable Player award for the Series.

The Cardinals clinched the title in Boston, but flew home to St. Louis to party. At a gathering some hours later, announcer Harry Caray dragged Gibson up to the microphone to say a few words to the celebrants. Gibson did not toot his own horn. "I'm just one guy on this great club. Give the other fellows the credit," he said.[15] With only four wins needed to clinch a Series, no pitcher has ever won more than three games. Gibson still shares that record.

In his talk, Gibson was not simply being diplomatic or modest. There was legitimacy to his sharing the wealth statement. Lou Brock batted .414 and stole seven bases in the Series. Roger Maris batted .385 and drove in seven runs. Gibson, who always prided himself on his capable hitting for a pitcher, poled a home run. There was much hilarity at the party, including the presentation of a $300 ham to manager Red Schoendienst by Missouri governor Warren Hearnes.

Schoendienst was a much-revered Hall of Fame second baseman who had terrific success as a manager, and who returned later as a coach for the Cards, too. In his half-century career in baseball, Schoendienst said of Gibson, "He had the greatest competitive spirit I ever saw. He was a tough guy who wanted to win more than anybody else in the game."[16]

Although Gibson told reporters he never intended to throw with a broken leg, and that he was not even in much pain until he collapsed off the mound, the incident helped flesh out a portrait of Gibson as a harder-than-nails guy who would sacrifice anything to win.

Gibson always contended that top black athletes lagged behind top white athletes in attention and endorsements despite their accomplishments. But elevating the Cardinals to the world championship and then claiming the *Sport* magazine Corvette for his showing kicked off a winter of rewards for Gibson, some on the national stage, some on the local level. His home city of Omaha declared a Bob Gibson Day and honored him. The powerful pitcher appeared on *To Tell the Truth* and shows hosted by comedian Joey Bishop and singer Pat Boone. Gibson even took an acting turn on an episode of a TV series called *Gentle Ben*. The off-season highlight, Gibson said, was being asked to a state dinner at the White House.

"I dropped everything, though, when President Johnson invited me in mid-November to the White House for a state dinner with Premier Sato Eisaku of Japan," Gibson said. "Vice President Hubert Humphrey, noticing that I was wearing a blue shirt under my tuxedo, as he was, commented that we were the only ones in the joint with any class."[17]

When Gibson arrived at spring training to start the 1968 season, he said a small batch of hate mail awaited him. The African American players on the team always received some, he said, but this time a sportswriter observed him reading and asked if he could print it. Gibson obliged, saying, "I didn't mind showing the world how ignorant some people could be." He was pleasantly surprised when 3,000 people wrote encouraging letters after the sportswriter's story ran.[18]

That was the prelude to Gibson's top season. His 1968 season was so extraordinary that four decades later historians and fans still marvel over it. It was a season declared "The Year of the Pitcher" by historians and among the pitchers having terrific years, Gibson was the most talked about in the National League. He was unhittable that season. His 1.12 earned run average was so unfathomable that it contributed to baseball officials altering the mound and seeking to even the contest with batters the next year.

Gibson's won-loss record of 22–9 was superb, but could have been much better with more run support. He threw thirteen shutouts that season, pitched more than 300 innings, and walked only sixty-two men while striking out 268. It was easily the best pitching season in the National League in more than forty years. Some of what Gibson accomplished was overshadowed because Detroit Tiger Denny McLain completed a season of 31–4. That marked the first time in thirty years anyone had won thirty games in a season. Nearly another forty years have passed without anyone else really coming close. Gibson and McLain are always remembered together for regular-season achievements and because the Cardinals and Tigers met in the 1968 World Series.

In the middle of the season, when the heat bore down from the sun and the heat flamed out of Gibson's right arm, he put together five straight shutouts. The zeros came to an end in an unlikely way—on a wild pitch in a game Gibson won against the Dodgers. He was chasing the record of six consecutive shutouts recorded by the Dodgers own Don Drysdale, who was the loser that day. Gibson ended up with a scoreless streak of 47 2/3 innings.

"It was a shame that I had to miss the doggone thing the way I did with a wild pitch," Gibson said. "But I don't care. We won. Pressure? Call it aggravation. There was more pressure on me when I was growing up as a kid."[19]

There was great anticipation for the 1968 World Series. The Cardinals were the defending champs and Gibson's 1967 Series domination was fresh in the minds of baseball fans. McLain's record was imprinted on their minds, as well. McLain was only twenty-four and Gibson was going on thirty-three at the time. McLain was the flavor of the month, a chatty, sometimes outrageous guy known for his love of drinking and having a good time, and a musician who was an excellent piano player. Some called him "Dennis The Menace," or "Mighty Mouth," but he earned his cockiness with the special, 30-win season. When a writer harkened back to the year before when Gibson outpitched the Red Sox, McLain declared, "Hell, I'm unbeatable, too! Maybe Gibson's worried about me."[20] McLain did his share, but the Cardinals should have worried more about the wild one's pitching partner, southpaw Mickey Lolich, who won three games, including the Series-deciding seventh game after the Tigers fell behind three games to one.

Gibson won the opener over McLain and struck out a World Series record seventeen batters. Lolich won the second game and Gibson captured the fourth game after a rain delay (he ate ice cream during the break) while hitting his second Series homer as a pitcher, something previously done only by Babe Ruth when he was throwing for the Red Sox. The Tigers tied the Series, setting up the seventh game matchup between Gibson and Lolich. On that day, Lolich was better. After the season, Gibson earned the National League Cy Young and Most Valuable Player awards.

Gibson's reputation was well established. Richie Ashburn, a Phillies star also on his way to the Hall of Fame, was another Nebraska native. He said there was never anything personal between him and Gibson, but he always felt Gibson threw with almost a hatred for him. "When the game started, I always had the feeling I was standing there as the Grand Dragon of the Ku Klux Klan. He was the toughest pitcher for me. Like Koufax and Marichal, Gibson dominated, but he did it longer and he did it with a vengeance that savaged the batters. His pitches were devastating." McCarver simply added, "I never saw anyone as compelled to win as Bob Gibson was. Gibson hated to lose, and because of that, he hated the competition. Hated them."[21]

Gibson proved he was willing to play with pain, but by 1969, age began afflicting his throwing arm. Koufax's career was famously cut short, forcing retirement at age thirty because of an arthritic elbow. Gibson's own arthritis was catching up with him and it was not clear how long he could go on. Bauman, the trainer, was aware of the problem. "There were times in the last couple of years you wouldn't have given two cents for Gibson's arm," he said. "He has the highest threshold of pain I've ever seen in an athlete."[22]

Gibson was on his way to a 20–13 season in 1969 when he made his second appearance at the White House. Because the All-Star game was held in Washington, D.C., President Richard Nixon hosted a player reception. Jackie Robinson, the first twentieth-century black ballplayer, was also in attendance—the first time Gibson met him—and the duo cornered Attorney General John Mitchell to discuss race relations in the United States. They decided Republicans had no viable plan to improve African American quality of life.

American race relations had improved over time, but unthinking whites still knowingly or carelessly insulted even the most famous black athletes in the country. Gibson told a story about how he was with Lou Brock in a hotel in Pittsburgh when a woman walked up to them, handed Brock her car keys, and asked him to put the vehicle in the garage for her. She assumed they operated the valet parking.

"I can sit here and laugh about it now," Gibson said sometime later, "but if it happened again I would get just as angry as I did the first time. It shows you how stupid people can be." Gibson said that even when he was dressed in a nice suit in hotel lobbies he was asked by older white women to bring their luggage up to their rooms, or to take them up in the elevator. At the time Gibson was making $125,000, and was a huge success in his field. A reporter asked how he could let small things get to him. "It's not small. It's a big thing. It happens every day of your life. It's one of the underlying reasons why you are not accepted and respected the same as everyone else. It's not to the point where I hate every white man I see, but I have to take a second look before I believe half of what he says is true."[23]

Gibson had at least one more super season left in him. In 1970, not only did he finish 23–7, but he also batted .303. It was the first recorded instance of a pitcher winning twenty games in a season while topping .300 in average. Most pitchers finish with averages closer to .030, or given that the American League employs the designated hitter rule, many are never even allowed to touch a bat.

A season later, Gibson achieved another on-field milestone, one he believed would forever elude him. Because he was a high fastball pitcher, Gibson never thought he would pitch a no-hitter, that some batter would always get a piece of a pitch. But during the 1971 season, he pulled it off, beating the Pirates, 11–0.

"This is the best game I've ever pitched—ever," a happy Gibson said afterward.[24] Gibson struck out ten batters and ended the game with a called third strike on Willie Stargell. Gibson and catcher Ted Simmons hugged on the field. For once, and perhaps the only time in his career, Gibson admitted being nervous as the innings passed and the zeros mounted. "You keep looking at the big scoreboard and see they don't have any hits," he said. Oddly, when Gibson was leaving his hotel for the ballpark that day, a little boy wearing a Cardinals jersey approached him and asked, "Are you going to shut out Pittsburgh tonight?" Gibson said, "Yes."[25] He was right and he did it in style.

LATER LIFE

Gibson was rapidly closing in on the end of his career when he passed 3,000 strikeouts in 1974. At the time Walter Johnson held the record with 3,508, though since then Nolan Ryan, Steve Carlton, and Roger Clemens have zoomed past the 4,000 mark. That was a last hurrah for Gibson, who retired after the 1975 season, with his arm, elbow, ankles, and knee worn out; his body let Gibson know it was time to go. On Labor Day, the Cardinals honored their premier pitcher with Bob Gibson Day and presented him a motor home.

Everyone knew Gibson was a future Hall of Famer and he did not have to wait very long to be inducted. He was elected in his first year of eligibility (a Nebraska congressman promptly read Gibson's deeds into the Congressional Record) and entered the Hall in Cooperstown in August of 1981.

In his acceptance speech in upstate New York, Gibson thanked family members, his first manager, the late Johnny Keane, who had enough faith to put him in the rotation in 1961 and told Gibson he was staying there no matter how hard he was hit, and Schoendienst, whom Gibson said would hardly ever take him out of games. "I want to be remembered as a person, a competitor, that gave one hundred percent every time I went out on the field," Gibson said.[26]

In an interview done in advance of the induction ceremony, a reporter asked Gibson which pitcher among the greats who starred while he played he would choose for one critical game. "Me!" Gibson proclaimed. It came off somewhat humorously, but there was no doubt Gibson meant it. Nor was there any reason to believe many would challenge the choice.[27]

In the years after his retirement, Gibson served as a coach for the Atlanta Braves, the New York Mets, and the Cardinals. He also did some broadcasting and worked on the American League executive office's staff. When his autobiography was released, Gibson did many interviews with sportswriters. A constant theme was how much he preferred to be seen as intense rather than mean, a pitcher who battled for his share of the plate, not one who was casual with his brushback pitches.

Gibson always fought for what he thought was right, whether that was on the baseball diamond or in life. All those childhood illnesses that made his mother fear for his survival just toughened him up. When his life came full circle in 2001, Gibson was dismayed with a diagnosis of prostate cancer, but knew how to fight back.

"I found out I had prostate cancer three years ago and I thought I was dead," Gibson told an audience in Springfield, Illinois, in 2004. Surgery and other treatment fixed him, but the disease also put him on the road as a guest speaker to push reluctant men to seek testing.[28]

Whenever Gibson speaks, talk turns to baseball and his Hall of Fame career. He has been consistent over the years highlighting the sweetest moments. Winning that seventh game over the Red Sox in 1967 is his greatest thrill, he said, but in a different way the entire season of 1968, with that unbelievable 1.12 earned run average, pushes to the forefront of his thoughts. "It was a once-in-a-lifetime year. I cherish that season."[29] In 1968, the pitching genius of Bob Gibson was on display for six straight months.

NOTES

1. Bob Gibson with Lonnie Wheeler, *Stranger to the Game: The Autobiography of Bob Gibson* (New York: Penguin Viking, 1994), ix.
2. Gibson with Wheeler, *Stranger to the Game*, 6.
3. Gibson with Wheeler, *Stranger to the Game*, 23.
4. Gibson with Wheeler, *Stranger to the Game*, 44–45.
5. Neal Russo, *St. Louis Post-Dispatch*, June 3, 1962.
6. Ibid.

7. *Pittsburgh Press*, "The Scoreboard," August 29, 1966.

8. Gibson with Wheeler, *Stranger to the Game*, 75–76.

9. Curt Flood with Richard Carter, *The Way It Is* (New York: Trident Press, 1971), 95–96.

10. Flood with Carter, *The Way It Is*, 75.

11. Gibson with Wheeler, *Stranger to the Game*, 83.

12. Gibson with Wheeler, *Stranger to the Game*, 135–136.

13. Brent Musberger, *Chicago American*, October 9, 1967.

14. Ibid.

15. Lowell Reidenbaugh, *Sporting News*, October 28, 1967.

16. Red Schoendienst, personal interview, November 6, 2005.

17. Gibson with Wheeler, *Stranger to the Game*, 151.

18. Gibson with Wheeler, *Stranger to the Game*, 151–152.

19. Neal Russo, *Sporting News*, July 13, 1968.

20. Lynn Hudson, *New York Daily News*, September 29, 1968.

21. Gibson with Wheeler, *Stranger to the Game*, 166–167.

22. Gibson with Wheeler, *Stranger to the Game*, 213.

23. George Kiseda, *Philadelphia Bulletin*, October 10, 1970.

24. Associated Press, August 16, 1971.

25. Neal Russo, *Sporting News*, August 28, 1971.

26. Bob Gibson, Hall of Fame induction speech, Baseball Hall of Fame library archives, August 2, 1981.

27. Hal Bock, Associated Press, August 2, 1981.

28. Don Trello, *Springfield State Journal Register*, September 17, 2004.

29. Associated Press, January 16, 1981.

Further Reading

Flood, Curt, with Richard Carter, *The Way It Is*. New York: Trident Press, 1971.

Gibson, Bob, with Lonnie Wheeler, *Stranger to the Game: The Autobiography of Bob Gibson*. New York: Penguin Viking, 1994.

CURT FLOOD

January 18, 1938–January 20, 1997

Curt Flood of the St. Louis Cardinals was renowned for sacrificing his own career to challenge Major League baseball's reserve clause binding players to teams indefinitely. Flood's case was the precursor to the dismantling of what was deemed to be an archaic system.

Flood was also an extraordinary player, who became a National League All Star, batted .293 for his fifteen-year Major League career between 1956 and 1971, and was regarded as a spectacular fielder who in 1966 played in 160 games without making an error.

☆　☆　☆

Curt Flood played center field with flair. He possessed the lithe athlete's body and speedy stride that reminded people of a deer. His glove was superb and he made the types of plays that few others could, patrolling the vast, empty pastures of the deepest section of Busch Stadium and other ballparks.

As a batter, Flood seemed too wiry to rely on home runs, but he did smack his double-figure share. He was a stroker, a hitter who peppered the outfield with line drives. The mix of his talents made him a valuable member of the St. Louis Cardinals for more than a decade.

Erudite, with many interests outside baseball—making him somewhat unusual in a clubhouse where education was sometimes at a premium—Flood was outspoken on issues, but enjoyed the time spent with his teammates and the socializing inherent while spending long summers with twenty-four other players.

To most who knew much about him, Flood was just another baseball player, an All Star, but not a dramatic boat-rocker. There was no advance evidence that he was someone who would put principle ahead of career. No one would have guessed that he was someone willing to make huge financial sacrifices to stick by his guns. Not many understood the Flood that churned inside. So when Flood challenged baseball in the courts for the right to stay with St. Louis rather than be traded to Philadelphia, fans, other ballplayers, sportswriters, and most of the known world, thought Flood had flipped and gone crazy.

Neither he nor his fellow players foresaw that when Flood refused to accept a trade from the Cardinals to the Phillies, his act of defiance would touch off an explosive chain of events. After Curt Flood, a century's worth of economic power held by owners would shift to players. After Curt Flood, baseball teams, players, rosters, loyalty, finances, and fan views would never be the same.

EARLY LIFE

Curt Flood was born in Houston, Texas, the youngest of six children. When he was two, his family moved to Oakland, California. The family was not well off. Between them, Flood's parents held four jobs at once, jobs he described as menial.

Young Curt Flood smiles after joining the St. Louis Cardinals. A gazelle-like outfielder for the Cardinals, Flood was an All-Star player, but was better known for taking on the baseball establishment when he sued to have the reserve clause overturned in contracts.

"We were not poor, but we had nothing," Flood said. "That is, we ate at regular intervals, but not much. We were not ragged."[1]

The family's spartan home was in the Oakland ghetto and Flood's perception was that many other families were worse off than his own. For that reason he never felt as if his own surroundings were shaped by poverty. There were no frills, but there was not plenty, either.

"Grits, beans, greens, and eked-out scraps of hog or fowl are now the basis of what is promoted as soul food at $6 a head," he said. "We called it midweek supper." Still, Flood said that the $2 Christmas tree his father purchased when the boy was a youngster was not disposable. "I think I must have been in my middle teens before I discovered that some folks buy new Christmas trees every year."[2]

One of the activities that Flood and his siblings used to amuse themselves with was drawing. In foreshadowing that would help define his life many years later, Flood realized he was pretty good at it.

He was also pretty good at baseball. He was the fastest kid in the neighborhood when there were foot races, and a coach named George Powles was a positive influence when Flood signed up for his first baseball team. Similarly, a junior high teacher named

Jim Chambers opened Flood's eyes to the world of art, harnessed some of his natural talent, and nurtured his creativity.

As a high school-aged baseball player, Flood teamed up with future Hall of Famer Frank Robinson and big-league star Vada Pinson to win American Legion championships. By the mid-1950s, all three of the outfielders were the property of the Cincinnati Reds.

In his prime as a major leaguer, Flood stood five-foot-nine and weighed 165 pounds. That did not make him a giant among sluggers. However, when he first examined his potential future in the game in a conversation with Powles, he was only five-seven and 140 pounds. Flood recognized that scouts looked for athletes with size and that he was small. He also realized that as an African American he probably had to be better than a similarly sized white player.[3]

After finishing high school, Flood did get that rare chance to play ball for pay. College was not in the cards because of the cost, and he decided that developing a career in art could wait. The Reds signed him for $4,000 and Flood joined the team in Tampa, Florida, for spring training in 1956. What he did not realize was that his true real-life education was just beginning, and not within the walls of any classroom.

It was possible for a youth who had grown up in California in the 1950s to be insulated from some of the worst racism of the period, to be aware of it more or less second hand, but not be victimized by it overtly. That changed the moment Flood stepped off the plane in Tampa. Racism was transformed from a that-happens-to-someone-else to in-your-face. Immediately, Flood noticed whites-only and colored-only water fountains. He mused that perhaps they meant club soda and Coca-Cola, but was not really fooled. Flood walked into a different world, one he had seen on television, read about, or heard about, but had not lived in. It was only the start. The Reds had mailed him a brochure showing the Floridian Hotel, where the team stayed. Yet at the hotel, Flood was escorted right out the door to a private home housing black players, including his old friend Frank Robinson. Flood said the realization of the discrimination made his knees knock.[4]

MAJOR LEAGUE CAREER

Although Flood made it into a handful of games for the Reds in 1956 (and 1957), he was only eighteen and considered to be in need of minor league seasoning. He may have devotedly worked on his batting stroke, but Flood's experiences in North Carolina and Savannah shaped a cynical outlook because of treatment away from the field.

In the first half of the twentieth century, before baseball was routinely televised, it seemed as if every town of any size operated its own minor league club. The modern minors consist of Class A up through AAA, but in the fifties the classifications ran all the way down through B, C, and D, for rank beginners. There was no Class F, presumably because it would be psychologically damaging to be sent to such a classification. It was not uncommon for teenagers with limited experience and who were not big-time bonus babies to start in Class D. Flood figured he lucked out. The Reds shipped him to High Point-Thomasville in the Class B Carolina League.

Pleased that the parent club regarded him highly enough for Class B, Flood was optimistic upon being farmed out and had visions of renting a nice apartment and having a productive summer. He sarcastically joked to himself that "substantial citizens would slap each other on the back, proud that good, old Curt had come to pay them a visit. I would have lunch with the mayor, dedicate the new library, endow an animal hospital, and give all the little children rides in my new Rolls-Royce. I was ready for High-Point Thomasville, but the two peckerwood communities were not ready for me."[5]

Fans in every stadium in the league called Flood "black bastard," "nigger," "eight-ball," and "jigaboo" from the stands. Most of Flood's teammates would not even talk to him. When the team bus stopped for food at restaurants, Flood was not allowed to eat with the club. He was forced to go to back doors.[6] The relentless negative pressure horrified Flood, alienated him from his fellow players, ate at his belly, and tormented his thoughts. "I used to break into tears as soon as I reached the safety of my room," he said. "I felt too young for the ordeal."[7]

Flood was angry most of the time. And he fought back on the field, where his talent provided a release. Flood had one squelching comeback. He could beat just about any-one with his baseball skills. He played with a fury and his statistics demonstrated just how much better he was than his belittling teammates. Flood may have been small of stature, but the others were small of mind and he made them seem smaller. Flood played everyday in the Carolina League, appearing in all 154 games. He batted .340 with 29 home runs, and scored 128 runs.

"Pride was my resource. I solved my problem by playing my guts out," he said. "I completely wiped out that peckerwood league."[8]

The next season, Flood was optioned by the Reds to Savannah in the South Atlantic League. Under Georgia law, a black man could not even dress in the same room as his white teammates. When Flood needed to eat out, the only place available to him "was the Jim Crow lunch room at the bus terminal." This was hardly a four-star establishment with Julia Child as resident chef. The food was greasy, of poor quality, and Flood was often concerned about just what he was ingesting. On road trips, Flood sat on the bus while his teammates ate at restaurants. One player, Buddy Gilbert, offering apologies for the world as it was, brought Flood meals on the bus.[9]

After a two-year tour of the American south, Flood wondered where the Reds might send him next. The answer fooled him. Cincinnati traded Flood to the St. Louis Cardinals, and in 1958 he became a Major League regular, playing in 121 games.

He also found a team he enjoyed. Until the Brooklyn Dodgers departed for Los Angeles and the New York Giants left for San Francisco, St. Louis was not only the southernmost team in the majors, but the westernmost. Many felt that St. Louis, in attitude, was not much different from the rest of the south. However, the Cardinals built something special. A team loaded with talent, but also with mature players who bridged original gaps between the races, St. Louis won big, won often, and became a family. Stan Musial, Tim McCarver, Bob Gibson, and Curt Flood, white and black, helped one another. Many of the players spent years together on the same roster through the late 1950s and the 1960s. The Cardinals were always contenders and in an era when there were no divisional playoffs, they won World Series championships in 1964 and 1967 and took the 1968 Series to seven games.

Gibson, the Hall of Fame pitcher, regarded Flood as his best friend. They were roommates on the road, often ate lunch together, shopped together, and talked together. Gibson admired Flood's wit and his braininess. They discussed the African American oriented writings of James Baldwin, yet were not above sharing practical jokes.

Once on the afternoon of a night game on a road trip to Philadelphia, Gibson and Flood were eating lunch in a small place across from the Warwick Hotel. Gibson was still wearing his sunglasses indoors and Flood whispered, "The guy in the next booth thinks you're Ray Charles." For the rest of the meal Gibson played the role of the blind singer. When it was time to pay the check, Flood helped Gibson find his wallet. Then Gibson let Flood lead him by the arm to the door. As they walked out, Gibson overheard one person in the nearby booth say, "See, I told you it was Ray Charles!"[10]

Flood flourished. He became a .300 hitter and in the sixties he won seven Gold Glove awards as the premier center fielder in the National League. He completed the entire 1966 season without making an error and once compiled a 226-game errorless streak. Flood participated in five All-Star games.

Flood improved as a hitter after coach Harry Walker suggested he record his history and impressions of pitchers. Flood's little black book contained notations about pitcher tendencies, rather than women's phone numbers. He played hurt, something that always gains the respect of teammates. He played with a sprained thumb, took a cortisone shot to play with a pulled leg muscle, another time tore a leg muscle by catching his cleats under a fence in spring training, but despite limping for three weeks, played most games. On another occasion, Flood cracked a toe, but did not miss a game.

"What a competitor!" said longtime Cardinals trainer Bob Bauman.[11]

Flood not only owned the vast open grounds of center field, but also batted .322 in 1961, .302 in 1963, .311 in 1964, .310 in 1965, .335 in 1967, and .301 in 1968. He was an integral member of the team, a star outfielder who was one of the keys to Cardinal success.

Flood married and after a while, giving free rein to his oil-painting urges, he and his wife Beverly opened an art gallery. The Floods moved to St. Louis sometime after a 1964 incident when a landlord sought to keep them from a rented home with threats in California. Flood had returned to his home area of Oakland and signed a home lease for a place fifteen miles away in Martinez. When the landlord realized he had rented the house to an African American, he reneged on the deal and threatened to keep Flood out at the point of a shotgun. The man and an accomplice actually stationed themselves at the end of the driveway and stated they would shoot any African American attempting to move in. Flood was backed up by the local sheriff's office and the courts.

In a life so frequently defined by negative racial attitudes, Flood felt he was part of something extraordinary with the Cardinals of 1967 and 1968. The United States was in the throes of racial turmoil at the time. The civil rights movement was front-page news in newspapers daily. Martin Luther King Jr. and other leaders were dragging America toward equality. College campuses were volatile. And a baseball team featuring white and black stars representing St. Louis was succeeding with harmony.

"The Cardinals of 1967 and 1968 must have been the most remarkable team in the history of baseball," Flood said. "I speak now of the team's social achievements, without which its pitching, batting and fielding would have been less triumphant than they were. The men of that team were as close to being free of racist poison as a diverse group of twentieth century Americans could possibly be. Few of them had been that way when they came to the Cardinals. But they changed."[12]

The California housing incident was long past and Flood was well established in St. Louis in 1969 when the Cardinals management informed him he had been traded to the Phillies. The Cardinals were not as tight as they had been, had dropped in the standings, and Flood hit .285. It was still a respectable average, but not what either he or the team was used to seeing etched next to his name in the season's final stats.

On October 8, Flood's life and career changed forever. He was at home, by then living alone after a divorce, contemplating his scheduled trip to Copenhagen in three days. His art-world contacts had told him he would love Europe and Flood had begun taking off-season trips. He was particularly fond of Denmark and had a vacation lined up.

When he picked up the phone, Flood heard the voice of Cardinals assistant general manager Jim Toomey. Toomey told him that he was being traded to the Phillies along with Tim McCarver, Joel Hoerner, and Byron Browne in exchange for Richie Allen, Cookie Rojas, and Jerry Johnson. The conversation was short and Flood said little. After sitting in a chair all day mulling over the news and his feelings both about being traded and leaving St. Louis, Flood resolved to refuse the deal. He not only would not report to Philadelphia, but was also determined not to accept the trade at all.

"At the age of thirty-one, and as a twelve-year veteran of the ballclub, he simply didn't want to go anywhere else," Gibson said.[13]

Gibson—and Flood—soon learned that not very many other people understood. Flood was happy in St. Louis and felt his employer should not be able to uproot him. If he worked in another field, he would not be shunted around. He wondered why baseball should be able to move him at will.

Yet all precedent, all signed contracts, and all courtroom proceedings had established that baseball did have that power. The player had no right to intervene in case of a trade. It was up to the team, the Cardinals, whether it wanted Flood's services or not. The Cardinals had complete freedom to transfer Flood's binding contract to another team of its choosing.

At the time Flood was in the middle of a baseball player's prime years. He was making $90,000 a year, a significant wage compared to most Americans, and even most ballplayers. Most observers believed he had nothing to gripe about. It was not the money but the principle that gnawed at Flood. Why should not the worker have more say in his future? Not only did Flood wish to stay in St. Louis and play for the Cardinals, but he was also irritated by the lack of freedom an American citizen in his profession enjoyed.

It was an option for Flood to retire at any time. That would void the trade. It would not do him much good because he did not want to retire; he desired to continue playing baseball. Others before him had been traded against their wills and after initial disappointment chose to report to new teams. Sometimes a raise was all it took to change minds.

Flood had been discriminated against, pushed around, cursed, mistreated, and bullied for much of his adult life in professional baseball. All that minor league abuse added up to a major league fuse being ignited.

If Flood had either played out his career in St. Louis without incident, or had chosen to retire rather than joining the Phillies, his career might only be a footnote in the game. He would be remembered as a prominent player of his time, though probably not of Hall of Fame caliber unless he ran up many more hits. At the least, he would be appreciated in St. Louis for helping the Cardinals win championships, and he would be admired among aficionados as a stylish fielder.

Instead, the steps Flood took to seek more rights for ballplayers make him a unique character in baseball annals, recalled for becoming the symbol of an economic struggle that prodded change in the way players and owners divvy up revenue and bargain over contracts.

At first, Flood told Cardinals management and newspaper reporters that he would retire rather than accept the trade. And then he hopped on a plane for Denmark, fulfilling his vacation plans. He relaxed, enjoyed himself, and investigated plans to open a restaurant in Copenhagen.

Meanwhile, Phillies general manager John Quinn tried to contact Flood. Ultimately, Quinn reached him upon his return to St. Louis. Quinn met Flood face-to-face to sell him on the Phillies and offered a $10,000 raise. A little later they also met in New York and shared drinks for four hours. Flood was favorably impressed, yet he was not appeased. At the same time he discussed the situation with Marvin Miller, the new executive director of the players' union.

Flood told Miller, a former negotiator for the United Mine Workers, that he wanted to sue baseball on constitutional grounds, to eliminate the reserve clause in all contracts that bound players to teams in perpetuity. Miller tried to talk him out of it, reminded Flood he would be persona non grata in baseball well after retirement, ruling out any type of coaching or managing career, and that such a court case might take years to resolve and cost him his salary along the way.

When Flood proved committed to going ahead, Miller invited him to address an executive board meeting of the players' association in San Juan, Puerto Rico. He was given ample time to state his case and to assure everyone that his idea was not just a negotiating ploy to wring more money out of the Phillies. He said he was going ahead, with or without the help of the association. The board voted 25–0 to support Flood and help with legal expenses.

Soon after, former Supreme Court Justice Arthur J. Goldberg—then just about the most famous lawyer in America—agreed to represent Flood. The filing of the suit to revamp the reserve clause set off a firestorm. Flood went on television and explained that he might be making $90,000 a year, but he was still "a slave. I don't think there is anything more damaging to a person's ego as a human being than to be traded, or bought and sold like a piece of property," he said.[14]

In 1922, Supreme Court Justice Oliver Wendell Holmes ruled that baseball was a sport, not a business, based on the premise that what the players did was not related to production. Holmes meant production, as in manufacturing production, but how a player performs on the diamond is almost always referred to as being his production with the bat or glove, or whether he is a "productive" player or not. Holmes' decision exempted baseball from antitrust law.

Publicly, baseball officialdom had clung to the reserve clause for decades under the protection of court rulings from antitrust legalities with the proclamation that the sport would devolve into chaos if players became free agents able to sign with the team of their choosing. This same argument was trotted out against Flood by American League President Joe Cronin, who said the reserve clause was part of the game and "it has stood the test of time."[15]

It was too soon to tell if it would stand the test of the court system. Flood's analogy to slavery did not resonate with some, but he was insistent on making the comparison. "A well-paid slave is nonetheless a slave," he said.[16]

Writing for the *St. Louis Post-Dispatch* in an article reprinted by the *Sporting News*, Cardinals scribe Bob Broeg dissected Flood's situation. "If the legality of the baseball reserve clause were being contested by a player less affluent than Curt Flood, the sympathy would be considerably greater," Broeg wrote. By asking for immediate release as a free agent and a $75,000 payment, or a $1 million-plus payment whenever the case was settled in the future, Broeg concluded, Flood made the suit a matter of principal rather than principle. "If principle were really involved in his legal assault on baseball's reserve clause as violating the federal anti-trust laws, Flood would have asked for $1 and the right to negotiate for himself." Yet Broeg admitted that the reserve clause did unjustly hold players back—ones who languished in a Major League team's minor-league system because they were owned by a team that had no room for them.[17]

Jim Murray, the *Los Angeles Times* sports columnist, had a different take on the matter. "The reserve clause, to be sure, is just another fancy word for slavery," Murray wrote. "The only thing it doesn't let the owners do is flog their help. You can't flee over the ice, there's no underground railway. All you can do is pick up your glove and hum spirituals.

You can wrap an old bandanna around your head and call the boss, 'Marse,' if you like. Lift that bat, chop that ball, git a little drunk and you land in sale.

"[The player] can be traded from one plantation to another, but only at the whim of the slaveowner or the overseer, otherwise known as the general manager, otherwise known as Simon Legree." Still, Murray foresaw removal of the reserve clause as promoting Major League anarchy and sinking the good ship baseball as players sold their services by the month or the inning. To prevent this disembowelment of the grand old game, he suggested an alternative—give players the right to veto any trade made against their will.[18] No one leapt forward to dance with Murray.

There was some behind-the-scenes maneuvering before Flood went to court. Flood had tried as a long-shot effort to bend Commissioner Bowie Kuhn to his way of thinking with a letter dated December 24, 1969. "After twelve years in the major leagues, I do not feel that I am a piece of property to be sold irrespective of my wishes," he wrote. "I believe that any system which produces that result violates my basic rights as a citizen and is inconsistent with the laws of the United States and the several States." "It is my desire to play baseball in 1970 and I am capable of playing. I have received a contract offer from the Philadelphia club, but I believe I have the right to consider offers from other clubs before making any decisions. I therefore request that you make known to all

Curt Flood was slightly built when he graduated from high school and first went into professional baseball, but bulked up during his prime as a .300 hitter.

Major League clubs my feelings in this matter, and advise them of my availability for the 1970 season."[19]

Kuhn was more likely to name a special contribution-to-baseball award after Flood. Instead of taking Flood's side and doing his bidding, Kuhn dispatched his chief assistant Monte Irvin to talk to Flood and try to avoid a messy court case. Years later, Irvin admitted that Flood's action initiated the free agency economic policies that have taken over baseball, but he did not believe, either at the time of the suit, or later, that Flood chose the right method.

"I tried to talk him out of going to Europe and into staying in baseball," Irvin said. "He's the reason why there became free agency. He started it all. He was going to make $100,000. I told him, 'Why don't you just go ahead and play for the Philllies? You can still have a lawyer and fight the case.' He was stubborn and stupid."[20]

Everyone from Miller to Irvin tried to talk Flood out of his commitment to carry the complaint through the courts. Everyone said he would be better off protesting in a way that would not jeopardize his career. Flood did not back down, went ahead with full knowledge of the potential consequences, and was determined to fight through the court system to the Supreme Court, if necessary.

Thus began Flood's time of anguish, a pariah in exile. A man without a career, he almost became a man without a country, as well. Flood's artistic career had gained some notoriety. In an ironic development, earlier in the same year he was traded, Flood painted a portrait of Cardinals owner August A. Busch Jr. Flood told reporters that the club chief liked the piece so much that he hired Flood to paint portraits of a dozen family members.

Flood had a special case made to hold and protect his paints and brushes on Cardinal road trips, saying that was an ideal time to get work done. "There's ample opportunity to paint on the road and I want to take advantage of it," Flood said. "I feel a lot of time is wasted in hotel rooms waiting for night games. I want to utllize these empty hours."[21]

Flood was particularly proud of a portrait he had painted of Martin Luther King Jr. after he was assassinated in 1968. It normally took Flood a month to paint a picture, but this one took him three. He gave the original to Coretta Scott King, King's widow, and a company printed a million copies of it on a calendar.

Once Flood filed suit, with no active baseball career, he had plenty of empty hours in front of him. Flood retained hope that he would be liberated in time for the next baseball season through an injunction sought from the U.S. District Court for the Southern District of New York. Judge Irving Ben Cooper presided and uttered such baseball bon mots as calling for "a seventh inning stretch" rather than a recess. After hearing arguments, Cooper said, "Now you have thrown the ball to me and I hope I don't muff it." Flood was not particularly amused. "My sense of humor was on the injury list," he said.[22]

Cooper refrained from issuing an injunction. On March 4, 1970, his order said there was no proper way for him to do so. Flood was benched from baseball by the judicial bench. The stress from the situation distracted Flood and his painting suffered. He was not even able to smoothly follow up on commissions, a handicap since he needed the income.

After a later hearing—Flood was cheered by the unsolicited appearance of Jackie Robinson and his support—Judge Cooper ruled that his courtroom was not the appropriate forum to determine the case. Cronin and National League President Chub Feeney both testified that the game would be ruined if Flood prevailed. Maverick owner Bill Veeck, who operated the Cleveland Indians, St. Louis Browns, and Chicago White Sox at various times and was considered a loose cannon by other owners, testified for Flood.

But Cooper said the only proper place for a decision was the Supreme Court. By then, Flood was living in Copenhagen, distancing himself from baseball, American newspapers, and as much as he could, the worry of his case. As he had been warned by Miller, the matter could take years to resolve and he lost out on substantial paydays.

Denmark stopped being a refuge, however, when Flood's business investments began courting bankruptcy. He was out of work in his chosen field, out of luck in his chosen retreat, and prospects were dim. Then, he received an overseas phone call that surprised him. Flood was informed that the Phillies had given up on him after his snub and that the Washington Senators had obtained negotiating rights. Soon after, Senators owner Robert Short telephoned and attempted to talk Flood into returning to the United States and playing ball for him in 1971.

Flood missed baseball and he fretted about his financial condition. The one thing that concerned him was making sure he could play again without jeopardizing his court case. If playing for Washington meant it was all wasted effort he would not play. Flood accepted the offer of a free plane ticket to New York to talk business with Short and while there sought out Goldberg for his opinion. At the time Goldberg was playing out a losing campaign for governor of New York, but he held a rendezvous with Flood and advised him that given the clearly documented damages suffered from sitting out the 1970 season as proof of his sincerity, there was really no reason why he could not suit up again.

It was tricky to even negotiate a contract, though. How could Flood sign a standard player contract at the same time that he was battling points contained in it on another front? It would be the height of hypocrisy for him to sign such a document and might demolish his own case. Instead, with legal advisors at his side, he drew up an alternative contract exempting him from provisions of the reserve clause. Short agreed to it and Flood was back in baseball. He was playing for the Senators at the same time that the justices down the street were deliberating his fate.

Professional athletes are always under pressure to perform. They must stay in peak condition, must stay mentally sharp, and must retain a stable equilibrium to succeed. While Flood thought he wanted to play baseball again, his year away from the game, consumed by the court case, appeared to erode his skills. Once a graceful fielder with great speed, once a skillful handler of the bat, Flood's instincts were out of kilter.

He came north from spring training with the Senators, but only played in thirteen games while batting a miniscule .200. Flood quit abruptly, leaving behind only a telegram of regret to Short citing mounting personal problems, fled to Spain, and terminated his Major League career. The second chance just did not work out.

"Neither his heart nor his reflexes served him in the tradition to which he was accustomed," Bob Gibson observed, "and he gave up the charade after about a dozen regrettable games."[23]

LATER LIFE

After this final flirtation as an outfielder, Flood became an expatriate. For five years he lived in Spain on the Island of Majorca. His painting developed and Flood gained the respect of critics. But his was an alternately peaceful and restless existence.

At last the decision of the Supreme Court was announced on June 18, 1972, in *Flood vs. Kuhn*. By a 5–3 vote, Flood lost. The reserve clause was technically upheld. However, the justices questioned the long-standing exemption from antitrust law and urged baseball to rewrite the reserve clause. On paper, that was the end, a baby step for players' rights and the ruination of one player's career. Flood disappeared from the spotlight—it was easy to do so in Europe.

But he had been a pathfinder. Rarely does revolution come overnight. In his case, Flood planted seeds of revolution rather than instigating one. It took others to add more floors to the platform he erected. In 1975, partially emboldened by Flood's efforts, pitchers Dave McNally of the Montreal Expos and Andy Messersmith of the Los Angeles Dodgers filed a grievance against the owners saying the reserve clause unfairly bound them to their teams. A federal arbitration panel presided over by Peter Seitz agreed and said the players who had played the entire preceding season with expired contracts were free to negotiate with all comers. That ended the owners' monopoly of players' lives based on retaining them perpetually through options.

"They received just about everything I was looking for," Flood said after the milestone ruling. "The only thing is, I was a little ahead of my time. I was right and the Supreme Court admitted I was, but they didn't want to take any action."[24]

Since then player-owner contracts have been collectively bargained, players have reaped a bonanza with multiyear free agency deals, and have established universal no-trade clauses based on time of service in the majors and with one team, as well as by negotiating private accommodations with their teams. Flood fought the establishment first, but reaped no tangible benefits.

One of the first prominent players to take advantage of the new landscape was Hall of Fame pitcher Jim "Catfish" Hunter, who was making $100,000 a year for the Oakland A's and signed a five-year, $3.75 million deal with the New York Yankees. The challenges did carry rewards.

Flood eventually returned to the United States and while maintaining an interest in art he also worked at a number of other jobs. Flood worked as a broadcaster for the Oakland A's during the 1978 season. In the early 1980s he worked for the city of Oakland developing sandlot baseball programs for kids. In 1981, Major League baseball went on strike over labor issues. Work stoppages were to become somewhat common in the ensuing years, but this one was very disruptive. Ron Bergman of the Oakland *Tribune* tracked Flood down and asked him to reminisce on his own strike of sorts years earlier.

"I'm very, very proud of what I did," Flood said. "Forget the money. Think of the dignity players have knowing that their contracts have a date to start and a date to end. I think I helped my colleagues a lot. They've paid their dues to get where they are." In 1989, Flood surfaced as the commissioner of the seventy-two-game season Senior Professional Baseball Association. "There will be no reserve clauses in the contracts," he said at the time. "There's life again in baseball after twenty years."[25]

Given that the league went belly-up rather quickly, there was not a great deal of time to savor the experience. Nor was there much time left for savoring anything, considering how young his own life would end.

Flood concluded his Major League baseball service with fifteen years credit and a lifetime batting average of .293. Once he was eligible after five years of retirement, his name was listed on the Baseball Hall of Fame ballot for fifteen years. Never did he come close to receiving the 75 percent of the vote necessary for election. Some, mindful of

Flood's fielding wizardry, thought his playing resume deserved the recognition. Some thought his actions as a pioneering player rights advocate made him worthy. But generally, the establishment does not embrace radicals very readily.

If fellow players were wary of joining his cause, speaking out on his behalf, or taking risks themselves when Flood filed his original protest and then the lawsuit, those who act as team representatives now, who work with the player's association, or monitor owner-player negotiations know the name Curt Flood.

If the tone of Flood's autobiography was at least cynical and arguably bitter in spots—and that is how some sportswriters saw him—he seemed mellow as his Major League days and the court case receded in the rearview mirror. Flood, a dashing man who was never large, contracted throat cancer in the 1990s and gradually shriveled from the ordeal. He was residing in Los Angeles when he died at the UCLA Medical Center on January 20, 1997—Martin Luther King Day. Flood was fifty-nine. Predictably, and inevitably, Flood's wrestling match with Major League baseball over the reserve clause was notably featured in obituaries. The sad occasion brought many of Flood's old teammates into the forefront, reminiscing more about what kind of man and player he was than dwelling on what type of freedom fighter he made.

"He was a sweet, warm-hearted fellow who always had time for a young player," said one-time Cardinals shortstop Dal Maxvill. "He was a heck of a ballplayer, an excellent center fielder and a consummate professional. I just hope people realize there was a lot more to Curt Flood than a guy who challenged a rule."

Maxvill said he still owned three portraits of his children that Flood painted for him and while he sometimes feared Flood was bitter because of the loss of his career, he really did not think it was true based on seeing him at old-timers games. "He was still the same friendly person, who always had a hug for everyone."[26]

Joe Torre, the manager of the New York Yankees, was a teammate of Flood's for a year, and knew him well. He said he too has a portrait of his daughter painted by Flood that he treasures. "Curt Flood was a very kind man," Torre said. "He was warm and sensitive, which may not coincide with the type of personality you'd expect if you simply read about his challenge to the game."[27]

Dan O'Neill, a sportswriter in St. Louis, supported Torre's assessment, noting that Flood was the first Major League player he ever met. O'Neill was eleven years old, taken with a group of kids by a priest to a Cardinals game in 1964 and led into the dugout and clubhouse. They stumbled upon a mostly naked Flood, wrapped in a towel on the trainer's table. Rather than being vexed by the intrusion, Flood made the kids welcome, chatting about school and baseball. "Thanks to Flood, it was a warm, positive experience, a memory I and those alongside, can cherish for a lifetime," O'Neill wrote.[28]

Yet for those who rushed to praise Flood's other positive traits, it still remained to be acknowledged that his suit against baseball was significant and important. At the time of Flood's death, team player representatives Tom Glavine and David Cone, two star pitchers, said in a statement that all players should remember Flood for the "profound impact of him on us."[29]

For all the rights won, Major League baseball and its players remain in a perpetual form of uneasy truce, essentially partners by a written collective bargaining contract that periodically expires. Fans of the game become enraged each time there is a work stoppage, or the threat of one. Congress' interest is piqued whenever there is a notable scandal, and muscle is flexed sometimes, such as on the occasion of steroid hearings in 2005. On January 21, 1997, the day after Flood died, members of Congress introduced bills attempting to completely eradicate baseball's remaining privileges under antitrust law. In the House, Rep. John Conyers (D-Michigan) introduced an act numbered to coincide with Flood's No. 21 Cardinals jersey number. In the Senate, Orrin Hatch (R-Utah) introduced a similar bill. The bill was entitled "The Curt Flood Act of 1997." "The hearts of baseball fans all over the country go out to Mr. Flood's family," Hatch said. "And let me suggest today that the time has come to finish what Curt Flood so courageously began."[30] There is much more balance in player-owner relations today, so much more revenue to split that both sides make fantastic sums. Officially, however, baseball still enjoys antitrust law protection.

About two months after Flood died, the cable television channel HBO aired a special about his life. Concurrent with its release, Flood's second wife Judy read some comments he wrote while he was dying that were reflections about the tumultuous lawsuit period in his life.

"I wanted to give every ballplayer the opportunity to be a human being," Flood said.[31]

During the long and often painful journey of his life, from the minor leagues to the major leagues, from discrimination to vindication, Curt Flood was a human being first. He just had to spend so much time and effort reminding others.

NOTES

1. Curt Flood with Richard Carter, *The Way It Is* (New York: Trident Press, 1970), 19.

2. Flood with Carter, *The Way It Is*, 21.

3. Flood with Carter, *The Way It Is*, 31–32.

4. Flood with Carter, *The Way It Is*, 34–35.

5. Flood with Carter, *The Way It Is*, 37.

6. Flood with Carter, *The Way It Is*, 38.

7. Geoffrey Ward and Ken Burns, *Baseball* (New York: Alfred A. Knopf, 1994), 339.

8. Flood with Carter, *The Way It Is*, 39.

9. Flood with Carter, *The Way It Is*, 43.

10. Bob Gibson with Lonnie Wheeler, *Stranger to the Game: The Autobiography of Bob Gibson* (New York: Viking Penguin, 1994), 220.

11. Baseball Hall of Fame Research Library Archives. *St. Louis Post-Dispatch*. (No date or byline in files)

12. Flood with Carter, *The Way It Is*, 86.

13. Gibson with Wheeler, *Stranger to the Game*, 218.

14. Lynn Hudson, *New York Daily News*, January 4, 1970.

15. Ibid.

16. Ibid.

17. Bob Broeg, *Sporting News*, February 7, 1970.

18. Jim Murray, *Sporting News*, February 7, 1970.

19. Flood with Carter, *The Way It Is*, 194–195.

20. Monte Irvin, personal interview, January 7, 2006.

21. Ed Rumill, *Christian Science Monitor*, June 14, 1969.

22. Flood with Carter, *The Way It Is*, 200.

23. Gibson with Wheeler, *Stranger to the Game*, 220.

24. *St. Louis Globe-Democrat*, May 26, 1982.

25. Baseball Hall of Fame Library Archives. St. Louis Globe-Democrat.

26. Dan Castellano, *Newark Star-Ledger*, January 22, 1997.

27. Ibid.

28. Dan O'Neill, *St. Louis Post-Dispatch*, January 24, 1997.
29. *USA Today*, January 21, 1997.
30. Orrin Hatch, *Congressional Record*, January 21, 1997.
31. Curt Flood/Judy Flood, March, 1997.

Further Reading

Broeg, Bob, *The Sporting News*, February 7, 1970.
Flood, Curt, with Richard Carter, *The Way It Is*. New York: Trident Press, 1971.
O'Neill, Dan, *St. Louis Post-Dispatch*, January 24, 1997.

HANK AARON

February 5, 1934–

Steadily, quietly, and with dignity, Hank Aaron emerged as a symbol of black pride as he pursued Babe Ruth's all-time home-run record. Aaron deflected messages of hate to assume the role of baseball's home-run king. He never forgot growing up in the south and starting his professional career in the Negro Leagues and has become an eloquent spokesman for African American issues in baseball.

Aaron played twenty-three Major League seasons, mostly with the Milwaukee and Atlanta Braves, compiling a .305 lifetime average stroking a record 755 home runs and driving in 2,297 runs. Aaron was a twenty-one-time All Star, who led the National League in homers four times while playing in 3,298 big-league games after a brief stay with the Indianapolis Clowns in black baseball.

☆ ☆ ☆

The most significant swat in Major League baseball history shot off of Hank Aaron's bat as a deep fly ball suspended against the night sky above Atlanta's Fulton County Stadium. But it landed as the linear descendent of every home run stroked in the Negro Leagues and as a punctuation mark to Jackie Robinson's smashing of the sport's color barrier.

It was a home run reviled and beloved, testimony to one man's steadiness and greatness, serving simultaneously as a symbol of the black ballplayer's twentieth-century steadiness and greatness. The 1–0 pitch from Los Angeles Dodgers southpaw Al Downing that Hank Aaron smote into the left-field home-team bullpen roughly 385 feet from home plate on April 8, 1974, represented an achievement previously thought impossible. It was the triumph of race over racism, and for Aaron was a personal step toward immortality.

The 715th home run of Aaron's lengthy and proud baseball career broke Babe Ruth's record for all-time home runs. The record that had lasted thirty-nine years was deemed unbreakable, and in a sport that relies more heavily on statistics to compare eras than other games was the most revered hitting accomplishment of them all. Babe Ruth, the most outsized, flamboyant great player of them all, was surpassed by Aaron, a soft-spoken, hardworking star for the Milwaukee and Atlanta Braves, who overcame poverty in his youth, racism early in his career, and the unrelenting glare of scrutiny later. Ruth was surpassed by a man who had begun his own baseball career in the Negro Leagues, a hope-giver organization that sent him into the world nurtured for the big time.

At the moment of Aaron's coronation as home-run king, it was impossible not to think back to the beginnings of African Americans in the major leagues. Less than thirty years had passed since Robinson's promotion to the Dodgers, and Aaron was a black man at the pinnacle of the sport feted from coast to coast. Still, as a reminder of the worst of times gone by, he was also someone disparaged by a vocal minority because of his skin color. If only briefly, Hank Aaron and Jackie Robinson (who had died two years before) intersected in a time warp. Aaron carried the cheers and admiration of black

A smiling Hank Aaron shows off the bat he did so much damage with. Aaron started his career with the Indianapolis Clowns of the Negro Leagues, but became the Major Leagues' all-time leading home-run hitter with 755.

Americans on his shoulders and trotted around the bases dodging the slings of racists. So much was similar to Robinson's quest as a pioneer. But also, so much was different because of the on-field achievements provided by Jackie Robinson, Roy Campanella, Willie Mays, Monte Irvin, and Aaron himself.

"It wasn't one of my better ones," Aaron said of the record-setting blast. "I hit it fairly good, though, and the wind helped to carry it." In the midst of the instant madness, with more than 52,000 fans providing a standing ovation, and a couple of teenagers sprinting onto the field and joining him on the record-setting jog, Aaron said he was focused. "I just wanted to make sure I touched them," he said of the bases.[1] He did. Hank Aaron was very good at touching all the bases.

Aaron had been chasing the ghost of Ruth, who died from throat cancer in 1948. Ruth was a giant among ballplayers, the type who commanded the spotlight and whose easy manner and innate joking capability made him a popular subject with the newsmen of his playing time between 1914 and 1935. He was a force of nature, and people were drawn to him because of his storytelling, ribaldry, and habit of puffing on big cigars and going on drinking binges. No one compared as a showman.

It took years of accomplishment for Aaron to outshine his contemporaries on the ballfield. Willie Mays and Mickey Mantle were complementary stars in New York.

Ted Williams was called the greatest pure hitter of all in Boston, and Stan Musial represented the entrenched aristocracy in the National League with the Cardinals. Hank Aaron played in Milwaukee, then Atlanta, away from major media centers. He was an All Star year after year, but only periodically led the league in anything. He was a quiet man, mostly interested in doing his job consistently and well and letting the results stand on their own.

In the end, Aaron eclipsed all of the best of those best when he blasted the home run for the ages directly into the glove of Braves relief pitcher Tom House just outside the fence, a teammate who delivered it Express Mail into Aaron's hands at home plate. The achievement was monumental by baseball standards and startling by societal standards—President Richard Nixon picked up the phone to call Aaron swifter than he ever had to chat with a Russian premier. The home run marked a key moment in the passage of the African American baseball player from All Star to icon. But it was no easier for Aaron to reach this moment in the spotlight than it had been for many of the earlier stars of black baseball to make names for themselves in the Negro Leagues. Aaron traveled at least as far.

EARLY LIFE

Henry Louis Aaron was born in 1934 in Mobile, Alabama, in one of the deepest pockets of the Deep South; though perhaps because of its location on the Gulf Coast, Mobile attracted a broader mix of people rather than just generations of ensconced Southerners. One of eight children, including brother Tommie, who also advanced to the major leagues, Aaron was raised by father Herbert, a boilermaker's assistant on the docks, and mother Estella, who supervised domestic tasks.

When Aaron was eight years old, the growing family moved to the outskirts of Mobile, to a village called Toulminville. With some help, the Aarons built their own new house, which, while sturdy, lacked amenities. Water was collected from a well, food was cooked on a wood stove, and the bathroom was an outhouse. The structure had no electricity and the only light came from kerosene lamps. Aaron wore hand-me-down clothes; meat on the menu was a rarity; and frequently the family dined on meals of beans, collard greens, and corn bread. Aaron said they never ate anything "store bought" and noted, "We were practically vegetarians before we heard of the word."[2]

The Mobile area was a hotbed of baseball. The south itself was better known for its high school and college football allegiances, a reputation well earned and perpetuated for decades. The University of Alabama team established a lengthy winning tradition before Paul "Bear" Bryant took over and raised the school's profile even higher. Baseball rates farther down the sports popularity chart. Mobile, where Satchel Paige grew up, was an exception. Willie McCovey, later a home-run hitting star with the San Francisco Giants, and Billy Williams of the Cubs, like the others a Hall of Famer, all got their start in the sport in Mobile.

"The black players eventually put Mobile on the baseball map," Aaron said, "but we weren't the only ones in town who took the game to heart. Mobile was one of the few places in the Deep South—maybe the only place—where baseball wasn't completely overshadowed by football." Mobile happened to be one of the cities where Major League teams just completing spring training played exhibition games on their way north to start the season. Aaron said that in 1928 his father had climbed a tree to watch a game and had seen Babe Ruth wallop a home run over the fence.[3]

When the greatest home-run hitter of all time began playing softball and baseball on the local playgrounds, his batting stance was incorrect. Aaron batted cross-handed.

A righty, he wrongly placed his left hand higher on the grip than his right hand. He also ran awkwardly, on his heels, and earned the name "Snowshoes."[4]

Aaron's other boyhood activities were playing marbles, roller skating, getting into fights with other boys, catching snakes, becoming a standout Boy Scout, and evolving into a devoted fan of Dick Tracy comics. He was not a particularly good student and did not apply himself to high school very much. By the time he was seventeen, Aaron was the shortstop for a local semipro baseball team named the Mobile Black Bears and was paid $10 a game.

Aaron was six feet tall and weighed a filled-out 180 pounds during his Major League years, but at eighteen in 1952, when he joined the Indianapolis Clowns, one of the leading clubs in Negro Leagues baseball, he was more slightly built. Although Jackie Robinson had integrated the majors five years earlier, many of the big-league ballclubs were slow to hire black players. Negro League teams had a little life left in them and for many African American players were still the best bet. Aaron was a teenager teaming with men. The Clowns were a distinctive franchise essentially because they still carried out a clowning tradition on the field. Indianapolis had two ex-players who traveled with the team to put on a show. The remainder of the players, Aaron included, were serious gamers, but indulged the fans in pregame warm-ups by playing shadow ball. This was a tried and true attention-getting formula with a long history in the Negro Leagues. The infielders would run through their paces scooping up grounders and throwing to the different bases—without using a real ball. It was as if Marcel Marceau had taken over at every position.

The Clowns were barnstormers, zipping around the country by bus to play exhibitions, and Aaron said the team never once stopped in the state of Indiana. The Clowns played and then traveled. Players slept on the bus, not in hotel rooms, and hardly ever stopped for a restaurant meal. Instead, they relied on portable groceries. On Saturday nights the Clowns got a weekly break for showering and laundering clothes and stayed in a hotel room. When the players went out on the town, Aaron joined them in the bars, but he needed better instruction in his drinking than playing habit, imbibing Scotch with milk and sugar.[5] He could have been the only player to develop cavities from his saloon habits and was lucky he did not endure next-day stomach aches from that concoction.

Whether traveling with a baseball team for backup or not, the United States circa 1952 was not a particularly warm place for a black man. The Clowns minimized their chances of encountering discrimination with their traveling habits and store-bought food, but incidents still occurred to remind the all-black team what majority white America thought. The Clowns ate breakfast at a Washington, D.C., restaurant, and afterward heard the sound of dishes being smashed in the kitchen. This was no accident, no dropping of a tray from a cleared table, but deliberate breakage. "What a horrible sound," Aaron said. "Even as a kid the irony of it hit me. Here we were in the capital of the land of freedom and equality, and they had to destroy the plates that had touched the forks that had been in the mouths of black men. If dogs had eaten off those plates, they'd have washed them."[6]

If the pace of integration among the sixteen Major League teams was not swift enough to satisfy many, there were indications many teams had wised up after being left behind in the original sweepstakes-like signings that stocked the best talent with the Dodgers and a few other teams. Aaron was courted by the Giants and then the Braves. The Braves, headquartered in Boston, but about to move to Milwaukee, won the talent scramble. Aaron spent less than a full season with the Clowns. It was midsummer when he signed with the Braves and was assigned to a Northern League farm club based in

Eau Claire, Wisconsin. Aaron's signing bonus was a cardboard suitcase and it held all his travel gear when he climbed the stairs for his first-ever plane ride. North Central Airlines, one of the legendary local air services of the Midwest during the second half of the twentieth century, hauled Aaron westward from Milwaukee on a two-engine plane that seemed to find every air pocket in the sky. "I'll never forget that plane," Aaron said. "It was the first flight of my life and the worst flight."[7]

There is no other way to describe Eau Claire of the early 1950s other than as white-bread Wisconsin. The Braves had sent black players there previously, so Aaron was not a trailblazer. But he said there was probably only one full-time African American resident of the community, so any Braves farmhands stood out like life preservers floating in a swimming pool. "Eau Claire was not a hateful place for a black person," Aaron said. "Nothing like the South. But we didn't exactly blend in. Wherever I went in Eau Claire I had the feeling that people were watching me, looking at me as though I were some kind of strange creature."[8]

Wes Covington, who later had a solid Major League career, was an Aaron teammate that season and the two young African Americans hung out together. Covington, a more outgoing personality, said Aaron was very content to spend his free time in peaceful pursuits. "Hank enjoyed quiet times," Covington said. "He'd bring a pocket radio with him on the road and just lay back and listen. Movies were always a big thing with Hank. He'd just sit there with his popcorn and be content. On game days Hank and some of the guys would bring fishing poles and just sit out there [nearby lake] fishing until it was time to get in uniform. Hank could get total relaxation out of things that other people would find boring."[9]

These habits and the style of young Hank Aaron noted by Covington are completely consistent with Aaron's later behavior. During his twenty-three-year Major League career Aaron rarely showed signs of being ruffled. He usually exhibited a calmness on the field and seemed perfectly content to stay out of the hubbub of the spotlight. If Aaron did not make news with his mouth or with any specific panache on the diamond, his statistics did not allow him to escape notice from reporters. In Eau Claire, Aaron batted .336 and was the Northern League rookie of the year.

Aaron was not outwardly demonstrative, yet he always seemed to have a sense of self. During that Northern League season, Covington observed how Aaron operated. He could take the razzing that came with being a slender, young, country-boy type, but when insulted, Aaron retaliated not overtly, but pointedly. Once, Covington said, a player seemed to laugh at Aaron. "Hank didn't do anything about it at the time," said Covington, who later was also a teammate of Aaron's with the Braves, "but he never ate with that fellow again. If somebody did something he didn't like, Hank would have nothing to do with them."[10]

In a way, young Hank Aaron had it easy in his first season of organized ball. He had a savvy friend in Covington, was basically accepted in the community where his team was based, and made an impression on the field. But the Braves did not feel Aaron was ready for the majors. In 1953, Aaron, joined by two other blacks, Felix Mantilla and Horace Garner, was sent to the Braves Class A team in Jacksonville. At the time Jacksonville was a member of the South Atlantic League, also known as the Sally League. The other teams in the league were located in Alabama, Georgia, and South Carolina. The Sally League was fifty years old that season and had never fielded a black player. Besides the Braves pioneers, Savannah hired two black players for the first time that season, as well.

The Braves housed all their minor league players at spring training at a military camp in Waycross, Georgia. The communal living arrangement offered game rooms and other services, and the players pretty much stayed away from town. On his first weekend there, however, Aaron got a haircut and missed a bus back to camp. He took a shortcut through some woods. Before he could get past the camp fence, the guard saw him. There was no "halt-who-goes-there" type of warning. "All he saw was a black kid sneaking up on the barracks," Aaron said. "So, without further ado, he opened fire." Bullets whizzed past Aaron's head, but he crawled to safety without being wounded.[11] When reminiscing, Aaron does not refer to his stay there as "good, old Waycross."

When Aaron, Mantilla, and Garner made their debut with the Jacksonville club, spectators shouted, "nigger," "burrhead," and "eight-ball." And those were home-team fans.[12] The flip side of the hostility was the wild embracing by black fans that helped league teams set attendance records. The African American players attracted African American supporters and had only to make a routine fielding play to gain considerable applause.

But the abuse was everpresent, and sometimes Aaron, Mantilla, and Garner gathered late at night and talked about the situation, exchanging stories about what transpired in various sections of the field that the others had not heard, or that everyone had heard. "Everything would be normal," Aaron said, "then it would get real quiet for a second, and out of the hush you'd hear something like 'Hey, nigger, why you running? There's no watermelon out there.' We had death threats in Montgomery. People would send us letters saying things like they were going to sit in the right-field stands with a rifle and shoot us during the game on a certain night. I don't recall ever feeling that our lives were in imminent danger, but we took nothing for granted."[13]

It was understood early that the black players would not take their meals with white teammates, and that they would not live in the same locations. Occasionally, white teammates might be heard disparaging the black guys, but Joe Andrews, a strong, white first baseman, stuck up for the trio, not only with teammates, but also with outsiders. Andrews knew that the black players could not defend themselves, even verbally, without causing a riot and risking their careers. So Andrews interceded often and said he was arrested at least three times that season "for arguing with people on Henry's behalf. It was amazing the way Henry and Horace and Felix could take it. I'd say, 'These sick Rebel suckers' and every now and then I'd wander over to the screen (the backstop) and see what I could do for 'em." Aaron later said, "Joe was our protector."[14]

Aaron may have been an inward-looking individual, but he never outwardly demonstrated a sense of bitterness toward Jacksonville. Two baseball things became clear during Aaron's one-year stint in the Sally League: his .362 average and 125 RBIs told people he was going places. And his thirty-six errors in the field told them it was not going to be as a second baseman. Aaron also met his future wife, Barbara Lucas, during the season. Lucas' brother Bill later became a major executive officer with the Braves.

MAJOR LEAGUE CAREER

In 1954, Hank Aaron was ready for the majors. The Braves relocated from Boston to Milwaukee and twenty-year-old Aaron relocated from Jacksonville to Milwaukee. Aaron had played winter ball in Puerto Rico and further sharpened his skills. Despite an advance buildup in the press, Aaron did not count on emerging from spring training with the big club. However, all the breaks went his way. He played well. One outfielder got injured and another was a contract holdout. Aaron became a starter right away and never gave up the job, eventually becoming an institution for the Braves in right field. He also wore the number five on his jersey initially. He made number forty-four famous a little while later.

Aaron was not a lonesome black player on the Braves. Holdout Jim Pendleton was there and so was center fielder Bill Bruton, an excellent player whose demeanor was much like Aaron's—reserved and serious. The Braves black players all called Aaron "Little Brother" since he was so young, but Aaron said, "Bruton was really my big brother."[15]

There had been a National League franchise in Boston for a half century when the Braves uprooted and moved to Milwaukee. Outside of the occasional upstart wooing by the Mexican League and limited other challenges, baseball had been stable since the turn of the century wars that established the American League. But in the first half of the 1950s clubs suffering in two-team markets hunted for new homes. The Philadelphia Athletics moved to Kansas City. The St. Louis Browns became the Baltimore Orioles. And the Braves moved to Milwaukee in 1953. This match produced one of baseball's memorable love affairs. Milwaukee had been home to an AAA minor league team and craved an association with a Major League ballclub. The city adopted the players and showered them with affection. Rookie Aaron walked right into a delirious reception at a time when the team could do no wrong. The party was still raging.

The Braves drew 2.1 million fans in 1954. The team featured Hall of Famer Warren Spahn on the mound and the power hitting of third baseman Eddie Mathews. In a town that knew its players well, Aaron suggested he could still walk to the ballpark unrecognized. But that could not have lasted long. Aaron hit 13 home runs, drove in 69 runs, and batted .280 in his rookie year. He played in 122 games, but missed the last three weeks of the season with a broken ankle. His initial season promised much more.

What disturbed Aaron that first year in the majors was what would be called casual racism now. Aaron did not have a natural sprinter's gait on the base paths, so sometimes it did not look as if he was running all out, and he did not hurry off the field, so it sometimes appeared that he was shuffling. Aaron resented the way he was portrayed in the media. Because he was black and from Alabama, he felt writers were quick to stereotype him, wonder about his intelligence, and suggest he hadn't quite taken the full step into the twentieth century.[16]

Mathews, like Aaron a future Hall of Famer, said black and white players mainly mingled while traveling on the train. They shared beers in a lounge area, although the black guys could not eat in the dining room. From the vantage point of maturity and age, an older Mathews said they all seemed naive, and he regretted not having stood up more forcefully for black players' rights. "It was rough on the black players," Mathews said. "We all knew it was ridiculous. I realize I should have done more about it than I did—we all should have. I wish I had been more indignant for our black players, but I had no idea how to approach something like that."[17]

What the best African American players did to answer insults was to play ever harder and produce ever grander results. Aaron had been an afterthought member of the roster originally during his rookie year, but his 1954 showing heralded good things. In 1955, they were great things. In his second season with the Braves, Aaron cracked 27 home runs, drove in 106 runs, and batted .314, All-Star numbers. The season marked Aaron's emergence as a special player. That was also the first season Aaron wore number forty-four. It truly was a magic number for him.

By 1956, new Braves manager Fred Haney was comparing Aaron favorably with Hall of Famer Rogers Hornsby. Hornsby retired with a .358 lifetime batting average and

With a powerful swing, Hank Aaron swats his record-breaking 715th home run on April 8, 1974, in Atlanta, surpassing Babe Ruth's career mark.

thrice hit over .400, including an incredible .424 in 1924. "Aaron is more like Hornsby than any other hitter I ever saw," Haney said. "And Rogers Hornsby was the greatest right-handed hitter I ever saw." What Haney liked was Aaron's all-around batting talent of hitting the ball to the opposite field, snapping his wrists in a blur of quickness to stroke a home run, and being patient at the plate.[18] The comparison to Hornsby was not casually made by the old-timer. It was a major league compliment for any major leaguer. In the end—years down the line—Hornsby proved better at hitting for high average, and Aaron proved better at hitting for power.

During the next season, 1956, Aaron increased his national profile by leading the National League in batting with a .328 average. His power statistics were good with 26 homers and 92 RBIs, but he collected 200 hits for the first time. In 1957, the fanatical Braves fans were rewarded with a pennant, and Aaron recorded a Most Valuable Player season. He crushed 44 home runs, equaling his uniform number, leading the league, and led the league in RBIs with 132 while batting .322. What amazed some was that Aaron was still only twenty-three.

Charlie Grimm, who was mostly associated with the Cubs during his half century in baseball, was the Braves manager when Aaron cracked the roster and foresaw much of what the player would become. "He's one in a thousand," Grimm said. "You can't make a Willie Mays out of him. He's not that spectacular. He does things his own way. But he'll probably be around a long time after Willie's gone. He was crude when he first came up, but it took only a little time to develop the polish."[19]

In an interview during the 1956 season, nearly two decades before Aaron would be crowned the all-time home-run champ, he was asked about his baseball ambitions. Home runs were less on his mind than hitting for average. "I guess the thing I would most rather do of all," Aaron said, "I'd rather hit .400. A lot of guys are hitting forty homers nowadays, but nobody is hitting .400 since Ted Williams a long time ago."[20] Nobody has equaled Williams since, either. But then, nobody has matched Aaron.

Grimm was correct about Aaron outlasting Mays on the field. Mays retired in 1973, Aaron in 1976. Aaron also stayed healthier and more productive for longer than just about any other baseball player. When Aaron stopped hitting he owned Major League records for most games played (3,298), plate appearances, including nonofficial appearances (13,940), official at bats (12,364), runs batted in (2,297), home runs (755), and other lesser batting marks. Aaron also set the National League record for runs scored (2,107, while accumulating 2,174 in all), had 3,771 hits (behind only Pete Rose and Ty Cobb), and batted .305. He was not the second coming of Rogers Hornsby, but the first coming of Hank Aaron.

Aaron won a second batting title by hitting .355 in 1959 and captured two more RBI titles. He hit a personal season's high of 47 homers in 1971, but hit over 40 homers eight times in all. Aaron's hallmark was All-Star consistency for more than two decades. He only sometimes had the most in a given year, but he had a lot of everything year after year. He was always there, always doing his job, and always compiling consistent numbers. But he did not hit more than 50 home runs, and he did not challenge either Ruth's 60-home-run record or Roger Maris' 61 once Maris bested the Babe in 1961. It is likely that Aaron's national renown would have mushroomed if he hit 59 home runs one year. It is likely that if he had stroked 175 RBIs one year in pursuit of Hack Wilson's record 191, he would have had a bigger following. During some of the time that he was battering the ball, Aaron was better known as Hank. Some of the time he was better known as Henry. His complicity in softening so many hardballs led others to call him "Bad Henry" as a nickname.

Similarly, Aaron did not make waves with contract holdouts. He did not utter controversial phrases. Unlike Jackie Robinson, who after his retirement became a well-known figure working for the NAACP, Aaron did not campaign for civil rights publicly while he played. In the modern age of hype, it has been suggested that Aaron would have been a far more appreciated ballplayer in his prime if he played in New York rather than Milwaukee. But Aaron was not eager to live in New York, and his personality was better suited to comfortable Milwaukee and Atlanta. What is misunderstood is that while Aaron was not marching in the streets for civil rights progress, in his own way he took many strong stands during his playing days. He did not call press conferences in New York, but made his case in the black press. He tackled the issue closest to him and something which had dragged on a long time bothering black players. Nearly a decade into his career, Aaron and other African American players were still forced into substandard living arrangements in southern spring training quarters.

Wendell Smith, the energetic African American sportswriter who received Baseball Hall of Fame recognition for his work, campaigned vigorously to overturn this embarrassing policy. In 1961, one of his pieces quoted Aaron's thoughts on the issue. "I'm sick and tired of being shoved into rooming houses and forced to eat in second-class restaurants," Aaron said. "If I'm a big leaguer, I want to live like one." That is neither a meek response, nor the voice of someone ducking an issue.[21] Many years later during the home-run-record pursuit, with reporters surrounding him daily, Aaron was asked why he was suddenly taking more forceful stands on civil rights issues. Aaron replied that he was just being listened to more.

At one time some critics thought that Aaron the young slugger swung at too many pitches outside the strike zone. Over the years Aaron proved he could swing at any pitch he liked and deposit it on the other side of the outfield wall. If Aaron swung at a pitch, low, high, or right over the middle, he was sure he could hit it. With thousands of at bats in his Major League career, Aaron had pretty much eliminated guesswork from his repertoire. He had seen it all, and even the best pitchers' efforts were subject to his scientific review.

Ron Perranoski, an outstanding Los Angeles Dodgers relief pitcher, was about to give up on the notion of ever getting Aaron out, and since he had faced Aaron over six seasons and been hit to the tune of an .812 average, it was not hard to see why. "He not only knows what the pitch will be," Perranoski said, "but where it will be. He hit one home run off me and he went after that pitch as if he'd called for it." One of Aaron's teammates, catcher-outfielder Gene Oliver, said Aaron was so good that he reversed the natural process in hitter-pitcher confrontations. "Pitchers don't set Henry up," Oliver said. "He sets them up. I honestly believe he intentionally looks bad on a certain pitch just so he'll get it again." Aaron was asked if that was true. "Well, not too often," Aaron replied.[22]

Aaron said he knew many opponents thought he practically fell asleep at the plate and that he couldn't run very fast. He said it was all deceptive. "I have the speed to shift gears," Aaron said.[23] That was probably also true at the plate. He was renowned for being able to get the bat around quickly to tatoo a fastball that looked too fast and was already past him. Even Hall of Famer Sandy Koufax said going one-on-one with Aaron exasperated him. "He's the last guy I want to see coming up there. Some guys give me more trouble one year than another. But Aaron is always the same. He's just Bad Henry."[24]

Even in the mid-1960s, as a far more visible and better known star in the National League than he had been during Sally League days, race reared up. "They don't give me a bad time because I'm somebody special," Aaron said of certain circumstances where he was accepted while other blacks wouldn't have been. "But that doesn't help my brothers and sisters, and anything that happens to any member of my race happens to me. I know how it feels because sometimes people don't know who I am. The South doesn't have any monopoly on prejudice. At least the people in Mississippi have the guts to tell you they don't like you and you know what to expect. But in the North they do it differently. I went into a restaurant in New York City one afternoon and they wouldn't serve me. They didn't say they wouldn't, they just left me sitting there."[25]

Season after season Aaron recorded All-Star numbers, but virtually no one talked about how someday he might catch Babe Ruth. Even teammates who loved his game-winning hits and his ability to take over a game in a variety of ways did not see the challenge coming. "I never dreamed he would hit a bunch of home runs because that wasn't the type of hitter he was," said Warren Spahn. "Henry was the type of hitter who would use the whole field. I always felt some year Hank Aaron would hit .400."[26]

The Braves never had more success on the field with Aaron in the lineup than they did in 1957 and 1958. Milwaukee won the 1957 World Series, four games to three over the New York Yankees and returned to the Series in 1958, though they lost to the same Yankees four games to three that time. Aaron was the Most Valuable Player in the 1957 event, hitting .393 with three homers. Aaron called 1957 "the best year of my baseball life, and it went along with the best year of baseball that any city ever had. It doesn't get any better than Milwaukee in 1957."[27] After the celebrations ended in the beer capital of the universe, Aaron was summoned to Mobile. His old hometown threw a "Hank Aaron Day." Aaron was presented the key to the city, and while such gifts are commonplace enough for big-time athletes, this had special meaning to him. He—and his supporters— recognized the significance. "I don't know it for a fact," Aaron said, "but I expect that I was the first black person to get the key to Mobile. It might seem like nothing more than a token, but believe me, that was a proud day for all the black people of Mobile."[28]

In the early 1960s, Aaron was joined on the Braves by his brother Tommie. Tommie Aaron was not the ballplayer his elder brother was. He played parts of seven seasons, but hit only .229. Hank Aaron called his brother a good roommate, except for the time the air conditioner exploded in their hotel room after little brother played around with the dials. Tommie Aaron was a successful manager in the Braves system, but died at age forty-five from leukemia without a chance to manage in the majors.

Sports fans and sportswriters love to make comparisons. Phrases like "He's the best quarterback since Joe Montana," or "He's the best scorer since Michael Jordan" creep into print regularly. It is no different in baseball. Best of all from the observer stand-point is if two greats are playing at the same time. Then the discussion revolves around, "Who's best now?" During the 1950s, New York had three Major League baseball teams and each of the teams had an outstanding center fielder. Mickey Mantle patrolled Yankee Stadium for the Yanks. Duke Snider covered the field for the Dodgers in Ebbets Field, and Willie Mays galloped around the wide expanses of the Polo Grounds for the Giants. The New York newspapers rode the "Who's best?" theme into the ground. To a lesser degree, but periodically brought up was "Who's better, Willie Mays or Hank Aaron?" Usually the answer was Mays. But with the passage of many years, twenty-twenty hind-sight, and a look at the historical record, there are many more voters for Aaron.

The case actually goes back to Charlie Grimm's half-century-old statement that Aaron would never be as spectacular as Mays. That was accurate. Mays seemed to run faster and he was always losing his cap in the effort. Aaron ran fast enough. Mays made flashier catches. But Aaron made all the catches he should have. Aaron hit more home runs, batted higher, drove in more runs, and played in more games. Mathews, another great slugger of the era, and a Hall of Fame third baseman, had a strong opinion on the Mays-Aaron scenario. "Willie Mays, in my opinion, wasn't as good a player as Hank Aaron," Mathews said. "But whenever Willie did something, the New York press and the skies lit up. I just felt that Hank was a touch better than Willie. Hank was a complete ballplayer. He never threw to the wrong base. He never missed the cutoff man. I'll bet you in a footrace Hank would have beaten Willie. It was hard to explain with Henry, but he could hit full speed in three steps and look like he wasn't even running."[29]

For the most part, Aaron dodged controversy, something much easier to do in Milwaukee than in New York. He was from the Teddy Roosevelt school of carrying a big stick and letting it do the emphasizing. Still, Warren Spahn sensed that Aaron was in part driven by Mays. "I think he wanted to be a better all-around player than Willie Mays," the old southpaw said.[30] Nothing changed for Aaron in the way of national atten-tion when the Braves abandoned Milwaukee for Atlanta after the 1965 season. At the time Atlanta was no more of a media Mecca than Milwaukee.

It would have been easier for Aaron to prove his case if he were flashier, or if he shouted about his stature with cockiness. But that was not Aaron's way. Even sportswriter Lonnie Wheeler, the coauthor of Aaron's autobiography, speculated about how the low-key nature of his personality restrained Aaron's fame. "Perhaps it was Aaron's lack of charisma," he wrote. "His reticence, the unassuming way he carried himself. Perhaps it was his playing in Milwaukee. Perhaps it was his walk. It was odd that Joe DiMaggio was also quiet and deliberate and yet in DiMaggio's case these traits were perceived as dignity and grace, which translated into American heroism. In Aaron's case, these traits translated into comparative invisibility."[31]

In the early 1970s, when it became apparent that Bad Henry had the staying power of Methuselah and was closing in on Babe Ruth's lifetime home-run record, lack of invisibility would become more of a curse. In a perfect world, Aaron's chase would have been pure and wonderful, the culmination of a long and terrific career, greeted by baseball enthusiasts with pleasure and support. In reality, one of the greatest moments in baseball history was far more complicated, with far less joy than relief attached to it.

In 1967, a *New York Times* columnist wrote of Aaron, "Aaron has long been one of the most overlooked superstars. His quiet competence over the years has lit few lights, started no pyrotechnic displays, and provoked no emotional outbursts."[32] With the advent of the 1973 baseball season that changed. Everything stated in the *Times* was true when it was written. By the end of that season the opposite had become truth.

An indefinable sort of public reassessment of Aaron had been building for a few years by the time he climbed within swinging distance of Ruth's career home-run record. By 1969, fans who had never rated Aaron so highly gave him standing ovations. It happened in Montreal when Aaron was introduced in French. It happened at home in Atlanta when Aaron hit critical home runs. Mickey Mantle said Aaron was the most underrated great hitter of all time. Clete Boyer, who played with Mantle, and then with Aaron, said public applause was starting to "get like it was for Mickey. And it's only right. Henry knows more baseball than any man I have ever met." Bill Lucas, Aaron's brother-in-law from his first marriage, and a Braves executive, saw the change. "The applause is louder when his name is announced and when he steps into the batter's box than it has ever been."[33] In 1972, Aaron became baseball's first $200,000-a-year player, so it was clear the Braves respected him.

Aaron did not always have his way with the best pitchers of his generation. They had Hall of Fame stuff, too, so the confrontations were more even. Aaron had special praise for Cardinals standout Bob Gibson, who was known to work games quickly and blow people away with his fastball. "When Gibson was working, you might as well come out hacking because you knew that either you would beat him or he would beat you in an hour and a half," Aaron said. "He didn't let the bars close on him. Most of the time, he was there before eleven o'clock with a victory under his belt."[34] Gibson was equally complimentary, saying something that most other pitchers had to agree with. "It was all but impossible to get a fastball past that man."[35]

Aaron had become the first player in history with more than 500 home runs and 3,000 hits before closing in on Ruth. The country seemed to be on his side, aware it was witness to history with each time at bat. In 1972, Fred Lieb, the longtime baseball writer who had known Ruth well, wrote a piece about a day he spent with the Sultan of Swat nine months before his death on August 16, 1948. During their time together, Ruth predicted that someone would break his record of 60 homers in a season. But he also predicted that his mark of 714 homers would stand forever. Lieb then said that he thought Aaron just might catch Ruth. "What makes Aaron's chances of passing Ruth look so good is that he improves with the years," Lieb wrote.[36]

The only question as the 1973 season began was whether Aaron—as long as he stayed healthy—would surpass Ruth that season or if he would have to wait until another winter passed. Aaron was aging, but gracefully. His once slender body was stockier, but his thighs looked super powerful in a tighter uniform than was worn in the 1950s. During the 1972 campaign Aaron hit 34 home runs. The Atlanta slugger entered the 1973 season needing 41 homers to tie Ruth and 42 to pass him. Midway through the season he smashed his 700th. The occasion should have been special to Aaron, but at a news conference at the All-Star game break he voiced displeasure. He was insulted because Commissioner Bowie Kuhn had not sent a congratulatory telegram and he said that the Baseball Hall of Fame, recipient of the ball from his 500th and 600th homers, had not sufficiently publicized them. Kuhn replied that he did not mean to snub Aaron. "I'm certainly sorry that Henry Aaron was disappointed, as I'm sure he knows that I am one of his biggest rooters. I want to lead the baseball celebration when he hits 714 and 715." Somewhat strangely, at about the same time, Claire Ruth, the widow of Babe Ruth, said that Aaron was trying to set a record of his own and that there was only one Babe Ruth.[37] From a strictly factual viewpoint, that was true. Aaron was trying to set a new home-run record and there has indeed been only one Babe Ruth.

This flare-up of mini-controversy was a prelude to what awaited as Aaron inched closer to Ruth. Irrational hatred revealed itself early in the 1973 season. As Aaron took his position in right field in some stadiums, rather than cheer him, some fans shouted racial slurs. Some yelled, "Nigger." Some yelled, "Son of a bitch." Some simply yelled that he was not as good a player as Babe Ruth. The sporting chase seemed to bring out the worst in some Americans—those who attended games in person and also some who communicated with Aaron by mail, sending vituperative letters. "All I want," Aaron said, "is to be treated like a human being. That's all I ask. Just let me do my job. I never said I was as good as Babe Ruth. But what am I supposed to do, stop hitting? I try to pass it off as ignorance, but the more it continues, it gets to the point that you say, 'What's the use?' I've enjoyed playing in Atlanta. I've loved playing here, but when you get this hatred and resentment. . . . Put it this way, the more they push me, the more I want the record."[38]

Aaron found the verbal assault unbelievable. Especially since some of it centered around his home park of Atlanta Fulton County Stadium. He could not fathom what touched the white tormentors' psyche so powerfully that they reacted so viciously. Aaron grew angry and he cultivated multiple motivations to break the record. "The most basic motivation was the pure ambition to break such an important and longstanding barrier," he said. "Along with that would come the recognition that I thought was long overdue me. I would be out of the shadows. I can't deny that I was also very interested in the financial benefits that the record would surely bring. Then there was the sense of doing something for my race. I felt stronger and stronger about that as the years went on. The hate mail drove me, too."[39]

The hate mail. Aaron said that nasty letters saying that no "nigger" had the right to go where he was going might have produced a benefit "There's no way to measure the effect that those letters had on me, but I like to think that every one of them added another home run to my total."[40]

By the 1970s, Atlanta was seen as the Renaissance city of the South. It was the hub of the region. If Southerners from North Carolina, South Carolina, Alabama, Georgia, Tennessee, or Mississippi wished to see major league sports of any type they had to travel to Atlanta. Atlanta, in its own way, had also been a hub of the civil rights movement and billed itself through a code phrase as being more advanced than other southern cities. Atlanta called itself "the city too busy to hate." As it turned out, that was not true.

An article in *Black Sports* magazine sarcastically ripped apart that image on Aaron's behalf. "The South still clings to Jeff Davis' faded grey," it read. "All of the sophisticated reassurances to the contrary, and well meaning liberals notwithstanding, the South is still in the nineteenth century. And Atlanta is part of the South."[41]

The hate mail did seem to emanate from an ancient, regressive, and repressive age. Most letters were unsigned and most were handwritten. Misspellings were common. One letter, preserved in Hank Aaron's file in the Baseball Hall of Fame research library, reads in part: "Hank Aaron. Are you trying to show off for your new girl friend? You must think people or [sic] dumb. We know you are trying to break Ruth's record, you dirty old Nigger man. We hope you don't this year. 1973 you will be too dam [sic] old to ever do it. We [unintelligible] wish you all bad luck. P.S. Playing ball is better than picking cotton and eating grits."

Another letter, reproduced in Aaron's autobiography, read, "Dear Nigger, Everybody loved Babe Ruth. You will be the most hated man in this country if you break his career home run record." Another letter in the book read, "Dear Black Boy, Listen Black Boy, We don't want no nigger Babe Ruth."[42]

Aaron and the Braves turned many hate letters over to the authorities for investigation. Others Aaron kept, to spur himself on. "I kept feeling more and more strongly that I had to break the record not only for myself and for Jackie Robinson and for black people," Aaron said, "but also to strike back at the vicious little people who wanted to keep me from doing it. All that hatred left a deep scar on me."[43]

For a long time Aaron kept mum about the hate mail outside Braves officials' circle. He did not talk about it with teammates, and he did not mention it to sportswriters. One day over breakfast with teammate Paul Casanova he spilled the word. Casanova was shocked and tried to assure Aaron that the letter writers were a lunatic fringe of crazies. Then Aaron told a sportswriter about the hate mail and he put it into a story. Other newspapers picked up the item and after that Aaron began receiving thousands of letters of support.[44]

The late cartoonist Charles Schultz, who drew the "Peanuts" comic, incorporated Aaron's pursuit of Ruth into a series of strips. So many of Schultz' wisdom-of-life strips told through Charlie Brown and other children revolved around baseball that it was a natural fit. Schultz had Charlie Brown and Linus discover that Snoopy was on the cusp of breaking Babe Ruth's record and was closer to it than Aaron. Snoopy, they found, was only one homer shy of the Babe. In a strip dated August 10, 1973, as Aaron closed in on Ruth, Charlie Brown handed a letter to Snoopy reclining on the top of his doghouse while wearing a baseball cap. Snoopy opened the letter and it read, "Dear Stupid, Who do you think you are trying to break Babe Ruth's record? Why don't you go back to where you came from? Drop dead! Get lost! Sincerely, A True Baseball Fan." Charlie Brown asked Snoopy, "Is it from anyone you know?" Snoopy suggested, "One of my admirers."

There was also much positive fan mail. Frank Sinatra sent a supportive telegram. Children wrote pleasant things, such as a note quoted in the *New York Times* reading, "I remember you when I bite into an Oh Henry candy bar," said one child. "I hope you beat that other guy in homers." Another wrote, "You are my idol. You always were and you always will be. I hope you get traded to the New York Mets."[45]

During the course of that year Aaron received 930,000 pieces of mail, the most by an individual nonpolitician in the country. The U.S. Postal Service even gave him a plaque to mark the occasion.

Equally mystifying was the cool reception Aaron received from baseball fans in Atlanta. Attendance was frequently horrible during the season, with at least one game luring barely 1,300 fans. It seemed as if more reporters were on hand than fans. With only days remaining in the season the Braves had a game rained out. It likely cost Aaron four more plate appearances. When the 1973 season ended, Aaron had hit 40 home runs, one more than his age. And he was left with a career total of 713, one shy of tying Ruth.

It could be philosophized that it was the worst of all possible situations. The drama would build in the off-season, and so would the pressure on Aaron. More than 30,000 fans sent Aaron off into winter with cheers after he made his last out of the season. "I'll do it next year," he said of the record.[46]

It was far from a restful winter. Aaron got married to his second wife, Billye, in November. He was invited to speak just about everywhere and had to be judicious accepting opportunities. By the time spring training rolled around, there was new controversy because the Braves opened on the road, at Cincinnati. The Braves wanted Aaron to tie and break Ruth's record at home where they could capitalize on what they expected to be many more fans turning out than the season before. There was mention that Aaron might not even play in the first few games against the Reds. Commissioner Bowie Kuhn intervened, ordering the Braves to put Aaron into the lineup if he was healthy and use him normally.

Aaron did tie Ruth's record in Cincinnati on April 4, 1974, on his first swing of the season. It was as if he declared, "Enough waiting." But then he went homerless until the Braves went home to Atlanta for a series against the Los Angeles Dodgers. Kuhn, who had threatened severe reprisals for then-manager Eddie Mathews if he did not heed the ruling and play Aaron appropriately in Cincinnati, was not very popular in Atlanta. But he increased tension with Aaron by honoring a speaking commitment in Cleveland rather than attending the first series. In his place he sent Monte Irvin, the one-time Giants star and former Negro Leagues player, as a representative of the office.

Aaron hit the record-breaking home run during the fourth inning of a night game off of Dodger pitcher Al Downing, who mistakenly believed he would not be much-remembered by history. The stadium hosted a sellout crowd of 52,870 fans that provided a long standing ovation, and Aaron's teammates flooded the field.

Years later, in his autobiography, Irvin said he thought Kuhn made the wrong decision. "I thought he should have gone to Atlanta, at least for the first series," Irvin wrote. "By not going he kind of offended Aaron and the fans in Atlanta, too. I thought that, since this was almost like a sacred record, the commissioner of baseball should have been there." The commissioner's office made up a $5,000 diamond-studded watch for Irvin to present on the occasion. But Aaron immediately asked, "Where's the commissioner?" Kuhn's absence started a feud between the two men and Aaron often criticized Kuhn in the press.[47]

Aaron completed the 1974 season with only 20 home runs. And once the season ended and the Babe was in his rearview mirror, Aaron played no more for the Braves. In an unthinkable twist, Aaron left the Braves after twenty-one seasons to join the expansion Milwaukee Brewers. The Brewers, the new team in Aaron's old town, welcomed him excitedly. At a banquet in Milwaukee over the winter leading up to the 1975 season, Aaron spelled out his feelings about the two cities. "I was farmed out for twelve years," he said of his time in Atlanta. "Now I'm back in the major leagues. For a long time, each time I attended Milwaukee dinners, I dreamed some day that I'd come back here to finish my career. I'm happy my dream came true."[48]

Aaron was not the Aaron of old, and the Brewers were not the Braves of old. Aaron was simply old, forty-one, and buying time in the designated hitter role. The Brewers were headed for a season of playing ball at a pace of twenty-six games under .500. Still, Aaron's name sold tickets and he had fun playing once again in a place that loved him. For the home opener, more than 48,000 fans showed up and sang, "Welcome Home, Henry" to the tune of "Hello, Dolly." Aaron singled, scored a run, and drove in a run.[49]

It was a nondescript statistical season for Aaron. He hit 12 home runs, but batted only .234. He gave it one more try with the Brewers in 1976, but when the results were similar he announced his retirement with an all-time best of 755 home runs. "I'm going to miss the competition, going one-on-one with the pitcher, trying to outguess him and the catcher," Aaron said.[50]

LATER LIFE

It was a given that as soon as Aaron was eligible following the mandatory five-year wait, he would be elected to the Baseball Hall of Fame, and he was. At the induction ceremony in Cooperstown in 1982, Aaron paid tribute to the black pioneers who set the stage for him in the majors, praising the Dodgers' Jackie Robinson and Roy Campanella. "They proved to the world that a man's ability is limited only by his opportunity," Aaron said. "The way to fame is like the way to heaven, through much tribulation."[51]

In the years after his retirement as an active player, Aaron appeared on a Wheaties box, was a Black History Month honoree, rang the opening bell at the New York Stock Exchange, started a Hank Aaron Foundation to help kids, was a member of the Atlanta Falcons football team's board of directors, served on the Hall of Fame's veterans' committee, owned a Krispy Kreme franchise (and numerous other fast-food restaurants), received an honorary doctorate degree from Bradley University in Illinois, owned a group of auto dealerships, and spent years working in management positions with the Braves.

In 1999, commemorating the twenty-fifth anniversary of the Aaron blast that passed Ruth, baseball inaugurated the Hank Aaron Award. It has been presented to the best hitter in each league each season since, paralleling the awarding of the Cy Young Award for pitchers. Aaron turned seventy-two in early 2006. While graying and heavier he had a distinguished bearing. Frequently sought for his thoughts on baseball issues, Aaron is treated as a wise elder statesman of the game, is outspoken when he thinks blacks are being overlooked for front-office positions, and is outspoken about players who take drugs to enhance their performances.

After Aaron's long pursuit of Ruth's record culminated on that long-ago April evening in Atlanta, after the years-long run-up and the nasty hate mail, he was asked how he felt. "I'm happy it's over," Aaron said. "I feel now I can relax."[52]

The home run was an achievement frozen in time; the video replayed on baseball shows for decades. The blast empowered Aaron to speak out on issues of concern more often. "Maybe the day will come when I can sit back and be content with the changes that have taken place in America, or, at least, in my part of it, which is baseball," he said. "Maybe in a few years baseball won't need somebody like me anymore."[53]

The clout that made Hank Aaron the greatest home run hitter of all time provided him with the clout to become the conscience of baseball. For a man who began his baseball life riding buses in the Negro Leagues, that is no small thing.

NOTES

1. Wayne Minshew, *Sporting News*, April 27, 1974.
2. Hank Aaron with Lonnie Wheeler, *I Had a Hammer: The Hank Aaron Story* (New York: HarperPaperbacks, 1992), 12.
3. Aaron with Wheeler, *I Had a Hammer*, 12–13.
4. Aaron with Wheeler, *I Had a Hammer*, 27.
5. Aaron with Wheeler, *I Had a Hammer*, 44–45.
6. Charlie Vascellaro, *Hank Aaron: A Biography* (Westport, CT: Greenwood Press, 2005), 17.
7. Aaron with Wheeler, *I Had a Hammer*, 54.
8. Aaron with Wheeler, *I Had a Hammer*, 55.
9. Aaron with Wheeler, *I Had a Hammer*, 65.
10. Aaron with Wheeler, *I Had a Hammer*, 66.
11. Aaron with Wheeler, *I Had a Hammer*, 74.
12. Aaron with Wheeler, *I Had a Hammer*, 76.
13. Aaron with Wheeler, *I Had a Hammer*, 82–83.
14. Aaron with Wheeler, *I Had a Hammer*, 84.
15. Aaron with Wheeler, *I Had a Hammer*, 125.
16. Aaron with Wheeler, *I Had a Hammer*, 132.
17. Aaron with Wheeler, *I Had a Hammer*, 133–134.
18. Vascellaro, *Hank Aaron*, 70.
19. Furman Bisher, *Saturday Evening Post*, August 4, 1956.
20. Ibid.
21. Vascellaro, *Hank Aaron*, 86.
22. Jack Mann, *Sports Illustrated*, August 1, 1966.
23. Ibid.
24. Ibid.
25. Ibid.
26. Aaron with Wheeler, *I Had a Hammer*, 153–154.
27. Aaron with Wheeler, *I Had a Hammer*, 179.
28. Aaron with Wheeler, *I Had a Hammer*, 183.
29. Aaron with Wheeler, *I Had a Hammer*, 169.
30. Aaron with Wheeler, *I Had a Hammer*, 168.
31. Aaron with Wheeler, *I Had a Hammer*, 206.
32. Arthur Daley, *New York Times*, August 8, 1967.
33. William Leggett, *Sports Illustrated*, August 18, 1969.
34. Bob Gibson with Lonnie Wheeler, *Stranger to the Game: The Autobiography of Bob Gibson* (New York: Viking Press, 1994), 170.
35. Gibson with Wheeler, *Stranger to the Game*, 174.
36. Fred Lieb, *Sporting News*, June 3, 1972.
37. Associated Press, July 24, 1973.
38. Wayne Minshew, *Sporting News*, May 26, 1973.
39. Aaron with Wheeler, *I Had a Hammer*, 308.
40. Aaron with Wheeler, *I Had a Hammer*, 308–309.
41. Sam Andrews, *Black Sports*, September 1973.
42. Aaron with Wheeler, *I Had a Hammer*, 315–316.
43. Aaron with Wheeler, *I Had a Hammer*, 328.

44. Aaron with Wheeler, *I Had a Hammer*, 331.

45. Dave Anderson, *New York Times*, September 29, 1973.

46. Dave Hirshey, *New York Daily News*, October 2, 1973.

47. Monte Irvin with James A Riley, *Nice Guys Finish First* (New York: Carroll & Graf, 1996), 212–214.

48. Lou Chapman, *Sporting News*, February 15, 1975.

49. Paul Delaney, *New York Times*, April 12, 1975.

50. Phil Pepe, *New York Daily News*, September 19, 1976.

51. Dick Kaegel, *Sporting News*, August 9, 1982.

52. Wayne Minshew, *Sporting News*, April 27, 1974.

53. Aaron with Wheeler, *I Had a Hammer*, 457.

Further Reading

Aaron, Hank, with Lonnie Wheeler, *I Had a Hammer: The Hank Aaron Story.* New York: Harper Paperbacks, 1992.

Bisher, Furman, *The Saturday Evening Post*, August 4, 1956.

Vascellaro, Charlie, *Hank Aaron: A Biography*. Westport, CT: Greenwood Press, 2005.

BIBLIOGRAPHY

The Baseball Hall of Fame Library Archives has massive amounts of material in individual player files. In many instances, especially if clips are older, newspaper articles may be missing dates, headlines, or bylines. In older newspapers, many stories appeared in the paper without bylines. That is reflected here.

Aaron, Hank, and Lonnie Wheeler. *I Had a Hammer.* New York: HarperPaperbacks, 1992.

Allee, Rod. *The Record* (Hackensack, NJ), July 14, 1994. "Baseball Pioneer Honored, Mr. Precedent, Team Retires No. 14 of No. 1 Black," On the occasion of the Cleveland Indians retiring Larry Doby's jersey number.

Allen, Maury. *New York Post*, December 16, 1980 (Baseball Hall of Fame Archives).

Anderson, Dave. "Robinson Looms as Indian Manager, on Frank Robinson Likely to Become First African-American Manager." *New York Times*, September 26, 1974.

Andrews, Sam. "A Bitter Pill. On Hank Aaron's Pursuit of Babe Ruth's Home-Run Record in a Southern Town." *Black Sports*, September 1973.

Arkansas Gazette, April 19, 1971 (Baseball Hall of Fame Archives). On Satchel Paige appearing in a movie.

Bankes, James. "Cool Papa Bell." From the Baseball Hall of Fame Library Archives, April 1982.

Banks, Ernie, and James Enright. *Mr. Cub.* Chicago: Follett Publishing Company, 1971.

Becker, Jeff. "War Slowed Monte Irvin's Early Race to the Majors." *St. Petersburg Times*, June 20, 1993.

Bell, James. "Cool Papa." *Black Sports*, June 1974.

Biederman, Les. "Banks Pays Back 'Debt' to Baseball Through Children." *Pittsburgh Press*, August 16, 1964.

———. "Sets Sparks Flying in His Giant Debut." *San Francisco Chronicle*, August 2, 1959.

Bisher, Furman. "Born to Play Ball." *Saturday Evening Post*, August 4, 1956.

———. "Something Willie Borrowed." *Atlanta Journal*, May 17, 1967.

Bloom, Barry. Robinson awarded Gold Medal, March 2, 2005. www.Major League Baseball.com.

Bock, Hal. "Gibson: The Pitcher Who 'Had to Win.' " *Associated Press*, August 2, 1981.

Bodley, Hal. "Doby Gets Hall of Fame Ticket." *USA Today*, March 4, 1998.

Broeg, Bob. "Banks Is Mr. Big at Hall of Fame Induction." *Sporting News*, August 20, 1977.

———. "Just What Prompted Flood Lawsuit?" *Sporting News*, February 7, 1970.

———. *St. Louis Post-Dispatch*, July 19, 1958 (Baseball Hall of Fame Archives); August 7, 1977, "Cool Papa to Swell with Pride As Ernie Enters Shrine," On the early connection between Cool Papa Bell and Ernie Banks; August 6, 1973, "Monte Irvin Comes Long Way To Cooperstown," On Irvin's Hall of Fame induction.

Brogan, John. "Campanella Sells Faith and Desire." *Philadelphia Bulletin*, March 10, 1964.

Brooks, Connie. "The Legendary James Thomas 'Cool Papa' Bell" (summary of life). Baseball Hall of Fame Library Archives, June 2002.

Brown, C. L. "His Time to Shine." *Cleveland Plain-Dealer*, July 27, 1998.

Burns, Ken (director, producer). *Baseball*, documentary film, 1995. On Cool Papa Bell hitting three inside-the-park home runs in one game; On Baseball Commissioner Kenesaw Mountain Landis refusing to allow blacks into the majors; On black players being exiled to the Negro Leagues.

Campanella, Roy. *It's Good to Be Alive.* Boston: Little, Brown and Company, 1959.

Cannon, Jimmy. "The Good Side." *New York Journal-American*, July 7, 1965.

————. *King Features Syndicate*, April 26, 1964. "Hutson 'Taught' Mays to Catch Ball."

Caruso, Gary. "Hustlin' Down the Stretch." *Atlanta Constitution*, June 5, 1977.

Castellano, Dan. "Mates Remember: There Was More to Flood Than Battle for Free Agency." *Newark Star-Ledger*, January 22, 1997.

Chapman, Lou. "Brewers' Fans Salute Returning Aaron." *Sporting News*, February 15, 1975.

Chere, Rich. "McCovey Fame Stretches to Cooperstown." *Newark Star-Ledger*, August 3, 1986.

Clark, Dick, and Larry Lester, eds. *The Negro Leagues Book*. Ohio: Society for American Baseball Research, 1994.

Cleveland, Rick. "Cool Papa's Roots: Starkville Honors Its Native Legend." *Clarion-Ledger*, May 11, 1999.

Condon, Dave. "In the Wake of the News." *Chicago Tribune*, June 18, 1958.

————. "In the Wake of the News." *Chicago Tribune*, August 12, 1964.

Cooke, Bob, and *Brooklyn Eagle*. "Fans Give First Baseman Auto and a Television Set." September 23, 1947.

Coughlin, Dan. "Second Chance Saves Newcombe." *Cleveland Press*, January 30, 1976.

Daley, Arthur. "A Welcome to the Hall of Fame." *New York Times*, January 22, 1969.

————. "It's Impolite to Point." *New York Times*, August 8, 1967.

————. "Ol' Satch Looks Back and Gains." *New York Times*, February 10, 1971.

Davidson, Craig (producer, writer). *There Was Always Sun Shining Someplace: Life in the Negro Baseball Leagues* (DVD), Refocus Films, Westport, CT, 1984. On Judy Johnson discussing his career; On Ted Radcliffe talking about life on the road as a black player; On Judy Johnson discussing Satchel Paige; On Buck Leonard as a black player traveling; On Buck Leonard discussing playing against white teams; On Buck Leonard discussing Jackie Robinson breaking the color line; On Buck Leonard discussing being elected to the Hall of Fame.

Delaney, Paul. "Aaron, Back in Milwaukee, Upstages Robinson." *New York Times*, April 12, 1975.

DeLeon, Clark. "Wilmington's Stadium Sets up a Shrine to Negro League Star." *Philadelphia Inquirer*, April 15, 1995.

Dickey, Glenn. "Catching up with Willie McCovey." *San Francisco Chronicle*, January 30, 2005.

Dolgan, Bob. "A Racial Milestone." *Cleveland Plain-Dealer*, April 26, 1998.

Durslag, Melvin. "Campy Is Winning the Battle." *Los Angeles Herald-Examiner*, March 20, 1958.

————. "Loss of 10 Pounds." *Los Angeles Herald-Examiner*, June 17, 1959.

————. "McCovey a Menace." *Los Angeles Herald-Examiner*, August 9, 1969.

————. "Ol' Satch Still Fishin' Around." *Los Angeles Herald-Examiner*, February 28, 1969.

————. "Souvenirs Are Not for Willie." *Los Angeles Herald-Examiner*, May 20, 1966.

Durso, Joseph. "Robinson Follows Robinson: 27 Years, One Hurdle Later." *New York Times*, October 4, 1974.

————. "McCovey, 42, Frets on Bench." *New York Times*, June 15, 1980.

Einstein, Charles. *Willie's Time: A Biography of Willie Mays*. New York: Penguin Books, 1989.

Enders, Eric. *The Scribner Encyclopedia of American Lives* (Volume 5). New York: Charles Scribner's Sons, 2000. On Buck Leonard late in his career.

Enright, Jim. "Wrigley Banks on Ernie's Day to Be Tops." *Sporting News*, August 22, 1964.

Erardi, John. "Robinson Touched by Statue." *Cincinnati Enquirer*, September 27, 2003.

"Ernie Banks' Three Triples in One Game Ties Record." *Houston Post*, June 12, 1966.

Eskenazi, Gerald. *Bill Veeck: A Baseball Legend*. New York: McGraw-Hill, 1988.

————. *New York Times*, October 4, 1974 (Baseball Hall of Fame Archives).

Etkin, Jack. "Still Cool Papa, Years Have Dimmed His Efforts, but Bell Has His Place in Baseball Lore." *Kansas City Times*, May 11, 1985.

Falkner, David. *Great Time Coming*. New York: Touchstone, 1996. A biography of Jackie Robinson.

Ferdenzi, Til. "Complete Catcher? Howard Fills the Bill." *Sporting News*, September 12, 1964.

————. "Howard, Frisky as a Freshman, Wants to Catch Until He's 40." *Sporting News*, June 5, 1965.

————. "MVP Honor Caps Career of Yank Star." *Sporting News*, November 30, 1963.

Flaherty, Vincent X. "Campanella Real Eager!" *Los Angeles Examiner*, January 26, 1958.

Foo, Rodney. "Newcombe Is Pitching New Inning." *Gannett News Service*, July 22, 1981.

Flood, Curt, and Richard Carter. *The Way It Is.* New York: Trident Press, 1971.

Flood, Curt/Flood, Judy. Reflection statement (Baseball Hall of Fame Archives), March 1997.

Forman, Ross. "Don Newcombe Makes Pitch for HOF." *Sports Collectors Digest*, June 3, 1994.

Fox, William Price. *Satchel Paige's America.* Tuscaloosa: University of Alabama Press, 2005.

Francis, Bill. "Buck O'Neil Thrills C-town Audience." *Freeman's Journal*, February 11, 2000.

Freedman, Lew. "Taking a Short Glimpse Back into Willie's Time, on Willie Mays' Visit to Alaska." *Anchorage Daily News*, July 13, 1984.

Friendlich, Dick. "Mays Crazy Catch." *San Francisco Chronicle*, August 23, 1963.

Frizzell, Pat. "McCovey a Super-Star in Merthiolate." *Sporting News*, August 9, 1969.

Frommer, Harvey. *Rickey & Robinson: The Men Who Broke Baseball's Color Barrier.* New York: Macmillan Publishing, 1982.

Furlong, Bill. "Ernie Banks in the Evening of His Career." *Sport*, August 1967.

Gibson, Bob. Hall of Fame induction speech (Baseball Hall of Fame Library Archives), August 2, 1981.

Gibson, Bob, and Lonnie Wheeler. *Stranger to the Game: The Autobiography of Bob Gibson.* New York: Penguin Viking, 1994.

Graham, Frank. "Why Leo Wouldn't Trade Mays." *New York Journal-American*, August 16, 1951.

Gregorian, Vahe. "Belated Respect, Baseball Says Goodbye to Cool Papa Bell." *St. Louis Post-Dispatch*, March 17, 1991.

Grieve, Curly. "The McCovey Story: Found by Bird-Dog." *San Francisco Examiner*, August 6, 1959.

————. "Willie's Long, Hot Summer." *San Francisco Examiner*, September 3, 1963.

Grimsley, Will. "Executive Example by Yanks and Elite." *Associated Press*, March 16, 1980.

Hano, Arnold. *The Say-Hey Kid: A Biography of Willie Mays.* New York: Bartholomew House, 1961.

Hatch, Orrin. "The Curt Flood Act Being Introduced as Possible Legislation." *Congressional Record*, January 21, 1997.

Hecht, Henry. "Satchel Paige Dead." *New York Post*, June 9, 1982.

Hirshey, Dave. "Aaron, the Best Years of His Life Arrive." *New York Daily News*, October 2, 1973.

————. "He Commands Full Respect." *New York Daily News*, October 4, 1974.

Hoffman, John C. "Minnie's What You Say 'Hokay!' " *Collier's*, April 5, 1952.

Holmes, Tommy. "We Looked at Him and There He Was." *Brooklyn Eagle*, June 27, 1949.

Holtzman, Jerome. "For Inspiration, Monte Irvin's Book Does Nicely." *Chicago Tribune*, May 12, 1996.

————. "Just Like Old Days, Minnie Hustling, Hitting for Chisox." *Chicago Tribune*, March 21, 1964.

————. "Mr. Cub Doffs Lid to GIs in Vietnam." *Chicago Tribune*, December 7, 1968.

————. "Veeck Taps 'Mystery Man' and He's Old Pal Minnie." *Sporting News*, January 31, 1976.

Holway, John. Interview on file (Baseball Hall of Fame Library Archives), 1969.

————. *Josh and Satch.* Connecticut: Meckler Publishing, 1991.

————. " 'They Made Me Survive,' Mays Says." *Sporting News*, July 18, 1981.

————. "Two GI Years Cost Willie Shot at Ruth Mark." *Sporting News*, February 16, 1974.

Howard, Arlene, and Ralph Wimbish. *Elston and Me: The Story of the First Black Yankee.* Columbia: University of Missouri Press, 2001.

Hudson, Lynn. "90G Still Slavery, Sez Flood." *New York Daily News*, January 4, 1970.

————. "World Series Pitchmen." *New York Daily News*, September 29, 1968.

Irvin, Monte, and James A. Riley. *Nice Guys Finish First: The Autobiography of Monte Irvin.* New York: Carroll & Graf, 1996.

Izenberg, Jerry. "Irvin Recalls Early Days with Doby in Newark." *Newark Star-Ledger*, June 19, 2003.

Jackman, Phil. "F. Robby Strictly Business No Idle Chatter With Foes." *Baltimore Sun*, April 10, 1971.

Judge, Walter. "Giant Star Retains Cohn as His Agent." *San Francisco Examiner*, November 18, 1959.

Kaegel, Dick. "Echoes of Jackie at Cooperstown." *Sporting News*, August 9, 1982.

Kahn, Roger. *The Boys of Summer.* New York: Harper and Row, 1971.

Katzman, Izzy, and Gary Soulsman. "Hall of Famer Judy Johnson Dies." *Wilmington News Journal*, June 16, 1989.

Kelly, Frederic. "Judy Johnson: From Snow Hill to the Hall of Fame." *Sun*, February 1, 1976.

King, Joe. "Elston His Old Pals: 'Going No Place.' " *New York World-Telegram*, June 25, 1965.

Kiseda, George. "Dash of Bitters Sours Gibby Success Saga." *Philadelphia Bulletin*, October 10, 1970.

Klores, Dan (director and co-producer), and Stuart, Charles (writer and co-producer). *Viva Baseball* (documentary film). New York: Shoot the Moon Productions, 2005. Documentary on early black Latin players in the majors.

Kornheiser, Tony. "It's Good to Be Alive: Campy." *Newsday*, February 19, 1974.

Kuenster, John. "Ernie Did Get Mad Once—in '59." *Chicago Daily News*, August 15, 1964.

Lang, Jack. "Johnson, 'Black Traynor,' Elected to Shrine." *Sporting News*, March 1, 1975.

———. " 'Not Bitter, Just Grateful,' Beams Shrine-Bound Monte." *Sporting News*, February 24, 1973.

Lardner, John. "Reese and Robinson: Team Within a Team." *New Yorker*, September 18, 1949.

Leggett, William. "Hank Becomes a Hit." *Sports Illustrated*, August 18, 1969.

Leonard, Buck. Hall of Fame induction speech (Baseball Hall of Fame Library Archives), August 7, 1972.

Leonard, Buck, and James A. Riley. *Buck Leonard: The Black Lou Gehrig.* New York: Carroll & Graf Publishers, 1995.

Leonard, Buck, with John Holway. "Buck Leonard: Lou Gehrig of Black Baseball." *Sporting News*, March 4, 1972.

Lieb, Fred. "Babe Thought 714 HRs Would Stand Forever." *Sporting News*, June 3, 1972.

Los Angeles Examiner, August 4, 1959 (Baseball Hall of Fame Archives).

Loverro, Thom. *The Encyclopedia of Negro League Baseball.* New York: Checkmark Books, 2003.

Mann, Jack. "Danger with a Double." *Sports Illustrated*, August 1, 1966.

Mays, Willie, and Lou Sahedi. *Say-Hey: The Autobiography of Willie Mays.* New York: Pocket Books, 1989.

McCovey, Willie. Hall of Fame induction speech (Baseball Hall of Fame Library Archives), August 3, 1986.

McCovey, Willie, and William Flynn. "Remembering McCovey." *San Francisco Examiner/Chronicle*, July 6, 1980.

Miller, Lou. " 'I Not Afraid,' Says Minnie, Back after 50th Plunking." *Cleveland Press*, June 15, 1955.

Minoso, Minnie, and Herb Fagen. *Just Call Me Minnie: My Six Decades in Baseball.* Illinois: Sagamore Publishing, 1994.

Minshew, Wayne. "Aaron Slurred as He Assaults Ruth's Mark." *Sporting News*, May 26, 1973.

———. "The Hammer Hails the Big One." *Sporting News*, April 27, 1974.

———. "Satchel Comes to Grips with Pop Time, Hangs 'Em Up." *Sporting News*, April 19, 1969.

Moore, Joseph Thomas. *Pride Against Prejudice.* New York: Praeger Publishers, 1988.

Moriah, Dave. *Sports Collectors Digest*, August 13, 1993.

Mullen, James. " 'Banks Too Nice' to Manage: Wrigley." *Chicago Sun-Times*, August 1, 1974.

Munzel, Edgar. "A Negro Skipper in Big Time? 'Bound to happen,' Says Banks." *Chicago Tribune*, May 21, 1966.

Murray, Jim. "Similing Ernie Banks Is Always an Optimist." *Los Angeles Times*, May 18, 1967.

———. "Uncle Curt's Cabin." *Sporting News*, February 7, 1970.

———. "Wonderful Willie." *Los Angeles Times*, May 23, 1962.

Musberger, Brent. *Chicago American*, October 9, 1967.

Myslenski, Skip. "Frank Robinson, Manager: Well, Nobody Said It Would Be Easy." *Philadelphia Inquirer*, August 3, 1975.

Newark Star-Ledger, September 28, 1971 (Baseball Hall of Fame Archives). "Nostalgia gets up 'at bat' in Ernie's last home game." On the end of Ernie Banks' playing career.

Newcome, Don. Interviewed by Tom Reed, Members Only Television. Printed as foreword to *Elston and Me: The Story of the First Black Yankee*, Arlene Howard and Ralph Wimbish, Columbia: University of Missouri Press, 2001.

New York Times, October 4, 1974 (Baseball Hall of Fame Archives). October 27, 1979, "Kuhn Tells Mays to Choose Casino Company or Mets."

New York World-Journal-Tribune, October 11, 1966. "When Robby Nearly Died."

New York World-Telegram, January 26, 1957 (Baseball Hall of Fame Archives). "Campy: Robinson Can't Hurt Me."

Nightingale, Dave. "Maxi Career for Minnie as Veeck Runs His Hands." *Chicago Daily News*, August 8, 1976.

Oates, Bob. "Coping: Some Days Are Good and Some Days Are Bad, but Any Day That Revolves Around Dodger Baseball Is Still His Favorite." *Los Angeles Times*, July 8, 1985.

O'Brien, Jim. "Buck's $50-a-Month Glory." *New York Post*, February 9, 1972.

O'Neil, Buck, Steve Wulf, and David Conrads. *I Was Right on Time*. New York: Simon & Schuster, 1996.

O'Neill, Dan. *St. Louis Post-Dispatch*, January 24, 1997, Court of Appeal: Flood, The Pro, Shouldn't Be Lost in Deluge of Anti-Memories. On remembering Curt Flood after his death.

Paige, Leroy "Satchel," and David Lipman. *Maybe I'll Pitch Forever*. New York: Doubleday and Company, 1962.

Patterson, Kelly D. "Towns, Teams Pay Tribute to Baseball Pioneer." *Arlington Morning News*, June 22, 1997.

Pepe, Phil. *New York Daily News*, August 6, 1979 (Baseball Hall of Fame Archives); April 8, 1977 (Baseball Hall of Fame Archives); August 21, 1971, Through the Press Gate; April 21, 1965, Ellie Confident; September 19, 1976, Finally, After 23 Years, Henry Aaron Is a Legend.

Pittsburgh Press, The Scoreboard, August 29, 1966, "Now Gibson Makes Batters Look Sick;" September 23, 1996 (Baseball Hall of Fame Archives).

Pluto, Terry. *Akron Beacon-Journal*, April 20, 1997. Robinson's trail-blazing didn't make Larry Doby's life any easier that July in 1947.

Poliquin, Bud. *Syracuse Herald-American*, June 15, 1997. Rachel Robinson says it's true, there was a black cat.

Powers, Jimmy. "Powerhouse." *New York Daily News*, October 18, 1956.

Purdy, Mark. "McCovey Cove to be Part of Pac Bell Park." *San Jose Mercury News*, August 26, 1999.

Pye, Brad, Jr. "Suitcase Superstar." *Black Sports*, July/August 1972.

Ratto, Ray. "Huge Crowd Honors McCovey on His 'Day.' " *San Francisco Chronicle*, July 7, 1986.

Reidenbaugh, Lowell. "Gibson, Redbirds—Second to None!" *Sporting News*, October 28, 1967.

Ribowsky, Mark. *Don't Look Back: Satchel Paige in the Shadows of Baseball*. New York: Simon & Schuster, 1994.

———. *The Power and the Darkness*. New York: Simon & Schuster, 1996.

Robinson, Frank, and Al Silverman. *My Life Is Baseball*. New York: Doubleday & Company, 1968 and 1975.

Robinson, Jackie. *I Never Had It Made*. New Jersey: Ecco Press, 1995.

Rogers, Thomas. "Elston Howard, Yank Star for Many Years, Dies at 51." *New York Times*, December 15, 1980.

Rogosin, Donn. *Invisible Men.* New York: Atheneum, 1987.

Rosenbaum, Art. "A's Buy McCovey from Padres." *San Francisco*, August 31, 1976.

———. "McCovey A Hero." *San Francisco Chronicle*, November 1, 1973.

———. "Why Willie Left Us." *San Francisco Examiner*, July 19, 1960.

———. "Willie Can't Dance." *San Francisco Examiner*, August 6, 1959.

Rosenthal, Harold. *New York Herald-Tribune*, November 18, 1959 (Baseball Hall of Fame Archives).

Rosenthal, Ken. "Early in Count, Robinson Fights Off Prostate Cancer." *Baltimore Sun*, August 30, 1999.

Rumill, Ed. "An Artist—on Field or off." *Christian Science Monitor*, June 14, 1969.

Russo, Neal. "Never a No-Hitter? Gibby Glady Eats His Words." *Sporting News*, August 28, 1971.

———. "A Wild Pitch by Gibson—And That Snaps the Streak." *Sporting News*, July 13, 1968.

———. "You Learn to Pitch by Doing, Not Watching, Says Gibson." *St. Louis Post-Dispatch*, June 3, 1962.

Salter, Stephanie. "McCovey Memories: Quiet Power." *San Francisco Examiner*, July 1, 1980.

San Francisco Chronicle, October 25, 1927 (Baseball Hall of Fame Archives).

Schotz, Andrew. "Willie Mays Forgives." *Herald-Mail*, August 10, 2004.

Schumach, Murray. *New York Times*, December 17, 1980 (Baseball Hall of Fame Archives).

Shaikin, Bill. "Roxie Campanella, 77; Dodger Great's Widow Continued His Work." *Los Angeles Times*, March 15, 2004.

Shea, Lois. " 'Newk' Celebrates in Nashua." *Boston Globe*, April 15, 1997.

Smith, Bob. *Chicago Daily News*, June 9, 1962 (Baseball Hall of Fame Archives).

Smith, Lyall. *Detroit Free Press*, September 6, 1945 (Baseball Hall of Fame Archives).

St. Louis Globe-Democrat, January 27, 1957 (Baseball Hall of Fame Archives); May 26, 1982.

Stainback, Barry. "Have the Yankees Held Back Howard?" *Sport*, December 1961.

"Stats Preserve the Real Cyclone, On Cy Young, the Winningest Pitcher, and Don Newcombe Winning the First Cy Young Award," *Anchorage Daily News*, November 11, 1992.

Stevens, Bob. "Big Man from Nicetown." *Time*, August 8, 1955.

———. "Jackie Can't Speak for Me—Says Mays." *Sporting News*, March 30, 1968.

———. "Mays Sets 600 Homers as Goal." *Sporting News*, February 17, 1968.

———. *San Francisco Chronicle*, May 2, 1961, "Mays Used Amalfitano's Bat." On Willie Mays four-home-run day; September 23, 1963 (Baseball Hall of Fame Archives).

———. "Stretching Soothes Barking Dogs with Red-Meat Home-Run Diet." *Sporting News*, June 12, 1965.

Trello, Don. "Gibson Proves He's Tougher Than Prostate Cancer." *Springfield State Journal Register*, September 17, 2004.

USA Today, May 23, 1997, South Carolina pays tribute to Doby. On the return of Larry Doby to his boyhood home; January 21, 1997 (Baseball Hall of Fame Archives).

Vanderberg, Bob. *Minnie and the Mick.* Indiana: Diamond Communications, 1996.

Vascellaro, Charlie. *Hank Aaron, a Biography.* Westport, CT: Greenwood Press, 2005.

Veeck, Bill, and Ed Linn. *Veeck—As in Wreck.* Chicago: University of Chicago Press, 1962.

Ward, Geoffrey C., and Ken Burns. *Baseball, an Illustrated History.* New York: Alfred P. Knopf, 1994.

Weiner, Richard. " 'Say Hey' Again to Willie Mays." *USA Today*, March 31, 2000.

West, Cornel. *I Never Had It Made.* New Jersey: Ecco Press, 1995.

Williams, Joe. "Minoso, Injured Cardinal, Recalls Old Cuba to Writer." *Pittsburgh Press*, May 20, 1962.

Winter, Jonah. *Fair Ball! 14 Great Stars from Baseball's Negro Leagues.* New York: Scholastic Press, 1999.

Wulf, Steve. "The Guiding Light." *Sports Illustrated*, September 19, 1994.

Young, Dick. "Tab M'Covey BB Greatness." *New York Daily News/San Francisco Examiner*, September 12, 1959.

Zucco, Tom. "Buck O'Neil: A Baseball Homecoming." *St. Petersburg Times*, March 9, 1995.

Web Sites

Baseball Hall of Fame Web site: www.baseballhalloffame.org

The Baseball Library Web site: www.BaseballLibrary.com

Great African American Baseball Players Web site: www.africanamericans.com/Baseballhtm

History of African Americans in Organized Baseball Web site: www.thebaseballpage.com

Jackie Robinson Web site: www.espn.go.com/sportscentury/features

The Negro Leagues Baseball Museum Web site: www.nlbm.com

Satchel Paige Web site: www.satchelpaige.com

INDEX

ABOUT THE AUTHOR

Lew Freedman is a sportswriter with the *Chicago Tribune*. He has worked as an award-winning journalist with the *Anchorage Daily News* and is the author of over 27 books.